DATE DUE

			PRINTED IN U.S.A.

CLIFFS NOTES

HARDBOUND LITERARY LIBRARIES

EUROPEAN LITERATURE LIBRARY

Volume 2

German Literature

7 Titles

ISBN 0-931013-21-6

Library distributors, hardbound editions:
Moonbeam Publications
18530 Mack Avenue
Grosse Pointe, MI 48236
(313) 884-5255

MOONBEAM PUBLICATIONS
Robert R. Tyler, President
Elizabeth Jones, Index Editor

FOREWORD

Moonbeam Publications has organized **CLIFFS NOTES**, the best-selling popular (trade) literary reference series, into a fully indexed hardbound series designed to offer a more permanent format for the series.

Hardbound volumes are available in a **BASIC LIBRARY**, a 24 volume series. The current softbound series (over 200 booklets) has been divided into five major literary libraries to help researchers, librarians, teachers, students and all readers use this series more effectively. The five major literary groupings are further subdivided into 17 literary periods or genres to enhance the use of this series as a more precise literary reference book.

Hardbound volumes are also available in an **AUTHORS LIBRARY**, a 13 volume series classified by author, covering 11 authors and over 70 Cliffs Notes titles. This series helps readers who prefer to study the works of a particular author, rather than an entire literary period.

**CLIFFS NOTES HARDBOUND
LITERARY LIBRARIES**
1990 by
Moonbeam Publications
18530 Mack Avenue
Grosse Pointe, MI   48236
(313) 884-5255

Basic Library - 24 Volume
ISBN 0-931013-24-0

Authors Library - 13 Volume
ISBN 0-931013-65-8

Bound in U.S.A.

EUROPEAN LITERATURE LIBRARY

Volume 2

German Literature

CONTENTS

All Quiet on the Western Front

Demian

The Diary of Anne Frank

Faust Pt. I & Pt. II

Kafka's Short Stories

Steppenwolf & Siddhartha

The Trial

ALL QUIET ON THE WESTERN FRONT

NOTES

including
- *Life and Background of the Author*
- *General Plot Summary*
- *Remarque's Introductory Note*
- *Critical Commentaries*
- *Remarque's Style*
- *Remarque as a Social Critic*
- *Character Analyses*
- *Questions for Review*

by
Rollin O. Glaser

Cliffs Notes
INCORPORATED
LINCOLN, NEBRASKA 68501

Editor

Gary Carey, M.A.
University of Colorado

Consulting Editor

James L. Roberts, Ph.D.
Department of English
University of Nebraska

ISBN 0-8220-0155-1
© Copyright 1965
by
C. K. Hillegass
All Rights Reserved
Printed in U.S.A.

1990 Printing

Cliffs Notes, Inc.   Lincoln, Nebraska

CONTENTS

AUTHOR'S LIFE AND BACKGROUND.................................... 5

GENERAL PLOT SUMMARY....................................... 7

CHARACTER SKETCHES

    Major 10

    Minor 11

REMARQUE'S INTRODUCTORY
NOTE...13

SUMMARIES AND COMMENTARIES

    Chapter 1 14

    Chapter 2 16

    Chapter 3 18

    Chapter 4 20

    Chapter 5 23

    Chapter 6 24

    Chapter 7 27

    Chapter 8 29

    Chapter 9 30

    Chapter 10 33

    Chapter 11 34

    Chapter 12 36

THE AUTHOR'S STYLE..37

REMARQUE AS A SOCIAL CRITIC............................38

MAJOR CHARACTER ANALYSES.............................40

QUESTIONS..43

SUGGESTED THEME TOPICS...................................44

ALL QUIET ON THE WESTERN FRONT NOTES

AUTHOR'S LIFE AND BACKGROUND

Erich Maria Remarque was born in Osnabrück in Westphalia, Germany, on June 22, 1898. His father, a bookbinder by trade, was German; his mother was of French descent. As a youth he attended the gymnasium (equivalent to our elementary school) and seminar in the town where he lived. While attending the University of Münster, he was drafted into the German army. He was eighteen years old at the time of his induction.

During World War I Remarque fought at the Western Front and was wounded five times, the last time seriously. Following his discharge from the army, he worked at a series of professions, all of which became the subject matter of later novels. The same "lostness" felt by Paul Baumer in *All Quiet on the Western Front* seems to have controlled its author in the decade following the Great War. After completing a teaching course offered by the German government to war veterans, Remarque taught school for a year in a town near the Dutch border.

His restlessness and physical energy led him to a job as a salesman for a tombstone firm. These experiences as a dealer in the "appurtenances of grief" can be found in a novel entitled *The Black Obelisk*. Having had his fill of the business world, Remarque joined a group of friends in a "gypsy caravan" touring Germany.

His wanderings temporarily completed, Remarque's future literary career gained momentum when he wrote articles for a Swiss automobile magazine and later advertising copy for the same tire company. During this period Remarque became passionately interested in automobile racing and automotive mechanics. These interests form the backdrop for his novel *Heaven Has No Favorites*.

Eventually Remarque's literary inclinations and enthusiasm for sports brought him to write *Sport im Bild*. It was at this time that *All Quiet on the Western Front* was written, the theme of which had disturbed Remarque since the war.

Published in 1928, the original manuscript had been refused by one publisher and only reluctantly accepted by another. The novel's success was immediate and overwhelming, selling almost 1½ million copies during the first year. The unusual appeal of the book is reflected in the book's first year sales by countries. German readers alone bought 800,000 copies. The United States sales were 240,000. French readers purchased 219,000 copies, and the British, 195,000 copies. It was subsequently translated and published in 25 languages. The book was later made into two different motion pictures and was equally successful in film form.

Despite its success, the book generated a storm of controversy in Germany. Some people charged that the book was "replete with effeminate pacifism;" others claimed that it was really "romantic propaganda for war." Remarque stated in an interview that these contradictory criticisms stemmed from his refusal to declare himself politically. He told one interviewer that he had been misunderstood only in those quarters where one would be misunderstood anyway. He felt no need to take part in the controversy.

Whatever political overtones the book did or did not possess have since been resolved. The novel continues to be a definitive exposé of war.

After his first successful work, Remarque devoted more of his time to writing. The following novels were written in subsequent years:

The Road Back	1931
Three Comrades	1937
Flotsam	1941
Arch of Triumph	1946

Spark of Life   1952

A Time to Love and a Time to Die   1954

The Black Obelisk   1957

Heaven Has No Favorites   1961

Night in Lisbon   1964

Because of his untenable position in Nazi Germany, Remarque went to live at Porto Ronco on Lake Maggiore in Switzerland where he later bought a house. His emigration became permanent when the Nazis came to power. Because he would not voluntarily return and continued to write critically of the Nazi party, his books were burned, his films banned, and in 1938 his citizenship was revoked.

Remarque first visited the United States in 1939. In 1947, he became an American citizen, dividing his time between New York and Switzerland.

Since the publication of *All Quiet on the Western Front,* only *Arch of Triumph,* the story of a love affair in Paris between a German refugee doctor and a Parisian actress just before the outbreak of World War II, has had the same international success. Most of his works' have enjoyed greater popular acclaim than critical success.

GENERAL PLOT SUMMARY

All Quiet on the Western Front is the record of seven schoolmates who are representative of a generation destroyed by the shells and pressures of World War I. Because of the urgings of their teacher, Kantorek, whom they trust, all seven enlist in the army to serve the Fatherland. Paul Baumer, a young and sensitive member of the group, narrates the story.

Chapter 1

The story opens behind the German front lines. Paul and his friends are less naive as a result of their battle experience. Josef Behm has already been killed. Franz Kemmerich has had his leg amputated. A letter from Kantorek stirs the group's anger and despair at their shattered lives.

Chapter 2

The experience of military training and the war has been disillusioning for Paul and his friends. Corporal Himmelstoss wrung much of their youthful idealism out of them during basic training. The comradeship and esprit-de-corps are the only worthwhile results of their military training. At the end of the scene, Kemmerich, Paul's childhood friend, dies from his amputation.

Chapter 3

The focus in this chapter is on Kat who typifies the shrewd, self-reliant soldier. No matter what the situation, Kat is able to find food and supplies for his friends. News of Himmelstoss' arrival at the front causes Paul and his friends to remember the night before they left and how they revenged themselves on Himmelstoss.

Chapter 4

The action of this chapter is at the front. Paul and his unit have been assigned the job of laying barbed wire. While returning to the waiting trucks, Paul's company undergoes a terrific bombardment. Chapter 4 is a complete description of front-line war.

Chapter 5

Himmelstoss appears at the front and tries to make friends with Paul and his friends. He is insulted and generally abused but succeeds in having Tjaden and Kropp given light company punishment. The comradeship theme is developed further when Kat and Paul steal a goose and share it with their friends.

Chapter 6

The battle pattern described in this chapter is typical of trench warfare during World War I. Paul and his friends remain on the "line" throughout the summer and return to the rear for a rest in the fall.

Chapter 7

Paul and his comrades are moved farther behind the lines for a rest. Their time is spent eating, sleeping, and being friendly with local girls. Paul is sent home for a seventeen day leave. His homecoming is disappointing because he feels that he no longer fits or belongs. The war has destroyed his ambition and youthful pleasures. In Paul's mind the despair brought about by the war is emphasized by what he finds while on furlough.

Chapter 8

Before returning to his outfit, Paul goes through a refresher military training course at a camp on the moors. There he discovers that the men in a Russian prison camp are also human beings. This revelation further confirms doubts about the war.

Chapter 9

Returning to his unit, Paul feels the sense of belonging he was unable to feel at home. After being inspected by the Kaiser, the company is sent again to the front. In a patrol action Paul is forced to kill a French soldier named Gerard Duval. This act brings him face to face with his enemy, and he is conscience stricken by his act of murder.

Chapter 10

For three weeks Paul's squad is given the duty of guarding a supply depot. This turns out to be plush assignment, for there is an abundance of food and items of comfort. While trying to evacuate a village, Kropp and Paul are wounded. They succeed in being placed in the same hospital. Kropp's leg must be amputated. Paul recovers sufficiently to be given a leave and then returned to active duty.

Chapter 11

The action of this chapter takes place during the last summer of the war. The German war machine is crumbling, and the front line no longer exists. All of Paul's schoolmates have been killed. In this chapter Paul's best friend, Kat, is wounded, then killed by a flying splinter while being carried to a dressing station. The death of Kat is a mortal blow to Paul.

Chapter 12

The time is the fall of 1918. Paul is killed one month before the armistice on an exceptionally quiet day on the Western Front.

CHARACTERS

MAJOR CHARACTERS

Paul Baumer

The soldier, narrator and focal point of the novel who volunteered with four others from his class for military duty. Paul's group included: Muller, Kropp, Leer, Kemmerich and Behm.

Tjaden (pronounced Jahden)

A thin soldier with an immense appetite. He is nineteen and a former locksmith in civilian life.

Muller

A soldier who carries his school books with him and often dreams of examinations. He is the first to inherit Kemmerich's fine leather boots.

Stanislaus Katczinsky

Kat is a forty year old soldier who becomes Paul's best friend. He is shrewd, good-natured and known for his remarkable ability to find good food and soft jobs for the group.

Albert Kropp

First soldier of Paul's group to make lance-corporal. He was regarded as the best student in Paul's school class. He is discharged after leg amputation.

Leer

Paul's youthful classmate who grows a beard. He is first of Paul's school group to have experience with women.

Franz Kemmerich

Paul Baumer's childhood friend and fellow volunteer. Early in the novel he dies following a leg amputation. He is the first of the group to wear the fine leather boots.

Haie Westhus

The soldier who prefers the army to digging peat in civilian life.

Detering

The soldier who was a peasant-farmer in civilian life and thinks constantly of his farm and wife.

Kantorek

The schoolmaster who urged Paul and his friends to enlist. He is later called into the reserves under Mittlestaedt, a former pupil.

Corporal Himmelstoss

The drillmaster for Paul and his comrades, hated for his sadistic treatment of recruits. He is a former postman.

MINOR CHARACTERS

Josef Behm

First of Paul's schoolmates to be killed in the war.

Lieutenant Bertinck

Paul's company commander who is a fine soldier, respected by his men.

Ginger

The company cook who is more concerned about his personal safety and accurate food portions than he is concerned about feeding the men.

Tiejen

The soldier briefly recalled when Kemmerich dies. He called for his mother while dying and held off a doctor with a dagger until he collapsed.

Sergeant Oellrich
A sniper who takes pride in his ability to pick off enemy soldiers.

Heinrich Bredemeyer
A soldier who has told Paul's mother about the increasing dangers in front line fighting.

Mittelstaedt
Paul's friend who has been promoted to company commander of a home guard. He has the opportunity to take revenge on schoolmaster Kantorek who is only an ordinary soldier.

Boettcher
The soldier who was the school porter at Paul's former school.

Josef Hammacher
The soldier who shares the hospital ward with Paul, Albert and others. He has a "shooting license" because of his mental derangement.

Little Peter
One of Paul and Albert's hospital ward mates. He is thought to be the only patient ever to return from the "Dying Room."

Franz Wachter
A hospital ward mate who dies of a lung wound.

Sister Libertine
One of the sister-nurses at the hospital where Paul and Albert recover from their wounds.

Berger
The strongest soldier in Paul's company. During the last days, Berger loses his sense of judgment. He is wounded trying to rescue a messenger dog under fire.

Gerald Duval
The French soldier who lands in Paul's shell hole. Paul stabs him. After he dies, Paul discovers Duval, the enemy, is also human

—a printer with a wife and child. Paul realizes the enemy on the other side of the barbed wires is just a lonely, frightened soldier like himself.

REMARQUE'S INTRODUCTORY NOTE

All Quiet on the Western Front is prefaced by a brief statement of the novel's purpose. Here the author makes it clear that the story is not an accusation of an individual or group. It was not Remarque's intention to align himself with any particular German political party. The reader is also warned against viewing the book as an exciting adventure. This is an account of a generation of young men destroyed physically and spiritually by the experience of the war.

The book is not concerned with depicting the events of the war. The essential point is to describe war's effects on a particular generation.

It was Remarque's contention that his generation had grown up in a way different from others before and after it. Their overwhelming experience was the war. Shortly after publication of his novel, the young author declared, "The generation of young people, which no matter from what motive, has been driven through this period must necessarily have developed differently from all former generations." The men who emerged from the trenches were marked for life by deep, irreparable psychic wounds. For these young disillusioned, the world could never again hold the same innocence it had when the century was just beginning. As Jacques Barzun has put it, "The energies born with the twentieth century had been sapped, misspent and destroyed."

In a mood characterized by despair, disgust and disquiet, the youth of Europe and America returned to their private lives in 1918 to attempt to live in a world that no longer held sacred the ideals and beliefs that prevailed prior to 1914. Gertrude Stein, when she said to young Ernest Hemingway in Paris, "You are all a lost generation," summed up the dilemma Paul Baumer and his comrades would have faced had they lived.

14

CHAPTER 1

Summary

The novel opens behind the German front lines. What remains of Paul Baumer's company has moved back from the Western Front for a short rest after fourteen days of heavy fighting. The soldiers have been well fed. Rations for twice as many men had been prepared.

Among the mail distributed to the soldiers is a letter from Kantorek, the teacher who had persuaded Paul and his classmates to volunteer for military service. Paul comments that Kantorek is one of the little men who seem to create much of the world's unhappiness.

One of the students Kantorek succeeded in recruiting was Josef Behm. Behm was the first of Paul's schoolmates to be killed in the war. Paul realizes that Kantorek was only indirectly to blame for Behm's death, for the world is filled with men like Kantorek who must share the guilt.

Thoughts of Behm and Kantorek lead Paul to a bitter observation of the older generation. He reflects, "The idea of authority, which they represented, was associated in our minds with a greater insight and a manlier wisdom." The first bombardment and the first killing shattered this faith in the adult world. Paul and his generation feel betrayed and alone in the world they have inherited.

The second scene of the chapter focuses on Franz Kemmerich, another of Paul's comrades. Kemmerich is at a dressing station where he has just had his leg amputated. It is obvious that Kemmerich will die. Motivated by practical considerations, Muller tries unsuccessfully to persuade Kemmerich to part with his airman's boots. Muller knows that the hospital orderlies will take them as soon as Kemmerich is dead. Outside the room Kropp and his friends bribe an orderly with cigarettes to give Kemmerich morphine to ease his pain. Even with the bribe Kropp must go along to see to it that the drug is given.

The last scene of the chapter takes place back at the huts. Kropp becomes savagely angry at Kantorek's letter referring to Kropp and his friends as the "Iron Youth." Paul reflects on the word, "youth." Although none of his comrades are more than twenty, they are old, prematurely aged by the devastating experiences of war.

Commentary

The purpose of Chapter One is to establish the novel's setting, point of view, atmosphere, themes and briefly introduce the characters. Plot development is relatively unimportant in this opening chapter.

The setting is behind the German front lines during the latter part of World War I. The tide of German victories has turned, and a tired Germany now faces reinforced Allied troops. Paul Baumer, the narrator of the book, will be the character through whom you will witness the war and its effects on the other characters. Paul is typical of the young German infantry soldier who fought in the war. Although he is only twenty, he has matured beyond his years because of his experiences in the trenches. Paul's viewpoint represents the viewpoint of the author.

Note that although the story is told from the German point of view, its message is universal and representative of the thoughts and feelings of the soldiers of all of the countries that participated in the Great War. As you read through the novel, you will not be conscious of the fact that the narrative is about Germans and German action. The horror of the war belonged to all men regardless of nationality.

The general mood of a work is referred to as atmosphere. The atmosphere of this novel is pervaded by death and destruction, hopelessness and desolation. Occasionally, moments of laughter or a bit of human warmth appear unexpectedly. The light contrast sharpens one's awareness of the terrifying destruction and dangers.

The center theme of the book is the vivid portrayal of the horror and stupidity of all war. Minor themes emerge from time to time. The theft of Kemmerich's watch while at the dressing station is an example of the general decay of moral value fostered by the war. This theme will be repeated. As the novel progresses, the reader, like the hospital orderly, becomes immune to these smaller acts of immorality. The moral decline, resulting from the war, was one of the great social wounds the post war world had to attempt to heal.

CHAPTER 2

Summary

The chapter begins with Paul's thoughts about his earlier life. His present existence at the front makes memories of his youthful experiences seem vague and unreal. Because they did not have the opportunity to begin families, careers or develop strong interests, Paul and his generation feel a sense of emptiness and isolation from their society. As a result, Paul concludes that his generation has become a wasteland.

It is clear to Paul that ten years of schooling have had far less effect than ten weeks of military training. While the school attempts to teach the value of thinking, the military swiftly crushes individuality and fits people to a system. Recruits quickly discover that rank deserves more respect than wisdom.

Kropp, Muller, Kemmerich and Paul were assigned to training under the command of Corporal Himmelstoss. Himmelstoss, a mailman in civilian life, took personal satisfaction from treating recruits harshly. Because of their youthful, defiant spirit, he took a special dislike to Paul and his friends. No amount of harassment, however, could conquer their spirit, and in the end Himmelstoss was forced to give up. Paul recognizes his training as having been necessary for survival at the front. From it grew comradeship and esprit-de-corps, two positive results.

The action of the chapter takes place in Kemmerich's hospital room. It is evident from the beginning of the scene that Kemmerich is about to die. He knows that his leg has been amputated, and his pathetic statement, "I wanted to become a head-forester once," reveals that his dreams are over. Paul tries to comfort him. Kemmerich senses the nearness of his own death. Although Paul as a soldier has witnessed many deaths, his childhood friendship with Kemmerich makes this death terribly personal.

While Kemmerich is in his death throes, Paul frantically searches for a doctor. The one he finds callously refuses to be bothered, having already amputated five legs that day. Upon his return with a hospital orderly, Paul finds Kemmerich dead. Haste is made to remove him so that others outside on the floor may take his bed.

Paul's reaction to Franz Kemmerich's death is expressed in thoughts of girls, flowery meadows and white clouds – images the reverse of the death scene witnessed minutes earlier. A strong sense of his own life force pours through him. He feels a great hunger to continue living as he returns to the hut.

Commentary

Kropp's ironic statement, "We are the Iron Youth," is echoed by Paul at the beginning of this chapter. In each of the chapters, there will be at least one angry expression of disappointment with the older generation and the chaos they have caused.

One of the purposes of Chapter 2 is to give the reader an opportunity to discover more about Paul, the seeing eye of the book. He appears sensitive and intelligent. He has written poetry and attempted a play. Although his thoughts appear to be unemotional, he is capable of strong feeling and compassion as illustrated by his reaction to Kemmerich's death. His experiences with death and destruction intensify his own desire to go on living. Though Paul does not fully comprehend everything he experiences, he tries to present it as truthfully as possible. The reader will probably find himself identifying with Paul as the novel progresses. That identification is important to the success of the novel because the central message of the book is carried by Paul.

Kemmerich's death illustrates part of the central message. The event provides Remarque with the opportunity to better ask one of the questions basic to the novel: "There he lies now – but why?"

Paul then declares that the whole world ought to be forced to pass Kemmerich's deathbed so that they will say, "That is Franz Kemmerich, nineteen-and-a-half years old, he doesn't want to die. Let him not die." The scene is designed to be an object lesson to the reader. How effectively this lesson hits its mark is in part related to how well the reader has identified with Paul Baumer.

CHAPTER 3

Summary

Reinforcements for Paul's unit arrive, providing an opportunity for Paul and his friends to feel and act like "stone-age" veterans. Kropp, having a bit of fun at the expense of the newcomers, calls the new recruits, "infants." Katczinsky tells one of them that he is lucky to have bread made from turnips instead of sawdust. As a joke, Kat then offers a new recruit some haricot beans. This, of course, is taken as kidding, but true to his reputation as a clever and successful scavenger, Kat produces a stew of beef and beans.

Kat is always able to find food and supplies, no matter where he happens to be. His abilities to provide for himself and his friends are nothing short of amazing. As Paul concludes, "If for but one hour in a year something eatable were to be had in some one place only, within that hour, as if moved by a vision, (Kat) would put on his cap, go out and walk directly there, as though following a compass, and find it." His masterpiece of scrounging is four boxes of lobsters.

While relaxing and watching a dog fight between a German and an Allied plane, Kat philosophizes that if everyone in a war were given the same food and pay, the war would be over in a day. Kropp proposes that war should be staged like a full fight with entrance tickets and bands. Ministers and generals of the two countries should be armed with clubs and sent into the arena. The survivor's country wins. Kropp felt that this would prevent the wrong people from doing the fighting.

Continuing his anti-war arguments, the author uses this opportunity to discuss power in general. Kropp maintains that man is essentially a beast. He points to the difference between a man in civilian society and the same man in the army. The more insignificant a man has been in civilian life, the more power goes to his head in the military.

The action of the chapter begins with Tjaden's announcement of Himmelstoss' arrival at the front. This causes Haie Westhus, Kropp, Tjaden and Paul to recall their revenge on Himmelstoss the day before they were sent to the front. Catching Himmelstoss returning to the barracks on a dark uninhabited road, they throw a blanket over his head and beat him unmercifully. Himmelstoss never discovers his assailants' identities. Paul and his friends are later described as "young heroes" by others in the barracks. Paul's wry observation, "We had become successful students of his (Himmelstoss') methods," is one of few humorous lines in the novel.

Commentary

Although Himmelstoss' punishment satisfies the reader's sense of justice, the entire incident is further proof of Kat's observation, "In himself man is essentially a beast." The real tragedy of the matter is recognized by Paul when he points out that his group's sole ambition is to "knock the conceit out of a postman."

The purpose of the chapter is to provide the reader with a more detailed description of the men who make up Paul's unit. Chapter 2 specifically examined Paul Baumer, the narrator of the story. Chapter 3 focuses on Kat and the others. Because the viewpoint of the novel is based on the experiences of the infantry soldier, Remarque feels that it is important to give the reader a better understanding of what the ordinary soldier thinks about, talks about and feels.

The relative inaction of the chapter acts as a bridge or an interlude between Kemmerich's death and the coming chapters about the front. Chapter 4 will immerse the reader directly in the battle. Like a camera dollying in on action, the first three chapters are merely an introduction to death. The author has talked of dying. Franz Kemmerich has died a comparatively "clean" death. Now the reader must prepare to be shelled, gassed, wounded, and slaughtered.

CHAPTER 4

Summary

The action of this chapter begins just after dark one day and ends the following morning. Paul's unit has been assigned the routine military task of laying barbed wire at the front line. Jammed into military trucks, the soldiers are carried as far as the artillery emplacements, just behind the front. The rest of the way must be traveled on foot.

The air is filled with acrid smoke and the roar of artillery. The nearness of the front brings about a change in every man. It is like a mysterious force which each can feel. Voices sound different; the body is in full readiness; and each man is thrown back on his animal instincts.

At the front, rockets and bursts of flame light up the area as Paul and the others complete their mission of rolling out and staking down the barbed wire. While waiting for the trucks to take them back, the men try to sleep. A sudden shelling puts an end to this.

Afterwards the air is filled with the horrible moaning of wounded horses. These sounds are especially difficult for Detering to endure because he is a farmer and fond of horses. Finally the horses are shot after the wounded men are treated. With the bombardment over, the men troop back toward the trucks.

The barrage starts again. Paul and his group are pinned down in a graveyard, the only cover being mounds of earth. Suddenly the fields become a surging sea of flame. Hit by splinters and shrapnel, but not seriously hurt, Paul crawls toward a shell hole. In the hole he finds a coffin and its corpse. A gas attack has started, and the shelling makes it impossible to escape.

When the bombardment ends, the graveyard is wreckage, the shells having unearthed the coffins and their occupants. The same recruit Paul comforted earlier lies wounded in the stomach and hip. It is clear to Paul and Kat that he will not live. He will be in agony as soon as the shock wears off and for as long as he lives. They quickly agree to perform a mercy killing. Before they can act, the rest of the group gather. The situation is parallel to the scene at Kemmerich's deathbed. Kat's comment, "Young innocents—" seems to be a plea addressed to the entire world and an echo to Paul's question, "There he lies now—but why?"

Commentary

Remarque speaks of the "front" in at least two senses; as a physical location and as a psychological force. German soldiers in World War I fought on two fronts, an Eastern and a Western Front. The fighting on the Eastern Front facing Russia was mild by comparison to that on the Western Front facing France. This novel is set on the Western Front, a fighting line approximately five hundred miles long. As the war progresses, this line gradually disintegrates. Toward the end of the novel, the final breakdown can be seen in the small sector where Paul and his company are fighting.

More than just a physical location, however, the front exerted a chilling, powerful influence over the soldiers who came within its "embrace." Paul describes the front as a "mysterious whirlpool" whose vortex he can feel sucking him "slowly, irresistibly and inescapably into itself." Moreover, this influence can be felt at some distance. As soon as Paul and his unit reach the artillery lines, the men feel it in their veins, in their hands, and there is "...a tense waiting, a watching, a profound growth, a strange sharpening of the senses..." It often seems to Paul that the air at the front shudders and vibrates, emitting an electric current of its own.

Chapter Four provides the reader some clear insights into the nature of World War I. Except for the naval battle of Jutland, this was mainly a land war. The trench became the soldier's home while at the front. Intricate tunnel networks were constructed by both sides. Paul acknowledges this basic relationship between earth and soldier when he states, "To no man does the earth mean so much as to the soldier." Later, Paul's reflections about the earth have a hymn-like quality. "Earth!—Earth!—Earth!" he chants. She is the soldier's only friend, his brother, and his mother. She may give him a new lease on life for another ten seconds, or she may receive him forever.

Continuing the development of the earth theme, the final scene of the chapter takes place in a cemetery. This place of death appropriately emphasizes the life-death existence of the soldier. During the shelling the relationship between the living and the dead becomes intimate. The living crawling into coffins with the dead to escape the bombardment. Paul points out that each of the dead that was flung up from a grave saved one of the soldiers. Finally, the living-dead theme is used to describe the state of the exhausted soldiers as they ride in the trucks back to the huts.

Remarque's use of horses in this chapter serves several purposes. (1) The presence of animals in the midst of battle dates the war. World War I was the beginning of modern mechanized warfare. Trucks, tanks, airplanes, and other modern weapons were in their early stages of development. Horses and donkeys were used extensively at the beginning of the war.

(2) The majestic bearing of the animals provides another contrast to the foolish, wretched activities of men. Just before moving into the front lines to lay the barbed wire, Paul encounters a column of men and horses. The horses are strangely beautiful as their backs shine in the moonlight and they toss their heads. The whole procession reminds Paul of a line of knights and their steeds. Later, however, after a bombardment, the same horses are wounded and dying. Their cries are terrible and unearthly. Some gallop into the distance, guts trailing in the dust, reminding one of the unfortunate horses used in bull fights.

(3) Paul comments that the sound of the dying horses is like the "moaning of the world...martyred creation, wild with anguish, filled with terror and groaning." It is as if all of creation has risen to accuse Man.

If you have ever wondered how an author creates a climax or moves a reader to a fevered pitch in a fictional account, this chapter is an excellent illustration. Beginning with the placid entry to the front lines and ending with the horror of horrors, the shelling in the graveyard, the selection of detail is deliberate and dramatic. Each is calculated to move the reader to a more intense emotional level. Notice the constant appeal to the senses: the color of the flares and rockets, the sounds emitted by all sizes of shells and bullets, the moaning of the dying horses, the cries of wounded men, the sense of suffocation felt when a man wears a gas mask after the air has been used up. All of these carefully placed details contribute to the impact of one of the most vivid chapters in the whole novel.

CHAPTER 5

Summary

Following the laying of barbed wire at the front, the soldiers in Paul's company are returned to the huts behind the lines. Time is passed in killing lice and anticipating the arrival of Himmelstoss, the harsh drillmaster.

While discussing Himmelstoss' reception, Muller poses a question often mused upon by the battle weary soldier: "What would you do if peace were declared tomorrow?" Each soldier in the group gives a different answer, representative of the spectrum of typical responses. Answers range from Haie Westhus' wish to remain in the peacetime army because it is better than digging peat for a living to Tjaden's vengeful desire to spend the rest of his life torturing Himmelstoss. The conclusion of the discussion is representative of the conclusion reached by the youth in German and Allied armies. Much of the trivial information drilled in the classroom had no practical application in the trenches.

Kropp expresses the feeling of the group when he says, "The war has ruined us for everything." It has squelched all ambition to become anything. Paul summarizes this loss when he concludes: "We don't want to take the world by storm. We are fleeing. We fly from ourselves. From our life. We were eighteen and had begun to love life and the world; and we had to shoot it to pieces. The first bomb, the first explosion burst in our hearts. We are cut off from activity, from striving, from progress. We believe in such things no longer, we believe in the war."

During the discussion Himmelstoss appears. The situation is reversed, and now Himmelstoss is the green new arrival. Insulted by Tjaden, Himmelstoss stalks off to the orderly room to have him arrested. The company commander, Lieutenant Bertinck, is sympathetic to Paul and his friends, but he is bound by duty to punish insubordination. Tjaden and Kropp are given light sentences of "open arrest."

The chapter ends with an episode in which Kat and Paul roast a stolen goose. Sitting together in the darkened hut, sharing the food and comradeship, they are described as "two minute sparks of life; outside is the night and the circle of death." The brotherhood that springs forth when men face a common danger is the only positive result of the war. The remaining food is shared with Kropp and Tjaden at the compound, and the circle of friendship is enlarged.

Commentary

One of the important laws of drama (and fiction) has to do with the use of contrast. Prudently used, contrasting scenes heighten the effect of essential scenes or those which advance the main action of the plot. Remarque purposively places scenes in the novel to produce the maximal emotional effect on the reader. Chapter 4 immersed the reader in the hell of warfare. Chapter 5 is relaxed and relatively free from the horror of the war. This is the pattern Remarque uses, his theory being that only through the hell of war can a man realize the absolute sweetness of peace. Again in Chapter 6, the reader is moved with Paul and his friends up to the front line to face an assault of the French troops. And so it goes all through the novel. Sometimes the contrast will be effected within a chapter, as in Chapter 6 when Paul dreams of childhood scenes after a bloody attack.

The purpose of Chapter 5 is to provide a relief from the action of Chapters 4 and 6. Two themes are developed further: the loss of ambition brought about by the war; the brotherhood that life in the trenches fostered.

CHAPTER 6

Summary

The action of this chapter is typical of the trench warfare of World War I. An offensive commonly began with a prolonged artillery bombardment. An infantry attack would follow. This usually forced a withdrawal to a second line of defense where the attack would be repulsed. A counter-attack would carry the battle back to the enemy front lines. Finally, both sides would return to their original positions. So it went throughout most of the war, the Western Front line remained relatively stable despite great loss of life.

Remarque sets the scene for a typical slaughter with a high, double wall of new coffins. Ironically, these mute symbols of death are stacked against a shelled schoolhouse, another symbol of Paul's former life.

Paul describes the front as a kind of "cage" in which everyone must fearfully wait for whatever may happen. Staying alive is recognized by every soldier as a matter of pure chance. The action of this chapter makes this perfectly clear.

The approaching offensive is signaled by the prevalence of corpse-rats, extra rations, increased supplies of ammunition, and rumors about new enemy weapons. Day after day the heavy bombardment continues until there is little left of the trench system. The tension caused by waiting for the attack drives many of the green recruits to madness.

When the attack finally comes, Paul and the others are transformed into animals defending themselves against annihilation. It is not fighting, but self-preservation that motivates the soldier in the midst of a fierce battle. Paul sums up the soldier's will to survive when he says, "If your own father came over with them you would not hesitate to fling a bomb into him."

The holocaust seethes and grows, gaining momentum like a charging steed until Remarque reaches the ultimate in descriptions of front line horrors—"men living with their skulls blown open... soldiers running with their two feet cut off..." and so on and bloodily on. The death of Kemmerich early in the novel seems cheerful by comparison. The battle subsides after the loss of a few hundred yards and many hundreds of lives.

Following a summer of this kind of fighting, the remaining thirty-two men out of 150 in Paul's company return to the rear lines.

Commentary

Chapter 6 focuses on the characteristic pattern of world War I front line battle. Remarque tries to demonstrate the futility of wholesale slaughter for the purpose of gaining a few yards of worthless earth. Rather than simply telling the reader that war is hell, which most people agree to intellectually, the author forces us to see and feel the experience from the viewpoint of the infantryman. No holds are barred in this chapter, as none should be. The sharpened spade and the saw tooth bayonet are examples of the terrible brutalities of this war. The horrors are endless, and Remarque makes this chapter more grim, more repugnant than any of the preceding. By the end of it, the reader has become numb to human suffering, a condition roughly akin to that possessed by the veteran after long exposure to death.

In contrast to the images of destruction in this chapter, there are many references to children and images of beauty and innocence. One morning, for example, Paul watches two butterflies at play in front of his trench. They offer a brilliant contrast to the stark, shell-torn landscape. Again in the next chapter Paul contemplates butterflies, but they are the ones he caught as a child. The butterflies serve both to contrast with Paul's present existence and to symbolize his lost childhood.

Paul sees his own childhood reflected in the young recruits sent to the front, poorly trained and outfitted in uniforms never intended for childish measurements. Between five and ten recruits are killed for every experienced soldier. The presence of these very young replacements was indicative of a crumbling Germany which had reached the bottom of her manpower barrel.

The image of forlorn children is used again to convey the feelings of Paul's generation. "We are forlorn like children, and experienced like old men, we are crude and sorrowful and superficial — I believe we are lost." The reference to the lost generation of the twenties is clearly intended.

CHAPTER 7

Summary
Chapter 7 consists of three basic scenes; the first two provide a transition to the most important scene, Paul's experience with his family and friends at home on leave.

Because two-thirds of his company were killed or wounded, Paul's unit is taken to a field depot where they are given an abundance of food and rest. Here the terror of the front is temporarily forgotten. The soldiers are even able to joke about their experiences, but this is really only a way to keep from thinking seriously about them. Paul knows that there will come a time when all of these memories will return to haunt those who survive.

An old movie poster with the figure of a pretty girl and a young man in white trousers reminds Paul and Albert Kropp that there is another side to life. While swimming, Paul and his friends strike up an acquantance with three enemy French women who live across the sentry-guarded river. By promising food, Tjaden and the others are able to arrange a rendezvous for that evening. The evening meetings continue until Paul receives a seventeen day leave, after which he must report to the moors for a training course before returning to his company.

The train ride home prepares Paul for his old life as he sees a panorama of meadows, farms, children and finally his own home town. The trip from the station to his home is filled with places and memories of childhood experiences. The transition from front to home is completed when Paul hears the voice of his own sister and sobs.

Early in his visit Paul finds that a distance has grown between him and his family. The change is not so much in the family as it is in Paul. Even his room and books, which were so painstakingly collected, fail to stir his former interest and ambition. Having not directly experienced the war, the people Paul meets have no real understanding of the German predicament. His old German master refers to Paul as a "young warrior" and talks of a breakthrough and final victory.

While on leave Paul visits Mittelstaedt, a former school companion who has been promoted to company commander. Kantorek, the teacher responsible for recruiting Paul and his classmates for the military, has been assigned to Mittelstaedt's company as an ordinary soldier. Mittelstaedt takes every opportunity to torment him. He taunts Kantorek with his own valiant phrases, ordering him to perform the most menial tasks. Boettcher, the former school porter, is a model soldier in the company. During his last four days, Paul pays a visit to Franz Kemmerich's mother. To assuage her grief, he is forced to invent a story and swear that her son's death was instantaneous and that he felt no pain.

When his leave is over, Paul can only conclude that his stay at home has made matters worse. Before coming home he was indifferent and hopeless. Now he is in agony for himself, for his mother who is dying of cancer, and for his lost youth.

Commentary

The technical handling of this chapter is worth a brief analysis. Artistically Remarque faces the difficult problem of orientating the reader from the battlefront to the homefront. The transition is made gradually by removing Paul's unit farther behind the lines, introducing a poster with the fresh, young girl who suggests a forgotten side of life, providing an episode involving Paul and his comrades with three French girls, and finally describing the familiar countryside and home town as it appears to Paul during his journey home. Within a few pages the reader scarcely realizes that he is now being presented with a scene offering the most important contrast in the novel.

The rest of the chapter is devoted to Paul's recognition of the changes that have taken place within himself as a result of his war experiences. The magnitude of the change is made clear when Paul puts on his civilian clothes. "I feel awkward," he says. "The suit is rather tight and short. I have grown in the army." The growth must be understood in a double sense, having direct reference to changes in Paul's inner life as reflected by a later comment, "...now I saw that I have been crushed without knowing it. I find I do not belong here any more, it is a foreign world." Like so many of his generation, Paul was irreconcilably isolated from his former life. Because leave only made him more acutely aware of this isolation, Paul concludes that coming home was a mistake.

In this chapter the reader can see a partial reason for the writing and teaching of this book. None of the home people show any real understanding of this specific war and the efforts of war in general. Consider the advice Paul's mother gives him: watch out for French girls and be careful at the front. Paul's father wants to hear of his son's war adventures. Former teachers talk of victory. The novel then is an attempt to dramatize the bitter truth.

CHAPTER 8

Summary

A military training camp on the moors provides the setting for Chapter 8. The camp is near enough to Paul's home so that his sister and father can visit him on a Sunday afternoon. Paul's days are occupied by routine company drill. Evenings are spent at the Soldier's Home, a place for relaxation when off duty, and a place where Paul can play the piano. The atmosphere of the camp is relaxed and undemanding. Paul makes no close friends, preferring to being alone with his thoughts. Many of his reflections concern nature. The fall colors and peace of the moors make the war seem remote.

Next to the training camp is a Russian prisoner-of-war camp. Because of the general scarcity of food, the prisoners are on the verge of starving to death. They are a docile, pathetic lot, spending much of their time searching the garbage for scraps of food. To obtain additional food, the Russians trade their personal belongings or carved trinkets, but the German peasants drive a hard bargain.

Daily contact with the prisoners causes Paul to reflect on the fact that a word of command has made these people his enemies. An unseen document has legalized mass murder. Paul is frightened by his own thoughts, but vows to give them further consideration when the war is over. He vaguely understands that he will crusade against war and spread the truth and that this task will be the only one that will make life worthy after the hideous years in the trenches.

Paul is visited by his sister and father on the last Sunday before he is to return to the front. It is a depressing, uncomfortable visit. He learns that his mother has gone to the hospital because of cancer and will be operated on shortly. Family funds are inadequate. Paul knows that his father will have to put in many hours of overtime to pay for the operation. When his father and sister leave, they give him some food from home which he shares with the Russian prisoners.

Commentary

Throughout the novel Paul continually makes discoveries about society and about himself. It must be remembered that Paul is young, his thinking has not matured, and that he is groping towards the truth. His thoughts about the Russian prisoners, for example lead him to some frightening conclusions, frightening because they contradict what he has been taught by the society in which he lives. "I dare think this way no more. This way lies the abyss," he concludes when he discovers that the Russians are really human beings like his own countrymen. At the same time Paul becomes aware of a vague obligation to tell the world of this revelation. He sees his future role in society as one where he spreads this truth. Interestingly enough, this is exactly how Remarque has spent the rest of his life. His stories change, but the themes are always the same.

CHAPTER 9

Summary

After several nights of searching for his unit, Paul finds that they have been designated the "flying division" to be used wherever the battle is heaviest. Reunited finally with Kat and the others, Paul feels a sense of homecoming and belongingness.

In preparation for an inspection by the Kaiser, new uniforms are issued. Everything is cleaned and polished for the coming review. Paul is disappointed when the Kaiser appears, having had the impression that his voice was deeper and that he was taller. The visit, however, generates another discussion of the causes of the war. Paul and his friends find it difficult to understand how both sides can be fighting for a just cause. One must be in error. Again the point is made that the participants in the war are ordinary people like themselves who would prefer to be leading peaceful lives at home. The real causes of the war are incomprehensible to the common man, and in the end he can only conclude that there is the front and he is there and that is that.

Paul's company is again sent to the front although there had been a rumor that they were to be sent to Russia. While on patrol, Paul becomes panicky and temporarily loses his courage. Hearing the voices of his friends talking in the trenches, he is calmed and feels a sense of identity with his comrades.

Later, on the same patrol, Paul loses his sense of direction and is pinned down in a shell hole during an enemy attack. Face down in the mud, he pretends to be dead as the first wave of troops pass over him. When the attack is repulsed, a retreating French soldier jumps into his shell hole to escape the German machine gun fire. Striking blindly, Paul stabs the man with his dagger. Throughout the next day Paul is forced to remain in the shell hole with the mortally wounded soldier. During this time the soldier gasps for air and looks terrorized at Paul when he tries to bandage his wounds and give him water. About three in the afternoon, the French soldier dies.

Wishing it had been otherwise, Paul is stricken by his conscience. The war has suddenly become terribly personal for Paul. Later he identifies the soldier as Gerard Duval, a printer with a wife and a child. In a moment of emotional agony, Paul vows to make amends to the man's family, to spend the rest of his life preventing the occurrence of another such war.

When it becomes dark again, Paul returns to his lines. The next morning he relates the incident to Kat and Albert. They assure him that it is not his fault and that he did the only thing he could. Above them at a firing stand, Sergeant Oellrich deliberately snipes at the enemy, taking pride and pleasure from picking off human lives. He will receive an award for having a high score. Observing this, Paul attempts to justify his killing of Duval by saying, "After all, war is war." This is an attempt to ease his stricken conscience.

Commentary

The most important value Paul finds in his life as a soldier is the comradeship with the men in his unit. But for these single human relationships, he might have been driven to madness. Two examples of the importance of this comraderie are found in this chapter. When Paul returns from his leave and training camp, he breathes a great sigh of relief and says simply, "This is where I belong." His return to camp is far more meaningful to him than his return home on leave. A second example occurs when Paul is on patrol and suddenly loses his control and courage. Hearing the voices of his own troops and thinking he hears the voice of Kat is enough to calm him and help him regain his composure. "I am no longer a shuddering speck of existence, alone in the darkness... we are nearer than lovers...," he comments. These friendships are the only solid elements of the soldier's life.

In the previous chapter Remarque placed Paul near a camp of Russian prisoners. Here he discovered that these creatures were human that they "look just as kindly as our peasants in Friesland." This experience leads Paul to see the war in more personal and human terms. Before this it had been a matter of ducking enemy shells and firing back from a great distance. The enemy remained faceless. Murdering him was a reasonable front line behavior. In this chapter Remarque deliberately brought Paul face to face with an enemy who suddenly has a name, a family, a past and dreams. He turns out to be an ordinary man—a printer by trade—a man who writes his wife each day and has a little girl. In a soliloquy after Duval's death, Paul asks, "Why do they never tell us that you are just poor devils like us, that your mothers are just as anxious as ours and that we have the same fear of death, and the same dying and the same agony—Forgive me, comrade; how could you be my enemy?"

After this experience, Paul's comment that war is war is only a half-believed statement—a mask for his real feeling which he still only partially understands.

CHAPTER 10

Summary
Paul's squad has been selected to guard the supply depot of an otherwise abandoned village. From the town's shell torn houses, they provision themselves with food and the comforts of home. For three weeks they glut themselves with food and sleep while the town is gradually leveled by shells.

A few days after this assignment, Albert Kropp and Paul are caught in the open, trying to evacuate a village. Both are wounded, Paul in the leg and arm and Albert in the leg. They are picked up by an ambulance and taken to a dressing station. There an army surgeon cruelly and unnecessarily probes Paul's wound.

By bribing a sergeant-major with cigars left over from the supply depot, Albert and Paul are able to get themselves placed on a hospital train returning to the rear lines. While on the train Albert's fever begins to rise, and he is in danger of being separated from Paul. By heating his temperature thermometer, Paul is able to pretend that he too has a fever, and both succeed in being put off at the same station.

Paul and Albert are placed in the same room in a Catholic hospital. Here they meet Josef Hammacher, who has a "shooting license" certificate saying that he is not to be held responsible for his actions; Franz Wachter, who later dies of a lung wound; and little Peter, the only patient ever to return from the "Dying Room," a place where patients who are about to die are sent.

Many patients come and go in Paul and Albert's room. Paul's bones will not knit, and they operate on him. Albert's leg is amputated. On recovery, Albert is sent to an institute for artifical limbs, Paul is given another leave, before he returns to the front lines.

Commentary

At this point in the development of the novel, it is appropriate for Remarque to devote an entire chapter to a tour of a wartime hospital. Working backward from the author's summary comment, "A hospital alone shows what war is," observe the presentation of details in this chapter. The opening scene, relatively happy, does not prepare you for what is to follow. Even the continual removal of wounded to the "Dying Room" does not pack much of a wallop in view of previous combat descriptions. When Paul is able to walk around the hospital, Remarque has opportunity to detail all of the various wounds and their consequences. It is so staggering that Paul at first can only comment, "Here a man realizes for the first time in how many places a man can get hit." To complete the calculated effect, Remarque then asks the reader to bear in mind that he is describing only one hospital and that there are hundreds of thousands in Germany and France and Russia. Clearly, one need go no further than the nearest military hospital to have a complete experience of what war is like.

All of this, of course, leads Paul to two questions: what is the logic of a thousand-year culture that permits these torture chambers? What is to become of my generation now that my knowledge of life is limited to death? These two questions are at the core of the novel.

The medical profession in this chapter is dealt a blow. Doctors seem cruel, interested in using patients for guinea pigs to further their own experimentation, and preferring amputation to surgical repair because it is easier. As Josef Hammacher put it, "...the war is a glorious time...for all the surgeons." Remarque exploits the example of the chief surgeon's experiments in correcting flat feet. He produces club feet instead. No doubt there was truth to these examples, yet the pressure of mass operations, inadequate supplies and personnel, and poor conditions for treatment of patients must have compounded the problem enormously.

CHAPTER 11

Summary

Chapter 11 records the final collapse of the German army and the Western Front. It also records the deaths of all of Paul's comrades, Muller, Bertinck, Leer and finally Kat.

Life for the soldier alternates between the front and the rest camps. The men are reduced to "unthinking animals," and only their strong sense of camaraderie helps them to endure their condition.

Detering sees a cherry tree in blossom in a garden. He is so deeply affected by memories of his own farm that he deserts and tries to go home. He is caught and court-martialed. The case of Detering is typical of the general madness overtaking the men.

Outnumbered, underfed, without supplies, the army continues to fight. Weapons newly discovered and invented at the beginning of the war, became perfected by the end of it. Tanks, planes and flame throwers are now brought in by Allied troops in abundance. As Paul puts it, there is no escape but the trench, the hospital or the grave.

Kat's shin is smashed by a bullet. Paul carries him on his back to a dressing station. Near the station Kat catches a splinter in his head. He is dead on arrival. This is the final blow for Paul.

Commentary

The main purpose of this chapter is to complete the destruction of Paul's inner life. The death of his best friend, Kat, is really the end of Paul's life. When his actual death comes in the next chapter, it is difficult to feel a sense of loss. Paul has depended on his comrades for a shred of security. One by one they have been killed. The death of Kat is the final blow that strips Paul of everything resembling human comfort.

This chapter also records the entry of America into the war, bringing with her fresh men and supplies and hurling them against an exhausted Germany. Everything goes to pieces in this chapter — even the front crumbles as the troops are reduced to crater warfare. The Germans bring up very young soldiers who only know how to die.

For those who have survived the war to this point, there is the sickening fear that death will come just before it's all over. Stephen Crane's short story, "The Open Boat," expresses the feeling of the German soldier during the last days of the summer of 1918: "If I am going to be drowned — if I am going to be drowned — if I am going to be drowned, why, in the name of the seven mad gods who rule sea, was I allowed to come thus far and contemplate sand and trees?" Paul is killed one month before the Armistice.

Two items in this chapter offer an excellent opportunity to observe the interaction of symbols and narrative: the cherry blossoms and the boots. The blossoms, of course, suggest spring, a of rebirth and life. For the farmer, spring is a time for planting and nurturing life. Detering, faced daily with death, goes suddenly mad when he encounters the fact and symbol of spring in the midst of the shell torn landscape of the front. The memory and attraction of spring is too great for him to resist. He follows his inner calling to his farm and spring plowing. In a sense, the tree was a call to life for Detering — a last chance to escape the perpetual winter and death of the front. It is small wonder that Detering responded.

The boots are woven like a thread throughout the novel. Kemmerich first possesses them, but even he got them from an airman. They are passed to Muller who gives them to Paul who promises them to Tjaden. In a sense the boots serve to unite the friends, being passed and worn by each in turn.

CHAPTER 12

Summary
It is the fall of 1918, and Paul is the only one of the seven classmates remaining. There is a great deal of talk about peace, and revolution is threatened if it does not come.

Paul has been given a fourteen day rest because of gas poisoning. He again reflects on the fate of his generation and his personal destiny. His prediction is that his generation is without hope and will fall to ruin because of the destruction of its spirit.

The last two paragraphs are written in the third person in the form of an epitaph or epilogue. Paul Baumer was killed one month before the Armistice. He fell "on a day that was so quiet and still on the whole front, that the army report confined itself to the single sentence: All quiet on the Western Front."

Commentary

The death of Paul is an anticlimax. The emotion experienced by the reader is probably a general feeling in response to the novel as a whole rather than specifically to Paul's death. Had he survived the war, he would have joined the frustrated, searching group of adults who were appropriately referred to as the Lost Generation of the Twenties.

The ideas expressed by Paul in the final chapter are a repetition of those voiced throughout the novel.

THE AUTHOR'S STYLE

With the exception of the last two paragraphs of the novel, *All Quiet on the Western Front* is written in the first person narrative point of view. As used in this novel, the first person has both advantages and disadvantages. It is a definite advantage to the author to use a method of telling his story that will force the reader to identify with the thoughts and conclusions of the main character. Use of the first person gives the impression of actual experience being transmitted to the reader without the usual interference from the mind of a third party.

On the other side of the coin, Paul, our narrator, is young and immature. We are asked to consider and accept some rather momentous conclusions based on the experience of a nineteen year old infantry soldier. In the case of this novel, however, the advantages of the first person point of view far outstrip the disadvantages. What Paul does not have in years is more than accounted for in what the reader interprets as honesty and devotion to a principle which transcends any national allegiance.

The outstanding feature of Remarque's style lies in his sense of the theatrical. Each of the twelve chapters in the book is carefully placed so that the subject of each draws the reader closer to the important conclusion Remarque wishes him to reach. By using contrasting scenes and chapters, the reader is paced so that individual scenes will produce the greatest possible effect. All this is lighted with the glare of rockets and flares, complete with the sound effects of shells, men and animals.

Coupled with Remarque's ability to handle description, images and symbols, the novel transcends ordinary battlefield fiction. Paul and friends come to life. The truth they speak is not limited to a single war in a century of wars.

REMARQUE AS A SOCIAL CRITIC

With firm belief in an early and complete military victory, both sides entered the First World War. Nine million lives and four wasted empires later, the great conflict ended. The cost in human life and property was staggering: 22 million were wounded, 7 million of them were permanently disabled; over 9 million civilians were killed. A total cost of 400 billion dollars financed the holocaust.

Could they have been reckoned, the hidden costs probably would have been even greater. The damage to a generation of men on both sides was inestimable. In a sense, *All Quiet on the Western Front* is a firsthand account of this "hidden cost" of war. Remarque, himself a front line soldier who experienced all he wrote of, seethed with despair and unrest for ten years before he brought himself to write his reactions.

The success of this first novel was immediate and enormous. A journalist for the Boston *Evening Transcript* reported that within the first year almost 1½ million copies of the book were printed and that 800,000 alone were sold in Germany. Clearly, Remarque's short novel, dramatizing the war experiences of a young German foot soldier, touched the heart of the matter for people on both sides of the Atlantic who ten years later still deeply felt the experience of the war.

It can only be concluded that Remarque was in tune with the general feeling of his generation and his times and that he was able to communicate this tragic event with honesty, precision and clarity.

Although the book is an account of World War I from the viewpoint of an ordinary soldier, the criticism of the German war machine and the Kaiser is apparent. In the beginning of the novel, and repeated in every chapter at least once, is a tirade against the boastful supremacy of German nationalism ideas preached by the elder, supposedly responsible members of society. It was this inflated viewpoint that was responsible for bringing the Behm's and the Kemmerich's into the military and up to the front where they quickly became cannon fodder. The guardians of the society — the teachers, the government, the military, the elders — conspired knowingly and unknowingly to nurture the myth of German supremacy. The falsity of this notion was revealed, as Paul puts it, when the first explosion came and the first of his schoolmates fell in battle.

The same disastrous nationalism could be seen growing again during the twenties and thirties. The bitter lesson of defeat had not really been learned. Remarque and others could see the mistakes of the Kaiser and the German Republic about to be repeated under Hitler's leadership.

In addition to his criticism of contemporary Germany, Remarque poses some penetrating questions regarding the very nature of Man. Contrasted to the animals in some of the scenes of the novel, Man looks foolish and shabby. Just before moving into the front lines to lay barbed wire, Paul encounters a column of men and horses. The horses are strangely beautiful as they toss their heads in the moonlight. The whole procession reminds Paul of a line of knights and their steeds. Later, after a severe bombardment, the same horses are wounded and dying. Their cries are terrible and unearthly. Some gallop into the distance, their entrails dragging in the dust. Paul comments that the sound of the dying horses is like the "moaning of the world...martyred creation wild with anguish, filled with terror and groaning." It is as if all of creation has risen to accuse Man, the great destroyer.

Despite the serious nature of Remarque's insights into both Man and Society, the tone of the novel is restrained and not overwhelmingly bitter. As a result, the emotional impact of the novel on the reader is apt to be great—perhaps greater than that felt after reading all subsequent books on war.

MAJOR CHARACTER ANALYSES

Paul Baumer

Paul Baumer is the character through whose eyes the reader views the action and thought of the novel. Through Paul, the author speaks of his experiences and reaction to the First World War.

Paul is typical of the young German infantry soldier who is brought to the front lines after a brief period of training. His growth to manhood is completed amid the wretchedness and despair of those who fight and died in the trenches.

At the time the story opens, Paul, although only twenty years old, is already a hardened veteran. One of his schoolmates, Josef Behm has been killed. Another, Franz Kemmerich will die shortly from a leg amputation. Most of Paul's youthful idealism, learned in school and fostered by his parents and teachers, has disappeared. Although he accepts his lot as a front line soldier, he becomes increasingly aware of the futility of the war and its colossal waste of human life.

Paul does not undergo a major character change during the novel. Much of the real destruction of his ambition and ideals has occurred before the first chapter begins. The subsequent action of the story sees this destruction completed as his few remaining values and hopes are shattered. His friends are killed, his past becomes meaningless, and he has no future. His net gain is a few fundamental truths about war and society. Beyond this Paul is emotionally and intellectually bankrupt.

Corporal Himmelstoss

Himmelstoss, the corporal responsible for the basic training given to Paul Baumer and his comrades, typifies the truism that power corrupts. Himmelstoss, a little man, uses his petty authority over recruits to satisfy his personal desire for power. A postman in civilian life, he takes every opportunity to make life miserable for green army recruits. Paul and his friends finally get their revenge, but only a front line shelling has any real effect on Himmelstoss' character.

Himmelstoss represents a military type universally hated and feared. A few stripes or insignia make these individuals tyrants of their own small worlds.

Stanislaus Katczinsky

Although not one of Paul's classmates, Katczinsky becomes Paul's closest friend. He is forty years old and a cobbler by trade. Their differences in age and background only serve to draw Katczinsky and Paul closer together. Called Kat by his friends, he has the uncanny ability to find food and the comforts of home in places where not so much as a crust of bread is available. Kat symbolizes the shrewd, self-reliant soldier who has turned his imagination and inventiveness to practical uses.

Above all Kat is warm and good natured. His death near the close of the war is the final shock for Paul. Kat is the last and best of his friends.

Kantorek

Kantorek is the teacher who persuaded Paul and his classmates to assume their patriotic responsibilities and enlist in the army. He uses his position as a teacher to spread the myth of the German Destiny. For Paul and his friends, Kantorek represents the betrayal of youth by the older generation.

Later Kantorek is called up as a reservist and placed in a unit under the command of Mittlestaedt, a former pupil. The situation provides Mittlestaedt with an unlimited opportunity to inflict all of the indignities on his former teacher which he had suffered as a former student. The pattern of revenge parallels that taken on Himmelstoss. The two situations indicate the loss of esteem suffered by the elder generation.

Albert Kropp

Albert Kropp is one of Paul's classmates. He has a reputation for being the best thinker in Paul's class. In group discussions, Kropp proposes the most profound solutions to problems. It is his idea, for example, to transform the institution of war into a kind of public festival held in an arena. Only the politicians and generals can be injured while the common man simply watches and awaits the outcome.

Both Albert Kropp and Paul Baumer are sent to a military hospital behind the lines because of wounds. Kropp's leg is amputated, and he is eventually sent home. He presumably survives the war, although he is not mentioned again.

Tjaden

He is described as skinny and having a sharp, mousy appearance. Nonetheless, Tjaden is the most voracious eater in Paul's company. He is like a growing adolescent who is never filled. The reader first meets Tjaden as he is ready to pick a fight with Ginger, the company cook, who appears to be welching on rations ordered for a full complement of soldiers. Because of heavy casualties, only a part of the company has returned for chow. This causes a superabundance of food. Tjaden sees this overage as rightfully belonging to him and the men remaining. Ginger is concerned because he has overdrawn. Each views the food in his characteristic manner, Ginger as a miser and Tjaden as a glutton.

Tjaden was not one of Paul's classmates. He was of the same age as the others and fits well in the group with Kropp, Muller and the others. In civilian life he had worked as a locksmith.

Detering

Detering is an example of the simple, peace-loving peasant farmer who cared more for his wife and farm than political philosophies and militarism. He spends most of his time dreaming of tilling the soil and harvesting crops. One spring when nature surrounds him with memories of his home, he becomes deranged and goes A.W.O.L. His desire to return to his farm is so strong that all caution and reason are ignored. He is caught and court martialed.

Haie Westhus

In private life Haie Westhus was a digger of peat, a job that would be comparable to that of a coal miner. For Haie, the peace-time army seems attractive. It offers him a clean place to sleep, three square meals and a cleaner job. Haie is the only one in Paul's group who would reenlist in the postwar army if given the opportunity.

QUESTIONS

1. What is the significance of the statement, "To no man does the earth mean so much as the soldier?"

2. How does the author's use of contrasting scenes make the novel's ideas more vivid and forceful?

3. Consider the actions of Paul's family and friends when he is home on leave. How do these individual situations illustrate the public's lack of understanding of the war?

4. Has Remarque fulfilled his purpose as set forth in the preface to the book? Illustrate your conclusion with examples from the book.

5. Contrast Paul's killing of Gerard Duval with Sergeant Oellrich's sniping at the enemy at the front. Wherein lies the difference in their actions?

6. What was Remarque's opinion of the medical profession during the war? Does this opinion appear to be justified?

7. The death of the main character provides the climax to the plot structure in many novels. Why isn't this true of *All Quiet on the Western Front?* Where is the climax of this novel?

SUGGESTED THEME TOPICS

1. Many of Germany's postwar problems are intimated in the novel. After reading Remarque's, *The Road Back,* trace the relationship of the problems in both novels.

2. Compare the emotional and intellectual growth of Paul Baumer to some other anti-war protagonist such as Henry Fleming in *The Red Badge of Courage,* the youthful foot soldier in Civil War battles.

3. Compare the overall effect of *All Quiet on the Western Front* with another literary form that develops the same basic theme. Wilfred Owen's poem, "Dulce Et Decorum Est" might offer a good comparison.

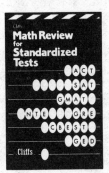 

DEMIAN

NOTES

ncluding
- *Life and Background*
- *Introduction to* Demian
- *List of Characters*
- *Critical Commentaries*
- *Character Analyses*
- *Review Questions*
- *Selected Bibliography*

by
Bruce L. Marcoon, M.Ed.
English Department
Upper Darby Senior High School

INCORPORATED

LINCOLN, NEBRASKA 68501

Editor

Gary Carey, M.A.
University of Colorado

Consulting Editor

James L. Roberts, Ph.D.
Department of English
University of Nebraska

ISBN 0-8220-0385-6
© Copyright 1974
by
C. K. Hillegass
All Rights Reserved
Printed in U.S.A.

1988 Printing

Cliffs Notes, Inc.   Lincoln, Nebraska

CONTENTS

LIFE AND BACKGROUND 5

INTRODUCTION TO "DEMIAN" 10

LIST OF CHARACTERS 12

CRITICAL COMMENTARIES 14

    Two Realms 14
    Cain 17
    Among Thieves 21
    Beatrice 24
    The Bird Fights Its Way Out of the Egg 29
    Jacob Wrestling 33
    Eva 35
    The End Begins 39

CHARACTER ANALYSES 41

    Emil Sinclair 41
    Max Demian 41
    Frau Eva 42
    Pistorius 42
    Knauer 42
    Franz Kromer 42

REVIEW QUESTIONS 43

ANNOTATED SELECTED BIBLIOGRAPHY 45

A HERMAN HESSE BIBLIOGRAPHY FOR THE ENGLISH-
SPEAKING STUDENT 48

Life and Background

Hermann Hesse was born in the little south German village of Calw on July 2, 1877. Situated on the edge of the Black Forest, Calw was to become the colorful setting of much of Hesse's writing. Hesse was the son of Johannes Hesse, who had been a missionary for the Lutheran Pietists to India. Forced to return to Europe after a short stay in India, Johannes worked in, and helped establish, a religious publishing house in Calw. Hermann's maternal grandfather, Hermann Gundert, also spent a major portion of his life as a missionary in India, acquiring a huge library of books about Eastern thought and becoming a master of Indic languages.

As a child, Hesse was greatly subjected to religious influences, both to the narrower views of Protestantism as well as to the wider scope of the Eastern religions and philosophies. Both views never left him; they became an integral part of his thought. His house in Calw was frequently the scene of visitations from foreigners, ranging from Buddhists to Americans. At his disposal was his grandfather's rich library. Hesse himself much later stated that all of his writing was religious in nature, not in the orthodox sense, but in a larger, universal way.

It was established early that Hesse would become a theological student. While showing intellectual promise as a student, young Hesse disliked school, especially the rigidity and the stifling of creativity of the German educational system of his time. His grades were never outstanding, and he disliked his teachers. He once stated that he had had only one teacher whom he liked. His reaction to this oppressive atmosphere is also reflected in his writings, especially in the bitter attack in *Unterm Rad (Beneath the Wheel)*. By the age of thirteen, Hesse had decided that he was going to be a poet. Great stress caused him to flee the Maulbronn Seminary, the setting of Mariabronn in *Narcissus and Goldmund.* He became so despondent that he considered suicide and a pistol for that end was purchased.

Causing great concern to his parents, Hesse was subjected to a variety of remedies for his rebelliousness. These ranged from a school for the disturbed to an attempt at exorcism. In 1894, Hesse became an apprentice in Perrot's tower clock factory in Calw. Needless to say, this was not satisfactory to him. Some progress was made in 1895 when he became an apprentice in the book trade in Heckenhauer's bookstore in Tubingen, although Hesse was still a rebel. A few years later he served in a similar capacity in Basel, from where he traveled through Switzerland and to Italy.

After writing a few minor works, Hesse achieved recognized literary success in 1904 with the publication of *Peter Camenzind,* a very popular book written in the tradition of the German Romanticists. In the same year he married Maria Bernoulli, and the couple took up a secluded residence at Gaienhofen, where Hesse became a free lance writer and a contributor to a number of journals.

Hesse's second successful novel, *Unterm Rad (Beneath the Wheel)* was published in 1906, followed by *Gertrud* in 1910 and *Rosshalde* in 1914. The latter work strongly depicts the plight of the temperamental artist and his wife. Meanwhile, Hesse had become associated with the pacifist Romain Rolland and had been writing numerous essays against the growing nationalism of the German people. Many of these writings have been translated into English and are available in a volume entitled *If the War Goes On....* The publication of *Knulp* in 1915 includes three stories about the life of a colorful vagabond.

A turning point in Hesse's life occurred in 1916 when his father's death, coupled with the illnesses of his son Martin and his wife, forced Hermann to seek refuge in a Lucerne sanatorium. His condemnation by his native Germany for his pacifistic views probably compounded his already serious problems. In 1916-17 Hesse had more than seventy sessions with a psychologist, J. B. Lang, who was a disciple of the famous Carl Gustav Jung. Supposedly these were more friendly conversations than attempts at serious psychoanalysis. The result was favorable for Hesse and of great importance to his future writings. The works following this period, beginning with *Demian*, cannot be fully understood without a recognition of the Jungian influence. Following *Demian* were *Marchen* (reprinted in English as *Strange News from Another Star*) and *Klingsor's Last Summer*, a collection of three excellent novellas, originally containing *Siddhartha*. At the same time, Hesse became co-editor of the newspaper *Vivos Voco* and decided to move, alone, to Montagnola. In 1920, he produced *Blick ins Chaos* which was referred to by T. S. Eliot in *The Wasteland*.

Hesse divorced his wife and adopted Swiss citizenship in 1923. He then married Ruth Wegner the following year. The years 1924-27 saw the publication of some of Hesse's best autobiographical pieces, namely *Kurgast* (1924), and *Die Nurnberger Reise* (1927), as well as his second divorce, which is reflected upon in *Der Steppenwolf* (1927). *Narcissus and Goldmund* was published in 1930, and shortly thereafter Hesse married Ninon Dolbin, who was to remain his companion until his death. In 1932, Hesse published *Die Morgenlandfahrt (The Journey to the East)*. The only other major novel to be produced was *The Glass Bead Game (Magister Ludi)*, which was published in 1943. Hesse was awarded the Nobel Prize in 1946.

During the course of World War II, Hesse was to relive the nightmare of World War I. Once again he became the subject of German ostracism because of his anti-nationalistic views. Following the war, however, his writings again became popular in Germany and have remained so until relatively recent times. After receiving many literary honors, Hermann Hesse died in seclusion of a cerebral hemorrhage in Montagnola on August 9, 1962.

Of immediate concern is the Hesse phenomenon now existent in the United States. Hesse's works have long enjoyed popularity outside of Germany, especially in southern Europe and Latin America. Indeed, of twentieth-century German writers, only Thomas Mann and Franz Kafka have been written about more than Hesse. However, Hesse has remained almost virtually unknown in the United States until the last decade. Only a handful of his works had been translated into English, and some of those had been very poor translations. Very few critical articles or references appeared in literary publications prior to the Nobel Prize of 1946. For a short time afterwards, his name was mentioned more frequently and some worthwhile critical material appeared. Largely though, Hesse was known only to a handful of individuals on college campuses. Hesse himself doubted greatly that he would ever receive popular recognition in the English-speaking world, particularly the United States.

Within the last ten years, Hesse has been worshiped by many college students who have made him a cult hero. *Siddhartha* and *Demian*, particularly, are now found in the curricula of some of the more progressive high schools. Ironically, *Siddhartha* is, among other things, one of the greatest criticisms of formal education that one could read, which is one aspect which makes it so appealing to today's alienated students. The novel has recently been adapted into a motion picture.

The reasons for Hesse's current popularity stem from several factors. Initially, his wide-spread acceptance in the United States was due to the youth culture which identified with his alienated protagonists. Both a rock group and a California discotheque owe their names to *Steppenwolf*, which has become a virtual Bible for the counter-culture. Also, a record album has been entitled "Abraxas," after the Gnostic deity who is an integral part of *Demian*. Youths frequently hear themselves echoed when Harry Haller condemns pre-World War II German society for building a dehumanizing military industrial complex and for destroying nature. When Haller uses drugs to achieve a state of intense awareness, they identify again, not realizing how little this aspect has to do with the essence of the novel. This generation, a great many of whom were witnesses to their country's involvement in what they considered to be an unjustifiable, immoral war (Viet Nam), found a spokesman against chauvinistic nationalism in Hesse. Today, when they see "progress" as a threat to the individual values and soul, they question the process deeply, as did Hesse. These individuals identify with the author in his own plight and have "turned within" to find their way. Hesse himself said that each of his writings was, in a sense, a spiritual autobiography. From the Nietzschean view of *Demian*, which questions the "herd instinct" and the "mass morality," to the concept of individual sacrifice for the sake of helping another person achieve a higher level of existence as depicted in the futuristic *Glass Bead Game (Magister Ludi)*, inspiration has been given and guidelines established.

Hesse, now the subject of much discussion, has been both highly praised and severely condemned. Whether he is a saint or whether his writings are just another fad certain to be forgotten remains to be seen. Because he deals with very real issues which are sensitive in our society today, he is rarely spoken of objectively. Because of conflicts in personal viewpoints, much of the intrinsic merit of his works has been neglected and not examined closely enough by both those of the "establishment" and those who seek to identify with Charles Reich's concept of "Consciousness III."

Introduction to "Demian"

Published in 1919, *Demian* is a crucial novel to an understanding of Hermann Hesse and his current popularity in the United States. *Demian*, whose title came to Hesse in a dream, is the direct outgrowth of his psychoanalysis of 1916-17. It marks a new direction in both the tone and message of his works. Dr. Timothy Leary has referred to Hermann Hesse as "the poet of the interior journey." *Demian* is the beginning of Hesse's introspection and his turning to the "inward way," as well as his discovery of "magical thinking" as answers to the dilemmas presented to us by modern life.

In its format, *Demian* could be classified as a *Bildungsroman*, a novel of education, popular in Germany's era of Romanticism. But, by combining with this traditional approach the surrealistic quality of "magical thinking," Hesse has far transcended the typical novel of this type. "Magical thinking" is a term difficult to define and would possibly be best handled by an example.

In a short, autobiographical essay, Hesse looked to the future and pictured himself in a jail cell for some act of immorality. In order to pass the time, he began painting a picture on the wall of the cell. (Painting was Hesse's life-long love.) In the picture there is a train travelling into a dark tunnel. Hesse imagines himself jumping onboard the train, going through the tunnel, thus escaping his captors. Somehow, this is the essence of his "magical thinking."

The combination of traumas of 1916-18 caused Hesse great mental anguish. His rejection by Germany, his father's death, and the illnesses of his wife and his son Martin caused Hesse to seek the aid of J. B. Lang, an associate of the famous psychologist Carl Gustav Jung. More than seventy sessions took place between Lang and Hesse from 1916 to 1917. One result was that Hesse began to reexamine his whole system of values and to formulate a new one. All of his novels subsequent to *Demian* reflect his new thinking and his increased awareness of the workings of the human mind. The latter aspect becomes more obvious after 1919, although it seems that even in his earlier works Hesse was intuitively aware, though not formally schooled, in such matters. After 1919, one cannot fully understand or appreciate Hesse without a knowledge of such terms as "unconscious," *anima*, and "archetype."

Demian was produced within two months' time in what one biographer and personal acquaintance of Hesse refers to as a "white heat." It was published under the pseudonym Emil Sinclair. One reason for the use of the pen name was the disfavor toward Hesse in Germany at the time. Had the novel been published under his real name, it would have been ignored. Under this guise, however, it was not only a success, but Sinclair was also awarded the Fontane Prize for new authors. Soon the truth became known through a careful style analysis. Hesse could not accept the prize, the monetary value of which he could have used, because he was already an established author. Even his friend, the renown Thomas Mann, could not believe that this was the work of Hermann Hesse, so radical was his departure from his earlier work.

Structurally, *Demian* is the beginning of a pattern followed in all of Hesse's novels after 1919. The book falls loosely into three sections. The first of these deals with the protagonist's awareness of an inharmonious world and some action which causes the loss of his innocence and can be paralleled with the biblical fall from grace. The second section, which is the longest, concerns itself with the period of anguish and despair which follows the fall. The third portion contains some degree of enlightenment for the protagonist. In one manner or other, he learns to come to terms with his life and with himself. However, this is not a permanent state and it can be assumed that the protagonist is able to achieve the heights of intense awareness and harmony only periodically, but, nevertheless, he is able to continue his existence in an easier manner than most people because he has occasionally tasted complete harmony. The only novel of Hesse's in which the protagonist both attains and maintains this concept of Nirvana is, appropriately enough, *Siddhartha*.

List of Characters

Emil Sinclair

The youthful protagonist of the novel who, in course of ten years, falls from childhood innocence, suffers great anguish in his search for self understanding, and finally achieves the awareness for which he has been striving.

Max Demian

A youth several years older than Sinclair who acts as Emil's guide in his search for fulfillment. Demian's name parallels his function; he is Sinclair's *daemon* or inner spirit. His function and human superiority is further related to his first name, as it is possibly a shortened form of "maximus." Demian and his actions frequently cannot be rationally explained as he is the product of "magical thinking."

Frau Eva

Demian's mother, also a product of "magical thinking." Appropriately named, she functions as a symbol for Eve, the universal mother. As Demian is leading Sinclair toward his goal, it is Frau Eva who actually is his goal. She is Sinclair's fulfillment, at least in a symbolic sense.

Pistorius

A radical renegade theologian, who, in the absence of Demian aids Emil in his inward journey by teaching him about various religions, instructing him in the art of meditation, and interpreting the meaning of his dreams. When he can be of no more service to Sinclair, he is cast aside by the former student.

Franz Kromer

Young Sinclair's first link with the dark world, who, in effect, causes Sinclair to begin his quest for self-knowledge and the cementing of his friendship with Max Demian.

Knauer

A fellow student at Emil's boarding school who looks to him for advice. In a certain aspect, he is reminiscent of an earlier Sinclair, and, as such, illustrates Sinclair's development in the direction of Demian and Frau Eva.

Critical Commentaries

I. "TWO REALMS"

Demian begins through the narration of the main character, Emil Sinclair, concerning his youth as of 1904 or 1905. The entire novel depicts ten years' activity, which takes us up to his involvement as a German soldier in World War I, at which point Sinclair is twenty years old. It is important for the reader to keep in mind constantly that it is not the child Sinclair telling the story, but a mature adult reflecting back upon various stages of his development, trying to present an understandable analysis of what was occurring to him both internally and externally. Although it is obvious that the major key of the novel is *individual* and deals with the internal development of one character, the outcome presents a minor key which transcends the individual aspect to arrive at a universal meaning.

At the age of ten, young Emil Sinclair begins to become aware of a division in the world into light and dark, and good and evil. Critics have traced the source of Hesse's choice for his protagonist's name to Isaac von Sinclair, who was a friend of Holderlin. Others have pointed out, additionally, that the name is of further importance symbolically because it is an Anglo-French compound with the first syllable "sin" meaning dark, and the last syllable "clair" meaning light. Thus the awareness of a dichotomized world by a young boy who is going to come to grips with it and whose name represents it is an appropriate beginning for the novel.

To young Emil Sinclair, the world of light is epitomized by his home, his family, and their customs and traditions. The dark world borders and even overlaps his world with servant girls, ghost stories, and scandals. Young Sinclair can imagine the Devil lurking on a neighborhood corner, but can never recognize his presence within his household. The recognition and awe of the potential evils waiting on the outside makes Emil appreciative of the security and warmth of his home. In his self-perspective at this time, Sinclair identifies with the world of the righteous because he is the child of "saintly" parents. Recognizing the overlap, however, he is aware that he also lives in the darker world, although he is a stranger to it.

In viewing his ambition to become a part of the good and righteous world on his own part, he senses that he will have to journey through the dark world and its temptations in order to obtain success. Emil reflects upon stories he has heard of sons who have gone astray and who have eventually returned home into the fold with much happiness. A great deal of Hesse's writing deals to varying degrees with such themes as the Prodigal Son. In reading and hearing such stories, however, Sinclair is most fascinated with the parts dealing with the hero's involvement with evil. Hence, without consciously being aware of it, the young boy has sensed something about the forbidden, yet enticing, aspects of evil.

As the son of a rather prosperous family, Sinclair attends the elite Latin school, but it is his involvement with a public school student, the drunken tailor's son, Franz Kromer, that is the beginning of Sinclair's journey.

In an attempt to impress the older ruffian, Kromer, with his bravado, Sinclair invents a lie about his heroic part in the theft of some apples, and thus he makes himself susceptible to blackmail by Kromer. The imagined theft of "apples" is what ultimately leads to his downfall, and his exclusion from the "garden." Sinclair frequently refers to the domain of his parents by this term. Hence, very early in the narrative, Hesse employed a biblical allusion and set a religious tenor for the novel. Both the symbolism and tone will remain quite religious throughout the remainder of the novel. This aspect of the book is one of the devices employed by Hesse to build tension, because when contrasted with the Nietzschean philosophy expressed, seemingly irreconcilable paradoxes result. The addition of the psychological aspect to the religious and Nietzschean aspects further complicates the novel. Indeed, the psychological factor leads into areas considered taboo by much of society. These factors have caused at least one of Hesse's critics to avoid discussing *Demian* because he feels such discussion might cause too much controversy. This, however, is not the case if the novel is analyzed logically and carefully.

Further description of the villainous young Kromer reveals that he has a habit of spitting through a space between his two front teeth which gives him a somewhat serpent-like aspect. Kromer's threat of exposure forces Emil into a more serious, and this time an actual, crime. In order to pay Kromer the amount of blackmail money which he demands, Emil steals, first, from his own piggy bank and, then, from wherever he can, especially when he finds money lying around the house.

Contemplating his plight, Sinclair feels that he has now made a covenant with Satan and that his life is ruined. Debating whether or not to confess his predicament to his father and take the resulting punishment, as he has at times in the past, Sinclair decides that he must solve this problem by himself. His deep guilt feelings effect a break in his family ties. Sinclair withdraws from the mainstream of family activity. Occasionally reprimanded by his father for trivial matters, Sinclair both transfers his father's anger to his greater wrong-doing, and at the same time feels a contempt toward his father because of his ignorance of Emil's real crime. This latter feeling, which is a new experience for Emil, is the beginning of his quest for independence.

Sinclair begins to feel like an outsider, something evil within his parent's realm of righteousness, certain that God's grace is no longer with him. Yet he is also intuitively aware that the end of his former life will lead to the beginning of a new one. Sinclair also realizes that in the process of rebirth he must also sever the cord binding him to his mother, an act which is much more difficult for him than leaving his father.

Because of his fear of meeting with Kromer, Sinclair frequently becomes conveniently ill and hides within the safe confines of his house.

When Sinclair does finally face Kromer, without the full payment required to buy his silence, Kromer continues his bullying tactics and, at times, even forces Emil to become his slave, performing menial tasks. From this point on, the terrifying shrillness of Kromer's whistle summons Sinclair to his evil master for further nameless tortures. When at home, Emil remains withdrawn from his parents and sisters, whom he cannot imagine guilty of any type of wrongdoing. It is emphasized that his alienation is strongest toward his father, to whom he is completely cold. By the conclusion of the first chapter, Emil Sinclair has been forced to leave the "garden" of his childhood innocence and to venture precariously into the realm of the dark world.

II. "CAIN"

At the beginning of the second chapter, Emil informs the reader that his "salvation" came from an entirely unexpected source. The key word here is "salvation." A new student, Max Demian, who is several years older than Sinclair, has enrolled at the Latin school. Demian is obviously an outsider. He is different from everyone else of Emil's acquaintance. The unexplained aura about him isolates him from the other students. Though not popular, Demian is respected by the students because of his great self-assurance, especially toward his teachers.

While walking home from school one day, Sinclair is joined by Demian, who engages the reluctant younger boy in conversation. Demian makes a reference to a weathered escutcheon above the doorway of the Sinclair residence. Emil himself is vaguely aware of its existence, although he has never really looked at it. Demian identifies the carving as a sparrow hawk, thus establishing the central symbol of the story.

Demian also makes reference to a lesson which his class has shared with Sinclair's, the subject of which was the story of Cain and Abel. Demian provides his own interpretation of Cain and his mark. Sensing that the awarding of a special mark for an act of cowardice, a mark that protects Cain and puts the fear

of God into others, is somewhat illogical, Demian states that
Cain is a different and superior human being. Because Cain is
"different" people are in awe of him and are suspicious and
afraid of him. Rather than admit their own inferiority, these
people invent stories about Cain and his people. Demian believes that Cain is guilty of murder, but does not pass a moral
judgment against his action. In short, Demian's view of Cain
emphasizes his nobility.

It is obvious in this discussion that the essence of Demian's
commentary about Cain can also be applied to Demian himself.
Demian's full name—Max Demian—provides insight into his
character. "Max" could well be a shortened form of "maximus"
meaning superlative. Demian is a name which came to Hesse
in a dream and can be linked to his function in the novel as Sinclair's *daemon*. Among ancient peoples, a *daemon* was a spirit
presiding over persons, places, and secret intentions. Ancient
philosophers believed that each person had two *daemons*—
one good and one evil. The term is frequently used in the writings of Carl Gustav Jung, whose influence on Hesse has already
been mentioned.

The concept of the superiority of certain individuals, which
Max has applied to the story of Cain, emphasizes the profound
influence of the early existential philosopher Friedrich Nietzsche
upon Hesse. In fact, Demian seems to be an enigmatic character
because his structural aspect in the story, which is decidely religious, and his functional aspect, which is Nietzschean, seem to
clash. This however, is not so and will be discussed later.

Demian's discussion of Cain greatly upsets Sinclair since
it undercuts the pillar of his fundamental religious beliefs which
he has never before questioned. Though Emil is disconcerted
with the ideas stated by Demian, he is nevertheless pleased by
Demian's manner and his aura of self-confidence manifested in
his voice and especially through his eyes.

Reflecting back on the time when he was chastised by his
father for his muddy boots and his secret feelings of superiority,

Emil recognizes his feelings as identifiable with Demian's interpretation of Cain. This realization and further thoughts of Demian's conversation forms the awakening of Emil's critical mind and his departure from a blind acceptance which is often said to be characteristic of childhood. For a time, at least, Emil has been so involved in thinking that he has forgotten about his predicament with Franz Kromer. Sinclair has begun to become involved in *living* and *thinking* about the total world in which he lives, encompassing both the light and the dark aspects of the dichotomized world of traditional Christianity.

Emil, however, has not been the only person to note the special qualities of Demian. Rumors are rampant. Some reports claim that the wealthy Demian is a Jew, or possibly Mohammedan. Later rumors will claim that he is an atheist, knows girls intimately, and is his mother's lover. One rumor concerning his physical prowess is confirmed when he humiliates and temporarily paralyzes the strongest boy in his class by a seemingly magical touch, probably directed at a vulnerable nerve. Thus to his less knowledgable contemporaries, Demian seems even more than unusual. He is almost god-like or demon-like.

Sinclair's short-lived escape from Kromer ends. But even in his dreams, he is tormented by Kromer. One dream initiates an Oedipus theme. Emil dreams that Kromer has forced him to wait in ambush, armed with a knife, for a certain person to pass by and this person always turns out to be his own father. However, Demian is also a subject of Emil's dreams and even takes Kromer's place as a torturer in two dreams.

The significance of the increased mention of dreams and dream-like states cannot be overstressed. As the story progresses, it becomes increasingly difficult to differentiate between what is reality and what is not reality because of Sinclair's constant dreaming. Ultimately, the question of the reality of Demian himself, as well as his mother arises. This problem will be discussed later.

Demian's next involvement in the story occurs while Kromer is once again terrorizing Sinclair, this time under Demian's analytical eyes. After Kromer's departure, it is only a matter of minutes and a few words until Demian is able to ascertain the reason for Emil's fear of Kromer. Emil is both repelled and fascinated by Demian's apparent psychic power. At this point, Sinclair notes that Demian seems to know him and understand him better than he does himself. He further adds that when Demian speaks, it is almost as though his own inner voice is conversing with him. Demian offers his assistance to Sinclair and tells him that he must free himself of Kromer's bondage if he wishes to have a meaningful life. Characteristically, Demian suggests that the most efficient method of achieving this would simply be to *kill* Kromer.

Approximately a week passes, during which time Sinclair has not once been bothered by Kromer's whistle. When Emil accidentally meets him on the street, Kromer turns aside to avoid facing Sinclair. Demian then admits that he has persuaded Kromer that it is in his best interest to stop plaguing Sinclair. He does not divulge his methodology, although he does say that he did not either pay Emil's debt or physically abuse Kromer. Emil remains perplexed.

His immediate problem and his necessary contact with the dark world at an end, Sinclair deserts his benefactor and returns to the womb—that is, back to his mother and the world of goodness; back to his lost paradise. The prodigal son has returned. The need now gone, Sinclair even confesses the whole episode to his parents and is subsequently forgiven and taken back into the fold. Sinclair, however, remains cognizant of the fact that things still are not and never will be as they once were. He also senses that Demian somehow, as well as Kromer, is a link to the dark world, although a different type of link.

Still dependent, still needing someone for support, Sinclair has returned to his parents. But he feels that possibly his confession, explanation, and gratitude should have been directed instead to Demian. His fear of Demian's encouragement toward independence has prevented him from seeking further contact. Demian's influence remains, nevertheless. A half year later, while walking with his father, he mentions Demian's interpretation of the Cain story. His father expounds upon it as a form of heresy and warns Sinclair about the dangers of entertaining such dangerous notions.

III. "AMONG THIEVES"

The title of the third chapter is once again a biblical allusion, which, once again, Demian will treat as a myth and interpret as he pleases. In this recurring practice, Demian reflects Hesse's own views. Hesse, as he stated in 1930, believed that biblical myths were useless unless they could be interpreted personally for the individual in his own time.

At this point, young Sinclair is just beginning to awaken sexually and is undergoing the agony of adolescence in coming to terms with those thoughts and desires deemed forbidden by society. As with most people at this point in their lives, Sinclair makes a further withdrawal from his family. Sinclair observes that leaving childhood and developing into adulthood is, for many people, the only time in their lives that they experience dying and rebirth, hinting that this should be a continual process if the individual is to attain the highest degree of fulfillment. Most individuals stop evolving, cling to their pasts, and dream of a lost state of innocence. It is implied that only superior beings — such as Demian — continue to evolve and seek their destiny. Again, obvious Nietzschean influence is observable.

While Franz Kromer has vanished from Sinclair's life, Demian will, from this point on, always be a part of his life. Reflecting back upon occasions when he has carefully observed Demian's uniqueness, Sinclair presents the first detailed physical description of his mentor.

Demian is described as having an ethereal appearance. His face contains characteristics of manliness, boyishness, and femininity. It is old looking, young looking and still ageless. He is handsome yet different. Sinclair observes that trees or animals could look this way but not people. Demian is extremely different from other people.

Several years pass before Sinclair again has close contact with Demian. Emil, now about fourteen years old, finds himself in the same confirmation class as Demian. Once again the lesson being taught is about Cain and Abel. Influenced by a fleeting glance from Demian, Sinclair this time is critical of the traditional interpretation given by the pastor. Soon Demian manages to move closer to Sinclair until he is sitting beside him. He accomplishes this feat even though the students have been alphabetically arranged by the pastor. The new bond established between the two boys enables Sinclair to fully understand just how remarkably different Demian is. He appears to control others with his thoughts. Even the pastor is subject to Demian's will, which he mysteriously manifests through his eyes. Demian also explains to Emil that his thought-reading and predictions of the actions of others are simply the product of intense observation.

Using the example of the night moth, Demian refutes the pastor's claim of free will. According to Demian, our will is free and we can obtain a particular goal only if the goal we have set is right and necessary to our individual needs and development. If the goal meets these criteria, we are capable of its attainment. Demian explains that he was able to accomplish changing his seat even though the pastor's will was in opposition to his by utilization of this principle.

Further development of Sinclair's independence is effected by Demian through the biblical account of Golgotha. Demian admires the unrepentant thief as a man of character and strength. The thief had been evil all his life and chose not to repent, but rather to follow his destiny in accord with the way he had lived. Demian believes that this thief might even have been a descendant of Cain, and labels the other thief a "sniveling convert."

At this time it is advisable to reflect upon all of Demian's characteristics as described up to this point. The first reference to him was in the words of Sinclair: "my salvation." Indeed, Demian did save Emil from the serpent-like Kromer, after Sinclair had caused his own expulsion from the "garden." Demian also seems to be almost magical, performing such "miracles" as thought reading and displaying uncanny knowledge of others, both physically and mentally. Subject of much suspicion, Demian is an unusual outsider who is, however, held in respect. He instructs Sinclair through parables and disputes things with his teachers. His difference is made even more apparent because of the unexplained aura which surrounds him. Later he will, in a sense, have a band of disciples. His physiognomy is, at the same time, masculine and feminine, possibly displaying the sensitive gentility frequently present in portraits of Christ. Even the chapter title could also refer as well as to Demian, who (figuratively) has been placed between two thieves, namely Sinclair and Kromer. There can be no doubt that Demian has been established as, and functions as, a Christ figure.

Yet, paradoxically, the essence of his words has been anything but Christ-like. Ironically, Demian is the mouthpiece for the "superman" doctrines of Nietzsche. To Hesse, this is not at all incongruous, as will be demonstrated later.

Demian's next attack on orthodox Christianity hits Sinclair harder and more personally than any of his previous tirades. Demian sees a serious weakness in any religion which arbitrarily sets up an attitude of attributing all that is good to God and all that is evil to Satan, when, in effect, God created the entire world and therefore deserves total responsibility. To make his argument more persuasive to Emil, Demian refers to God as the father of all life, and then to the religious and societal repression of all sexual matters. The clergy frequently refers to such matters as being the work of the devil. Demian's suggestion is that *all* of life should be affirmed and the arbitrary, illogical, and artificial dichotomy dispensed with.

Sinclair is now suddenly aware that his secret agony concerning the dark and light worlds is not uniquely his, as he previously thought, but rather a problem common to all mankind. Demian also informs Sinclair that now that he has begun to think critically, he will no longer be able to repress all of his darker urgings. Frustrated by all of this sudden illumination, Sinclair becomes defiant, asserting his belief that merely because evil exists as a fact of life, one cannot justify participation in it. Demian's concluding Nietzschean response is that Sinclair must realize the relativity of morality, citing the ancient Greek celebration of sexuality as a contrast to the Christian repression of it. Therefore, it is for each person to decide for himself what is permitted and forbidden for *him*, and then to stand by his own beliefs. It is possible here to observe some influence of Dostoevsky. Hesse was very familiar with his works, and this train of thought parallels Raskolnikov's thoughts in *Crime and Punishment*.

Sinclair's next reminiscence of Demian is again set in their confirmation class. Gazing at Demian, he observes his friend in a trance-like state resembling death, his face like a mask of stone. Demian is obviously deep within himself in the process of meditation. Meditation is a recurrent step in the search for self in all of Hesse's subsequent novels from *Siddhartha* to *The Glass Bead Game (Magister Ludi)*. Shortly after this scene, Sinclair makes unsuccessful attempts at emulating Demian. Meditation remains an art which Sinclair will need to master on his journey to his own interior.

Emil's childhood is now gone and his confirmation completed. It is determined that following his vacation he will be sent away from home to further his education at a boarding school. He soon finds himself alone, in a strange situation, in a strange town, without the crutches of his family, with whom he has long been severing ties, and without Demian.

IV. "BEATRICE"

At the boarding school, Sinclair soon finds himself an outsider, as Demian was previously viewed at the Latin school. He is at first neither liked nor respected by his classmates. His adolescent awkwardness has even caused him to dislike himself. Agonizingly alone, Sinclair soon finds the road to his much needed acceptance through a friendship with Alfons Beck, the oldest boy in his boarding house. Under Beck's tutelage, Sinclair once again finds himself immersed in a dark world. He begins to frequent bars and to associate with the disorderly crowd. Rebelling against all forms of authority, he is soon in academic difficulties. His reaction to this and to everything that happens to him, even his father's admonitions, is indifference. Despite his resultant feeling of self-hatred, Sinclair revels in his degradation, enjoying a new-found reputation of being an impressive character in this world of debauchery. The only significant difference between Sinclair and his comrades is that Emil maintains his sexual innocence. Yet with his loneliness terribly acute and his expulsion from school a near certainty, Sinclair finally finds his way back to himself.

His salvation this time is self-effected. During a spring walk in a park, Sinclair observes an attractive young girl whom he names Beatrice, after Dante's first love. Although Emil never meets or talks to the young lady, he sets her upon a pedestal and worships her from afar. Beatrice is described as being tall, slender, and boyish looking. Sometimes when added to past discussions, such as Demian's feminine aspect and Sinclair's sexual innocence, young readers think that his attraction to a boyish looking girl is indicative of a latent homosexual trait. Here again, the explanation and understanding must be sought in Jung's influence on Hesse.

Jung believed that no human being was entirely masculine or feminine, but rather that all humans possess characteristics of each sex in varying degrees. The female aspect in a man's personality was labelled the *anima* by Jung. Correspondingly, each woman has an *animus* which is her masculine aspect. The *anima* consists of such traits as the irrational, the sensual, the intuitive, and the sensitive, which Western men have been forced to repress by society in order to develop such traits such as the mechanical, the logical, the practical, and the rational.

These repressed aspects of the male, however, are not totally benign. They simmer beneath the surface somewhere in the collective unconscious, and they manifest themselves by influencing the conscious ego. Hence, a man, intuitively aware of his peculiar female aspect, sometimes projects it upon actual women, recognizing in an actual woman characteristics complementary to himself. Beatrice can therefore be considered Sinclair's *anima*.

The second Jungian archetype concerning the collective unconscious is the self. The self is an inner voice, which frequently manifests itself in the form of dreams which speak to and influence the conscious ego. In dream form, it usually appears as a person of the same sex as the dreamer, although it can appear as an animal or even a hermaphroditic figure. Recalling Sinclair's earlier description of Demian as combining both masculine and feminine features, or even his observation that "animals could look like that," it becomes apparent that Demian represents Sinclair's self. Thus only through the synthesis of Sinclair, Demian, and Beatrice can Sinclair be complete or fulfilled.

Sinclair realizes that in his state of degradation he is not worthy of Beatrice and he decides to repent of his evil ways. Consciously correcting his bad habits, he soon solves his academic difficulties and begins to enjoy better acceptance by the other students.

Still plagued by loneliness, because he lacks a real friend, he finds it necessary to create new ways of occupying his time. Inspired by Beatrice, he decides to paint. His first conscious attempts to reproduce her face fail. Sinclair then gives way to his imagination and allows his brush to flow at will. In this way the *anima* aspect of his unconscious manifests itself. It might be added that artistry, or creativity in an aesthetic sense such as painting is, of course, one of those characteristics considered to be largely feminine. Sinclair himself emphasizes the "dreaming" aspect of his painting activity, and likens its product to the manifestation of his subconscious mind. Finally, one day a

face which intrigues Sinclair is completed. The painted counte-
nance is stiff and masklike, half masculine, half feminine, and
yet somehow ageless. Awakening from a dream one morning,
Sinclair imagines that the face seems to know him, like a mother,
and calls to him. Emil, staring at the strange brightness of the
forehead and the expression of the eyes, recognizes the portrait
as being that of Demian. Pinning the painting to his window and
allowing the sunlight to shine through it, Emil further senses
that the painting is not actually of Beatrice or Demian, but
rather it is a reflection of himself, his inner self, his *daemon*,
symbolizing the essence of his whole future life.

Once again it should be emphasized that all of this activity
occurs in a dream-like state. Whether or not he actually ever pins
the portrait to the window could be debated.

Thinking of his sorely missed friend, Emil reflects back
upon their last meeting during one of his school vacations. Over
a glass of wine, the two boys are discussing Emil's school life
and his then existent period of rebellion. Demian appears to
accept but frown upon Emil's drinking habits, but adds that
sometimes a life of hedonism can be a type of preparation for
sainthood. He cites St. Augustine as an example of this principle.
As a final consolation to Sinclair, Demian adds that we are all
fortunate because within us there is someone who knows all
and wills all. This is an obvious reference to the subconscious;
Emil, through Demian's carefully selected words, identifies with
St. Augustine's example and realizes that this is the direction in
which his life has gone.

On the night of the flashback, Sinclair has a terrifying dream.
He remembers the coat of arms above the doorway to his house
and dreams that Demian forces him to swallow it. He feels
the heraldic bird coming to life within him. The bird then begins
to eat away from within. Horrified, he awakens from the dream.

Once again, the central symbol of the novel becomes important. Remembering his dream, Sinclair decides to paint a
picture of the heraldic bird. It should be remembered and noted,

however, that as he himself previously stated, Sinclair has never really looked carefully at the details of the coat of arms, which are not readily observable anyway because it has been obscured by age and many coats of paint.

When the painting is completed, it is of a sparrow hawk with half its body enclosed in a dark globe from which it is struggling to free itself, as if hatching from an egg. The fact that the bird is identifiable as a sparrow hawk indicates that it is a grown bird, not a chick. The picture therefore is representative not of birth but of rebirth. The question arises as to why the painting took this specific form when Sinclair did not really know what the coat of arms looked like specifically. The answer concerning this most important symbol of the novel is again to be found in the influence of Jung, filtered to Hesse by his many psychoanalytic sessions with Joseph B. Lang.

Hesse has emphasized the dream aspect of the painting. The dream-like state has also been connected to the subconscious. The term "subconscious" is a Freudian term, replaced with "unconscious" by Jung, who felt the prefix "sub" to be demeaning to what he felt was a higher form of innate awareness. According to Jung, the human mind contains two aspects of the unconscious. The first and most obvious consists of memories of actual events which have happened to the individual and have been either forgotten or repressed. The second, and, in this case, the most important aspect of the unconscious, he termed the "collective unconscious." This concept is absolutely necessary in the discussion of *Demian*, as well as all of Hesse's later novels.

The "collective unconscious" does not consist of memories specific to the individual, but rather consists of intuitive knowledge concerning universal human experiences, passed along in the species during the evolutionary process. In other words, there are certain symbols which convey similar intuitive meanings to all people. Such a symbol is called an "archetype." The egg (the dark globe of Sinclair's sparrow hawk painting) is such a symbol; it can be traced back to ancient Roman times when, according to the late anthropologist Bachofen, it represented the two poles of the world. Thus the sparrow hawk, breaking out of the egg, to be reborn, is shattering the world of unreal, arbitrary, and false polarities — much as Sinclair himself is trying to do. Hence, the symbol is an internal one for Sinclair at this point, although at the end of the novel it will be external and universal.

In a "dream-like" state, Sinclair mails this painting to Demian although he does not know his present whereabouts. To the painting Sinclair adds no message at all, not even his name.

V. "THE BIRD FIGHTS ITS WAY OUT OF THE EGG"

One day, shortly after mailing the painting, during a break between classes, Sinclair notices a note tucked into one of his books. Recognizing that the note is folded in a special manner peculiar to his classmates, he does not immediately open it. During his next lesson, while obviously "daydreaming," Sinclair opens the note. He is struck dumb by its message: "The bird fights its way out of the egg. The egg is the world. Who would be born must first destroy a world. The bird flies to God. That God's name is Abraxas." Sinclair interprets the note as being Demian's response to his gift of the painting. A logical question now arises. How did Demian get the note into Sinclair's book, and even if he did, how did he know how to fold it in the special manner of Sinclair's classmates? The answer can be approached in two different ways which provide insight on two different levels.

As the chapter progresses, Sinclair is startled out of his reverie (caused by the note) when his teacher mentions the name Abraxas during a lecture on Herodotus. Abraxas is the name of an ancient Gnostic deity. It is not, however, referred to in the writings of Herodotus. The young teacher, Dr. Follens, has just completed his university training. It has been mentioned previously in the novel that Demian is somewhere attending a university. Perhaps the young instructor is the messenger who delivered the message. Possibly he has had some contact with Demian. If such contact has occurred it could explain the oddity of the messages of the note and the corresponding lecture.

Another way of viewing this strange episode is to reflect upon the past emphasis on the "dream" aspect or potential unreality of some of the previous events. Possibly, this whole sequence of events took place only in Sinclair's mind. Maybe he actually wrote the note himself in one of his dream-like moments or maybe it didn't even exist outside of his dream world. This becomes the noticeable beginning of a sequence of events when Demian (self) and, later, his mother *(anima)* become increasingly internalized within Sinclair, thus indicating Sinclair's process of attaining a harmony of his various parts. This has been hinted at from the beginning when, in his amazement at Demian's ability to see inside others, Emil stated that it was as if Demian knew more about him than he himself. Perhaps, then, Demian is, or has become, Emil's own unconscious. Hesse himself offered a comment about trying to rationally analyze the characters of Demian and Frau Eva when he stated that they were figures "that encompass and signify far more than is accessible to rational consideration; they are magical conjurations."

Abraxas becomes the second important symbol of this novel. Abraxas is Demian's answer to the previously stated problem of a God who represents an arbitrarily selected half of the world. Abraxas is a deity who serves to unite the entire world, the light and the dark, the godly and the devilish. He does not represent either; rather, he is the affirmation of both.

Sinclair experiences an intensification of his sexual drive. His longing for meaningful love seems hopeless. Sinclair again retreats into his dream world, which has become as active during his waking hours as during his sleep. A new dream occurs which he explicitly and emphatically identifies as the most significant dream of his life.

In this dream Sinclair is entering his father's house beneath the heraldic hawk on the escutcheon. His mother is walking toward him with outstretched arms. As they are about to embrace, she suddenly changes. She now resembles Demian, or, more accurately, Emil's portrait. Sinclair is taken, enveloped in a passionate embrace which leaves him with feelings of both ecstacy and horror. He sees the embrace as both a crime and an act of worship. Utterly confused, he awakens, sometimes elated, sometimes guilt ridden. Here the motif of incest is clearly presented. One of the strongest taboos of every human society has been touched upon. It should be pointed out, however, that the dream is not of actual incest. Later, it will become more clear that the female figure is not Sinclair's mother, but, rather, is Demian.

Jung, in discussing the sun myth, which can be related to the Gnostic god Abraxas, explains that the basis of incestuous desire lies in the wish to become a child once more, to return to the protective womb of the mother for rebirth. This, however, is forbidden because the mother's body would have to be entered in order for the impregnation necessary for the reproduction of oneself to occur. The rebirth myths invent various substitutes for the mother in order to prevent the libido from sinking to actual incest. Hesse will, therefore, replace and make clear that the figure in question is Demian's mother and that the desire shown in the dream is symbolic rather than actual. Frau Eva will represent various things but mostly what her name indicates, the concept of a universal mother.

Sinclair is now near the end of high school and is soon to enter the university. Despite his adequacy as a student, however, he is still plagued by a lack of direction. His only goal is to come to terms with himself. Through his narration, it is obvious that despite his sense of futility, he has progressed a great deal. Emil actually now possesses some of the traits peculiar to Demian when he was first introduced to him. Sinclair also can intuitively analyze people and occasionally startles his fellow students with his mystical skills.

Still in the habit of taking evening walks to pass the time, Sinclair is attracted one night to a small church by the sound of some rather unorthodox organ music. After listening outside for a number of nights, he finally gains enough courage to follow the organist to a tavern. During the conversation with the organist, Pistorius, Sinclair states that the quality he admires most about his music is its amorality: it combines both heaven and hell and he associates it with Abraxas, whose name he mentions.

Pistorius, the son of a respected clergyman, and a renegade theologian himself, is shocked by Sinclair's mention of Abraxas and is further drawn to Emil. Pistorius is also familiar with Abraxas; in fact, he knows a great deal about him, which he promises to discuss with Sinclair at a later time. During the course of an evening at the house of the organist's father, Pistorius explains his interest in studying all religions and his fascination concerning what sorts of gods people have created. His viewpoint of religion as mythology is what has made it inappropriate for him to serve as a clergyman. It is here in his room, before the fireplace, that Pistorius teaches Sinclair the art of meditation.

At their next meeting, Pistorius assumes his role as a psychologist, again utilizing Jung's concept of the collective unconscious. Many critics have stated that Hesse is actually portraying his own period of psychoanalysis and that Pistorius represents, in actuality, Dr. J. B. Lang. Pistorius teaches Sinclair that all human possibilities and potentialities are contained within each one of us. Sinclair's reaction to this is to question. If all things are complete within us, why do we keep striving? The answer Pistorius provides is that most people are simply unaware that his completeness and potential exists. It is this very awareness that should be sought after.

The psychological skills of Pistorius also include the interpreting of dreams. Sinclair's dream of fear, at finding himself able to fly, is interpreted by Pistorius. The ability to fly in dreams is common to many people. Its source is our own innate awareness of our power. However, most people are afraid to recognize their own potential and thus they refuse to fly. The earth offers more security. Others become too exhilarated with the free feeling and soar off into infinity and are subsequently labeled insane.

Still others, like Demian and Sinclair, become aware of their power and develop means to harness it and use it effectively. The means of control, however, is not invented; it comes from within. Pistorius concludes with an analogy of certain types of fish which possess a type of air bladder which can function as a type of lung left, a relic ages ago, still remaining after thousands of years of evolution.

VI. "JACOB WRESTLING"

At the onset of chapter six, Emil Sinclair is a young man of eighteen. Because of the teachings of Pistorius, he has learned a great deal about self-acceptance and self-reliance, as well as about human nature in a more universal sense. With Pistorius, Sinclair has been very open, sharing his inner feelings and dreams. There is one exception, though. Sinclair has never told Pistorius about his one dark dream, the haunting dream of his return home and of the forbidden embrace of the half-masculine, half-motherly figure.

Pistorius continues to encourage Sinclair to listen to his dreams, to seek after them, and above all, not to fear them. Much earlier Demian had told Sinclair that he had to learn what was permitted and what was forbidden for him individually. This brought up the concept of individual morality, and Emil's statement that evil acts are not justified simply because they exist. Sinclair questioned whether a wrong such as murder could be justified. Demian did not provide a definite answer at that time, saying only that Sinclair had to sense and do what he thought he should do. Pistorius and Sinclair also touch upon this concept. This time, however, it is discussed from a psychological point-of-view, rather than as a purely philosophical concept. Concerning the justification of murder, Pistorius claims that, at times, it could be permissible although most often not. He tells Sinclair that he must discern whether or not such urges are simply Abraxas interacting with the individual. His rationale is that if an individual hates another so much that he wants to kill him, it is usually because there is some specific characteristic in the other person that he hates. Pistorius adds that the hatred is directed toward that specific aspect which is also present in the person himself. What is not part of ourselves doesn't bother us. Therefore murder would be a mistake. Again though, Pistorius stresses that all of reality is relative to the individual.

During his final term in high school, Sinclair is suddenly approached one day by a younger student named Knauer. Knauer has been carefully observing Sinclair and is aware of his unique qualities, his "mark of Cain." It is Knauer's desire to befriend Sinclair and to learn whatever Sinclair can teach him, while he himself offers some interesting concepts to Emil. Knauer knows a bit about the mystical world and such things as white magic. Knauer's deepest problem is his fear of his own sexuality. He expresses his belief that continence is necessary for spiritual purity. Sinclair disagrees with this idea. Although he has never had any sort of sexual contact with a woman, he feels that he should and would have sex under the proper conditions, namely mutual love. Sinclair informs Knauer that he can tell him nothing; he must find his own way by listening to his inner voice. Disappointed and disillusioned, young Knauer leaves in a fit of anger after insulting Sinclair.

After painting another picture, once again in a dream-like state, of his dark dream image, Sinclair begins to worship it. The words of the biblical Jacob exhorting the blessing of the angel he has wrestled into submission come to Emil's mind. This partly explains the significance of the chapter title. Emil is clinging to the figure he has imprisoned on canvas, and is asking its blessing. During this particular trance Sinclair's mind flashes to the remote past, even pre-existence, and then to the future.

Waking from his deep sleep, he finds the painting mysteriously missing. He is unable to remember what happened to it, but thinks he might have burned it, and that possibly in his dream he burned it in his palm, and then ate the ashes. The most probable answer is that the painting existed only in Sinclair's mind.

Restless, Sinclair ventures into the night and finds himself hurriedly drawn through the town by some unidentifiable force until he arrives at a new, partially constructed building. The setting is reminiscent of Sinclair's earlier liaison with Kromer. Here, inside the building, he finds the student Knauer, cowering in the dark, waiting for daybreak to implement his plan of suicide. Sinclair has saved Knauer's life. There is no rational explanation for this event. However, keeping in mind the chapter title, the occurrence seems fitting because Jacob also saved a life through his struggle with the angel. Once again Sinclair's progression, both inward and upward, is apparent through this scene, which is comparable to Demian's earlier salvation of Emil.

In the subsequent conversations with Pistorius, Sinclair learns a great deal more about religions. He learns about Abraxas, reads from the Vedas, and even speaks the sacred "Om." Shortly, however, Sinclair realizes that he has absorbed all the knowledge that Pistorius has to offer. Knowledge is communicable but wisdom is not. Pistorius has been of great value in presenting knowledge, but when one considers Pistorius's utilizing or living all that he endorses, Pistorius is a failure. Unable to resist a sudden impulse caused by a moment of frustration, Sinclair blurts out this opinion to Pistorius, deeply wounding him and causing a breach between the two which will never really heal. Despite his immediate guilt feelings, Sinclair is unable to apologize because he feels the fundamental truth of what he had said. Thus, the student has surpassed his teacher.

Sinclair comes to believe that each individual has but one real function in life: he must find the way to himself. What his vocation might turn out to be, whether the person turns out good or evil is of no real consequence. The important concern is simply for the individual to seek his own destiny. Any other approach to life leads to shallowness and unfulfillment.

VII. "EVA"

During vacation, prior to entering the university, Sinclair travels to Demian's former residence in his home town to inquire as to his whereabouts. The old woman now living there shows Sinclair a photograph of Demian's mother. It is here that he realizes that this is the woman of his disturbing dream; she is his *daemon* and she does exist.

Encouraged by this realization, Sinclair begins to look for her everywhere. Shortly after this event, in the university town, Sinclair once again, seemingly by accident, meets Demian, who informs Sinclair that the meeting was anticipated and that the initially attracting "mark of Cain" is now much more prominent on Emil's forehead. While talking about their respective pasts, the conversation is suddenly shifted to the state of affairs in Europe. Demian speaks of the inward rottenness of the various European societies and maintains that their collapse is inevitable. Once again Demian functions as a Nietzschean mouthpiece. The "herd instinct" of the fearful masses is condemned, and the shallow meaninglessness of the Europeans' lives is emphasized. Demian senses that Europe will collapse and then be reborn. The year is now 1913 and what he actually senses is the fast approaching holocaust of World War I.

It is at this point that the larger and most important aspect of the story becomes externalized. Throughout the novel, Sinclair and Demian have been compulsively concerned with themselves. Possibly they have been viewed as very egocentric. But it is only now that the several apparent paradoxes can be resolved. Demian now reveals the purpose of those with the "mark of Cain" when he visualizes the aftermath of the forthcoming chaos. It will revolve around those with the "mark," those who will determine the future. After the war, there will be no more oppression of the individual will and the further development of the human species will once again be possible. Demian states that this goal, the ultimate perfection of the human race, is one expressed by both Jesus and Nietzsche. Now it is clear that Hesse has made a parallel in these two diverse doctrines, and the fact that the Christ figure, Demian, speaks the existential doctrine of Nietzsche is no longer a problem once it is clear that their respective goals are the same. Nietzsche had implored the isolated individuals, who were a chosen

people, to seek solitude and self-understanding in order to benefit many others later. Thus Hesse's emphasis on self-knowledge
is not really selfish in nature. Through a thorough understanding
of self, one becomes more able to serve. Indeed, this idea of
service is contained even more obviously in Hesse's other
works: *Siddhartha, Narcissus and Goldmund, The Journey to
the East,* and *The Glass Bead Game (Magister Ludi).*

The next day Emil's dream becomes reality. He finally
meets Demian's mother, Frau Eva, in the hallway of their home
beneath his sparrow hawk painting. Momentarily speechless,
Sinclair takes Frau Eva's hands, kisses them, and finally feels
fulfillment. When Sinclair announces that his whole life has
been a journey toward this goal and he has now reached home,
Frau Eva smiles at him like a "mother." The first description of
Frau Eva stresses the same characteristics possessed by Demian,
only magnified infinitely.

During his first conversation with Frau Eva, she stresses to
Sinclair that dreams must be followed until realized, but that
each dream is replaced by another.

Emil's reaction to the meeting and to Frau Eva is manifold. He is totally in awe of her, worships her, and yet, as suggested in his dream, he also loves her in a physical sense and
desires her. Through Frau Eva, he comes to realize that his quest
for awareness and harmony is different from the goals of the
masses because the masses seek to preserve humanity as it was,
while those with the "mark of Cain" sought an unknown distant
goal for humanity which transcended the human condition at
present.

The Demian residence serves as a meeting place for many
types of intellectuals and philosophers, varying from astrologers
to Buddhists to a disciple of Tolstoy. Those with the "mark of
Cain" remained still somewhat isolated, forming an inner circle,
concentrating on achieving such a level of awareness that no
matter what would happen to the world, they would be able to
understand it, remain stable, and if called upon to do so, to lead.

Demian speaks about the soul of Europe and in doing so is very reminiscent of Hesse himself in *Blick in Chaos*. In his essay on *The Brothers Karamazov*, he refers to the concept of a new breed of "Russian man." This peculiar being is a type of amoral beast not subject to any existing laws, combining the ferocity of an animal with the gentility of a saint, the splendor of God and the horror of Satan. Those with the "mark" must be ready.

Paralleling an earlier sensation in the story concerning Demian, Sinclair notices that when Frau Eva is present at the conversations of the group, that all of his thinking seems to come from her and eventually to return to her. He gradually begins to sense that she seems, also, like a reflection of his inner being.

Sinclair's physical longing for Frau Eva grows in intensity. Sensitive to his feelings, Frau Eva guides Sinclair through stories. She feels that in order to find fulfillment in love, one must not consciously seek to be loved, but rather must learn to manifest his own love first. When a person becomes able to love, then the love of others, sensing this quality, will be attracted to that person.

One day in early spring, Sinclair, upon entering Max's room, observes him in a trance-like state resembling that which occurred during their confirmation class. Disturbed, he questions Frau Eva, who assures him that there is no need for alarm. Still upset, Sinclair goes for a walk. While walking in a gentle rain, he observes a strange phenomenon in the distant sky. Watching colliding cloud banks, he sees a gigantic bird emerge and take flight, causing thunderous sounds with its beating wings. The storm then becomes violent, mixed with hail, for a brief moment. It is followed by a sudden burst of sunlight and an unreal serenity. Once again, the symbolism of the sparrow hawk and the egg is employed. This time, however, the hawk is not just an internal symbol for Sinclair's development, but it is external and universal, and it foreshadows the literal destruction of a world — that is, the destruction of pre-World War I Europe and the rebirth which is to follow. The bird becomes a harbinger of the war.

Sinclair describes his vision to Demian. Understanding Sinclair's vision, Demian associates it with a recent dream of his in which he visualized a vast, blazing landscape. Frau Eva also appears to have had a similar presentiment.

VIII. "THE END BEGINS"

Just prior to the end of the summer semester, after which Sinclair is scheduled to reluctantly return home, he is in his room, thinking about Frau Eva, willing her to come to him with as much psychic force as he can muster. Responding to the sudden sound of a horse in the street below, Sinclair descends to meet Demian, who announces the beginning of the war and his commission as a lieutenant. Demian also informs Sinclair that it was Frau Eva who sent him and that she sensed his call.

Sinclair has that evening's meal as Frau Eva's only guest. Just as he is about to leave, she informs him that whenever he needs her, all he need to do is appeal to her in the same manner as he had that day.

The following winter finds Sinclair on the front lines. As a participant in the war, he senses that the horrible fighting and death that he observes all around him is merely a different type of sign for the same principle represented by his sparrow hawk. The manifested hatred is not in actuality directed toward the enemy, but is rather directed violently at the divided individual soul which must first be destroyed before it can be reborn.

One night while on guard duty in Belgium, Sinclair is gazing at the sky while braced against the trunk of a tree. The tree as a location for the occurrence of an enlightening experience becomes a strong motif in Hesse's writings from *Demian* on. In the clouds Sinclair visualizes a city, teeming with people. Suddenly there appears a godlike giant figure resembling Frau Eva. She swallows up the people, figuratively taking them back into the womb. In resultant agony, she falls to the ground, the "mark" bright on her forehead. As she utters a terrifying scream, thousands of stars spring from her forehead. One of these stars, actually a piece of shrapnel from an explosion, reaches Sinclair, seriously wounding him. Hesse's source for this scene is obviously the account of the Daughter of Zion in the Book of Revelations.

After a period of vague consciousness, Sinclair finds himself in a field hospital. Turning on his mattress, he notices that the mattress beside his is also occupied. It is Demian. Quietly making brief references to the past, even to the long, unmentioned Kromer episode, Demian calmly tells Sinclair that he will soon depart, but that the next time he is needed, all Emil need do is to listen within and he will find him. As a final gesture he gives Sinclair a kiss from Frau Eva.

Upon reawakening, Emil finds the neighboring cot occupied by a stranger. The transubstantiation complete, Sinclair has now internalized Demian. The synthesis is finished; Demian and Sinclair are one. The conscious ego (Sinclair) has merged with the self (Demian) and through Demian, with the *anima* (Frau Eva). At least to as great a degree as possible for Sinclair, harmony is achieved. In his last comment he states that dressing the wound hurt as has everything that has happened to him since. Sinclair has not attained the perfect rapture which he has sought, but he has had a taste of it. The answer to the pain of living, he has learned, now lies within him. He has achieved awareness and inner peace and can subsequently draw upon this when life places obstacles in his path.

It should be noted that the only Hesse hero to achieve complete, permanent fulfillment or a state of Nirvana is Siddhartha. In conclusion, it is important for the reader to remember Hesse's own statement about Demian and Frau Eva. While they certainly are real characters in the story, they also have a profound influence on Sinclair's mind, and at times necessarily seem like only parts of his mind. Their existence and activities cannot always be rationally explained, but they need not be; they are the products of Hesse's "magical thinking."

Character Analyses

EMIL SINCLAIR

The young protege of Demian is far from being an average person. Recognized by Max Demian as a possessor of the "mark" of uniqueness at the age of ten, Sinclair is guided by Demian and others in his search for complete cognition of what it is to be a human being and to subsequent fulfillment. Hesse, in his prologue, has told us that every individual is special. In each, nature is attempting to complete the human evolutionary process by creating the ultimate human. Sinclair follows the triadic development constantly utilized by Hesse. He falls from childhood innocence, suffers much of the anguish of life and finally, through his acute self-knowledge, transcends his despair to a state of semi-harmony with life and self. As all of Hesse's writing is autobiographical to varying degrees, Sinclair in describing his attitudes, sufferings, and search for self, can be considered the voice of the author himself.

MAX DEMIAN

Demian is a puzzling figure. He is obviously very important but only in terms of his relationship to Sinclair. Serving in the novel as a Christ-like figure who leads Sinclair in his quest, Demian is also the spokesman for the philosophical influence of Nietzsche upon Hesse. Demian seems at times like a real character with supernatural qualities. At other times he seems more like a figment of Sinclair's imagination or perhaps his subconscious rather than as a real person. He is probably somewhere in between. He does, however, serve as Sinclair's *daemon,* or inner voice, possibly only through his inspiration, which serves to activate the deeper recesses of Sinclair's mind. The reader should not be discouraged if he finds that Demian defies logical explanation. Hesse intended Demian to be this way.

FRAU EVA

Demian's mother's major function is related to her name. She represents the concept of the "universal mother." Possessing all the qualities of Demian, but in greater intensity, she comes to represent that very goal for which Sinclair is striving. She also frequently seems more like a part of Sinclair's subconscious than like an actual person. Subsequently she, like her son, defies rational explanation.

PISTORIUS

Pistorius is a character whom Sinclair meets while in high school and apart from Demian. He also serves as a guide for Sinclair, providing him with a vast background of religious knowledge, particularly about the Gnostic deity Abraxas. Serving also as an amateur psychologist, the character of Pistorius is probably based upon Dr. J. B. Lang, who aided Hesse during his period of mental strife. Pistorius is finally surpassed by his student and is cast aside because Sinclair must ultimately find his own way.

KNAUER

Knauer is a high school student a few years younger than Sinclair. His only important function in the story is as a device by which Sinclair's growth toward his goal can be illustrated. When Sinclair saves Knauer's life, Sinclair can be compared to an earlier Demian, who figuratively effected Emil's salvation.

FRANZ KROMER

Kromer is Sinclair's first human link with the dark world. When he blackmails the young Sinclair, he, in effect, begins Sinclair on his journey. His bullying tactics also serve to cement a friendship between Sinclair and Demian, who comes to his rescue.

Review Questions

1. Demonstrate how Demian's function as a Christ figure can be reconciled to his being a spokesman for Nietzsche's ideas.

2. Discuss whether or not Demian and Frau Eva are real characters or whether they exist only in Sinclair's mind.

3. Explain the terms "collective unconscious," "*anima,*" and "archetype."

4. How does the heraldic bird function as a symbol for Sinclair and how does it eventually transcend its individual nature to become universal?

5. Discuss various aspects of Demian and Frau Eva which can be attributed to Hesse's concept of "magical thinking."

6. Demonstrate by specific references why the goal of those with the "mark" is not an egocentric one.

7. List various characteristics of Demian which identify him as a Christ figure.

8. In what ways do both Demian and Pistorius emphasize that morality is relative to the individual?

9. Discuss Sinclair as the "conscious ego," Demian as the "self," and Beatrice or Frau Eva as "*anima.*"

10. Discuss the various biblical allusions and what function each one serves.

11. Show how Sinclair's life can be divided into three distinguishable periods.

12. Discuss the various stages of Sinclair's struggle for independence from his family.

13. Discuss the importance of the concept of human evolution as depicted in the novel.

Annotated Selected Bibliography

Baumer, Franz. *Hermann Hesse*. New York: Frederick Ungar Publishing Company, 1969. This translation of the German edition of 1959 is a useful and easily read short work dealing with the latter part of Hesse's life. It is more useful as a biographical piece than as a source of criticism of Hesse's works.

Boulby, Mark. *Hermann Hesse: His Mind and Art*. Ithaca, New York: Cornell University Press, 1968. This book, available only in hardback, is an exhaustive study of Hesse's works in all their aspects. Its coverage spans the entire literary life of Hesse and shows great objective insight.

Casebeer, Edwin F. *Hermann Hesse*. New York: Warner Books, Inc., 1972. This paperback edition concerns itself only with the works following *Demian*. It is, however, well written and extremely useful in its discussion of the psychological aspects of Hesse's later works.

Field, George Wallis. *Hermann Hesse*. New York: Twayne Publishers, Inc., 1970. This paperback is a comprehensive study of Hesse's entire literary life and is extremely useful for its biographical information, as well as for its criticism.

Fleissner, Else M. *Hermann Hesse: Modern German Poet and Writer*. Charlotteville, New York: Story House Corp., 1972. This short pamphlet is useful for a quick account of Hesse's life and the introduction of some of his major themes. It is also extremely easy to understand.

Freedman, Ralph. *The Lyrical Novel: Studies in Hermann Hesse, Andre Gide, and Virginia Woolf*. Princeton: Princeton University Press, 1963. This paperback approaches Hesse as a poetic writer who frequently bares his soul through the autobiographical aspects of his works. It treats especially Hesse's Romantic imagination and his use of allegory.

Mileck, Joseph. *Hermann Hesse and His Critics*. New York: AMS Press Inc., 1972. This hardback by one of the leading Hesse scholars is useful primarily because of its summations and criticisms of various writers, and especially because it contains an extensive bibliography which lists all literature by and about Hesse up to 1957. References in German might prove difficult.

Rose, Ernst. *Faith from the Abyss: Hermann Hesse's Way from Romanticism to Modernity*. New York: New York University Press, 1965. One of the most readable works on Hesse, this volume, now in paperback, is excellent in its correlation between biographical incidents and their resultant influence on Hesse's literary production.

Serrano, Miguel. *C. G. Jung and Hermann Hesse: A Record of Two Friendships*. New York: Schoken Books, 1968. This paperback is interesting in its Latin insight into both men by the author, a Chilean diplomat, who was a friend to both. There is, however, little discussion of the relationship between Hesse and Jung.

Wilson, Colin. *The Outsider*. New York: Dell Publishing Co. Inc., 1956. One chapter in this important book, now in paperback, concerns itself with Hesse's protagonists as fringe characters alienated from the mainstream of society.

Zeller, Bernhard. *Portrait of Hesse*. New York: Herder and Herder, 1971. This translation from the German biography is easy to read and provides great insight into its subject. It is also profusely illustrated with interesting photographs.

Ziolkowski, Theodore. *Hermann Hesse*. New York: Columbia University Press, 1966. This pamphlet by the leading Hesse authority provides the best brief overview of Hesse and his works. It places Hesse in perspective as an extremely important writer of the twentieth century.

Ziolkowski, Theodore. *The Novels of Hermann Hesse: A Study in Theme and Structure*. Princeton: Princeton University Press, 1965. This critical masterpiece by Ziolkowski combines thoroughness with easy reading and is extremely interesting. Unfortunately, it deals only with the works from *Demian* to *The Glass Bead Game* (Magister Ludi).

A Hermann Hesse Bibliography for the English-Speaking Student

Writings by Hermann Hesse in English Translation

Peter Camenzind	Farrar, Straus and Giroux Noonday Press
Beneath the Wheel	Farrar, Straus and Giroux Noonday Press Bantam Books
Gertrude	Farrar, Straus and Giroux Noonday Press Bantam Books
Rosshalde	Farrar, Straus and Giroux Noonday Press Bantam Books
Knulp	Farrar, Straus and Giroux Noonday Press
Demian	Harper & Row Bantam Books
Strange News from Another Star	Farrar, Straus and Giroux Noonday Press
Klingsor's Last Summer	Farrar, Straus and Giroux Noonday Press Bantam Books
Wandering	Farrar, Straus and Giroux Noonday Press

Siddhartha	New Directions Bantam Books
Steppenwolf	Holt, Rinehart and Winston Modern Library Bantam Books
Narcissus and Goldmund	Farrar, Straus and Giroux Noonday Press Bantam Books
The Journey to the East	Farrar, Straus and Giroux Noonday Press Bantam Books
The Glass Bead Game (Also published as *Magister Ludi*)	Holt, Rinehart and Winston Bantam Books
If the War Goes On...	Farrar, Straus and Giroux Noonday Press
Poems	Farrar, Straus and Giroux Noonday Press
Autobiographical Writings	Farrar, Straus and Giroux Noonday Press
Stories of Five Decades	Farrar, Straus and Giroux Noonday Press
My Belief	Farrar, Straus and Giroux
Reflections (to be published June 1974)	Farrar, Straus and Giroux
Gerbersau (publication set for late 1974 or 1975)	Farrar, Straus and Giroux
Hesse's Letters (publication set for 1976)	Farrar, Straus and Giroux

50

I. Books, Pamphlets, and Articles in Books about Hermann Hesse

Andrews, Wayne. "The Achievement of Hermann Hesse," *Siegfried's Curse: The German Journey from Nietzsche to Hesse*. New York: Atheneum, 1972. 274-329.

Barrett, William. "Journey to the East," *In Time of Need: Forms of Imagination in the Twentieth Century*. New York: Harper and Row, 1972. 187-213.

Baumer, Franz. *Hermann Hesse*. New York: Ungar Publishers, 1969.

Boulby, Mark. *Hermann Hesse: His Mind and Art*. Ithaca: Cornell University Press, 1967.

Casebeer, Edwin F. *Hermann Hesse*. New York: Warner Paperback Library, 1972.

Devert, Krystyna. "Hermann Hesse: Apostle of the Apolitical Revolution," *Literature in Revolution*. Edited by George Abbot White and Charles Newman. New York: Holt, Rinehart and Winston, 1972. 302-17.

Engel, Eva J. "Hermann Hesse," *German Men of Letters*. Edited by Alex Natan. London: Oswald Wolff, 1963. Vol. II, 249-74.

Farquharson, Robert H. *An Outline of the Works of Hermann Hesse*. Toronto: Forum House, 1973.

Field, George W. *Hermann Hesse*. New York: Twayne Publishers, 1970.

Fleissner, Else M. *Hermann Hesse: Modern German Poet and Writer*. Charlotteville, New York: Sam-Har Press, 1972.

Freedman, Ralph. *The Lyrical Novel: Studies in Hermann Hesse, Andre Gide and Virginia Woolf.* Princeton: Princeton University Press, 1963.

Friedrichsmeyer, E. S. *Hermann Hesse's "Narcissus and Goldmund": A Critical Commentary.* New York: Monarch Press, 1972.

Glenn, Jerry. *Hermann Hesse's "Siddhartha": A Critical Commentary.* New York: Monarch Press, 1973.

Glenn, Jerry. *The Major Works of Hermann Hesse: A Critical Commentary.* New York: Monarch Press, 1973.

Hanlon, James. "Siddhartha," *Creative Approaches to Reading Literature.* No. 7. Edited by Robert Burns. Middletown, Conn.: Xerox Education Publications, 1974. 97-102.

Hatfield, Henry. "Accepting the Universe: Hermann Hesse's *Steppenwolf,*" *Crisis and Continuity in Modern German Fiction.* Ithaca: Cornell University Press, 1969. 63-77.

Mayer, Hans. "Hermann Hesse's *Steppenwolf,*" *Steppenwolf and Everyman.* Translated by Jack D. Zipes. New York: Thomas Y. Crowell, 1971. 1-13.

Mileck, Joseph. *Hermann Hesse and His Critics.* Chapel Hill: University of North Carolina Press, 1958.

Reichert, Herbert W. *The Impact of Nietzsche on Hermann Hesse.* Mt. Pleasant, Michigan: The Enigma Press, 1972.

Rose, Ernst. *Faith from the Abyss: Hermann Hesse's Way from Romanticism to Modernity.* New York: New York University Press, 1965.

Secundy, Claudia. *Teacher's Guide to Hermann Hesse.* New York: Bantam Books, 1973.

52

Serrano, Miguel. *C. G. Jung and Hermann Hesse: A Record of Two Friendships*. New York: Schocken Books, 1966.

Simonns, John D. *Hermann Hesse's "Steppenwolf": A Critical Commentary*. New York: Monarch Press, 1972.

Welch, Carolyn R. *"Steppenwolf" and "Siddhartha" Notes*. Lincoln, Nebraska: Cliff's Notes Inc., 1973.

Whiton, John. *Hermann Hesse's "Demian": A Critical Commentary*. New York: Monarch Press, 1973.

Wilson, Colin. *The Outsider*. New York: Dell Publishing Co., 1956. 46-68.

Zeller, Bernhard. *A Portrait of Hesse: An Illustrated Biography*. New York: Herder and Herder, 1971.

Ziolkowski, Theodore. (Ed.) *Hesse: A Collection of Critical Essays*. Englewood Cliffs, New Jersey: Prentice-Hall, Inc., 1973.

_____. *Hermann Hesse*. New York: Columbia University Press, 1965.

_____. "Hesse, Myth, and Reason: Methodological Prolegomena," *Myth and Reason: A Symposium*. Edited by Walter D. Wetzels, Austin: University of Texas Press, 1973. 127-55.

_____. *The Novels of Hermann Hesse: A Study in Theme and Structure*. Princeton: Princeton University Press, 1966.

II. Articles in Periodical Literature about Hermann Hesse

Abood, Edward. "Jung's Concept of Individuation in Hesse's *Steppenwolf*." *Southern Humanities Review*, 3(1968), 1-13.

Andrews, R. C. "The Poetry of Hermann Hesse," *German Life and Letters* 6 (1952-53), 117-27.

Anolt, V. "Hesse: An Existential Thinker," *Contemporary Education*, 44 (Feb., 1973), 212-14.

Bandy, Stephen C. "Hermann Hesse's *Glasperlenspiel:* In Search of Joseph Knecht," *Modern Language Quarterly*, 33(Sept. 1972), 299-331.

Bauke, Joseph P. "Narcissus and Goldmund," *Saturday Review of Literature*, 51(May 4, 1968) 32-33.

Beerman, Hans. "Hermann Hesse and the Bhagavad-Gita," *Midwest Quarterly*, I(1959), 27-40.

Benn, Maurice. "An Interpretation of the Work of Hermann Hesse," *German Life and Letters*, 3(1949-50), 202-11.

Boulby, Mark. "Der Vierte Lebenslauf as a Key to *Das Glasperlenspiel,*" *Modern Language Review*, 61(1966), 635-46.

Bretensky, Dennis. "*Siddhartha:* A Casebook on Teaching Methods," *English Journal*, 62(March, 1973), 379-82.

Bronson, John. "Death and the Lover," *Bookman*, 76(June, 1933), 91-92.

Butler, Colin. "Hermann Hesse's *Siddhartha:* Some Critical Objections," *Monatshefte*, 63(1971), 117-24.

———. "Literary Malpractice in Some Works of Hermann Hesse," *University of Toronto Quarterly*, 40(1971), 168-82.

Cohn, Dorrit. "Narration of Consciousness in *Der Steppenwolf,*" *Germanic Review*, 44(March, 1969), 121-31.

Cohn, Hilde. "The Symbolic End of Hermann Hesse's *Glasperlenspiel,*" *Modern Language Quarterly*, 11(1950), 347-57.

Colby, Thomas. "The Impenitent Prodigal: Hermann Hesse's Hero," *German Quarterly,* 40(1967), 14-23.

Crenshaw, Karen O. and Lawson, Richard H. "Technique and Function of Time in Hesse's *Morgenlandfahrt:* A Culmination," *Mosaic* (Spring-Summer, 1972), 53-59.

Engel, Monroe. "Magister Ludi," *Nation,* 169(Dec. 24, 1949), 626-27.

Enright, D. J. "Hesse vs. Hesse," *New York Review of Books,* (Sept. 12, 1968), 10.

Farquharson, Robert H. "The Identity and Significance of Leo in Hesse's *Morgenlandfahrt,*" *Monatshefte,* 55(1963), 122-28.

Farrelly, John. "Demian," *New Republic,* 118(Feb. 23, 1948), 24.

Fickert, Kurt J. "The Development of the Outsider Concept in Hesse's Novels," *Monatshefte,* 52(1960), 171-78.

Field, G. W. "Hermann Hesse: A Neglected Nobel Prize Novelist," *Queen's Quarterly,* 65(1958), 514-20.

_____. "Hermann Hesse as Critic of English and American Literature," *Monatshefte,* 53(1961), 147-58.

_____. "Music and Morality in Thomas Mann and Hermann Hesse," *University of Toronto Quarterly,* 24(1955), 175-90.

_____. "On the Genesis of Hesse's *Glasperlenspiel,*" *German Quarterly,* 41(1968), 673-88.

Flaxman, Seymour H. *"Der Steppenwolf:* Hesse's Portrait of the Intellectual," *Modern Language Quarterly,* 15(1954), 349-58.

Foran, Marion. "Hermann Hesse," *Queen's Quarterly,* 55(May 9, 1948), 180-89.

55

Ford, Richard J. "Hermann Hesse: Prophet of the Pot Generation," *Catholic World*, 212(Oct. 1970), 15-19.

Freemantle, Anne. "Good and Evil: *Demian*," *New York Herald Tribune Weekly Book Review*, (Feb. 29, 1948), 27.

Freedman, Ralph. "Hermann Hesse," *Contemporary Literature*, 10(Summer, 1969), 421-26.

_____. "Romantic Imagination: Hermann Hesse as a Modern Novelist," *Publication of the Modern Language Association*, 73(June, 1958), 275-84.

Goldgar, Harry. "Hesse's *Glasperlenspiel* and the Game of Go," *German Life and Letters*, 20(1966), 132-37.

Goldman, Albert. *"The Glass Bead Game:* Fanned by Youth," *Vogue*, 155(Jan. 1, 1970), 82.

Gowan, B. "Demian," *Monatshefte*, 20(1928), 225-28.

Gropper, Esther C. "Literature for the Restive: Hermann Hesse's Books," *English Journal*, 59(Dec., 1970), 1226-28.

_____. "The Disenchanted Turn to Hesse," *English Journal*, 61(Oct. 1972), 979-84.

Gross, Harvey. "Hermann Hesse," *Western Review*, 17(1953), 132-40.

Hallamore, Joyce. "Paul Klee, H. H. and *Die Morgenlandfahrt*," *Seminar*, 1(1965), 17-24.

Halpert, Inge. "The Alt Musikmeister and Goethe," *Monatshefte*, 52(1960), 159-64.

_____. "Vita Activa and Vita Contemplativa," *Monatshefte*, 53(1961), 159-66.

Halsband, R. "Siddhartha," *Saturday Review of Literature*, (Dec. 22, 1951), 38.

Hanlon, James. "Siddhartha," *Senior Paperbacks*, (April, 1973), 3-4.

Heller, Peter. "The Creative Unconscious and the Spirit: A Study of Polarities in Hesse's Image of the Writer," *Modern Language Forum*, 38(1953), 28-40.

_____. "The Masochistic Rebel in Recent German Literature," *Journal of Aesthetics and Art Criticism*, 2(1953), 205-6.

_____. "The Writer in Conflict With His Age: A Study in the Ideology of Hermann Hesse," *Monatshefte*, 46(1954), 137-47.

Hill, Claude. "Hermann Hesse and Germany," *German Quarterly*, 21(1948), 9-15.

_____. "Herr Hesse and the Modern Neurosis: *Steppenwolf*," *New York Times Book Review*, (March 16, 1947), 5.

_____. "The Journey to the East," *Saturday Review of Literature*, (June, 1957), 12.

Hirsch, T. E. "Demian," *Library Journal*, 72(1947), 1685.

Hughes, Kenneth. "Hesse's Use of Gilgamesh Motifs in the Humanization of Siddhartha and Harry Haller," *Seminar*, 5(1969), 129-40.

Irvine, L. "Steppenwolf," *Athenaeum*, (May 11, 1929), 208.

Jaeger, Hans. "Heidegger's Existential Philosophy and Modern German Literature," *Publication of the Modern Language Association*, 67(1952), 655.

Jehle, Mimi. "The 'Garden' in the Works of Hermann Hesse," *German Quarterly*, 24(1951), 42-50.

Johnson, Sidney H. "The Autobiographies in Hermann Hesse's *Glasperlenspiel*," *German Quarterly*, 29(1956), 160-71.

Koch, Stephen. "Prophet of Youth," *New Republic,* 159(July 13, 1968), 23-26.

Koester, Rudolf. "Hermann Hesse: Portrayal of Age in Hesse's Narrative Prose," *Germanic Review,* 61(March, 1966), 111-19.

————. "Hesse's Music Master: In Search of a Prototype," *Forum for Modern Language Studies,* 3(1967), 135-41.

————. "Self-Realization: Reflections on Youth," *Monatshefte,* 57(1965), 181-86.

Kronenberger, Louis. "Death and the Lover," *New York Herald Tribune Books,* (Dec. 11, 1932), 18.

Lazare, Christopher. "A Measure of Wisdom: *Siddhartha,*" *New York Times Book Review,* (Dec. 2, 1951), 52.

Lesser, J. "Hermann Hesse: Nobel Prize Winner," *The Contemporary Review,* 171(1947), 31-34.

MacDonald, Dwight. "Books," *New Yorker,* (Jan. 23, 1954), 98.

Malthaner, J. "A Visit with Hermann Hesse," *Books Abroad,* 21(1947), 146-52.

————. "Herman Hesse: *Siddhartha,*" *German Quarterly,* 25(1952), 103-9.

Maurer, Warren R. "Jean Paul and Hermann Hesse: Katzenbergen and Kurgast," *Seminar,* 4(1968), 113-28.

Middleton, Drew. "A Literary Letter from Germany," *New York Times Book Review,* (July 31, 1949), 2.

Middleton, J. C. "An Enigma Transfigured in Hermann Hesse's *Glasperlenspiel,*" *German Life and Letters,* 10(1956-57), 298-302.

_____. "Hermann Hesse's *Morgenlandfahrt*," *Germanic Review*, 32(1957), 299-310.

Mihailovich, Vasa D. "Hermann Hesse as a Critic of Russian Literature," *Arcadia*, 2(1967), 91-102.

Mileck, Joseph. "A Visit with Hermann Hesse and a Journey from Montagnola to Calw," *Modern Language Forum*, 41(1956), 3-8.

_____. *"Das Glasperlenspiel:* Genesis, Manuscripts, and History of Publication," *German Quarterly*, 43(1970), 55-83.

_____. "Hesse Bibliography," *Monatshefte*, 49(1957), 201-5.

_____. "Hesse Collections in Europe," *Monatshefte*, 47(1955), 290-94.

_____. "Hermann Hesse and Romain Rolland: Briefe," *Modern Language Notes*, 70(1955), 627.

_____. "Hermann Hesse's *Glasperlenspiel*," *University of California Publications in Modern Philology*, 36(1952), 243-70.

_____. "Names and the Creative Process," *Monatshefte*, 53(1961), 167-80.

_____. "The Poetry of Hermann Hesse," *Monatshefte*, 66(1954), 192-98.

_____. "The Prose of Hermann Hesse: Life, Substance, and Form," *German Quarterly*, 27(1954), 163-74.

Misra, Bhabagrahi. "An Analysis of the Indic Tradition in Hermann Hesse's *Siddhartha*," *Indian Literature*, 11(1968), 111-23.

Morris, A. S. "The Will to Perish: Demian," *New York Times Book Review*, (Feb. 1, 1948), 6.

Mueller, Gustav. "A Hermann Hesse Reminiscence," *Books Abroad*, 21(1947), 287.

_____. "Hermann Hesse," *Books Abroad*, 21(1947), 146-52.

Naumann, Walter. "The Individual and Society in the Works of Hermann Hesse," *Monatshefte*, 41(1949), 33-42.

Negus, Kenneth. "On the Death of Joseph Knecht in Hermann Hesse's *Glasperlenspiel*," *Monatshefte*, 53(1961), 181-89.

Norton, Roger C. "Hermann Hesse's Criticism of Technology," *Germanic Review*, 43(1968), 267-73.

_____. "Variant Endings of Hesse's *Glasperlenspiel*," *Monatshefte*, 60(1968), 141-46.

Park, C. W. "Notes on Hermann Hesse's Verse," *Poetry*, 70(1947), 206-8.

Pasinetti, P. H. "Novels from Three Languages," *Sewanee Review*, 56(1948), 171-4.

Paslick, Robert H. "Dialectic and Non-Attachment: The Structure of Hermann Hesse's *Siddhartha*," *Symposium*, (Spring, 1973), 67-75.

Pawel, Ernst. "Stories of Five Decades," *New York Times Book Review*, (Feb. 11, 1973), 7.

Peppard, Murray. "Hermann Hesse's Ladder of Learning," *Kentucky Foreign Language Quarterly*, 3(1956), 13-20.

Peters, Eric. "Hermann Hesse: The Psychological Implications of His Writings," *German Life and Letters*, 1(1948), 209-14.

Pick, Robert. "Cryptic Game of Beads," *Saturday Review of Literature*, (Oct. 15, 1949), 15-16.

60

_____. "Demian," *Saturday Review of Literature*, (Jan. 24, 1948), 18.

_____. "Nobel Prize Winner Hesse," *Saturday Review of Literature*, (Dec. 7, 1946), 38-40.

Plant, Richard. "Magister Ludi," *New York Times Book Review*, (Oct. 30, 1944), 52.

Porterfield, A. W. "Mozart Still Lives: *Steppenwolf,*" *New York Herald Tribune Books*, (Sept. 8, 1929), 4.

Resnik, Henry S. "How Hermann Hesse Speaks to the College Generation," *Saturday Review*, 52(Oct. 18, 1969), 35-37.

Sammons, Jeffrey. "Notes on the Germanization of American Youth," *The Yale Review*, (Spring, 1970), 342-56.

Schludermann, Brigette. "Mythical Reflections of the East in Hermann Hesse," *Mosaic*, 2(1968/69), 97-111.

Schneider, Christian I. "Loss of Soul Without Nature," *National Parks and Conservation Magazine*, 44(August, 1970), 20.

Schwarz, Egon. "Hermann Hesse: The American Youth Movement, and Problems of Literary Evaluation," *Publication of the Modern Language Association*, 85(October, 1970), 977-87.

Seidlin, Oscar. "Hermann Hesse: Exorcism of the Demon," *Symposium*, (Nov. 1950), 325-48.

_____. "Hermann Hesse's *Glasperlenspiel,*" *Germanic Review*, 23(1948), 263-73.

Shaw, Leroy. "Time and the Structure of Hermann Hesse's *Siddhartha,*" *Symposium*, 11(1957), 204-24.

Shuster, G. W. "A Comment on the Soul of an Artist," *New York Herald Tribune Book Review*, (March 16, 1947), 1.

Sklar, Robert. "Tolkien and Hesse: Top of the Pops," *Nation,* 204(May 8, 1967), 598-601.

Smith, B. "Steppenwolf," *New York World,* (Oct. 27, 1929), 11.

Stanck, Lou Willett. "Hesse and Moffett Team-Teach the Theory of Discourse," *English Journal,* 61(Oct. 1972), 985-93.

Steiner, G. "Eastward Ho!" *New Yorker,* 44(Jan. 18, 1969), 87-90.

Taylor, R. "Steppenwolf," *Spectator,* (May 18, 1929), 290-93.

Timpe, Eugene F. "Hermann Hesse in the United States," *Symposium,* 23(Spring, 1969), 73-79.

_____. "Hesse's Siddhartha and the Bhagavad-Gita," *Comparative Literature,* 22(Fall, 1970), 346-57.

Townsend, S. "The German Humanist Hermann Hesse," *Modern Language Forum,* 32(1947), 1-12.

Vonnegut, Kurt Jr. "Why They Read Hesse," *Horizon,* 12(Spring, 1970), 28-31.

Werner, Alfred. "Nobel Prize Winner," *New York Times Book Review,* (Dec. 8, 1946), 56-57.

_____. "Hermann Hesse," *South Atlantic Quarterly,* 52(July, 1958), 384-90.

Weyr, Thomas. "Hermann Hesse and the American German Review," *American German Review,* 35:2(1969), 1.

Wilson, A. L. "Hesse's Veil of Isis," *Monatshefte,* 55(1963), 313-21.

Wood, Ralph Charles. "Hermann Hesse," *American German Review,* 43(1956), 3-6.

Ziolkowski, Theodore. "Hesse's Sudden Popularity with To-day's Students," *University: Princeton Quarterly*, (Summer, 1970), 19-25.

_____. "Hermann Hesse's Chiliastic Vision," *Monatshefte*, 53(1961), 199-210.

_____. "Saint Hesse Among the Hippies," *American Germanic Review*, 35:2(1969), 19-23.

Miscellaneous Articles about Hermann Hesse

"A God Within," *Time*, 86(July 30, 1965), 68-69.

"Hermann Hesse's *Briefe*," *The Times Literary Supplement*, (Dec. 28, 1951), 838.

"The Novels of Hermann Hesse," *The Times Literary Supplement*, (Dec. 19, 1952), 835.

"Outsider," *Time*, 92(Oct. 18, 1968), 111-12.

"Siddhartha," *Nation*, (Nov. 17, 1951), 430.

"Steppenwolf," *Bookman*, (Oct. 1924), xxii.

"Teaching Guide for *Siddhartha*," *Campus Book Club Publication*, (Jan. 1974), 2-3.

"The Wolf Man," *New York Times Book Review*, (Sept. 29, 1929), 7.

NOTES

NOTES

THE DIARY OF
ANNE FRANK
NOTES

including
- *Introduction*
- *Historical Background*
- *List of Characters*
- *Critical Commentaries*
  The First Year
  The Second Year
- *Character Backgrounds and Fates*
  Anne Frank
  Margot Frank
  Otto Frank
  Mrs. Frank
  The Van Daans
  Mr. Düssel
  The Dutch "Protectors"
  Lies
- *Essay Topics*
- *Selected Bibliography*

by
Dorothea Shefer-Vanson, M.A.
Hebrew University of Jerusalem

INCORPORATED

LINCOLN, NEBRASKA   68501

Editor	Consulting Editor
Gary Carey, M.A.	*James L. Roberts, Ph.D.*
University of Colorado	*Department of English*
	University of Nebraska

ISBN 0-8220-0390-2
© Copyright 1984
by
C. K. Hillegass
All Rights Reserved
Printed in U.S.A.

1990 Printing

Cliffs Notes, Inc.   Lincoln, Nebraska

CONTENTS

INTRODUCTION 5

HISTORICAL BACKGROUND 7

LIST OF CHARACTERS 14

CRITICAL COMMENTARIES
    The First Year: June 1942–May 1943 16
    The Second Year: June 1943–August 1944 24

EPILOGUE 38

CHARACTER BACKGROUNDS AND FATES
    Anne Frank 38
    Margot Frank 46
    Otto Frank 47
    Mrs. Frank 49
    Mr. Van Daan 50
    Mrs. Van Daan 51
    Peter Van Daan 51
    Mr. Düssel 52
    Lies 53
    Mr. Kraler 54
    Mr. Koophuis 56
    Miep 57
    Elli 59

ESSAY TOPICS 60

SELECTED BIBLIOGRAPHY 61

THE DIARY OF ANNE FRANK
Notes

". . . ideals, dreams, and
cherished hopes rise within us
only to meet the horrible truth
and be shattered . . . yet in
spite of everything I still believe
that people are really good at heart."

Anne Frank
July 15, 1944

INTRODUCTION

Anne Frank's *Diary* is not a novel or a tale of the imagination. It is the diary kept by a young Jewish girl for the two years she was forced to remain in hiding by the Nazi persecution of the Jews of Europe. Between June 1942 and August 1944, from Anne's thirteenth birthday until shortly after her fifteenth birthday, Anne Frank record- ed her feelings, her emotions, and her thoughts, as well as the events that happened to her, in the diary which her father had given her as a birthday present. Together with her parents and her sister, Margot, the Van Daan family (consisting of a husband, a wife, and a son, Peter, two years older than Anne) and, later on, an elderly den- tist named Mr. Düssel, Anne lived in a set of rooms at the top of an old warehouse in Amsterdam, Holland, concealed behind a hidden door and a bookcase. During the day, when people worked in the office and in the warehouse below, Anne and the others had to keep very quiet, but at night they could move around more freely, though of course they could not turn on any lights nor show in any way that the house was inhabited.

The *Diary* is many things at one and the same time. It is an amusing, enlightening, and often moving account of the *process of adolescence*, as Anne describes her thoughts and feelings about herself and the people around her, the world at large, and life in general. It is an accurate record of the way a young girl grows up and matures, in the very special circumstances in which Anne found herself throughout the two years during which she was in hiding. And it is also a vividly terrifying description of *what it was like to be a Jew* — and in hiding — at a time when the Nazis sought to kill *all* the Jews of Europe.

Above all, Anne was an ordinary girl, growing up, and eventually dying, but she was an *ordinary* girl growing up in *extraordinary* times. She loved life and laughter, was interested in history and movie stars, Greek mythology, and cats, writing, and boys. In the few entries which she wrote before the family went into hiding, we discover something of the world of a child growing up in Holland in 1942. Anne went to school, had girl friends and boyfriends, went to parties and to ice-cream parlors, rode her bike, and *chattered* (an understatement) in class. In fact, Anne chattered so much that, as a punishment for her talkativeness, she had to write several essays on the subject of "A Chatterbox." Much of this chatty quality of hers, however, spills over onto the pages of her diary, where we often feel as if she is a good friend who is confiding in us. Although the world of that period is divided from us by more than mere years, Anne's voice is very contemporary, and many of her thoughts and problems are very much like those of any youngster growing up both then and now.

Anne Frank did *not* survive the concentration camps to which she was sent after her little group was discovered. Of all the eight people who hid in the "Secret Annexe" in Amsterdam, only Anne's father survived. The pages of Anne's diary, which the Nazis left scattered on the floor when they arrested the group in hiding, were kept by the two young women who had worked in the office and had faithfully supplied the little group with food and other provisions. When Mr. Frank returned after the war, they gave him the pages of Anne's diary, and he eventually published them. And so, although Anne died, as the Nazis had intended, her spirit lives on, through her *Diary*, stronger and clearer by far than any brute force or blind hatred.

HISTORICAL BACKGROUND

The events recounted in Anne Frank's diary take place during World War II, in which almost all the countries of Europe, as well as the U.S.A. and Japan, were involved to a greater or lesser extent between 1939 and 1945. The reasons for the war are many and varied, and even the historians are not fully in agreement as to the precise causes, some blaming the harsh conditions and economic penalties imposed on Germany after its defeat in World War I, others claiming that it was the weakness of the European countries after Hitler's rise to power in Germany that was the indirect cause. All are agreed, however, that had it not been for Hitler and his policies, the war would *not* have taken place.

In addition to the various military engagements, however, the Nazis were engaged in a systematic attempt to kill off certain sections of the population – primarily Jews and Gypsies – both within Germany and in the countries which they occupied, claiming that they were "racially inferior." The murder of mentally retarded and psychologically disturbed people, as well as homosexuals, was also official Nazi policy. In some cases, these people were made to work as slaves before they were killed, so that the Germans could benefit as much as possible from their labor. To implement this scheme, the Germans established huge "concentration camps," or death camps, throughout Europe. Jews and other people were sent there in cattle trains, and upon arrival, their heads were shaved and their arms were tattooed with numbers; in addition, they were stripped of their clothes and whatever possessions they still had. They were made to work and were subjected to the strictest discipline and the most inhumane conditions before they were gassed in special chambers and their bodies burned. In those parts of Europe which were occupied by the Nazis, but where these methods of killing large numbers of people had *not yet* been established, the Nazis assembled large numbers of Jews and machine-gunned them all as they stood on the edge of huge pits which they had dug themselves, or beside natural, deep ravines, as was the case at Babi Yar, in Russia. In other places, the Nazis herded all the local Jews into the synagogue and then set it on fire.

Throughout World War II, the Nazis devoted considerable thought, equipment, and manpower to the wholesale slaughter of Europe's Jewish population, and by the time the war had ended, they had succeeded in killing six million of them, two-thirds of the total number of Jews in the world.

How could it come about that one nation regarded itself as *racially superior* to another, to the extent that it felt that it was its *right* and its *duty* to kill all the members of that other nation? How could huge "factories of death," manned by thousands of people, systematically kill off millions of people in the midst of inhabited areas without anyone protesting or even knowing what was happening? How could Hitler, a homicidal maniac, become the ruler of a country whose civilization had produced some of the world's greatest thinkers, writers, composers, and statemen? In order to obtain answers to these questions, we have to go back to the nineteenth century.

Germany was not always one united country. During the Middle Ages, Germany consisted of a series of small kingdoms and principalities, often rivals, and often even at war with one another. The language which they all shared was German, but the people differed on matters of religion, so much so that these differences occasionally erupted into wars between the Catholics and the Protestants. In the mid-nineteenth century, Bismarck (the Chancellor of Prussia, the largest German state) made it his objective to unify the various German states. This he achieved by judicious policies, arranging marriages between various royal families and obtaining treaties which were mutually beneficial to the parties concerned. By the end of the nineteenth century, Germany was united under one monarch, Kaiser Wilhelm I; it possessed colonies in Africa and was ruled by an Emperor (the German term *Kaiser* is derived from the Latin word *Caesar*).

World War I, in which Germany fought against France and England, from 1914 to 1918, was largely a result of the structural weakness of many European states and the growing military and economic strength of Germany. After four years of bitter fighting, Germany was defeated, the Kaiser fled to Holland, and a peace treaty, the Treaty of Versailles, was drawn up. This stripped Germany of its foreign colonies, imposed heavy economic penalties on the country in the form of fines and disarmament, and it changed many of the borders of the countries of Europe. This policy gave rise to severe economic problems in Germany. Hunger and poverty were widespread, and galloping inflation caused prices to rise at a dizzying rate. The middle class, which had been the chief support of the German

Republic, which was established after World War I, became embittered, and many Germans longed for the old autocratic kind of government that had formerly dominated the country.

It was during the years after World War I that Adolf Hitler, a house painter who had experienced the bitterness of defeat as a soldier in the German Army, developed his ideas of the Master Aryan Race, the need to rid Germany of "inferior" peoples, such as Jews and Gypsies, and the need to expand Germany's borders and build a Germany that was militarily strong. He gathered around him a group of people who supported his ideas and used the tactics of bullying and terrorism to obtain publicity and intimidate his opponents. His National Socialist – or Nazi – party advocated the establishment of a totalitarian state, the redistribution of the nation's wealth and the provision of jobs for everybody.

Hitler used inflammatory rhetoric in his speeches, and he was able to arouse huge audiences to hysterical enthusiasm. He claimed that Germany's problems and the decline in its power were the fault of Jews and radicals, and that the German, or Aryan, race was the Master Race, the creators of all civilization, and fitted by *nature* to rule the world. In order for this Master Race to have adequate living space, *Lebensraum,* Hitler intended to expand Germany's frontiers in the East, taking from the lands of Poland, Czechoslovakia, and Russia. The inhabitants of those countries, the Slavs, were also "inferior," according to Hitler, fit only either to serve the Master Race as slaves – or to be killed.

Hitler's Nazi party, regarded initially by most Germans as merely a lunatic fringe, began to gain ground and support within Germany after the world's economic depression, which began in 1929. In the German parliament, the *Reichstag,* the Nazis were represented alongside the various other political parties. Hitler continued to fulminate against the Jews, describing them as an alien, inferior race despite their distinguished contribution to German cultural and economic life throughout many centuries. He regarded them as being responsible for all the movements which the Nazis opposed, communism, pacifism, internationalism, and Christianity, as well as being a threat to "German racial purity." The Jews, who had resided in Germany for a thousand years and constituted half a million people, a small fraction of the population, watched in horror as Hitler's party gained power throughout the country. Many believed that the political hysteria would soon pass, that the common people would soon see Hitler for what he really was, or that, once in power, Hitler would modify his extreme views. After all, they seemed to think, Germany is a civilized country; anti-Semitic riots could never happen here. They could not imagine that millions of people would be murdered for no other reason than that they were Jews.

Hitler's racial theories and nationalism had deep roots in Germany's past. The Christian tradition of anti-Semitism and Jewish responsibility for the death of Jesus also played a role in the reluctance to regard Jews as equal members of society. When, through various parliamentary maneuvers, Hitler became the Chancellor of Germany in 1933, he immediately took measures to establish an absolute, totalitarian regime. He outlawed *all* political parties other than his own, banned *all* literature that did not support his party or that was written by Jews or communists, and introduced a set of laws, the Nuremberg Race Laws, prohibiting Jews from interacting with, or marrying, Aryans. Most Germans quietly accepted Hitler's regime, and those who did not were confronted with arrests, beatings, torture, and imprisonment.

Hitler's new laws prevented Jews from holding public office, being teachers, practicing law or medicine, working in journalism or engaging in business. Jews were forbidden to employ Aryans, and Aryans were discouraged from patronizing Jewish stores. Jewish property was confiscated, collective fines were imposed on Jewish communities, and even emigration was made difficult for Jews. The countries of the world gathered at Evian, France, in 1938 to discuss ways of absorbing the Jewish population of Germany, but no country was willing to provide a home for more than a handful of Jews. The U.S. government declined to increase its immigrant quotas, and the British, who controlled Palestine, refused to allow large numbers of Jews to go there, fearing Arab opposition to this move. Even countries like Australia and Canada, with vast tracts of uninhabited land, refused to allow large numbers of Jews to enter.

After gaining power, Hitler set about rearming Germany, even though this was *strictly prohibited* by the terms of the Treaty of Versailles. In doing so, he strengthened Germany's economy, created full employment, and restored a sense of pride to the German population. The countries of Europe, however, turned a blind eye to this flagrant disregard of the Versailles Treaty, refrained from taking any action, and thereby allowed the stage to be set for Hitler's next acts.

In 1938, encouraged by the inaction of the European nations, Hitler proceeded to invade and annex, first, Austria, and then Czechoslovakia, each time assuring the world that all he wanted was "peace," and that this would be his "last demand." By the end of 1939, when Hitler was obviously preparing to adopt a similar take-over policy toward Poland, and the efforts of Chamberlain, Britain's prime minister, to find a peaceful solution had evidently failed, France and Britain declared war on Germany.

The years since 1933 that Hitler had spent rearming Germany had not been militarily paralleled by the Allies (the European countries, the United States, and Russia) so that the outbreak of World War II found Germany vastly superior in military strength. This enabled German forces to rapidly overrun Poland, Denmark, Norway, Holland, Belgium, and France within a short space of time in 1939 and 1940, so that *within less than a year,* most of Europe was occupied by Germany. The German troops were highly mobile and mechanized, strictly disciplined, and motivated by theories of national and racial superiority. Britain's island status enabled it to withstand German threats, and although it suffered considerable devastation as a result of German bombardments, its people rallied, manufacturing arms and defending its shores and skies.

Not content with being master of most of Europe, Hitler then launched an attack against Russia in June, 1941, *despite* the non-aggression pact that Hitler had signed with Stalin in 1939. For over five years, Europe was a virtual slave empire under the Nazis. The people of Europe worked long, hard hours in farms and factories, receiving little more than subsistence rations in return, and millions of people were taken to Germany to work there. In occupied countries, any resistance was crushed ruthlessly; hostages were executed in retaliation for the killing of a single Nazi soldier, listening to British broadcasts, or possessing anti-Nazi literature were all made punishable by death. Harboring Jews was punishable either by death or by being sent to a concentration camp.

The Nazis were as efficient in setting up the machinery of death as they were in manufacturing arms. Over the years, they perfected a system of obtaining lists of *all* the Jewish inhabitants of a particular place and making them all wear a distinguishing mark in the form of a yellow star, herding them into "ghettoes" and then loading them into crowded cattle cars and dispatching them by train to concentration camps. There, they were either worked until they dropped, starved to death, or were gassed. All through the war, the long trains of Jewish prisoners rolled through Europe, taking their human cargo to be killed. Even at the end of the war, when Germany's defeat was obvious to everyone, the death trains continued to cross Europe, and the gas chambers continued to operate. Later, Jews were marched, or transported, from concentration camps outside Germany to other camps farther inland, many dying on these forced marches. The Nazis made sure that these Jews would be dead before the Allies could rescue them.

Both prior to the war and throughout the war years, the Nazis continuously depicted the Jews as "vermin" and as "sub-human." Their propaganda machine produced endless articles, caricatures, and films portraying Jews as greedy, grasping people who secretly "ruled the world," or as criminals who should be exterminated. It did not matter that the events of the war years proved decisively that the Jews were poor, weak, and powerless. In many countries of Europe, the inhabitants were rewarded for handing over Jews who had not yet been arrested. Here and there, however, some Europeans *did* risk their freedom, and even their lives, in order to help Jews and help conceal them from their Nazi oppressors. In Denmark, the king himself declared that he and the entire population would wear the yellow star, in sympathy with the Jews.

The Nazis used special terms, or euphemisms, to disguise their intentions and their treatment of the Jews. These constituted a "code," which sounded fairly harmless to those – including the victims – who were not fully aware of their real meaning. Thus, the cattle trucks and trains in which Jews were sent to the concentration camps were only "transports." Jews who had been designated for death in the camps underwent a "selection process," and the mass murders in the gas chambers constituted "special treatment." The total annihilation of the Jews of Europe was the "final solution of the Jewish problem."

Clearly, throughout World War II, from September 1939 until June 1945, Europe was ravaged by incessant war, its human and natural resources used by the German occupiers for their own ends, its cities bombarded and laid waste, and its population terrorized. By the time that the war had ended, millions of people had been killed or made homeless, exiled from their homes and separated from their families. Meanwhile, the systematic murder of six million Jews by the Nazis continued steadily and with brutal efficiency throughout all this chaos. When the war ended, the Jewish populations of Germany, Poland, Hungary, Czechoslovakia, Greece, Italy, France, Holland, Yugoslavia, and part of Russia, embodying a unique and age-old culture, had been virtually wiped out.

Despite the efforts which the Nazis made to keep their systematic murder of the entire Jewish and Gypsy populations of Europe secret, most people knew, at least in rumored theory, if not in detail, what fate awaited those Jews who were "sent East." The Nazis' brutality, their disregard for the sanctity of human life, as well as their efficiency and ingenuity, made it obvious to anyone of even moderate intelligence that the Jews were being sent to a bitter fate. Many people closed their eyes to the truth, refusing to admit even to themselves the full horror of what was happening, or perhaps unable to grasp to what depths human bestiality could descend, while others, such as the Franks' "protectors," did what they could to help Jews evade the Nazis. Anne writes in her diary that it was apparent to a number of "outsiders" — for example, the man who supplied their bread, as well as the greengrocer who provided their vegetables — that people were in hiding, but these Dutch people kept the group's secret, and even added extra rations when they could. Throughout Holland, some Jews, whether as individuals or as families, were kept in hiding in circumstances similar to those of the Frank family. There was a fairly active Dutch resistance movement, and this also played a part in ensuring that Jews were kept hidden and that their whereabouts did not become known to the Nazis. In every country which was occupied by the Nazis, a handful of that country's courageous individuals concealed Jews, and this happened even inside Germany itself, but the individuals who were capable of putting conscience above fear, prejudice, or envy were few and far between. In some cases, Jewish people managed to place children who looked "Aryan" — that is, those who were fair-haired and blue-eyed — in the homes of non-Jews who, whether for money or out of humanitarian considerations, sheltered them in their homes.

The Germans' euphemistic phrase, "the final solution of the Jewish problem," in fact, referred to the *total annihilation* of the Jewish population of Europe. Anne Frank's family, having moved to Holland from Germany in an attempt to escape Nazi persecution, and after living in hiding in the middle of Nazi-occupied Holland for two years, was discovered by the Nazis and sent to various concentration camps. All the members of the group in hiding, with the exception of Anne's father, Otto Frank, perished in those camps.

LIST OF CHARACTERS

The Group in Hiding

Anne Frank

The thirteen-year-old Jewish girl who writes a diary while she is hiding in Amsterdam from the Nazis during World War II.

Margot Frank

Anne's sister; she is three years older than Anne.

Otto Frank

Anne's father; he is a Jewish businessman who left Germany after Hitler's rise to power, hoping to find refuge in Holland.

Mrs. Frank

Anne's mother; she is the source of many conflicts with Anne during the two years that the family spends in hiding.

Mr. Van Daan

A Jewish businessman and an associate of Mr. Frank's. He and his family share the "Secret Annexe" with the Franks.

Mrs. Van Daan

Mr. Van Daan's wife; a rather interfering person. Anne finds it difficult to get along with her.

Peter Van Daan

The Van Daans' son; he is two-and-a-half years older than Anne, and his calm, quiet nature contrasts with her more excitable, vital personality. At first, Anne thinks that Peter is dull, but later on, they develop a warm and loving friendship.

Mr. Düssel

An elderly dentist who joins the group in hiding in November 1942. He shares Anne's room, and his pedantic nature continually irritates her.

The Dutch "Protectors" or "Helpers"

Mr. Kraler

A Dutch Gentile businessman who has been an associate of Mr. Frank and Mr. Van Daan and who takes over the running of the business when they are no longer able to do so. He works in the office in the building where the "Secret Annexe" is located, and he helps with technical, logistical aspects, such as obtaining food for the people in hiding.

Mr. Koophuis

A Dutch Gentile business associate of Mr. Frank and Mr. Van Daan. He also takes over the running of the business after all Jews have been forbidden to employ Gentiles, and he helps to conceal the group in hiding and obtain supplies for them.

Miep

A young woman who works in the office below the "Secret Annexe." She helps with obtaining food and supplies for the group in hiding and keeping their spirits up.

Elli

A young typist who also works in the office below the "Secret Annexe." She also helps obtain food and supplies for the group in hiding and comforts them psychologically.

CRITICAL COMMENTARIES

THE FIRST YEAR

June 1942–May 1943

Anne has just turned thirteen, and she lists the birthday presents which she has received, including the diary, which she says is "possibly the nicest of all." She then gives us a brief description of her personal history, mentioning her birth in Frankfurt, Germany, the family, their emigration to Holland after Hitler's rise to power and his persecution of the Jews in Germany, the Nazi occupation of Holland, among the Nazis' occupation of other European countries, plus the various, severe restrictions imposed upon Jews there. Anne describes all this in a very matter-of-fact way, listing the sorts of things that Jews must and must not do: "Jews must hand in their bicycles, Jews are banned from trains and are forbidden to drive. Jews are only allowed to do their shopping between three and five o'clock, and then only in shops which bear the placard 'Jewish Shop,'" and so on. She points out, however, that "life went on in spite of it all," and "things were still bearable" (June 20, 1942). Thus, in the midst of persecution and restrictions, Anne still describes her feelings about boyfriends and about girl friends, about school and her teachers, and also describes meeting Peter Wessel, a boy whom she apparently was rather fond of (June 30, 1942).

Anne's father tells her that at some future date the family will have to go into hiding in order to avoid being sent to concentration camps; to Anne, this all seems to be vaguely distant. Yet, suddenly, less than one month after the diary begins, the family does suddenly have to go into hiding because Anne's older sister, Margot, has been summoned by the Nazis to be sent to a concentration camp. All Jews knew that the concentration camps were terrible places of imprisonment, although the full extent of what was actually done there was not yet known. And so, the family had no choice; they packed a few basic possessions into shopping bags, put on as many items of clothing as they could, made arrangements for their cat to be looked after, and they set off on foot – in the rain – for the "hiding place" that Anne's father had been arranging and preparing for some time.

Straightaway, Anne and her father set about arranging and tidying the place, while Anne's mother and Margot lie down on their beds, too tired and emotionally drained and miserable to help (July 9–10, 1942).

The process of settling in and arranging a daily routine takes up several pages of the diary. At first, the Franks are alone, and the strange situation strikes Anne as "more like being on vacation in a very peculiar boardinghouse" than like being in hiding (July 11, 1942). Fear is an ever-present reality, however, as Anne writes, "It is the silence that frightens me so in the evenings and at night . . . I can't tell you how oppressive it is *never* to be able to go outdoors. Also, I'm very afraid that we shall be discovered and be shot" (July 11, 1942).

Anne then describes her surroundings and the considerable precautions which the family must take not to be seen or heard by anyone other than their "protectors" – namely, the workers in the office downstairs.

The second family, the Van Daans arrive, bringing new faces into the little group, but also new sources of irritation and conflict. Anne does not think very highly of young Peter Van Daan, who strikes her as being lazy, hypochondriacal, and boring. She is also shocked by the noisy quarrels between Mr. and Mrs. Van Daan, remarking rather self-righteously: "Mummy and Daddy would never dream of shouting at each other" (September 2, 1942).

Very perceptively, Anne describes the Van Daans' foibles and quirks. For example, Mrs. Van Daan is piqued that *her* dinner service – *and not the Franks'* – is put into communal use. Secretly, Anne knows, Mrs. Van Daan has removed three of her sheets from the collective linen cupboard. Mrs. Van Daan, who continually scolds Anne for her continuous chatter, also does her best to leave the washing up of the pots and pans for others to do (September 21, 1942). Mr. Van Daan tries to discipline Peter in a particularly overbearing way, but he is not very successful in this.

These may seem like small matters, but when people are confined within a small space, they get on one another's nerves so much more easily and for smaller causes. It is Anne's father who is always the "peacemaker" in the "Secret Annexe," the one who always has to assume the responsibility for "pouring oil on troubled waters" and soothing ruffled feelings.

In fact, Anne's father does his best to keep the younger members of the group busy, assigning them study tasks to do and ensuring that there is a constant supply of books for them to read as well. They all follow events in the outside world on a clandestine radio, and Anne struggles valiantly with French lessons. She also quarrels with her mother and complains to her diary that she cannot understand her mother and that her mother cannot understand her. Anne also resents the interference of the other members of the group. To illustrate this, Anne quotes a "squabble" with Mrs. Van Daan during dinner one night, ending with Mrs. Van Daan's saying to Anne's father, "I wouldn't put up with it if Anne were my daughter." According to Anne, these *always* seem to be Mrs. Van Daan's first and last words: "if Anne were my daughter." Understandably Anne confides to her diary, "Thank heavens I'm not!" (September 27, 1942).

Anne suffers a great deal from the constant criticism of the other members of the group in hiding; she is confused herself, and unable to understand fully the emotional suffering and horrible fears of both her own family and the Van Daans. In particular, though, Anne feels that her mother is not defending her sufficiently, and Anne resents the fact that she has *always* to keep so very quiet and restrain her adolescent impulse to "sass people back."

Anne also gives us a fairly detailed description of the washing and lavatory arrangements, which are far from ideal. Again, the stress in her relations with her family is not easy. Clearly, she feels a greater affinity with her father than with her mother, and it appears that there are various "scenes" and quarrels because of what her mother perceives as Anne's faults and failings. As always, Mr. Frank attempts to improve the situation and asks Anne to be more helpful in the house, but Anne stubbornly declines, preferring to concentrate her efforts on her schoolwork.

The war news filtering in from the outside is bad, and the little group in hiding hears that many of their Jewish friends have been taken away, crowded into cattle trucks and sent off to concentration camps, first in Holland, and then farther east, into Poland. Anne asks herself, "If it is as bad as this in Holland, whatever will it be like in the distant and barbarous regions they are sent to? We assume that most of them are murdered. The English radio speaks of their being gassed" (October 9, 1942).

An admirable attempt is made to celebrate the birthdays of the little group, and everyone tries to procure a little gift, through the people in the office, who constitute their only link with the outside world. Generally, these gifts consist of items of food, but also, they occasionally include such "luxuries" as flowers and books – things we take for granted, but which were precious for the little group in the "Secret Annexe."

Anne's relations with her family continue to fluctuate. On October 16, 1942, she writes, "Mummy, Margot, and I are as thick as thieves again. It's really much better," and then she describes how she and Margot squeezed together into bed, letting one another read parts of their diaries – and also, girl-like, discussing their "looks."

Then on November 7, Anne writes: "Mummy is frightfully irritable and that always seems to herald unpleasantness for me. Is it just a chance that Daddy and Mummy never rebuke Margot and that they always drop on me for everything?"

Clearly, the situation of being in hiding in the midst of a busy city produces many hours of extreme fear and tension – especially for an adolescent girl. When a workman comes to fill the fire extinguishers in the house, his noises terrify the unsuspecting, frightened little group, and they fear that their hiding place has been discovered. Anne writes: "My hand still shakes, although it's two hours since we had the shock" (October 20, 1942).

Anne further reveals the turmoil of her feelings about her family with startling frankness. "I'm not jealous of Margot, never have been. I don't envy her good looks or her beauty. It is only that I long for Daddy's real love: not only as his child, but for me – Anne, myself" (November 7, 1942). Anne feels again and again that her mother is unfair to her, and occasionally she feels that her mother is inadequate as a mother, yet Anne does try very hard not to pass too severe a judgment on her for this. Her remarks here, however, reveal a very perceptive and sensitive girl of thirteen: "Mummy and her failings are something I find harder to bear than anything else. I don't know how to keep it all to myself. . . . I have in my mind's eye an image of what a perfect mother and wife should be; and in her whom I must call "Mother" I find no trace of that image. . . . Sometimes I believe that God wants to try me, both now and later on; I must become good through my own efforts, without examples and without good advice. . . . From whom but myself shall I get comfort? As I need comforting often, I frequently feel weak, and dissatisfied with myself; my short-comings are too great. I know this, and every day I try to improve myself, again and again" (November 7, 1942).

Anne finds a great deal of solace in her diary; it is, in effect, her best friend, her confidante; she calls it "Kitty," and on its pages she feels absolutely free to complain of her sense of frustration at not being able to give vent to her feelings. But, most of all, she feels frustrated because she has no real person whom she can truly confide in – and receive encouragement from – just through expressing her feelings. Only her diary can do that for her.

Under normal circumstances, Anne would probably have confided her feelings to a friend, but these were *not* normal circumstances, and the only outlet for Anne's emotions lay within the pages of the small, red-checkered, cloth-covered diary.

In addition, Anne also gives factual accounts of some humorous events that occur, such as the splitting of a seam on a sack of beans which Peter was carrying up the stairs, so that "a positive hailstorm of brown beans came pouring down and rattled down the stairs . . . [I was] standing at the bottom of the stairs, like a little island in the middle of a sea of beans!" (November 9, 1942). She also recounts the serious discussion which precedes the decision as to whether or not they should take in an eighth person, an elderly dentist, Albert Düssel, who will have to move into Anne's room because of a lack of space.

Living in such cramped conditions with seven other people is bound to take its toll on anyone, particularly when discovery means almost certain death, yet Anne always tries to accept their situation in a positive way and to keep her spirits up: "Quite honestly, I'm not so keen that a stranger should use my things, but one must be prepared to make some sacrifices for a good cause, so I shall make my little offering with a good will. 'If we can save someone, then everything else is of secondary importance,' says Daddy, and he's absolutely right" (November 19, 1942).

That very evening, bad news from outside reaches the group in the "Secret Annexe," and Anne describes it vividly in her diary: "When it is dark, I often see rows of good, innocent people accompanied by crying children, walking on and on, in charge of a couple of these chaps, bullied and knocked about until they almost drop." Despite the difficulties and privations of living in hiding, however, Anne *realizes* that she is far more fortunate than a great many of her friends: ". . . who have now been delivered into the hands of the cruelest brutes that walk the earth. And all because they are Jews!" (November 19, 1942).

The Jewish festival of lights (Hannuka) occurs almost at the same time as the Dutch Festival of Saint Nicholas Day, and the members of the little group exchange gifts and light the traditional candles of the festival, although the group keeps them alight for only ten minutes because of the shortage of candles. Their "protectors" give them presents for the Dutch Festival of Saint Nicholas Day, attaching a little poem for each person and trying their best to lighten the tedium of their caged lives. And tedium it is – rarely, but occasionally, relieved. For instance, Anne describes the lengthy, prudent process whereby Mr. Van Daan prepares sausages, and then she tells in hilarious detail how the dentist, Mr. Düssel, examines the hysterically nervous Mrs. Van Daan's teeth, reminding Anne of "a picture from the Middle Ages entitled 'A Quack At Work'" (December 10, 1942). She also describes the scene which she can see in the street below the window and the joy of the group in hiding at receiving extra rations of butter for Christmas. To divert themselves, they all talk about what they will do "when the war is over" although they do not forget to feel sorry for the people outside who are taken away from their homes each day, or are unable to obtain enough food.

As the weeks grow into months, the little group in the "Secret Annexe" has, as might be expected, its ups and downs, quarreling with one another and incessantly criticizing its youngest member, the spirited Anne (who often cries at night because of the group's irritable remarks). The members of the group also talk about their respective childhoods and occasionally laugh at funny remarks made – whether intentionally or not – by one or another of their number. The fact that the building in which they are hiding and which serves as offices is being sold to a new owner (the offices were only leased from the former owner) gives the group some cause for alarm, but the problem is finally overcome.

And then more tedium sets in again, and as a diversion Anne and Margot are given card index boxes so that they can keep an account of the books they have read; Anne is also given a little notebook for foreign words she masters. Butter and margarine are distributed carefully and in rationed quantities to each person. At one point, Anne writes, "Lately Mummy and I have been getting on better together, but we still *never* confide in each other" (February 27, 1943). It is sometimes painful to read these intimate confessions.

On March 10, 1943, Anne mentions the bombing of Amsterdam by the planes of the Allies and the firing of the anti-aircraft guns, which disturb their sleep almost every night while they are in hiding. Although Anne knows that it is childish, she always creeps into her father's bed for comfort, unable to overcome her fears by herself.

The news from the outside world continues to raise – and then dash – the hopes of the group. On March 18, 1943, Anne writes excitedly that Turkey has entered the war, but the next day, it is announced that this is not, in fact, the case. Anne also describes a visit made by Hitler to wounded soldiers, a visit which is broadcast over the radio. She remarks, "Listening in to it was pitiful. . . . One of them [the wounded] felt so moved at being able to shake hands with the Führer (that is, if he still had a hand!) that he could hardly get the words out of his mouth" (March 19, 1943).

Because of the circumstances of being in strict hiding during the midst of the outside world's "ordinary life," every small noise or sudden suspicion of being discovered is a cause for serious alarm for the group. Although the men of the group try to be chivalrous and protect the women from becoming so anxious, it is not always possible. Since the group is in the habit of using the offices downstairs in order to listen to the radio there, or go to the bathroom after the office and warehouse staff have gone home, they are more exposed to being discovered than if they had remained in their hiding place, behind the false bookcase, all the time. Whether or not the alarms and fears of a burglary which they occasionally experience are genuine or imagined, real terror is struck into the hearts of everyone, causing them all to cower in dread, trying to keep quiet. Anne recounts the effect which this has on them all and how none of them can sleep afterward because they are so afraid (March 25, 1943).

After Anne confides to her diary, in a rather contemptuous way, about the real (or imagined) sickness of Mr. Van Daan, she changes the tone of her diary entry, giving the essence of a speech made by one of the German leaders in the Netherlands, declaring that the Nazis have decreed that a new objective within Holland will soon be "cleaning out" the various Dutch provinces of Jews. Anne notes that the terms which the "German big shots" use are reminiscent of those employed in getting rid of cockroaches, and then she revealingly remarks, "These wretched people are sent to filthy slaughterhouses like a herd of sick, neglected cattle. But I won't talk about it, I only get nightmares from such thoughts" (March 27, 1942).

Once again, the topic of Anne's relationship with her parents is discussed in her diary. She has unintentionally hurt her mother's feelings by refusing to say her prayers with her (because Anne's father cannot do so that night). Anne tries to reason with herself, feeling sorry for her mother, yet she refuses to apologize for saying what she considered to be the *truth* at the time about how she felt. Anne states quite clearly that her mother has alienated her with her "tactless remarks and crude jokes, which I don't find at all funny" (April 2, 1943). Later, that same month, Anne lists her quarrels with her mother as just one of the various clashes going on amongst *all* the members of the group, adding that "everyone is angry with everyone else" (April 27, 1943). At that time, the Allied air raids were increasing in intensity, and Anne writes, "We don't have a single quiet night. I've got dark rings under my eyes from lack of sleep." In addition, the shortage of food is beginning to be even more acute although in her following entry (May 1, 1943), Anne reminds herself: ". . . it is a paradise compared with how other Jews who are not in hiding must be living."

Nevertheless, despite her realization that their situation is better than that of many other Jews, Anne is horrified by the *drastic* decline of *their own* standards. The comfortable life which they had lived beforehand, and even, to some extent, in the "Secret Annexe" has declined rapidly. Their former life contrasts starkly with the privations which they are suffering now, ranging from a lack of food, to the inability to change their sheets, or even to renew their diminishing stock of underwear. The nightly air raids continue, and Anne prepares a suitcase with the basic things she would need if she had to escape, though she realizes, at her mother's prompting, that there would be nowhere for her to escape to – absolutely nowhere.

The last entry before Anne's fourteenth birthday contains news from the outside world relating to an air battle between German and British planes. The group also learns about strict new regulations concerning Dutch university students which have been imposed by the Nazis. Anne also mentions the fact that the group in the "Secret Annexe" must burn its vegetable peelings and refuse every other day, even though the weather is quite warm, because they must not put *anything* in the garbage pails for fear that even this might lead to their discovery. She remarks: "How easily one could be betrayed by being a little careless!" (May 18, 1943).

This innocent remark is bitterly ironic in view of the group's eventual fate.

The air raids continue to be as frightening as usual, but Anne and the others find relief in nervous laughter at the comical remarks of Mr. Düssel, especially when Mrs. Van Daan goes downstairs to Mr. Düssel's room, ". . . seeking there the rest which she could not find with her spouse," and Düssel receives her with the words, "Come into my bed, my child!"

Anne remarks, "This sent us off into uncontrollable laughter. The gunfire troubled us no longer, our fear was banished!" (May 18, 1943).

This first year of Anne's diary has been eventful, to put it mildly. From being a normal Dutch girl going to school and having fun with her friends, she has been forced to go into hiding and to be shut up with another seven individuals, unable to go outside, and live as other youngsters do. Apart from the problems which she experiences in her relations with her mother and her sister – problems which are fairly normal for any adolescent – she is also obliged to contend with the problems of being confined in a rather small area with a group of people who generally irritate and annoy her.

In addition to the difficulties of coping with her emotions and the changes in her body – another normal feature of adolescence – Anne has had to come to terms with the privations, the crowded and insanitary conditions and – most especially – with the ever-constant fear of being discovered and hauled away to one of the Nazi death camps.

The voice of the somewhat spoiled young girl who begins the diary changes by the end of this first year to the voice of a young girl who is able to analyze situations and characters, find amusement rather than annoyance in the little incidents of daily life, and put them all down on paper in a vivid, graphic way. She decidedly has a way with words, and her delicate irony, the way she records conversations, and her ability to describe scenes all enable *us* to experience and see and feel what she herself is undergoing.

THE SECOND YEAR

June 1943–August 1944

Anne's fourteenth birthday is celebrated with little gifts from the members of her "family in hiding," as she calls them, and she also receives a poem from her father. This was a German tradition, and as Anne's family had originally come from Germany, moving to Holland only after the rise to power of the Nazis in Germany, Anne's father wrote the poem in German. Margot, Anne's sister, translated it "brilliantly" into Dutch, and the English translator has also done a good job.

The Nazis have begun to move quickly; new regulations have been imposed. All civilians are ordered to hand in their radio sets (listening to stations other than those of the Nazis had been forbidden since the beginning of the war, but the Dutch people, nevertheless, listened to the BBC secretly, drawing encouragement from it), and the little group in the "Secret Annexe" is reluctantly obliged to forfeit the large set which was in the office downstairs. One of their "protectors," however, promises to provide them with another, substitute radio, and Anne concludes this entry by saying, "It is really true that as the news from the outside gets worse, so the radio with its miraculous voice helps us to keep up our morale and to say again, 'Chins up, stick it out, better times will come!'" (June 15, 1943).

Almost a month passes without an entry in Anne's diary, and then we read that Anne has decided to control her public remarks about the people whom she must be confined with, even if this involves shamming (or fraudulent behavior) ". . . so that the rain of rebukes dies down to a light summer drizzle" (July 11, 1943). Thus, the routine life of the group goes on, and Anne and Margot are even allowed to help a little with the work of the office downstairs, making them feel quite important. Anne mentions again how very important books are to her, as she is shut up in the "Secret Annexe" and has no other amusements.

She then describes—in a very detailed entry—how she approached her roommate, Mr. Düssel, very politely, after having first discussed the matter with her father. She asks Mr. Düssel if she may use the work table in their room for an extra hour-and-a-half twice a week. She explains that there is too much going on in the common room, and that although she is able to work on the table every day from half-past two until four, while Düssel sleeps, she needs more time to work. She is very disappointed and angry when Düssel absolutely refuses her request without giving any explanation. Yet, Anne keeps her temper and asks him to reconsider. She then recounts Düssel's selfish, melodramatic, and false tirade against her, again describing her own self-restraint and the immense mental effort that this discipline represents for her. Eventually, at her request, her father intervenes on Anne's behalf, and Düssel gives in. Anne concludes: "Düssel . . . didn't speak to me for two days and still had to go and sit at the table from five till half-past – frightfully childish. A person of fifty-four who is still pedantic and small-minded must be so by nature, and will never improve" (July 13, 1943).

Various events occur to alarm the group in the "Secret Annexe." The offices downstairs are burglarized, although this is noticed only after it has occurred sometime during the night (July 16, 1943). The air raids continue by day as well as by night, so that there is a constant fear of both fire and discovery. The news that Mussolini has resigned provides some encouragement, but the emotional and physical exhaustion resulting from the sleepless nights of the air raids continues (July 26, 1943).

In the following entry, Anne describes her efforts to find a neutral topic of conversation while she is doing the dishes with Mrs. Van Daan and Mr. Düssel, and how this tactic not only fails, but backfires because of a critical comment that Anne makes of a book which Düssel has recommended. This sets off Düssel and Mrs. Van Daan on a long tirade about how badly brought-up Anne is and how her ideas and opinions are *all wrong.* Anne comments perceptively: "I suppose it's their idea of a good upbringing to always try to set me against my parents, because that is what they often do" (July 29, 1943). Anne then allows herself to note all of her criticisms of Mrs. Van Daan, describing her as "very pushing, selfish, cunning, and calculating," but adds in a postscript: "Will the reader take into consideration that when this story was written the writer had not cooled down from her fury!"

Anne begins to give a detailed account of the group's daily routine, starting on August 4, 1943, with an account of their evening and night-time routines, who sleeps where, who washes when and how Anne leaves hairs in the bathroom sink. She also describes the strange noises which the house and its "inmates" make during the night. There is also a graphic description of Anne using the potty in the middle of the night, waking up from a dream to the sound of an air raid and scampering into her father's bed in fear. This last episode is illustrated by a verse from the poem which Margot wrote for Anne's birthday. Anne continues her account the following day with a description of lunchtime. Her review of the evening meal becomes an analysis of the characters of the people sitting around the table, their eating habits, their ways of talking, and their general traits. On the whole, these are not very complimentary.

In the passage for August 18, 1943, Anne manages to give a vivid and entertaining account of a rather mundane task, potato peeling. She has a keen eye, and she carefully observes the little nuances of speech and the physical gestures which characterize the various members of the group. There is also a touching description of what Anne calls "a little bit of real family life" (August 23, 1943).

The members of the group are up before half-past eight, when the workers begin their duties in the warehouse, and even though the office staff has not yet arrived, so that it is necessary for the group to be particularly quiet, Anne and Margot and their parents sit, read, or work in their room until it is time for breakfast, at nine o'clock.

The news about Italy's capitulation raises everyone's spirits (September 10, 1943), but this is offset by the illness of one of their "protectors," Mr. Koophuis. Another cause for concern is the fact that one of the workers in the warehouse appears to suspect something, and thus the already strained nerves of the members of the group lead them to virtually refrain from speaking to one another because "whatever is said you either annoy someone or it is misunderstood." Anne takes sedatives to calm her nerves (and so presumably do the others), but she notes that "it doesn't prevent me from being even more miserable the next day. A good hearty laugh would help more than ten Valerian pills, but we've almost forgotten how to laugh" (September 16, 1943). This remark, "but we've almost forgotten how to laugh," is but one of the many of Anne's comments that suggests that here is a person of a sensitivity, an intelligence, and a maturity far beyond her chronological years.

Mrs. Van Daan's birthday is celebrated, and the members of the group, as well as the "protectors," give her presents of things to eat, as well as some food coupons. Anne remarks: "Such are the times we live in!" (September 29, 1943). The strained relations between the members of the group continue, and Anne's words, "Oh, what kind of explosion is hanging over us now? If only I wasn't mixed up so much with all these rows! If I could only get away! They'll drive us crazy before long!" (September 29, 1943), are desperate cries from her heart.

One day, Mrs. Van Daan is obliged to sell her fur coat to raise money for food, and this leads to additional quarrels. Anne remarks, ironically: ". . . and now the reconciliation period of 'Oh, darling Putti' and 'precious Kerli' has set in." Then she adds: "I am dazed by all the abusive exchanges that have taken place in this virtuous house during the past month. . . . Quite honestly, I sometimes forget who we are quarreling with and with whom we've made it up. The only way to take one's mind off it all is to study, and I do a lot of that" (October 17, 1943).

Sundays – when there is no one working in the office, and when there is no relief from the tedium of the group – are particularly depressing days for Anne. She describes them with a telling phrase: "The atmosphere is so oppressive, and sleepy and as heavy as lead" (October 29, 1943). We can feel her painful desperation at being "jailed" for over a year when she writes: "I wander from one room to another, downstairs and up again, feeling like a songbird whose wings have been clipped and who is hurling himself in utter darkness against the bars of his cage" (October 29, 1943).

With an admirable sense of self-awareness, Anne writes, "If you were to read my pile of letters one after another, you would certainly be struck by the many different moods in which they are written. It annoys me that I am so dependent on the atmosphere here, but I'm certainly not the only one – we all find it the same" (November 8, 1943). She also gives us a very vivid account of her fears and nightmares, remarking that although she talks about the concept of "after the war," ". . . it is only a castle in the air, something that will never really happen." In this, she is being prophetic without even realizing it. Anne's diary entries now begin to show an increasing sense of sadness, desperation, and, occasionally, the loss of hope, although there is an entertaining interlude entitled "Ode to my Fountain Pen: In Memoriam," in which Anne recounts how she received her fountain pen as a gift from her grandmother when she was nine and how it was accidentally burned in the stove that day (November 11, 1943).

One night, Anne dreams about her best schoolfriend, Lies, and she is shot through with guilt at living in comfort and being unable to help Lies in any way. In her dream, Anne sees Lies "clothed in rags, her face thin and worn. Her eyes were very big" (November 27, 1943). This is an accurate description of the appearance of most of the concentration camp inmates, although Anne did not know – *and* could not have known – Lies' condition (sadly, ironically, Lies really was in a concentration camp).

The Dutch Festival of Saint Nicholas Day is celebrated with little poems which Anne and her father have written for everybody, and Christmas is marked by the exchange of small gifts. Anne has recovered from a bad bout of flu and comments that they "are all getting on well together for a change! There's no quarrelling – we haven't had such peace in the home for at least half a year" (December 22, 1943).

Anne's account of her feelings is extremely, almost achingly, honest in the entry for December 24, 1943, when she writes at length about her longing to go outside, to walk about freely, to do the things that young people all over the world do and, above all, to simply "have fun." This futile wish leads her once again to the sad topic of what she considers to be the inadequacies of her mother, and Anne vows to behave differently when she has children of her own. Anne seems to have expected too much of her mother, who would probably have functioned well enough in normal circumstances, but here – in this horrible situation – Mrs. Frank appears to be almost unable to understand her mercurial daughter, a girl of high intelligence and sensitivity. Remember that these are exceptional and dangerous conditions in which the Franks are trying to survive, and Mrs. Frank is just an ordinary, middle-class person with, perhaps, a limited imagination.

Anne mentions the fact that the mere act of writing her thoughts down in her diary has improved her mood a little. She also refers to her father's phrase "the love of his youth" (December 25, 1943), realizing that her father had confided in her concerning this person the previous year, but then she had not been able to understand "the meaning of his words" because he had to "express his own feelings for once" rather than coping with those of others. Anne adds that her father "has become very tolerant. I hope that I shall grow a bit like him, without having to go through all that [suffering]." This entry reveals Anne's sensitive awareness of her own faults and her desire to improve herself, as well as showing us Anne's acute consciousness of the feelings of others.

Anne's moods continue to swing back and forth between grief, compassion, and guilt. She grieves for the past and for loved ones who are gone, and there is also Anne's ever-growing compassion for those Jews whose suffering is greater than hers; in particular, she thinks about her girl friend Lies (December 29, 1943). She also feels guilty for having negative feelings about her mother (January 2, 1944). Anne seems to be becoming more aware of what it is that she believes that her mother lacks (January 5, 1944) – namely, a certain sensitivity to the feelings of her lively, moody adolescent daughter, and although this does not really ease Anne's pain at being misunderstood, it does help her to cope with it.

Anne's longing for a girl friend (January 5, 1944) is partly fulfilled when, on January 6, 1944, Anne decides to go up to Peter Van Daan's room and talk to him. Peter is a rather shy boy, two years older than Anne, and it seems that he is not averse to having Anne come and talk to him. Anne, however, is torn between her need for someone to confide in and her fear of seeming to be "too forward," but she concludes, "Don't think I'm in love with Peter – not a bit of it! If the Van Daans had had a daughter instead of a son, I should have tried to make friends with her too."

That night, Anne dreams about a former boyfriend, also called Peter, dreaming about him in a rather romantic way, and she feels certain, upon waking, that "Peter was still the chosen one." This leads her, in her next diary entry, on January 7, 1944, to relate the history of all her boyfriends at the various stages of her life. We realize here that her relationship with Peter Van Daan compensates for many of the difficulties of her daily life, for Anne writes, "What do I care about the lot of them! Peter belongs to me and no one knows anything about it. This way I can get over all the snubs I receive. Who would ever think that so much can go on in the soul of a young girl?" (January 12, 1944).

After writing rather antagonistically about the faults of the Van Daans, Anne comes to realize that the faults which she sees in them might not necessarily be theirs alone. It is a very perceptive and mature Anne who writes, "Until now I was immovable! I always thought the Van Daans were in the wrong, but we too are partly to blame. We have certainly been right over the subject matter; but handling of others from intelligent people (which we consider ourselves to be!) one expects more insight. I hope that I have acquired a bit of insight and will use it well when the occasion arises" (January 22, 1944).

Another milestone of maturity is passed when Anne manages to have a conversation with Peter about sex, when he shows her his cat's male organs. Anne feels strange, but she admires Peter for being able to talk about it in a matter-of-fact way. Other than that, the normal daily routines of the little group continue. Anne is still involved in her studies, but she also occupies herself with compiling the family trees of the royal families of Holland and England, as well as collecting pictures of the various movie stars of the time. The adults continue to annoy her by repeatedly telling the same anecdotes, and, in a telling phrase, she marvels at the fact that "we are quite as used to the idea of going into hiding, or 'underground,' as in bygone days one was used to Daddy's bedroom slippers warming in front of the fire" (January 28, 1944). Their "protectors" continue to help and encourage them, even though this involves danger for them, and Anne regards this as being on a par with all other acts of heroism performed during the war, vowing never to forget them.

The probability of an invasion of Europe by the Allies (the forces fighting against the Nazis) increases, and all sorts of rumors and speculations are talked about and considered. The group in the "Secret Annexe" is aware of all this through their "protectors," as well as through listening to the BBC. Anne gives examples of the kinds of conversations conducted by the members of the group, concluding rather fatalistically, "I myself keep very quiet and don't take any notice of all the fuss and excitement. I have now reached the stage that I don't care much whether I live or die. The world will still keep on turning without me; what is going to happen, will happen, and anyway it's no good to resist. I trust to luck and do nothing but work, hoping that all will end well" (February 3, 1944).

Anne's growing relationship with Peter continues to excite and console her, even though she remains terribly frustrated by having to remain inside—especially now, when spring is beginning, filling her with longings "to talk, for freedom, for friends, to be alone!" (February 12, 1944). Peter confides in her about his frustration at being unable to express himself clearly, as he claims she does, and even though she feels that this is not justified, and that she is equally tongue-tied or unnecessarily verbose, she feels glad "because I sensed a real feeling of fellowship, such as I can only remember having had with my girlfriends" (February 14, 1944). On another occasion, Peter helps Anne find the smallest and sweetest potatoes, and Anne feels that he is looking at her with "such a gentle warm look which made a tender glow within me. I could really see that he wanted to please me, and because he couldn't make a long complimentary speech he spoke with his eyes" (February 16, 1944).

Although Anne now feels much happier and is always hoping to see "him" when she goes upstairs, she still experiences sudden moods of unhappiness, when the tears simply roll down her cheeks, and she feels uncertain of Peter's affection for her (February 19, 1944). Anne does find some solace, though, in going up to the attic, where Peter works, and from where she can look up through the skylight at "the bare chestnut tree, on whose branches little raindrops shine, appearing like silver, and at the seagulls and the other birds as they glide on the wind" (February 23, 1944). From that room, Anne can also look out over Amsterdam, gaze at the roofs, and at the horizon, and in her misery, she finds that this communion with nature, and with the things that seem *more permanent than man,* bring peace to her soul.

As her concern with Peter increases steadily, so that she "hardly does anything else but think of Peter" (February 27, 1944), Anne realizes that there are a great many similarities between them. Both of them, she feels, have mothers who are inadequate, and both she and Peter wrestle continually with their inner emotions. She notes, however, that whereas *her* reaction is to be noisy and boisterous, Peter is more likely to sink into silence. In a sad mood, Anne ends this entry for February 28, 1944, with the plaintive cry, "I'm sentimental—I know. I'm desperate and silly—I know that too. Oh, help me!"

A burglary in the office downstairs alarms the members of the little group again, although fear does *not* seem to play such a large part in their lives as it did at the beginning of their period of hiding. Anne, *in particular,* appears to be less fearful about things than she was before, possibly because she has developed a more fatalistic attitude, as her entry for February 3, 1944, shows. Still, though, she continues to resent the fact that grownups treat her, Margot, and Peter as "children" and prevent them from expressing their opinions about such subjects as overcoming depression and feelings of discouragement, which they feel as well-equipped as the adults to discuss.

Anne finally admits to herself that her feelings for Peter are "pretty near to being in love with him" (March 3, 1944), and each entry in her diary records another topic of conversation discussed or another meeting between them. Anne realizes that Peter is very shy, and she does not want to appear too eager herself, so both of them seem to be hovering on the brink of declaring their love. She writes, "Who will be the first to discover and break through this armor?" And she then adds, "I'm glad after all that the Van Daans have a son and not a daughter; my conquest could never have been so difficult, so beautiful, so good, if I had not happened to hit on someone of the opposite sex" (March 6, 1944).

In one of her more introspective moods, Anne looks back to the girl she was and to the life which she led before she went into hiding, noting that ". . . it all seems so unreal. It was quite a different Anne who enjoyed that heavenly existence from the Anne who has grown wise within these walls" (March 7, 1944). While recognizing that her life beforehand had been enjoyable, she admits that she was certainly more superficial then, and that she will never again be able to live like that, at least not for long stretches of time. She maintains that even then she felt a certain emptiness, but disguised it with a constant flurry of activities and friends. She also analyzes the various phases which she has gone through after going into hiding. She speaks of her initial confusion, followed by depression and then, as she began to mature, both physically and emotionally, she describes her growing self-awareness, and finally, her discovery of her inward happiness through her close relationship with Peter Van Daan.

The daily problems of obtaining and preparing food, getting along with the various members of the group, contacts with the outside world and news of the progress of the war still occupy Anne's thoughts to a considerable extent. But some things have changed. Anne's feelings about Peter, for example, cause her to be very reserved with her family, and she says, ". . . the brightest spot of all is that at least I can write down my thoughts and feelings, otherwise I would be absolutely stifled!" (March 16, 1944).

As we read, we realize that Anne continues to resent being cooped up with the other members of the group and that she still objects to being treated as a child, for she says, "Although I'm only fourteen, I know quite well what I want, I know who is right and who is wrong, I have my opinions, my own ideas and principles, and although it may sound pretty mad from an adolescent, I feel more of a person than a child, I feel quite independent of anyone" (March 17, 1944).

More and more, Peter and Anne confide in one another, and Anne records their conversations in her diary. As they open their hearts to one another, talking about their initial impressions of one another when the group first went into hiding, they realize that they have even more in common than they had ever imagined. Anne, however, is sad at the thought that Margot is made wretched by Anne's relationship with Peter, since Margot also likes him, but Margot assures Anne, in a letter, that it is not that *she herself* loves Peter, but, rather, that she regrets not having found anyone for herself yet. This sets off a touching exchange of letters between Margot and Anne, in which each one shows her concern for the other's feelings. It was obviously easier for them both to set their emotions down on paper than to talk about them face-to-face.

Both Anne and Peter have to take a fair amount of teasing from the adults about the fact that Anne goes up to Peter's room in the evenings, and Anne remarks that "we don't take much notice of all this parental chatter, their remarks are so feeble. Have the two sets of parents forgotten their own youth? It seems like it, at least they seem to take us seriously, if we make a joke, and laugh at us when we are serious" (March 23, 1944). In this, she is probably speaking for a great many teenagers who have often felt misunderstood and mistreated by their parents.

Although Anne states quite clearly that politics do *not* interest her, she nevertheless describes the reactions of the various members of the group to the news which they hear over the radio or from their "protectors." For example, she depicts one scene as they all sit around the radio, listening to a speech given by Winston Churchill; yet, following the speech, the heated arguments that ensue horrify and anger her (March 27, 1944).

Anne continues to be more preoccupied with Peter and with the growing closeness between them. She also continues to resent her mother's interference, although she admires her father's restraint at his daughter's obvious interest in Peter.

One day, one of the BBC broadcasts contains a suggestion by one of the Dutch leaders in exile that after the war the diaries and letters of people who have been through the war should be published. This causes quite a stir among the members of the group in hiding, and Anne starts to entertain serious thoughts of publishing her diary at a later stage, remarking that "it would seem quite funny ten years after the war if we Jews were to tell how we lived and what we ate and talked about here" (March 29, 1944). This sentence is strangely prophetic, as Anne's diary is, indeed, one of the most vivid documents – and perhaps the best-known – that has survived from that period, giving us a painfully honest, human "inside view" of what it was like to be Jewish and to be hiding in perpetual fear during the war years.

Time and time again, Anne wrestles with depression, struggling to hold back tears when she is with Peter, bravely endeavoring not to sob out loud when she is alone. She tries to reason with herself, and eventually she succeeds, writing, "It was over!" (April 4, 1944). On the same occasion, she gives us a far more hopeful and more positive account of what she wants her future to be, so that the gloomy entry which began – "For a long time I haven't had any idea of what I was working for any more; the end of the war is so terribly far away, so unreal, like a fairy tale" – becomes more optimistic: "I must work, so as not to be a fool, to get on, to become a journalist, because that's what I want! I know that I can write."

This same entry reveals Anne becoming a more mature young woman, one who is able to appraise herself and her surroundings clearly and also critically. She knows that *she* is the best judge of her own work, and she also realizes that she wants more from life than being just a homemaker, as her mother is, and as the women of her class generally were. Here, too, Anne exhibits an awareness of the position of women, an attitude which is *far ahead of her time* and her immediate environment.

Anne also expresses her desire to go on living after her death, and she thanks God for her ability to write, declaring that it is writing that consoles and encourages her. How ironic it is to read Anne's heart-searching entries and her assertions about the future when we know, as she could not, that these hopes of hers were indeed fulfilled, but not in the way she expected, and that *the very words* which she was writing at that moment were to bring her far greater immortality than she could ever have imagined.

Another attempt by burglars to break into the warehouse downstairs forces the members of the group to cower almost motionless for hours, afraid that they have finally been discovered. Anne gives us a graphic description of their whispered conversation and the various sights, sounds, and smells of these long hours. The incident causes Anne to wonder at their fates as Jews; again, she states her belief that the suffering which they are undergoing is so that they may emerge stronger. She also affirms her love for the Dutch nation, its people and its language, asserting that she intends to remain in Holland after the war (April 11, 1944).

Anne is, figuratively, "up in the clouds" when Peter kisses her for the first time (April 16, 1944), although her doubts regarding the propriety of this, and the probable reactions of her parents and sister if they had known about it strike us as rather odd in this age of permissiveness. Although Peter and Anne would put their arms around one another, and, later on, occasionally kiss, their physical relationship was very innocent, a far different situation from the behavior of many teenagers today. In the space of only a few years, and with the help of medical advances in methods of birth control, sexual morality has changed tremendously. Once again, Anne displays astonishing maturity for a girl of fourteen by refusing to accept completely the extremely strict moral standards of her time, writing, ". . . we are shut up here, shut away from the world, in fear and anxiety, especially just lately. Why, then, should we who love each other remain apart? Why should we wait until we've reached a suitable age? Why should we bother?" (April 17, 1944).

Anne's happiness with Peter is not overshadowed by the daily trials of life in the "Secret Annexe." But perhaps Anne's awareness of what maturity means has been heightened, for it is a very perceptive, if disenchanted, Anne who writes that the ordinary man in the street is as much to blame for the war as are the politicians, and that there is a destructive urge in everyone, so that unless this changes, bloodshed will always continue. Nevertheless, her *irrepressible optimism* causes her to write: "I am young and I possess many buried qualities; I am young and strong and am living a great adventure; I am still in the midst of it and can't grumble the whole day long. I have been given a lot, a happy nature, a great deal of cheerfulness and strength. Every day I feel that I am developing inwardly, that the liberation is drawing nearer and how beautiful nature is, how good the people are about me, how interesting this adventure is! Why, then, should I be in despair?" (May 3, 1944).

Following the advice that Margot has given her, Anne writes a letter to her father, explaining her feelings about him and her mother, the difficulties she has been through during the period they have been in hiding and speaking honestly of her refusal to knuckle under to what she knows has been his silent disapproval of her relationship with Peter (May 5, 1944). Anne's father has a long and emotional talk with her after this letter, and Anne regrets having wounded his feelings, acknowledging that she might have misjudged him.

Various setbacks – such as the arrest of the man who brought them vegetables, rumors that there is growing anti-Semitism among the Dutch people, and Anne's fears that, having been born in Germany, she and her family will not be able to remain in Holland once the war is over – cause Anne's spirits to fall. She wonders if they might not all be better off dead, but still she clings to her hope that *something will happen,* and that the war will end soon (May 26, 1944). The news of the Allied invasion of Europe revives the optimism of the group, and Anne's fifteenth birthday is celebrated in a spirit of greater cheerfulness (June 13, 1944).

The last few entries in Anne's diary are concerned with the various daily events that Anne has written about all along – the moods of the members of the group, their preoccupation with food, the books they read and discuss, Anne's relations with her parents, and her feelings toward Peter.

Anne's last entry, on August 1, 1944, three days before the "Secret Annexe" is raided by the police and its occupants are sent to concentration camps, is one in which Anne analyzes herself and her situation, displaying considerable powers of perception. She concludes, after acknowledging that her flippant behavior is just a front to help her cope with the people around her, with the statement that she keeps on "trying to find a way of becoming what I would so like to be, and what I could be, if . . . there weren't any other people living in the world."

At the end of the period of hiding, Anne is clearly a very different person from the girl who started out to write in the red-checkered diary; especially during the second year, she has matured greatly. Of course, there has been the growing love between her and Peter, and this has certainly left its mark. But in addition to the self-confidence she has acquired, Anne is less quick to judge the other people around her; she has a greater self-awareness now, and she has thought deeply about a great many subjects.

Anne has not wasted her time while she has been in hiding. Under her father's guidance, she has continued studying various subjects, skills, and languages. She has developed her writing, especially, so that the style in her diary has become more varied and vivid. In fact, her diary contains descriptive passages, conversations, character analyses, and honest introspection that we would not expect from such a young girl; this is one of the reasons why it has managed to capture the interest of so many people over such a long period of time; very simply, it is well-written. Anne's ability to analyze people and situations has grown as we watch, so to speak, so that we do not feel that we are reading the maudlin confessions of a "mixed-up" teenager; rather, we are eager to find out what this intelligent young woman has to say about the varied subjects which she chooses to write about. Being forced to remain in hiding for two years is obviously too high a price to pay for precocious maturity, but how much poorer our world would have been had we not been granted this glimpse into the inner workings of a young girl's mind in the years that were so fateful for her and for the whole world.

EPILOGUE

Of the eight people hiding in the "Secret Annexe," only one, Anne's father, survived. All their Dutch "protectors," or helpers, managed to live through the war, and even Anne's schoolfriend, Lies, about whom she thought and dreamed, and whom she mentions in the *Diary*, survived. In his book *Anne Frank: A Portrait in Courage,* Ernst Schnabel has retraced Anne's life. It starts in the town of Frankfurt, in the house where Anne spent her early childhood; Schnabel interviewed people who knew the Frank family in Frankfurt and, later, those who knew them in Amsterdam.

After the group's capture by the Nazis, they were taken back to Germany and were sent to concentration camps. Ernst Schnabel also interviewed people who had been in the camps with the Franks and had witnessed their final moments, as well as those of the other members of the group in hiding. In the following pages, you will find brief accounts of the backgrounds and fates of the characters in the poignant human drama revealed to us through Anne Frank's *The Diary of a Young Girl.*

CHARACTER BACKGROUNDS AND FATES

Anne Frank

Anne was born on June 12, 1929, three years after her sister,

Margot, in the town of Frankfurt-on-Main in Germany. Four years later, in the summer of 1933, the Frank family moved to Holland because Hitler had come to power in Germany and had introduced strict laws which discriminated against Jews. In addition, gangs of Nazi thugs would roam the streets, beating up Jews for no reason – except that they were Jews.

Anne attended the Montessori kindergarten and grade school in Amsterdam after the Germans invaded Holland in May, 1940, but the anti-Semitic regime from which the Frank family had sought to escape in Germany caught up with them. Anne and Margot, along with thousands of other Jewish children, were no longer allowed to attend schools of their own choosing and were obliged to go to only Jewish schools. Anne herself did not mind this, readily adapting to the new environment, making new friends and finding old ones among her classmates.

Realizing how dangerous the political situation was becoming, Mr. Frank prepared a refuge where his family could go into hiding, rather than submitting to arrest by the Nazis and being dispatched to concentration camps and to almost certain death. At the beginning of July, 1942, when it would have been foolish to delay not going into hiding, the Franks, and then a few days later, a family called the Van Daans, moved into the "Secret Annexe" in the building where Mr. Frank's offices and warehouse were situated; overnight, they simply vanished from sight.

As a child, Anne was bright and lively, not considered by her parents and their friends to be as intelligent and as beautiful as her sister, Margot, but nonetheless loved for her humor and personality. Anne does *not* conceal her awareness of this attitude in her diary, and her resentment of it perhaps adds to the irony that it should be Anne's name, rather than Margot's, that has become known to posterity. Perhaps this early, slight adversity strengthened in Anne a resolve to shine in some way and to prove to her family and to the world that she was not *just* the younger sister of the beautiful and talented Margot Frank.

As anyone who has read Anne's diary knows, she was immensely gifted, both as a writer and as a person of great sensitivity. She could feel things deeply, sense the feelings of others and communicate all this to paper. Anne's personality sparkles and shines on every page of the diary – whether Anne is in the heights of ecstasy over her budding relationship with Peter Van Daan or whether she is in the depths of despair over the grim realities of her life in hiding; whether she is describing the constant irritation of being confined to the house and having to live at such close quarters with people whom she dislikes, or whether she is confessing her ambivalent feelings toward her parents and her sister.

Above all else, Anne's feelings are ordinary and so akin to those experienced by any teenager growing up and being confronted by situations and with individuals which he or she is not yet capable of dealing with in a detached or adult way. One of the most striking features that emerges from Anne's diary is the sense of the *intensity* of the emotions that she experiences as an adolescent.

On August 4, 1944, the Gestapo, apparently acting on information provided by an informer, probably one of the workers in the warehouse, arrived at the building where the Franks were hiding, entered the office and began to search the building. Although Mr. Kraler tried to convince them that there was nothing behind the bookcase at the end of the corridor, the Nazis pulled it away, and the secret door to the Franks' hiding place was exposed.

No one acted hysterically or violently when they realized what had happened; in numbed silence, they simply put together a few basic possessions which they thought they might need and left with their captors. The notebooks in which Anne had written her diary were scattered on the floor and left there when one of the Gestapo men emptied a briefcase in an attempt to find money or any other "valuables." Another instance of the irony of fate.

The members of the Jewish group in hiding, together with Mr. Kraler and Mr. Koophuis, were taken to Gestapo headquarters in Amsterdam and locked in a room with other people who had been arrested. Later in the day, the Jewish prisoners were separated from the rest, and after being kept at headquarters for a few days for questioning, they were taken to the railroad station and transported to the Westerbork reception camp. They rode in a regular passenger train, and, according to the evidence of Mr. Frank, they were relatively cheerful. *They were together.* Moreover, they knew where they were going, although they did not know if they would be permitted to remain there for long, and they were aware that there was the possibility of deportation to Poland and the concentration camps there. But they also knew that the Allies were advancing, and they hoped that luck and faith would keep them out of the death camps until the war was over.

Throughout the journey, Mr. Frank relates, Anne remained glued to the window, seemingly absorbing as much as she could of the scenery of the summer countryside. Remember: Anne had not been outside for two whole years.

When the group arrived at Westerbork, they were made to stand in a long row in the mustering square while one of the clerks entered their names on a list. The conditions were bad, but not unbearable. Westerbork, after all, was merely a reception camp, and although there was overcrowding, deprivation, and undernourishment, there were no gas chambers or crematoriums, as there were at the concentration camps.

An eyewitness who was at Westerbork says, "I saw Anne Frank and Peter Van Daan every day in Westerbork. They were always together, and I often said to my husband: 'Look at those two beautiful young people.' . . . In Westerbork, Anne was lovely, so radiant that her beauty flowed over into Peter. She was very pallid at first, but there was something so intensely attractive about her frailty and her expressive face."

Seemingly, Anne was happy at Westerbork, despite everything. She could see new people and talk to them, after having been cooped up with the same seven people for over two years. The thought that occupied her mind most of all was whether they would be sent to Poland and whether or not they could live through the trying days ahead. Anne's father would visit her in the women's barracks sometimes in the evenings, standing by her bed and telling her stories. Similarly, when a twelve-year-old boy who lived in the women's barracks fell ill, Anne stood by his bed and talked to him in the same way.

On September 2, Anne, together with the other members of the group in hiding, was gathered into a group of one thousand persons and sent to Germany. They traveled in sealed railway cattle cars, seventy-five people crowded in each car, with only one, small, barred window, high up. The journey took several days, and on the third night, the train suddenly came to a stop. The doors of the car were jerked open, and blazing searchlights, SS men with dogs, and the bustling Kapos (prisoner-guards) constituted the prisoners' first glimpse of the Auschwitz concentration camp. As the passengers streamed out of the train, the men were ordered to go right, and the women were ordered to go to the left. Children and sick people were told to enter trucks painted with big red crosses to spare them the hour's march to the camp, but the trucks never arrived. The children and sick people who entered them were *never seen again.*

Anne, her mother, Margot, and Mrs. Van Daan all marched with the rest of the women to the camp, hustled along at a brutal pace by the SS guards and the Kapos. On arrival at the camp, everyone's head was shaved; yet a woman who was with Anne at that time said of Anne; "You could see that her beauty was wholly in her eyes. . . . Her gaiety had vanished, but she was still lively and sweet, and with her charm she sometimes secured things that the rest of us had long since given up hoping for.

"For example, we had no clothing aside from a gray sack, and under that we were naked. But when the weather turned cold, Anne came into the barracks one day wearing a suit of men's long underwear. She had begged it somewhere. She looked screamingly funny with those long white legs, but somehow still charming.

"We were divided into groups of five for roll call, work, and distribution of food. You see, we had only one cup to each group of five. Anne was the youngest in her group, but nevertheless she was the leader of it. She also distributed the bread in the barracks, and she did it so well and fairly that there was none of the usual grumbling."

With the sensitivity which she reveals in her diary, Anne must have suffered greatly, having to witness the daily acts of cruelty and suffering in the concentration camp. Many prisoners became immune to the torment of those around them, but Anne retained her sense of compassion, and she could still shed tears of pity and perform acts of kindness for others.

On October 30, 1944, there was a "selection," and all the women had to wait naked on the mustering ground for a long time, then march in single file into the barracks, where each one had to step into the bright beam cast by a cold searchlight. The infamous Dr. Mengele ordered those prisoners who were not too sick or too old to step to one side, and it was obvious to everyone that the others would be gassed. Anne and Margot passed the exam; they were deemed fit enough to be sent to the Belsen concentration camp, while their mother was not.

Once again, the prisoners were crowded into sealed cattle cars and sent on a long journey which lasted for several days. The train stopped and started, sometimes waiting for an hour at a time. Many passengers died of hunger or disease along the way.

When the train arrived in Belsen, SS guards were waiting on the platform with fixed bayonets. The prisoners were told to leave the dead lying in the cars and to line up in marching order. In the words of someone who was there at the same time as Anne, Belsen was different from Auschitz. "There was no regular work, as there had been at Auschwitz, although the prisoners were given the task of removing the dead, dragging them over the ground to the cremation area. There were no roll calls, nothing but people as fluttery from starvation as a flock of chickens, and there was neither food nor water nor hope, for it no longer meant anything to us that the Allies had reached the Rhine. We had typhus in the camp, and it was said that before the Allies came, the SS would blow us all up."

It was at Belsen that Anne and her schoolfriend, Lies, met again, for Lies and her family had been sent there earlier and had been placed in a separate section for "neutral foreigners." In that "privileged position," Lies was still able to receive packages through the Red Cross Organization. When she heard that a group of people had arrived from Auschwitz, Lies managed to make contact with Anne, across the barbed wire fence that separated them, and Lies describes her thus: "She was in rags. I saw her emaciated, sunken face in the darkness. Her eyes were very large. We cried and cried."

Anne was freezing and starving, and Lies attempted to get some extra food across the fence to her friend. She packed up a woolen jacket, zwieback (rusks), sugar, a tin of sardines, and threw it all across the fence. All she heard, however, were screams, and Anne crying. When she shouted and asked what had happened, Anne called back, weeping: "A woman caught it and won't give it to me." Lies told Anne to come back again the following night, and that time, Anne caught the packet, but this time it contained only zwieback and a pair of stockings.

Anne's sister, Margot, died of typhus at the end of February (or the beginning of March), after having been critically ill and in a coma for days. Anne was already sick at the time, and she was not informed about her sister's death. After a few days, however, Anne sensed what had happened, and soon afterward, she herself died, peacefully, feeling that nothing bad was happening to her, shortly before the camp was liberated by the Allies.

In summary, when the Nazis occupied Holland in 1940, Anne was only eleven years old. Like many parents, Mr. and Mrs. Frank tried to protect their children from the edicts issued by the Nazis, and although the girls knew that they had to change schools and wear the "yellow star" (signifying that they were Jews) on their clothes, they did not have any direct contact with Nazis. In general, the Dutch people were sympathetic to the plight of the Jews, and many of them helped them with a kind word or little gifts. The grisly, wholesale murder of Jews in concentration camps did not really get underway until 1942, and in 1940 no one could imagine that the annihilation of an entire people was possible.

By the time Anne and the others went into hiding, in June 1942, they knew that Jews were rounded up, beaten, stripped of their possessions, and sent East. They suspected that the conditions out there were not good, but Nazi propaganda insisted that the "resettlement" was to the Jews' benefit, and there was no clear information to be obtained as to what really went on there. In her diary, Anne writes: "Our many Jewish friends are being taken away by the dozen. These people are treated by the Gestapo without a shred of decency, being loaded into cattle trucks and sent to Westerbork. . . . Most of the people in the camp are branded as inmates by their shaven heads. . . . If it is as bad as this in Holland, whatever will it be like in the distant and barbarous regions they are sent to? We assume that most of them are murdered. The English radio speaks of their being gassed" (October 9, 1942).

From this, and other remarks which Anne makes, we know that she and the other members of the group in hiding knew what was happening to the Jews on the outside, to a greater or lesser extent. There was a radio in the office, and they would creep downstairs at night and listen to the BBC broadcasts, so that they had a fairly good idea of what was going on.

The windows of the "Secret Annexe" allowed its inmates to see something of what was going on in the streets outside, and on December 13, 1942, Anne writes, "I saw two Jews through the curtain yesterday; it was a horrible feeling, just as if I'd betrayed them and was now watching them in their misery." The members of the group of "protectors" (or helpers) also brought eyewitness accounts of what was happening to Jews outside.

Every sudden, unexplained noise, every real or imagined break-in by burglars, and every stranger who visited the office and the warehouse was a continuous source of fear and concern for the people in the "Secret Annexe." There were several occasions when they sat up all night, afraid to make a sound, fearing that they had heard someone moving around downstairs.

The Allies' air raids on Amsterdam, the anti-air cannon fired by the Nazis, and the aerial dog-fights between Nazi and Allied aircraft in the sky also constituted a source of alarm for the group in hiding. The building was old and could easily catch fire. For that reason, they had each prepared a small bag of basic necessities to grab in case they had to leave the building in a hurry. But that, of course, was the greatest danger, as it involved their worst fear of all: discovery by the Nazis.

"We had a short circuit last evening, and on top of that the guns kept banging away all the time. I still haven't got over my fear of everything connected with shooting and planes, and I creep into Daddy's bed nearly every night for comfort." That is how Anne's entry for March 10, 1943, begins. This kind of remark recurs at intervals through the diary, but it would seem that eventually the inmates of the "Secret Annexe" *did* become accustomed to the situation. After all, two years in hiding is *a long time,* and they knew that the Allies were advancing and the situation of the Nazis was deteriorating. By the time the diary ends, in August 1944, Anne had every reason to be optimistic, and she was even thinking about going back to school.

By the time they were arrested, the occupants of the "Secret Annexe" no longer seriously thought that they would be discovered. Although they had been frightened at the beginning, they had become used to their situation and hoped to continue in that way until the war ended. The news from the various war fronts was very good, and it was obvious that the Nazis *would* be defeated. If the discovery had only come a little later, if the group had not been included in the last shipment of people to leave Westerbork, if Anne had not been sent first to Auschwitz, and then to Belsen, who knows what might have happened?

When Anne's father returned to Amsterdam after the war had ended, Miep and Elli (the young workers in the office where the "Secret Annexe" was located) gave him the notebooks and papers in Anne's handwriting which they had found strewn over the floor of the "Secret Annexe" after the Gestapo police had left. At first, Otto

Frank had copies of the diary circulated privately, as a memorial to his family, but he was finally persuaded by a Dutch professor to publish it. After the *Diary*'s initial appearance in Dutch in 1947, it quickly went through several editions and was translated into dozens of languages. The *Diary* was dramatized, and the play was presented on Broadway, winning the Pulitzer, Critics Circle, and Antoinette Perry Prizes for 1956. It has been made into a movie and has been adapted for television. The Anne Frank Foundation, founded by Otto Frank, maintains the building on the Prinsengracht Canal where the Franks hid for twenty-five months as a museum and memorial to Anne Frank. Each year, the house is visited by thousands of people from all over the world. The Foundation is trying to promote better understanding between young people from every part of the world, and it has established the International Youth Center, which serves as a meeting place for young people and holds lectures, discussions, and conferences covering a wide range of international problems.

The Montessori School in Amsterdam is now renamed the Anne Frank School, and there are other memorials to her in Germany, Israel, and elsewhere. But, above all, it is Anne's *Diary*, in which her unique, yet representative, voice is preserved, that constitutes the most eloquent memorial of all.

Margot Frank

Margot was three years older than Anne, so was probably more aware of the family's move from Germany to Holland, which took place when she was seven years old. Margot was a quiet, obedient child, who always kept her clothes neat and clean, unlike her younger sister. She was considered the more beautiful and the more intelligent of the two, and Anne resented her for this sometimes, as she notes in her diary.

Margot did well at school and was often used as an example for Anne by the Franks, who wanted Anne to copy Margot's good behavior. During the two years that they were confined in the "Secret Annexe," the two sisters grew very close, learned to be more patient with one another, and eventually became close friends.

After the group in hiding was discovered and sent to the concentration camps, Anne and Margot managed to remain together almost until the end. After surviving the Westerbork reception camp and the Auschwitz concentration camp, however, Margot became sick with typhus at the Belsen concentration camp in the winter of 1944–45. After being gravely ill and lying in a deep coma for days, Margot died at the end of February (or the beginning of March), 1945. While unconscious, she fell out of bed, and she was found dead when her friends tried to lift her back into her bed.

Otto Frank

The Franks were an old German-Jewish family. Otto Frank's father, a businessman, came from Landau in the Palatinate (a section of Germany). His mother's family can be traced in the archives of Frankfurt back to the seventeenth century.

Otto Frank was born and grew up in Frankfurt-on-Main and, after graduating from high school, went into business, like his father. He fought in the German army during World War I in an artillery company. He impressed his superiors and was promoted in the field to the rank of lieutenant.

After the war, he settled down in Frankfurt as an independent businessman, specializing in banking and the promotion of brand-name goods. He was a member of the comparatively prosperous middle class when he married Edith Holländer of Aachen. He was thirty-six years old, and she was twenty-five. In 1933, when Anne was four years old and Margot was seven, the family moved to Holland, following the rise of the Nazis to power and the introduction of harsh laws against all Jews in Germany. When Mr. Frank brought his family to Holland, he became managing director of an established firm and did well for seven years. When the Nazis invaded Holland in May 1940, however, they introduced the same anti-Jewish laws which had caused the Franks to leave Germany. Times became very difficult for the Franks, and Anne's father soon began to form a plan whereby they could "disappear" – that is, enter a hiding place that had been prepared in advance.

Otto Frank took his colleagues and employees at work into his confidence, and they all helped him prepare the upper rooms (at the back of the building where his business was situated) as a hiding place for his family. Items of furniture, bedding, and kitchenware – in fact, everything needed for a regular household – were taken there, little by little, so as not to arouse the attention or suspicion of anyone who was not a party to the pre-planned secret move. After the Franks had moved into the secret hiding place on July 8, 1942, a bookcase was attached to the door leading to the annexe so that the entrance was concealed. The "Secret Annexe" was a reality.

Throughout the two years that the Franks were in hiding, Mr. Frank was a pillar of strength for the group. It was he who tutored Anne, Margot, and Peter, it was he who always tried to soothe members of the group when tempers flared up and nerves were frazzled, and it was he who consoled and encouraged Anne and, presumably, the other members of the group, when the strain of being cooped up, in hiding, and under nightly bombardment became almost too much for them to bear. He readily shared his hiding place with another family, the Van Daans, and later on with another man, Mr. Düssel, even though this meant that the Franks' own living conditions were even more cramped and their food rations far more limited than before.

When the Nazis discovered the hiding place, all the members of the group, together with the two business associates who had been helping them, Mr. Koophuis and Mr. Kraler, were taken to Gestapo headquarters. Mr. Frank told Mr. Koophuis how bad he felt, knowing that his friend was being imprisoned for helping him. Mr. Koophuis told him not to give it another thought, that it had been his decision and he would not have done anything else. The group traveled together, without their Gentile helpers, by train to the reception camp at Westerbork. Although conditions there were bad, the families were still together, so their spirits were not too low. They knew the possibility of deportation to Poland existed, and they were aware of what happened at Auschwitz, Treblinka, Maidanek, and other concentration camps. On the other hand, they knew that the Allies were advancing and that the Russian Army was already deep in Poland, so that if luck were on their side, they *might* survive until the war was over.

Although the sexes were housed in separate barracks at Westerbork, Mr. Frank was able to visit his wife and daughters in the women's barracks. His presence was reassuring, and when Anne fell sick, he came over every evening, stood beside her bed for hours and told her stories. After being kept in the Westerbork camp for a few weeks, the Franks, the Van Daans, and Mr. Düssel were herded into a shipment of one thousand persons and sent to Auschwitz. This was the very last shipment to leave Holland. The people traveled in crowded, sealed cattle cars for three days and nights. At Auschwitz, men and women were separated, and that was the last Mr. Frank ever saw of his family.

When the SS guards left Auschwitz in January 1945, in order to escape the approaching Allies, they took most of the inmates of the camp with them, forcing them to march through the countryside barefoot, in rags, and without proper food. Mr. Frank was in the camp infirmary, and so he was spared. He was in Auschwitz when it was liberated by the Russians in February.

After the war, Mr. Frank returned to Holland via Odessa and Marseilles on board the New Zealand ship *The Monaway,* which brought concentration camp survivors from East to West Europe. He contacted the people who had helped him and his family while they were in hiding in Amsterdam, and Elli and Miep (as noted above) handed over to him the papers in Anne's handwriting which they had found on the floor of the "Secret Annexe" the day the Gestapo had come and taken the group away.

Otto Frank, as described by the writer Ernst Schnabel, was: ". . . a tall, spare man, highly intelligent, cultured and well-educated, extremely modest and extremely kind. He survived the persecutions, but it is difficult and painful for him to talk on the subject, for he lost more than can be gained by mere survival."

He survived until he was in his nineties and died in Amsterdam in 1980.

Mrs. Frank

Mrs. Frank was born Edith Holländer, and her family came from Aachen, a town on Germany's western border, near Belgium. Like her husband, she came from the comfortable middle classes and was accustomed to a life of relative ease, with most of the work in the house being done by servants. Her husband was eleven years older than she was, being thirty-six to her twenty-five when they were married in 1925. They lived in Frankfurt-on-Main, Germany, and their daughters, Margot and Anne, were born in 1926 and 1929, respectively. When the Nazis came to power, in 1933, and the persecution of the Jews of Germany began, the Franks moved to Holland.

For seven years, the Franks lived peacefully and prosperously in Amsterdam, but things changed when the Nazis invaded and occupied Holland in 1940. The Franks tried to continue living a normal life under the Nazi regime, but this became increasingly difficult, and in the summer of 1942, they went into hiding.

In the "Secret Annexe," Mrs. Frank was obliged to perform various tasks which she had not formerly been accustomed to doing. In addition, she was living in cramped quarters, together with her family and another four people. This obviously was not easy for her, and possibly much of the bad feeling between Anne and her mother may have been due to this and the effect that the cramped living conditions had on everyone's nerves.

After her arrest, Mrs. Frank was taken with her family to Gestapo headquarters in Amsterdam and the Westerbork reception camp. There, according to an eyewitness, she was very quiet. "She seemed numbed all the time. . . . Edith Frank could have been a mute. She said nothing at work, and in the evenings, she was always washing underclothing. The water was murky and there was no soap, but she went on washing, all the time."

Like the other members of the group, Mrs. Frank was included in the last shipment of people to be sent to Auschwitz from Holland in early September 1944. At Auschwitz, she was still with Anne and Margot, though separated from Mr. Frank.

On October 30, 1944, there was a "selection" among the women at Auschwitz, and the younger and healthier ones were sent on to the Belsen concentration camp. Anne and Margot were included in this group, while Mrs. Frank was left behind. The events which she had been through, the hunger, and the privation, had unhinged her mind, and she refused to eat. She began collecting what few crusts of bread she could find and hiding them in her bed, saying that they were for her husband. The bread spoiled, but still she continued to hoard it, unwilling or unable to eat. She was forty-five years old when she died in her bed in Auschwitz on January 6, 1945, ten days before the SS guards fled from the camp.

Mr. Van Daan

A business associate of Otto Frank's, Mr. Van Daan was, as someone who knew him put it, "a highly intelligent and well-bred man, but in time his nervous strength gave out." This is supported by Anne's account of him in her diary; his wife appears to have been the more domineering of the two, at least during the period while they were in hiding.

Once the group was discovered, like the rest, Mr. Van Daan was taken first to Gestapo headquarters in Amsterdam for questioning, and then he was sent to the Westerbork reception camp. He, too, made the long journey by train to Auschwitz, and once there, he was separated from his wife, whom he never saw again.

Mr. Van Daan was gassed at Auschwitz, and he was seen by Mr. Frank marching to the gas chamber together with a group of other men. The exact date is not known.

Mrs. Van Daan

Mrs. Van Daan was described by one of the group of Dutch "protectors" as: ". . . a very uncomplicated person, anxious and cheerful at the same time, as temperamental people often are." Anne's account of her in her diary is generally unflattering and intolerant, and we often feel that there was a great gulf of character and intelligence between them. What is evident is that Mrs. Van Daan was not a stoical person who shines in adversity.

Mrs. Van Daan was included in the last group of one thousand prisoners sent from Westerbork in Holland to Auschwitz in Poland on September 2, 1944, as the Nazis retreated before the advancing Allies. At Auschwitz, she was separated from her husband and son. She was sent to Belsen, separately from Anne and Margot, who were surprised to meet her there later on. It was she who heard Anne's friend, Lies, calling from another part of the camp, and who summoned Anne to their meeting.

Mrs. Van Daan died at Belsen, although it is not known whether she was gassed or succumbed to hunger or disease. The date of her death is not known, although it must have been after February, when Anne and Lies saw one another for the last time.

Peter Van Daan

One of the Dutch "protectors" has described Peter as a ". . . simple, lovable boy, whom Anne would sometimes tease for his slow, methodical ways." It is clear from Anne's diary that she loved him, although it is possible that she loved her dream of love rather than the boy himself. Peter was a quiet, handsome boy with a forest of brown curls and blue-gray eyes.

At the Westerbork reception camp, Anne and Peter were still together, and they made a striking and handsome pair. At Auschwitz, however, men were separated from women upon arrival, so we must presume that after their dispatch there, on September 2, 1944, they did not see one another again. When the women were ordered to go to the left, at the Auschwitz railway station, Peter, Mr. Frank, Mr. Van Daan, and Mr. Düssel had to turn to the right.

Peter was taken along by the SS guards when they left Auschwitz in January 1945. Mr. Frank, who was in the infirmary at the time, tried to persuade Peter to hide there too, but Peter did not dare to do so. It was bitterly cold and the roads were covered with ice as thousands of prisoners marched out of the camp, together with their guards. Many died of the cold, of hunger, and of exhaustion, and many were shot by the SS guards for lagging behind. Most of them were never heard of again. Peter Van Daan was among these.

Mr. Düssel

Mr. Düssel, the elderly dentist who joined the group in hiding in November 1942, had formerly lived in Berlin and was married to a Catholic woman. He and his wife emigrated to Holland after the anti-Semitic riots of November 1938 which took place throughout Germany.

When Mr. Düssel went into hiding, his wife was informed that he had managed to get out of the country, so she never knew that her husband was in Amsterdam, near her, until the group was discovered by the Nazis. The information was conveyed to her then by a member of the Dutch group of "protectors."

Life in the confined quarters of the "Secret Annexe" had made Mr. Düssel rather difficult, and Anne describes him with great severity in her diary. If life in hiding was uncomfortable and annoying, it was much more so if one had to share one small room with a somewhat pedantic, older man. The experience obviously was not a pleasant one for either Anne or Mr. Düssel.

Mr. Düssel went with the other members of the group first to Westerbork and then to Auschwitz. He was later separated from the other men in the group and was sent back to Germany. He died at the Neuengamme camp.

Lies (pronounced "Lees")

In her diary entry for Saturday, November 27, 1943, Anne writes: "Yesterday evening, before I fell asleep, who should suddenly appear before my eyes but Lies! I saw her in front of me, clothed in rags, her face thin and worn. Her eyes were very big and she looked so sadly and reproachfully at me that I could read in her eyes: 'Oh, Anne, why have you deserted me? Help, oh, help me, rescue me from this hell!' And I cannot help her, I can only look on, how others suffer and die, and can only pray to God to send her back to us."

Lies' father, who had been press chief of the last pre-Nazi administration in Prussia, had emigrated to Holland with his family in 1933. They lived near the Franks in a suburb of Amsterdam, and Anne and Lies went to school together and were good friends. Together with Anne, Lies had to leave the Montessori school and attend the Jewish school, wear the yellow star on her clothes, and have her movements increasingly restricted by the edicts of the Nazi authorities after 1940. The Jewish children, however, continued to go to school, meet their friends for ice cream, conduct themselves as normally as they could, and lead as carefree a life as possible under the circumstances. Their parents, and the Dutch population, did all they could to protect them from the harsh reality of life under the Nazis, until this was no longer possible.

Lies and her parents did not go into hiding because Lies' mother was expecting a baby. Relations in Switzerland had obtained South American passports for the family; thus, they hoped that they could remain unmolested. Nevertheless, they were sent to Westerbork in 1943, and later to the Belsen concentration camp. There, they lived in a block for "neutral foreigners," and they were occasionally permitted to receive a Red Cross package. Lies' mother died, and later, in the winter of 1944–45, Lies' father fell ill and died also.

The same winter, Lies heard that in the next block of the camp, which was separated from hers by a barbed wire fence, a group had arrived from Auschwitz, and that among the prisoners were Margot and Anne Frank. Lies waited until night, then stole out of the barracks, went over to the barbed wire fence, and called softly into the darkness: "Is anyone over there?"

As chance would have it, the voice which answered her belonged to Mrs. Van Daan, whom both Lies and the Franks, of course, knew, and it was she who went and called Anne. Both Anne and Lies were very weak and emaciated by then and simply cried upon seeing one another across the barbed wire fence. They told one another what had happened to their families, but Anne did not know where her father was, only that her mother had stayed behind in Auschwitz. She also told Lies that Margot was still with her, but that she was very ill.

Lies tried to get a little extra food and clothing across the fence to Anne, and she succeeded, in part. But this, it seems, was not enough to save Anne from the typhus that was raging in the camp, and from which Margot died a few days before Anne herself perished.

Lies was told that Anne had died of typhus, and she believes this because she never saw her after the February night when she attempted to throw a package across the wire fence to her. Lies was sent out of Belsen in a shipment destined for Theresienstadt, but their train traveled right into the middle of a Russian offensive, and the Russians liberated the prisoners. Today, Lies is a mother and housewife and lives in Jerusalem, Israel.

A woman who was in the camps at that time has said: "In Auschwitz we had had visible enemies: the gas chambers, the SS, and the brutality. But in Belsen we were left to ourselves. There we had not even hatred to buoy us up. We had only ourselves and our filthy bodies; we had only thirst, hunger, and the dead, the corpses lying all around, who showed us what a little thing life is. There it took a superhuman effort to remain alive. Typhus and debilitation – well, yes. But I feel certain that Anne died of her sister's death. Dying is so frightfully easy for anyone left alone in a concentration camp."

Mr. Kraler

After Mr. Van Daan's withdrawal from his firm, Mr. Kraler took over the management of dealings between Travis, Inc. and the affiliated firm of Kohlen and Co. He was an Austrian by birth, fought in the Imperial Navy during World War I, and he moved to Holland afterward. He was a business associate of Mr. Frank, whom he met in Amsterdam in 1933. When Jews were no longer allowed to own business enterprises, Mr. Kraler took over those run by Mr. Frank and Mr. Van Daan. This alone involved a certain amount of risk, as under the Nazi regime even the fact that they had formerly been Jewish-owned made them liable to be confiscated.

Mr. Kraler helped the Franks to prepare the "Secret Annexe" as a hiding place. While the group was in hiding, he was instrumental in obtaining supplies, keeping them secret and providing moral and psychological support. He was in the downstairs office when the police came to take the Franks, the Van Daans, and Mr. Düssel away. They asked Mr. Kraler for the owner of the house, and he gave them the name and address of their landlord. They insisted that they wanted the person in charge there, and when he said that it was he, they ordered him to come with them as they searched the building.

The police were acting on information passed to them by an informer, possibly one of the workers in the warehouse, and they would not allow Mr. Kraler to put them off the trail as they approached the bookcase which hid the door leading to the "Secret Annexe." And so, Mr. Kraler was the first one to ascend the steps, a pistol held against his back; he entered the Franks' room, where Mrs. Frank was standing at the table. He said, "The Gestapo is here," and Mr. Frank did not start in fright or say anything. The police gave the group in hiding enough time to collect a few possessions, then they, together with Kraler and Koophuis, were taken to Gestapo headquarters for questioning.

Because the year was 1944, and not 1943 or 1942, the Gestapo was more careful in its treatment of non-Jewish prisoners. It was evident by then that the Nazis would lose the war, and so, instead of treating them strictly and sending them to one of the death camps, they were treated more leniently. Mr. Kraler, like Mr. Koophuis, did not attempt to defend himself; he remained silent, and the officials obviously did not think it worthwhile to force them to talk.

Mr. Kraler was sent to a camp near Amersfort in Holland, and from there to a forced-labor camp in Zwolle. In March 1945, the inmates of the Zwolle camp were supposed to be removed to Germany. Four hundred men were marched under guard along the highway from Arnhem to Zevenaar. During the march, the column was strafed by planes, and in the confusion Kraler and another man managed to escape. They crawled off into the underbrush, and when the firing stopped, they slipped into a house. After an hour, they ventured out again and hid with a farmer for two days. Traveling by night over back roads, Kraler made his way to Hilversum, where his relatives lived. After the war, he moved to Canada.

Mr. Koophuis

Mr. Koophuis had met Mr. Frank in Amsterdam in 1923, when they both had business dealings there. This association continued intermittently until 1933, when the Franks moved to Amsterdam and the business relationship and personal friendship between the two men grew. In 1941, Koophuis took over Mr. Frank's place in the Travis company – otherwise, the firm would have been confiscated or liquidated as a Jewish business. It was Koophuis, together with Kraler, who proposed that the Franks use the back of the business building as a refuge. They helped the Franks move furniture and household items there, by stealth and at night, in order to avoid detection.

When a postcard reached the Franks in 1942, ordering Margot to report to the reception center at the Westerbork camp, everyone knew that the time to act had finally come. Mr. Koophuis was instrumental in ensuring that the secret of the group in hiding was kept, even though this raised many technical difficulties, particularly when the ownership of the building changed hands and the personnel in the warehouse also changed. Food had to be obtained for the group in hiding and paid for, extra food ration stamps had to be obtained, and in many cases, this aroused people's suspicions. Nevertheless, the baker, the vegetable man, and most of the other people with whom Koophuis had dealings, did not ask embarrassing questions; they simply cooperated in silence.

Mr. Koophuis has described the arrest by the Gestapo in the following words: "It was a Friday, and a fine August day. The sun was shining; we were working in the big office, Miep, Elli, and myself, and in the warehouse below us the spice mills were rumbling."

While Mr. Kraler accompanied the police in their search of the building, Mr. Koophuis and the two girls were ordered to remain at their desks. His first concern was to protect the two girls, and he told them to leave the building and insist that they had been unaware of what was going on, if asked. He was taken with the others to Gestapo headquarters, but largely because of his presence of mind, Miep and Elli were not taken too.

As they left the building, Mr. Koophuis relates: "I was the first to step out on the street. People were standing around on the sidewalk, staring as if there had been a traffic accident. They all looked stunned. I was also the first to get into the van and sat down way up in front, behind the driver."

As they waited in the cell at Gestapo headquarters, Mr. Frank told Mr. Koophuis how bad he felt that this had happened to them. Mr. Koophuis replied: "Don't give it another thought. It was up to me, and I wouldn't have done it differently." Koophuis and Kraler did not talk to their captors, who did not invest very much effort in forcing them to do so.

Fortunately, an international welfare organization intervened on behalf of Koophuis, pointing out that he was ill. He was released for medical care after a few weeks of imprisonment, and then he returned to Amsterdam.

Miep

Miep has been described by someone who met her after the war as "a small, delicate, intelligent young woman." She was born in Vienna, and she was sent to Holland after World War I as an "undernourished child" in whom a welfare organization had taken an interest.

She remained in Amsterdam, and in 1933 she met Mr. Frank, who hired her to work for the Travis company. When Austria was absorbed by Germany, she was given a German passport, and after the Germans occupied Holland, in 1940, she was asked to join a new club called "The German Girls Club in the Netherlands." She declined, stating quite bluntly that she did not want to join. A few days later she was summoned to the German Consulate, her passport was stamped as being invalid after three months, when she would have either to become a Dutch citizen or emigrate as "a stateless person."

At that time, Miep and Henk van Santen, a young Dutchman, intended to get married, and the situation created by the Nazis obliged them to move the date forward. There were various technical and bureaucratic difficulties, but in the end, with the cooperation of other Dutch citizens, Miep and Henk were married in July 1941, and Miep was legally able to remain in Holland.

Henk, like many Dutch people, worked in the Dutch underground resistance organization, which helped Jews and opponents of the Nazis hide from their oppressors. Miep and Koophuis knew or guessed what Henk was doing, but neither ever tried to stop him.

Throughout the period when Anne and the other members of the group were in hiding, Miep helped and encouraged them. She brought them food and visited them in their hiding place, bringing news from the outside and a breath of fresh air when she came. Anne longed for someone new to talk to, and Miep was a good friend to her. Together with Elli, she arranged little gifts and surprises on birthdays and festivals, brought wild flowers, and generally did her best to make the situation of the group in hiding a little more tolerable.

Miep and Henk even spent a night in the "Secret Annexe," because the children wanted "to have guests" so badly. It was a night of terror for them, however, and only the others slept soundly, having grown accustomed to the fear and discomfort.

When the police came to take the group in hiding away, Miep was in the office, together with Mr. Kraler, Mr. Koophuis, and Elli. They were all, except Mr. Kraler, ordered to remain where they were, while the search for the "Secret Annexe" was conducted. Mr. Koophuis tried to persuade Miep to leave, because it was obvious that they would all be arrested too, but she refused to go. Then Mr. Koophuis gave her the office keys and told her to insist that she had not known what was going on. "You can't save us," he said. "Save what can be saved. First and foremost, make sure that you are not involved."

Miep was in the office when the group in hiding went down the stairs, under police guard. She said, "I could hear the heavy boots, the light footsteps [of the others], and the very light footsteps of Anne. Through the years, she had taught herself to walk so softly that you could hear her only if you knew what to listen for. I had seen her only the day before, and I was never to see her again, for the office door was closed as they all passed by."

After the Franks and the others had been driven away in a police van, Miep was questioned by one of the policemen. She did as Mr. Koophuis had told her. She claimed that she had not known about the group in hiding. The policeman accepted her story, but told her to continue to come to the office every day, threatening that if she did not, her husband would be arrested and hinting that he knew about his resistance activities.

Henk and Miep sat up until late at night, discussing what action to take, but there was nothing they could do. When Miep was in the office the following day, one of the firm's traveling salesmen phoned, and Miep told him what had happened. He suggested that Miep try to bribe the police, and that she should do this quickly, while the prisoners were still in Amsterdam. He offered to contribute his own savings, and the baker from whom Mr. Koophuis had been buying bread for the group in hiding also offered to contribute something.

Miep went to Gestapo headquarters in Amsterdam a few days later and attempted to secure the prisoners' release for money but was told that although that had been possible in the past, that was no longer the case.

Today, Miep and Henk live in Amsterdam.

Elli

Elli was a young girl who worked in the office as a typist and was the closest to Anne during the period she was in hiding. She is a gentle, warm, shy person, and although she was eight or nine years older than Anne, she often discussed her personal problems with Anne. Elli also helped Anne and the others both practically and psychologically throughout the period they were in hiding.

Elli has said that Anne was sometimes bad-tempered and nasty, and at those times only her father, to whom she was very close, could bring her to her senses. He did it by saying the magic word, "Self-control!" This caused her to stop whatever it was she was doing and regain her composure.

Elli also spent a night in the "Secret Annexe," sleeping on an air mattress. This was in October 1942, and she claims that she did not sleep a wink that night and almost died of fright. The noises of the night, the bell of the clock tower nearby, and the fear of arrest or an air raid kept her awake all night. The other members of the group slept undisturbed, however.

When the Gestapo came to arrest the group in hiding, Elli became extremely distraught and cried like a little child. She stood at the window, crying and wringing her hands, while the police searched the house. Mr. Koophuis went over to her, gave her his briefcase, and told her to take it to the corner druggist, with a message that his brother would come and pick it up.

Elli made an immense effort to do as she was told and got to the druggist's store. She made up a story about their having been found possessing a radio set (they were illegal under the Nazi regime), and the druggist believed her. He took the briefcase and promised to give it to Mr. Koophuis' brother when he came. Elli then called Mr. Koophuis at the office and asked him what she should do, although she could hardly talk. Mr. Koophuis told her to go home, but she started crying again, and eventually remained with the druggist, crying and praying, for over an hour.

This is Elli's account of the events of that afternoon: "All afternoon I wandered through the city, not knowing where I was going, and did not reach home until dusk. My father was in bed. He had been operated on some time before. But when the doctors saw that he had cancer of the stomach, they could do nothing for him.

"I sat down beside his bed and told him everything. He was deeply attached to Mr. Frank, whom he had known a long time. He said nothing. But then he suddenly asked for his clothing, dressed and went away. When he came back after dark, he said there was nothing to be seen, that the building looked just as it always had. He had peered into the windows for awhile, but everything was deserted and still."

Today, Elli lives in Holland, together with her husband and children.

ESSAY TOPICS

1. Try to keep a diary for a week. Can you make it interesting and varied?

2. Imagine that you are in hiding with your family. Write descriptions of everyone's character, your feelings, conversations you have, and things you do.

3. What kind of a girl do you think Anne Frank was? Describe her character.

4. What do you think makes Anne's diary interesting?

5. What would you do if laws were passed against you because of, say, the color of your hair, eyes or skin, your grades in school, or your height? How would you feel and react?

6. Which character of the group in hiding do you like best? Why?

7. Pretend that Anne survived the concentration camps. Write an account of what she did when she grew up.

8. What can ordinary people do to make sure that other ordinary people within their society are not persecuted?

SELECTED BIBLIOGRAPHY

BETTELHEIM, BRUNO. *The Informed Heart.* Glencoe, Ill.: Free Press, 1960.

BIRENBAUM, HALINA. *Hope Is the Last To Die.* New York: Twayne, 1971.

COHEN, ELIE A. *Human Behavior in the Concentration Camp.* New York: Norton, 1953.

FRANK, ANNE. *Tales from the Secret Annex.* New York: Washington Square Press, 1983.

FRANKL, VIKTOR E. *From Death-Camp to Existentialism.* New York: Farrar, Straus, 1958.

GINZBURG, EUGENIA SEMYONOVNA. *Journey into the Whirlwind.* New York: Harcourt, Brace & World, 1967.

GLATSTEIN, JACOB, and SAMUEL MARGOSHES. *Anthology of Holocaust Literature.* New York: Atheneum, 1973.

GOLDSTEIN, BERNARD. *The Stars Bear Witness.* New York: Viking, 1949.

HART, KITTY. *I Am Alive.* New York: Abelard-Schuman, 1962.

KLEIN, GERDA WEISSMAN. *All But My Life.* New York: Hill & Wang, 1957.

KUZNETSOV, A. *Babi Yar.* New York: Farrar, Straus & Giroux, 1970.

MANDELSTAM, NADEZHDA. *Hope Against Hope.* New York: Atheneum, 1970.

MANN, GOLO. *The History of Germany Since 1789.* New York: Praeger Publishers, 1972.

PAWLOWICZ, SALA. *I Will Survive.* New York: Norton, 1967.

RAPPAPORT, ERNEST A. "Survivor Guilt," *Midstream,* XVII, August – September, 1971, pp. 41-47.

SCHNABEL, ERNST. *Anne Frank: A Portrait in Courage.* New York: Harbrace Paperback Library, 1958.

THORNE, LEON. *Out of the Ashes.* New York: Rosebern, 1961.

UNSDORFER, S. B. *The Yellow Star.* New York: Thomas Yoseloff, 1961.

VRBA, RUDOLF. *I Cannot Forgive.* New York: Grove, 1964.

WEISS, RESKA. *Journey Through Hell.* London: Vallentine, 1961.

WIECHERT, ERNST. *Forest of the Dead.* New York: Greenberg, 1947.

WIESEL, ELIE. *Night.* New York: Avon, 1969.

_____. *A Beggar in Jerusalem.* London: Weidenfeld and Nicolson, 1970.

_____. *One Generation After.* New York: Avon, 1972.

_____. *The Oath.* New York: Random House, 1973.

NOTES

NOTES

GOETHE'S FAUST
PARTS I AND II

NOTES

including
- *Introduction*
- *Summaries and Commentaries*
- *Character Sketches*
- *Critical Notes on the Plays*
- *Select Bibliography*
- *Examination Questions*

by
Robert Milch
Brooklyn College

INCORPORATED

LINCOLN, NEBRASKA 68501

Editor	Consulting Editor
Gary Carey, M.A.	*James L. Roberts, Ph.D.*
University of Colorado	*Department of English*
	University of Nebraska

ISBN 0-8220-0479-8
© Copyright 1965
by
C. K. Hillegass
All Rights Reserved
Printed in U.S.A.

1990 Printing

Cliffs Notes, Inc.   Lincoln, Nebraska

CONTENTS

INTRODUCTION 5
    Goethe's Life 5
    The Faust Legend 8

BRIEF OUTLINE OF "FAUST" 11

SUMMARIES AND COMMENTARIES
    Part One 12
    Part Two 40

THE PRINCIPAL CHARACTERS
    Faust 60
    Mephistopheles 61
    Gretchen 62

SPECIAL PROBLEMS
    Relationship of the Two Parts 63
    Theatrical Productions 64

MAIN THEME: A METAPHYSICAL QUEST 65

"FAUST" AND ROMANTICISM 67

BIBLIOGRAPHY 68

EXAMINATION QUESTIONS 68

FAUST

INTRODUCTION

Faust, Goethe's great dramatic poem in two parts, is his crowning work. Even though it is based on the medieval legend of a man who sold his soul to the devil, it actually treats modern man's sense of alienation and his need to come to terms with the world in which he lives.

This theme has always been an important one in western literature, but it has gained in urgency during our own century. Each generation must explore anew the problems of human estrangement and fulfillment — the best way to begin such a search is to see what the past has to offer. Goethe's vision may not provide the perfect or the only answer, but it has been a source of inspiration to many readers for more than a hundred years and reflects the thoughts and experiences of one of the 19th century's most active and gifted minds.

This book will help you to understand and remember Goethe's poem, but it is not a substitute for the complete work. Use this outline as a guide while you are reading *Faust* and as a review afterwards. By all means, though, take advantage of your opportunity to read the poem in full. It has much real beauty and philosophical value to offer, and you will never regret the small effort it requires.

GOETHE'S LIFE

Johann Wolfgang von Goethe was one of the rare giants of world literature. Throughout a long and full life he demonstrated his prolific genius in many different areas. Goethe composed literary works and established artistic principles that had a profound influence on his contemporaries throughout Europe, and which are still looked to as models. The position he holds in the development of German literature and thought is like that which Shakespeare has in the English-speaking countries.

Goethe was born August 28, 1749, in Frankfurt-am-Main, Germany, to a wealthy, middle-class family. He was educated at home by his father and tutors until 1765, when he was sent to Leipzig to study law, his father's profession. Goethe had shown his literary talent even as a child. While at Leipzig he began to write brilliant lyric poetry and completed his first two full-length plays, although these were not produced until some years later.

After a serious illness and an extended convalescence at home, Goethe resumed his legal studies at Strasbourg and completed the course in 1771. He continued his literary activities there and became acquainted with several of the younger German poets and critics.

Following his graduation, Goethe returned to Frankfurt. His mind was filled with many exciting ideas, and he devoted himself to philosophical studies, mainly of Spinoza, and literature. It was here that he wrote his first important metrical drama, *Gotz von Berlichingen* (1772), and then the superb short novel, *The Sorrows of Young Werther* (1774). These aroused widespread interest and admiration, and established Goethe's place as an important literary artist and leader of the "Romantic Revolt" in Germany. During this period he also began work on the earliest version of *Faust, Part One* (now known to scholars as the *Urfaust*).

In 1775 Goethe was invited by the young Duke Karl August of Weimar to accept a position at his court. In the next ten years Goethe held several responsible administrative and advisory posts in the government there, serving at various times as privy counsellor, and as head of the Ministries of Finance, Agriculture, and Mines. He showed much skill in the problems of government administration, and his practical knowledge and good sense were soon respected, even by those who had originally resented his presence at court. Goethe and the Duke became good friends, but the poet always maintained his independence of thought and action, and did not allow his sovereign to dominate him.

Karl August was an enlightened ruler who gathered many talented writers and artists at his court. The atmosphere at Weimar was stimulating, but Goethe was a conscientious public servant and gave most of his energy to official business. The security and responsibility of his position at court was an asset to him in solving some of his personal problems, but he eventually found that it interfered too much with his literary work. During this period he was often unable to complete manuscripts he had begun or to bring to maturity many pressing ideas. Finally in 1786 he left Weimar on a two year trip to Italy in order to come to terms with himself and his art.

On his return to Germany Goethe lived in a state of semi-retirement and concentrated on his studies and writing. His friendship with the Duke continued and he kept his affiliation with the Weimar court, but aside from the directorship of the Wiemar State Theatre and other cultural matters, Goethe was no longer involved in public matters. Despite this the Duke went on paying all the emoluments to which Goethe had formerly been entitled, thus giving him the material security his work required.

Goethe continued to cultivate his wide interests. His scientific studies included original researches in botany, anatomy, geology, and optics. He also maintained an active interest in current political and social developments, and accompanied the Duke on a military campaign against the French in 1792. Later on he wrote commentaries on the French Revolution and the Napoleonic Wars.

In 1806 Goethe married the woman who had been his mistress for many years, and by whom he had a son in 1789. His material and domestic stability, as well as an intimate friendship with the poet Schiller, helped Goethe to maintain his emotional serenity and artistic dedication. As the years passed he became acquainted with many of the most prominent men of his time and was highly regarded by all. Napoleon Bonaparte was among his most famous admirers, and remarked when they first met, "Vous êtes un homme," (You are a man).

The complete edition of Goethe's vast and uneven literary production comprises 143 volumes. This diverse collection contains *Faust, Part One* (completed 1808), *Faust, Part Two* (completed 1832), and many other dramatic works, including *Torquato-Tasso*

(1780), *Iphigenia in Tauris* (1787), *Egmont* (1788), and *Pandora* (1810). There are also the novels, *Wilhelm Meister's Apprenticeship* (1796), *The Elective Affinities* (1809), and *Wilhelm Meister's Journeys* (1829); and such varied prose works as *The Italian Journey* (1817), *The Campaign in France* and *The Siege of Mainz* (1821); scientific papers like *The Theory of Colors* (1810); his autobiography *Poetry and Truth* (1811-1833), and a collection of reminiscences and literary criticism, *Conversations with Eckerman* (posthumously, 1837). Goethe's many volumes of poetry include *Reynard the Fox* (1794), *Roman Elegies* (1795), *Hermann and Dorothea* (1798), *West-Eastern Divan* (1819), and *Xenien* (1797), in collaboration with Schiller). He also found time to translate many foreign works into German and participated in the editing and publication of several literary reviews. In addition, numerous sizeable fragments of works which he never completed still survive.

By the time of his death, Goethe had attained a position of unprecedented esteem in the literary and intellectual circles. His works and opinions made a deep impression on most of the writers and poets of the early 19th century. His great work, *Faust,* is still deemed the most important masterpiece of German literature.

Because of the breadth of his thought, his comprehension of human nature and optimistic faith in the human spirit, and his intuitive grasp of universal truths, Goethe is regarded by many as the outstanding poet of the modern world. He died March 22, 1832, but his work lives in its meaning and value for modern day readers.

THE FAUST LEGEND IN EUROPEAN THOUGHT

The Faust legend first flourished in medieval Europe and is thought to have its earliest roots in the New Testament story of the magician Simon Magus (Acts 8:9-24). During the superstitious Middle Ages, the story of the man who sold his soul to the devil to procure supernatural powers captured the popular imagination and spread rapidly. At some point the name of Faust was definitely attached to this figure. A cycle of legends, including some from ancient and medieval sources that were originally told about other magicians, began to collect around him. One of the most widely-read magic texts of the period was attributed to Faust and many others referred to him as an authority.

A famous German sage and adventurer born in 1480 was thought by many of his contemporaries to be a magician and probably did practice some sort of black magic. Few details of his life are certain, but it is known that he capitalized on the situation by calling himself "Faust the Younger," thus acquiring the occult reputation of the legendary character.

After a sensational career, this Faust died during a mysterious demonstration of flying which he put on for a royal audience in 1525. It was generally believed that he had been carried away by the devil. One of the scenes of Goethe's tragedy is set in Auerbach's Cellar in Leipzig, the city of this fatal exhibition, because the walls of the old tavern were decorated with representations of Faust's exploits, and the place was traditionally connected with him.

A biography of Faust, the *Historia von D. Johann Fausten,* based upon the shadowy life of Faust the Younger, but including many of the fanciful legendary stories, was published in Frankfurt in 1587. That same year it was translated into English as *The Historie of the damnable life and deserved death of Doctor John Faustus.* In both these popular editions of the "Faust-Book," the famed magician's deeds and pact with the devil are recounted, along with much pious moralizing about his sinfulness and final damnation. It was in this version that the legend took on a permanent form.

When the Renaissance came to northern Europe, Faust was made into a symbol of free thought, anti-clericalism, and opposition to Church dogma. The first important literary treatment of the legend was that of the English dramatist, Christopher Marlowe.

Marlowe's *Tragical History of Doctor Faustus* (1588, now usually referred to as *Doctor Faustus*) was the forerunner of all later English tragedies and had a revolutionary effect on the development of dramatic art. It is still renowned for its exciting theatricality, its beautiful blank verse, and its moving portrayal of a human soul in despair because he cannot accept God and so is condemned to damnation.

Marlowe used the English translation of the 1587 Faust-Book as his main source, but transformed the legendary magician into a figure of tragic stature and made his story a powerful expression of the main issues of Elizabethan thought. As in the earlier versions, Marlowe's Faustus signs a pact with the devil which consigns his soul to hell in return for 24 years of unlimited power and pleasure. Up to the moment of his death, however, this Faustus is free to resist his seduction by the forces of evil, despite having signed the pact. In the final scenes Faustus becomes terrified by the thought of his impending damnation and desperately wants to save himself, but his faith in God's merciful love is not strong enough and he cannot repent. After a painful struggle with himself, Faustus is carried off by the devil at the end of the play.

In addition to the difference in the fate of the protagonist, Marlowe's drama varies from Goethe's in other significant ways. At the outset Faustus does not invoke the devil because of moral or philosophical alienation, as does Faust, but only from a crass desire for power, and in his adventures afterward there is little effort made to explore the many kinds of human experience and ways to personal fulfillment that are examined in Goethe's poem. Both characters are torn by conflicts within their own souls, but Faustus is trying to believe in God, while Faust seeks a way to believe in himself. Finally, the theology and morality of Marlowe's play is that of traditional Christianity. In *Faust* Goethe tends to use orthodox religion only as a source of imagery. He tells his story in the context of an abstract pantheistic religious system and a fluid moral code that gives precedence to motives and circumstances rather than deeds as such.

Marlowe's rendition of the legend was popular in England and Germany until the mid-17th century, but eventually the Faust story lost much of its appeal. The legend was kept alive in the folk tradition of Germany, though, and was the subject of pantomimes and marionette shows for many years.

The close of the 18th century in Germany was a time very much like the Renaissance. Before long the old Faust story with its unique approach to the period's problems was remembered. The German dramatist Lessing (1729-1781) wrote a play based on the legend, but the manuscript was lost many generations ago and its contents are hardly known.

Goethe's great tragedy struck a responsive chord throughout Europe and reinforced the new interest in the Faust story. Since his time it has stimulated many creative thinkers and has been the central theme of notable works in all fields of expression. In art, for instance, the Faust legend has provided fruitful subjects for such painters as Ferdinand Delacroix (1798-1863). Musical works based on the Faust story include Hector Berlioz's cantata, *The Damnation of Faust* (1846), Charles Gounod's opera, *Faust* (1859), Arrigo Boito's opera, *Mefistofele* (1868), and the *Faust Symphony* (1857) of Franz Lizt. Even the newest of art forms, the motion picture, has made use of the ancient story, for a film version of Goethe's *Faust* was produced in Germany in 1925. But most important, the legend has continued to be the subject of many poems, novels, and dramatic works. Among the more recent of these are the novel, *Doctor Faustus* (1948) by Thomas Mann and the poetic morality play, *An Irish Faustus* (1964) by Lawrence Durrell.

Each succeeding artist has recast the rich Faust legend in terms of the intellectual and emotional climate of his own time, and over the past few centuries this tale has matured into an archetypal myth of man's aspirations and the dilemmas he faces in the effort to understand his place in the universe. Like all myths, the Faust story has much to teach the reader in all its forms, for the tale has retained its pertinence in the modern world. The history of the legend's development and its expansion into broader moral and philosophical spheres is also an intellectual history of mankind.

Students who are interested in a more detailed study of the Faust theme should begin by consulting E. M. Butler's *Fortunes of Faust,* available in any good library.

BRIEF OUTLINE OF FAUST

Heinrich Faust, a learned scholar, feels that none of his many achievements has provided him with satisfaction or a sense of fulfillment. He yearns to gain knowledge of absolute truth and the meaning of existence. Faust turns to magic in the hope of finding a solution and finally makes a pact with the devil. He agrees to sell his soul if the devil can give him one moment of experience which is so rewarding that his sense of alienation disappears and he calls upon that moment to stay as it is forever.

In Part One of the poem Faust attempts, with the devil's help, to find happiness through emotional involvement. His tragic love affair with Gretchen ends in her death, but Faust is much chastened by this experience. In Part Two he tries to satisfy his craving through temporal accomplishments and exposure to all that the world can offer in terms of ideas and externalized gratifications. He attains an important position at the Imperial Court, learns much from the figures of classical antiquity, woos Helen of Troy, wins great victories, and is renowned for his public works, but none of these things gives him lasting peace of mind.

Faust dies bitter and disillusioned. He is finally admitted to heaven by God's grace, in reward for his endless striving after knowledge of goodness and truth, and his courageous resolution to believe in the existence of something higher than himself.

SUMMARIES AND COMMENTARIES: PART I

DEDICATION

Summary

In this short poem preceding the main action of the tragedy, Goethe describes the thoughts that run through his mind as he sits in his study, preparing to work on the manuscript of *Faust* after a lapse of many years. He seems to see vague forms and shadows floating in the air before his eyes, ghosts that have haunted him all his life, but now they press upon his consciousness with more intensity than ever before. As these forms become charged with greater emotional significance for him, the world of reality in which Goethe lives seems to fall back into distant recesses of his mind.

Commentary

These forms represent the long gone friends and loved ones of Goethe's youth, as well as the ideas he hopes to voice in *Faust*.

A mood of sad but firm resolution comes over him as he determines to give new life to these shadows — ideas he cannot escape, which have a sort of independent existence. Despite the melancholy tone of his words, Goethe communicates a feeling of firmness and strength that will be maintained throughout the poem.

PRELUDE IN THE THEATRE

Summary

A discussion takes place on the stage of a theatre between a director, a poet, and a clown. They argue about what constitutes a good play. Three points of view are presented. The director is interested in those things which make the play a commercial success: action and novelty. The poet is concerned with the artistry and ideas that make the play's meaning universal and give it value for posterity. The clown asserts that these views are not contradictory. He points out that the needs of art and the needs of the moment can be reconciled, for that which attracts the general public need not be worthless. The artist can maintain his integrity and still be successful if he stops feeling superior and develops a proper appreciation for the values of everyday life.

Finally the director ends the discussion, reminding the others that there is still much work to be done if they are to put on any play at all. He describes the techniques of producing a play and promises the audience that the whole universe will be presented on his stage — beginning with Heaven and proceeding through the world to Hell.

Commentary

At first glance this prelude seems only indirectly connected to the tragedy itself, but Goethe uses it to sketch in commonplace terms some of the essential themes that will be treated in *Faust*. The poet represents the idealist who strives to comprehend eternal values, the clown is the realist who is concerned with the here and now, but both personify important principles of life. The director of the theatre is like the god of a universe of the mind (conscience) of a single individual. He must blend these disparate elements to create a harmonious world or well integrated personality. The problems he faces on his stage foreshadow those which Faust will strive with.

14

In making this analogy between the universe and the individual soul, Goethe draws upon the medieval philosophical conception of the microcosm and the macrocosm. The individual and the cosmos are related to each other as the inner "small world" and the outer "great world," vastly different in size and scope, but having the same basic essence and responding to the same eternal laws. This is also the relationship between the two parts of *Faust*.

On a more topical level, the director's final speech is an analysis of the problems of the playwright, and demonstrates Goethe's thorough knowledge of stagecraft, derived from many years as a dramatist and director of the State Theatre at Weimar.

PROLOGUE IN HEAVEN

Summary
The Lord and all the hosts of heaven are assembled. The three archangels, Raphael, Gabriel, and Michael, individually step forward and recite eloquent praises of the beauty and perfection of the universe and the omnipotence of God. Then Mephistopheles (also called Mephisto, the devil) enters. He cannot imitate the songs of the others, he says, for he lacks their skill. Furthermore, he has seen that the possession of reason and intelligence has made mankind unhappy, and this troubles him.

The Lord counters this criticism of humanity by citing the example of Faust, a man who is not debased by reason and who will ultimately be guided by it to a knowledge of the truth. God and Mephisto differ in evaluating Faust's potential. The devil censures Faust's present indecisive confusion, but the Lord excuses it by saying, "Men make mistakes as long as they strive." He asserts that Faust in the end will attain understanding and peace of mind.

The Lord and Mephisto make a wager to settle this dispute. As long as Faust lives, the devil may attempt to influence and conquer him, but if Mephisto's judgment of Faust is shown to be wrong, he will have to admit that "A good man with his groping intuitions/ Still knows the path that is true and fit." Mephistopheles and the Lord are both confident of winning and the bargain is sealed. The heavens close, and the Lord and the archangels disappear.

Commentary

The songs of the three archangels express Goethe's belief that the universe is a dynamic continuum where action is the law that dominates Nature and man. This doctrine will be illustrated in the story of Faust. In this system the only absolute sin is nonaction; man, despite many errors of judgment or wrong turns can find the path of righteousness, but only if he continues striving. He eventually will succeed if he keeps up the struggle because striving is itself a moral act and his intuitive yearnings all point toward a good end.

Mephisto represents the spirit of negativistic cynicism, of endless denial. He can be a force for good or evil—inducing a man to surrender to his lowest instincts and give up the quest, or driving him by persistent prodding and frustration to find the fulfillment of his ideals, *i.e.* salvation. The Lord is the paragon of perfection toward which men strive. He is unmoved by Mephisto's threats to Faust because He knows that man has an innate will for good, and that errors or backsliding are natural incidents in the human progression toward righteousness.

The conversation and bargain between God and Mephistopheles are reminiscent of a similar scene at the opening of the Book of Job. This Biblical connection is emphasized by Goethe's use of an archaic German style in this section. It creates an exalted and sacred background for the worldly tribulations of Faust and invites the reader to compare Goethe's conception of the universe, where man is free to err and strive, with that of Job, where he must blindly accept his fate.

The setting of the prologue to the poem in Heaven implies that the life and fate of Faust are matters of universal significance, which will clarify the relationship of God and man, good and evil, existence and nonexistence. Aside from this important purpose, the prologue presents another crucial question, which is symbolically expressed in Mephisto's wager—whether the Lord has been competent as a Creator and whether his creation, the world and its inhabitants, is worthy of survival.

NIGHT • FAUST'S STUDY (i)

Summary

In a narrow, vaulted Gothic chamber Dr. Heinrich Faust sits at his desk, surrounded by a clutter of books and scientific instruments. It is Easter Eve.

Now fifty years old, Faust is depressed and frustrated. He has mastered all the important academic disciplines — Philosophy, Medicine, Law and Theology — has fearlessly inquired into everything that interested him, and is not afraid of the devil or Hell, but he is unsatisfied and believes himself trapped by the limitations of human understanding. Moreover, he feels that his achievements have been of no use to mankind and have brought him no earthly rewards. Now he plans to turn to magic in the hope of at last attaining ultimate knowledge.

Faust studies the esoteric symbols in an old magic book and meditates on their meaning, then invokes the Earth-Spirit. Accompanied by various spiritual phenomena, the Spirit of Earthly Reality appears, but it rebukes Faust, denies their kinship, and vanishes again.

Commentary

This incident indicates that man's higher nature makes it impossible for him to be accepted into the gross sphere of complete earthliness, of abstract and formless being. Whatever his wishes, a human being cannot separate existence and consciousness.

Faust begins to despair of ever satisfying his aspirations when Wagner, his famulus or assistant, enters the room and interrupts him. In the conversation which follows both men speak at cross-purposes. Faust is critical of Wagner's conventional attitudes and Wagner is unable to understand Faust's unhappy alienation.

The dull, unimaginative but honest Wagner is a parody of bourgeois pedantry. His characterization emphasizes the differences between the search after knowledge for its own sake or for worldly rewards and the search for true understanding.

After Wagner departs, Faust returns to bitter thoughts about human impotence. The sight of a skull makes him think of suicide as the solution to his problems. He is about to drink a glass of poison when the pealing of church bells and the melodious singing of a choir remind him of the Easter message of resurrection and eternal life. Faust does not literally believe in these concepts, but they bring back memories of his childhood religious faith and their symbolic meaning restores his self-confidence.

The Easter message that inspires Faust is the hope of life's rebirth from corruption and death. It predicts the course that Faust will follow—first sinking lower and lower into the depths of personal degradation, then rising to the highest level of human fulfillment and salvation.

OUTSIDE THE CITY GATE

Summary

It is Easter Sunday afternoon. The townspeople are all strolling into the countryside to welcome the advent of Spring. Their mood is gay and youthful. It is as if they are celebrating the world's resurrection from winter, Faust remarks to Wagner, for the two scholars have joined the throng on this beautiful day.

Faust eagerly attunes himself to the holiday atmosphere and shares the peoples' happiness, but Wagner is too stiff and formal to enjoy himself. They stand watching while a group of youngsters sing and dance. Faust says:

> Here is the plain man's real heaven—
> Great and small in a riot of fun;
> Here I'm a man—and dare be one.

A peasant comes by and respectfully praises Faust's skill as a physician. This reminds Faust of his own feelings of futility. He tells Wagner that he is torn between two currents in his soul; one is tied to the pleasures of the world, but the other reaches out to the stars. Faust says he would forego all earthly joys if he could satisfy his lofty, spiritual desires. Wagner is frightened by Faust's talk of spirits and warns him against such thoughts.

The men return to town. On the way they notice a mysterious black poodle following them. To Wagner it seems only a harmless little dog, but Faust senses something occult about it.

Commentary

The simple and joyous life of the common people depicted in this scene is the result of their humble, unthinking acceptance of the world. Faust envies them, but is prevented from following their example by the highly developed spiritual side of his character.

FAUST'S STUDY (ii)

Summary

Evening finds Faust in his study. The poodle is still with him. Faust's soul is tranquil after his happy afternoon, and he feels confident of finding peace. He says:

> Ah, when in our narrow cell
> The lamp once more imparts good cheer,
> Then in our bosom—in the heart
> That knows itself—then things grow clear.
> Reason once more begins to speak
> And the blooms of hope once more to spread;
> One hankers for the brooks of life,
> Ah, and for life's fountain head.

But Faust's depression begins to return with these last words. To renew his inspiration he sets about translating into German the Gospel of Saint John, but cannot get past the first line, "In the beginning was the Word." After making several attempts to select a rendition that satisfies him, Faust finally decides on, "In the beginning was the Deed."

Commentary

This episode crystallizes one of the main philosophical themes of the poem—Goethe's conception that action is the creative and ruling force of the universe. This is the metaphysical meaning of Faust's final translation.

The poodle begins to growl and continues to do so as long as Faust goes on reading the Bible. Faust realizes that some mysterious spiritual presence has taken on the form of the dog. He uses a magical incantation to force it to appear. In an instant Mephistopheles stands before him in the guise of a travelling scholar.

This is a crucial moment. Mephisto has been in pursuit of his intended victim ever since making the wager with God, but it was up to Faust to take the first step in his own seduction by recognizing and invoking the devil. This act confirms Mephisto's suspicion of Faust's disgust with positive methods of finding satisfaction and illustrates Faust's movement toward the nihilistic cynicism which characterizes the devil. Mephisto's costume is purposely chosen to make Faust feel at ease with him, and to prevent him from becoming frightened as he had been by the terrifying supernatural appearance of the Earth-Spirit.

Faust senses his visitor's identity, but Mephistopheles refuses to reveal his name. Instead he describes himself by explaining his function in the divine plan, saying he is:

> A part of that Power
> Which always wills evil, always procures good...
> ...the Spirit which always denies.

A metaphysical debate follows concerning Mephisto's description of himself as only a part of a whole—a concept which Faust finds hard to accept. After their talk Faust invites Mephistopheles to visit him again. The devil prepares to leave but cannot go because Faust has not released the spell that invoked him. Faust refuses to free Mephistopheles. The unexpected discovery that even the devil is subject to a form of law makes him wonder about the possibility of making a contract with him. He intends to force Mephistopheles to buy his freedom.

The devil is not as powerless as he has been pretending, however. He calls up a choir of spirits who lull Faust to sleep with an idyllic song about the sensual pleasures of pagan, southern lands. Next Mephistopheles summons the aid of some mice and makes his escape. When Faust awakens the room is empty. He wonders whether he has been dreaming.

Faust's belief that Mephisto's appearance was only a dream is one of many hints that the devil is partly a symbolic representation of hidden aspects of Faust's personality (*i.e.* of human nature in general).

FAUST'S STUDY (iii)

Summary

The next day Faust is alone in his study again. Mephistopheles enters, dressed as a nobleman. He tries to tempt Faust by offering him a life of limitless wealth and pleasure, but Faust sadly declines the offer, saying that the world's pleasures cannot end his doubts or satisfy his needs.

Mephistopheles taunts Faust for his failure to commit suicide on Easter Eve and drives him to voice a rejection of the value of life and the traditional Christian virtues. The devil urges Faust to begin a new life with his assistance, and to exist no longer as an ordinary human being. If Faust agrees to become his servant after death (*i.e.* to sell his soul), Mephisto will be his during life and will guarantee to provide all that Faust desires.

Faust accepts this offer with some hesitation, for he doubts Mephisto's ability to fulfil his end of the bargain, but makes a significant change in the wording of the pact. Faust promises that if any moment, however brief, is so charged with pleasure for him that he says, "Linger a while! Thou art so fair!" that will be the day of his death and he will serve the devil forever after.

Commentary

Mephisto's costume in this scene is a reminder to Faust of the narrow limitations on the world in which he has been living until now. Faust's change in wording recalls the divine law that action is the ruling force of the universe, and raises the story of this Faust to a higher philosophical level than that of the hero of the old legends. The terms of the new pact mean that only when Faust is so satiated with pleasure that he chooses to be in a state of rest or nonaction will he be damned. In other words, the primal sin is to absolve oneself of the responsibility for motion and activity. This idea is in full accord with Mephisto's nihilistic principles so the devil accepts the amended pact. In Goethe's religious thought, movement, action, and striving are equated with virtue, while nonmovement, passivity, and resignation are sin. Since Faust does not believe in the traditional heaven and hell, he is really offering little in his own terms, and is betting his life rather than selling his soul. In Faust's mind there is no certainty that eternal life really exists, so he is merely stating his willingness to give up an existence that he is already dissatisfied with. Faust's desire is not intrinsically an evil one, despite his pact with the devil. As the Lord said in the "Prologue," striving and error are the path of even the righteous man. At this point Faust's final end is still uncertain, but his opportunity to redeem himself is undiminished by his alliance with Mephisto.

The devil is unsure of his ability to fulfil Faust's request, but he accepts the challenge and their pact is signed in blood. Faust is filled with eagerness to taste all those aspects of life that he has neglected until now. He has found that reason and magic were unable to console him, but hopes to find understanding and knowledge through emotional and physical experience. Faust and Mephistopheles are interrupted when a student knocks at the door. Faust is in no mood to see him and asks Mephisto to take his place. The devil puts on Faust's academic gown.

The young freshman has just arrived in town and wants the advice of the great scholar Faust on his studies, but Mephisto confuses him by a bitter, satirical attack on pedantry and academic learning. The devil's analysis of the traditional learned disciplines parodies Faust's in the first scene. Before the student departs, Mephistopheles sarcastically writes in his album, *Eritis sicut Deus, scientes bonum et malum* ("You shall be like God, knowing good and evil"), the advice given by the serpent to Eve in the Garden of Eden.

The devil as portrayed by Goethe performs a necessary function in the execution of the divine purpose. Despite his cynical belief in the futility of learning and the grossness of mankind, Mephisto often speaks the truth. His advice to the student is important for understanding God's attitude toward Faust's moral errors—one comes to know good partly through knowing evil, and one cannot come to know God without this knowledge. Moreover, true knowledge is gotten only from experience.

After the student goes, Faust re-enters the room. Mephistopheles cheerfully congratulates him on his new life and they set out on their adventures.

AUERBACH'S CELLAR IN LEIPZIG

Summary
Four men, Frosch, Brander, Siebel, and Altmayer, are drinking in a tavern in the city of Leipzig. Mephistopheles has offered to show Faust the pleasures that can be gotten from convivial company and good cheer. They enter and join the others.

After observing their coarseness and watching Mephistopheles befuddle them with magic tricks, Faust realizes that this is not the answer to his longing. He voices his disgust and urges that they go. Before they leave, Mephisto works another spell, to demonstrate to Faust the inherent bestiality of human beings.

Commentary
For the significance of Auerbach's Tavern as the setting for this scene, see the section on "The Faust Legend in European Thought," page 8. The mood of this scene is comic, but there is an undertone of seriousness, for in their drunken revelry the four men are desperately seeking an escape from frustration and boredom. Faust's disgust with their bestiality is an ironic portent of the low state to which he will fall before the play ends. Faust's intellect and conscience are too highly developed for him to find satisfaction in the animalistic "freedom" and irresponsibility of drunkenness, but this is not because his moral sense is so secure; rather, he has not yet been tempted at his real weak spot—lust. This episode establishes the pattern of all the events in Part One, where, except for the restoration of Faust's youth (which can be interpreted symbolically), Mephisto does nothing for him that he could not have done himself.

WITCH'S KITCHEN

Summary

Now Mephistopheles brings Faust to the mysterious lair of a witch. A brewing cauldron tended by a weird family of monkeys occupies the center of the room, and the place is filled with the occult symbols and paraphernalia of black magic and sorcery. A strange vapor permeates the air. The mood of the place is grotesque and ugly.

The devil has promised that the witch will concoct a potion to remove thirty years from Faust's age so he can more easily enjoy sensual pleasures. At first Faust is repelled by what he observes around him, but then, in a mirror on the wall, he sees the image of a beautiful young woman and all his ardor is aroused. The restoration of his youth now becomes such an exciting prospect that he soon overcomes his distaste for his surroundings.

After a while the witch returns to her den. Following some repartee with Mephistopheles, she prepares the potion and Faust drinks it. The brew is immediately effective. Faust eagerly looks into the mirror again to recapture his vision. Mephisto repeats his promise to introduce Faust to many new delights and predicts that he will soon meet his vision in the flesh. In an aside the devil remarks that:

> With a drink like this in you, take care —
> You'll soon see Helens everywhere.

Commentary

The devil's reference is to Helen of Troy, the legendary paragon of womanhood. He implies that Faust's natural desires have been so heightened by the magic aphrodisiac potion that he will be attracted by any woman he meets. The most important point is that Faust's initial desire arose spontaneously before he took the drink.

Throughout this scene there are symbolic allusions to an evolutionary theory of human development. It is implied that in regaining his youth, Faust is moving backward toward the primeval world from which human reason and civilized institutions once developed.

He is abandoning the highest human attainments to find fulfilment in his baser animal instincts. Evolutionary symbolism will be used many times in both parts of the poem to put Faust's personal adventures into a broader perspective that has reference to all mankind.

A STREET

Summary

Later, on the street of a typical German town, Faust sees Margareta (usually called Gretchen, her nickname in German), recognizes the maiden of his vision, and develops a great passion for her. He tries to strike up a conversation, but Gretchen refuses to respond to his advances and walks away.

When Mephistopheles joins him, Faust excitedly describes Gretchen's youthful beauty and asks the devil to get her for him. Mephisto replies that he has no power over Gretchen because of her innocence and piety. Undaunted, Faust boasts that he will seduce her without help and asks Mephistopheles to cooperate by getting him jewelry and other expensive gifts for the girl.

Commentary

In this scene Faust's sordid lust is contrasted with Gretchen's chastity and feminine warmth. As their romance progresses in the remaining episodes of Part One, Gretchen will develop into a character of genuine tragic stature.

EVENING

Summary

Alone in her small bedroom Gretchen braids her hair and wonders about the strange man who accosted her so boldly on the street earlier in the day. Then she goes out to visit a neighbor.

Faust and Mephistopheles enter the room, for Faust has expressed the wish to see where Gretchen lives and sleeps. He is moved by the simple furnishings and asks Mephisto to leave. Alone, Faust soliloquizes about the strange sense of calm he feels among Gretchen's things and the passionate love welling up within him.

For a moment the wholesome purity of his surroundings causes Faust to waver in his plan to seduce the maiden. Mephistopheles returns with a chest of jewels, however, and quickly turns Faust's thoughts away from such moralizing. They leave the jewels and go out.

Gretchen comes in again. After commenting to herself about the oppressive atmosphere of the tiny room and the odd tension she feels, the maiden prepares for bed. While undressing she sings a charming little song, "There was a king in Thule/Was faithful to the grave..." Suddenly she discovers the jewels. She is so delighted by their beauty that she barely wonders about the significance of their unexplained presence in her room.

Commentary

Gretchen's song, with its theme of fidelity in love, reveals her naivete and idealism. Its innocence foreshadows the deep impression which Faust, in the guise of a handsome and generous young nobleman, will make on her, and her complete devotion to him once he has won her love.

A WALK

Summary

Faust is pacing back and forth, deep in thought, when Mephistopheles enters. The devil angrily reports that Gretchen's mother has learned about the jewels and, suspicious of their origin, has turned them over to the priest as an offering. He comments that:

> The Church has an excellent appetite.
> She has swallowed whole countries and the question
> Has never risen of indigestion.
> Only the Church...can take
> Ill-gotten goods without stomach-ache!

Commentary

The theme and conclusion of this poem are religious, but Goethe believed that man's salvation was dependent on his own efforts and individual relation with God. Faust's life illustrates this doctrine. Therefore, Goethe felt, there was no need for a church to act as an intermediary for man. In addition, he despised the Church because of its corruption, materialism, and worldliness. He felt it maintained a religious facade but was irreligious and rotten at its core. Mephisto's remarks here are typical of many anti-clerical gibes and accusations throughout the poem.

In this scene Faust asks Mephisto to get new jewels to replace those which were given away by Gretchen's mother. This definitively establishes Faust's guilt for the tragic events to come, and shows that the second thoughts he had while meditating were not very sincere. The action of Gretchen's mother and the priest has given him a chance to give up his attempt to seduce the maiden, but Faust decides to go ahead with his original plans.

NEIGHBOR'S HOUSE

Summary
Martha, the neighbor, is Gretchen's friend. At the opening of the scene she is alone, thinking about the long absence of her husband. Gretchen runs in and tells Martha that she has found another casket of jewels, but this time has not told her mother. Martha advises that she continue to keep it a secret, otherwise these will be taken from her also.

Mephistopheles enters the house and attempts to win the friendship of the women by flattery. He pretends to be a traveler, then claims he knew Martha's husband in Italy and was a witness to his death. Martha is not upset by the news, particularly since her husband left no estate, but wants definite proof so she can be free to remarry.

Mephistopheles flirts with Martha and says he will return with a young companion (Faust) who will attest to the death. He asks that Gretchen be present also, saying that his friend has an eye for attractive girls. Though embarrassed, Gretchen agrees, and a meeting is arranged for that evening in Martha's garden.

Commentary

Martha's worldliness and materialism make her an effective contrast to the innocent and romantic Gretchen, and a human counterpart to Mephistopheles. This scene is important because it shows Gretchen's first moral lapse in her decision to keep the second casket of jewels a secret, and thus is the first step leading to her eventual downfall. Gretchen's motives are not evil—she is moved by a naive joy in what seem to her only pretty baubles. Gretchen's sins will become more serious, but the simplicity and innocence of her motives will not change. She will be victimized by her lack of experience and her faith in human nature.

A STREET

Summary

Faust objects to Mephisto's scheme, protesting that they cannot lie about the death of a man they have never even seen. The devil presses him to consent anyway. He points out that Faust, as a scholar, often made definitive statements about matters in which he had no precise knowledge. Faust sees through this sophistry, but finally agrees to the ruse.

Commentary

Faust knows full well that there is a difference between premeditated lies and innocent errors caused by ignorance, but he is beginning to lose faith in all human moral responsibility. In addition, Mephisto has convinced him that he is really at base motivated by animal instincts and his moral protests are a poor attempt at rationalization. He accepts Mephisto's plan, despite his initial reservations, because of his desperate need to find love and give his life meaning, but at the same time Faust is overwhelmed by skepticism about whether any such positive values really exist.

IN MARTHA'S GARDEN

Summary

In the garden behind Martha's house, Faust courts Gretchen, and Mephistopheles courts Martha. The two couples stroll back and forth, on and off stage, so that only parts of each conversation are overheard. Gretchen tells Faust about her life at home and her love for her baby sister. Faust is charmed by her tale and the general tone of the scene is idyllic, although this mood is repeatedly broken by bits of the cruder conversation between Mephisto and Martha.

Commentary

This unique scene is known as the "quartet." Through the device of the alternating conversations, the outlooks of Faust and Mephistopheles are contrasted. The devil is cynical and material-istic, but Faust still possessed some degree of spirituality and ideal-ism. These are momentarily reinforced by his exposure to Gretchen. As he comes to know her virtues, Faust's original lust is transcended by feelings of real love. At the same time this scene reveals that Gretchen is already deeply in love with Faust and ready to do any-thing he asks her. The differences between them as individuals con-trast the peace of mind produced by natural innocence and a simple life with the mental turmoil caused by a complex, introspective mind and familiarity with a vast body of knowledge.

A SUMMER-HOUSE

Summary

In a sheltered bower in the garden, possibly a few days later, Faust and Gretchen kiss and pledge their newly discovered love for each other. Mephistopheles and Martha interrupt them and say it is time for the men to leave. Gretchen does not allow Faust to escort her home because she fears her mother's disapproval, but she promises to meet him again. After he has gone, Gretchen won-ders whether it can be true that a gentleman like Faust really loves a simple girl like herself.

Commentary

Some editions of *Faust* do not separate the last scene from the one preceding it, but it seems justified by the implications in the conversation that there has been a short lapse of time between them. This scene is the culmination of the first stage of Faust's romance. At this point he is unable to decide whether love or lust is dominating his actions, but it is no longer possible for Faust or Gretchen to turn back now, whatever his decision. Because of the submissive character of her love for Faust, Gretchen's future is entirely in his hands. This scene also establishes the convention- ality of Gretchen's mother, a factor which will be a partial cause of unfortunate events later on in the story.

FOREST AND CAVERN

Summary

Torn by the ambivalence between his unselfish love for Gretch- en and his passionate desire for her, Faust seeks the solitude of the woods for his thoughts. He is grateful for the new joy in life which his love for Gretchen has given him, but he is undergoing severe emotional pain also because of his unsatiated lust. He realizes de- spondently that he is becoming dependent on Mephistopheles for the fulfilment of his wishes.

The devil enters and urges Faust to stop brooding. He reminds Faust that it was he who saved him from suicide and who is respon- sible for his present ecstasy. Furthermore, Mephisto goes on, Faust is only rationalizing when he tries to make his love for Gretchen seem exalted. His interest in the girl is carnal; he ought to admit this and take advantage of the situation.

Faust protests this callous indifference to his feelings, but Mephisto's continued erotic references to Gretchen have stimu- lated his passion. Still confused by his doubts, Faust can no longer control himself and hurries away to see Gretchen, saying:

> ...I, the loathed of God...
> Her too, her peace, I must undermine...
> This was the sacrifice I owed to Hell!
> Help, Devil, to shorten my time of torment!
> What must be, must be; hasten it!
> Let her fate hurtle down with mine,
> Let us go together to the pit!

Commentary

In this crucial transitional scene Faust wrestles with himself and the dual aspects of his nature strive to gain dominance. He is tormented by self-doubts and torn between spirituality and sensuality, conscience and desire, idealism and nihilism—in effect, between the ways of life represented by Gretchen and Mephisto. Faust reproaches himself but cannot maintain his balance. Mephisto is unable to convince Faust that his feelings for Gretchen are only physical. Faust is so confused and demoralized that he retreats from further debate and follows the path of least emotional resistance—that to Gretchen's bed—with no concern for the possible consequences, her welfare, or his own ethical qualms.

MARAGARETA'S ROOM

Summary

Alone in her room, Gretchen sadly thinks that Faust has abandoned her. She sits at her spinning wheel and sings:

> My peace is gone,
> My heart is sore,
> I shall find it never
> And never more...

Commentary

The "Spinning Wheel Song" is one of Goethe's best-known lyrics. It expresses Gretchen's overwhelming love for Faust. Her words indicate that her coming "seduction" will not be an unwilling one.

MARTHA'S GARDEN

Summary

Faust and Gretchen are together in the garden. She has noticed that he never participates in any religious rites, and she is concerned about the state of his soul. She asks whether he believes in religion.

In answer, Faust states his tolerance for the beliefs of other people, despite his contempt for conventional religion and orthodox theology. He defines God as the creative spirit of the universe and describes his personal faith in Nature and human emotions as manifestations of this cosmic guiding force. He explains:

Then call it what you will—
Happiness! Heart! Love! God!
I have no name for it!
Feeling is all;
Name is mere sound and reek
Clouding Heaven's light.

Commentary

Faust's answer is an equivocating one and demonstrates a contempt for reason and analytical thought. His creed, as given here, visualizes God as a dynamic force that imbues all of life with vitality and form. It can only be known by feeling and intuition, and not through artificial rituals or systems of belief. To recognize this force is to worship it, and the name one uses is of no importance. To a certain extent this is a statement of Goethe's own beliefs, but Faust overemphasizes the importance of sensory experience because of the influence Mephisto has on him. Faust's real concern here is not to give a complete or even a truthful answer, although he is truthful, but only to overcome a potential barrier between himself and Gretchen.

Faust's reply has not fully satisfied Gretchen, but she turns to another source of anxiety—her intuitive distrust and fear of Mephistopheles. Faust reassures her, then asks permission to come to her room that night. Gretchen's only objection is that her mother might overhear. Faust gives her a sleeping potion for the old woman. They arrange their rendezvous and Gretchen leaves.

Mephistopheles enters and comments sardonically about Gretchen's concern for Faust's religious status. Faust defends her, but Mephisto responds with some caustic remarks about Faust's interest in the girl. He adds that he will share Faust's pleasure with her in the coming night.

The devil's keen understanding of Faust's character is shown by his observation that Faust is really not loathe to violate Gretchen's trust and that the spirituality in her, that Faust continually praises, is just another source of her sensual attraction for him. The devil's final remark implies his belief that the damnations of

Faust and Gretchen will be ensured by their tryst that night. He will enjoy snaring both their immortal souls, and, as a result, winning his wager with God.

AT THE WELL

Summary
An uncertain period of time has gone by since the last scene. Gretchen and Lisbeth, another young woman, are at the town well drawing water. Lisbeth gossips about a maiden of their acquaintance who has been made pregnant by her lover. She makes some bitter comments about the girl's character and predicts that the man will not marry her. Gretchen reacts to this story with sympathy.

After Lisbeth leaves, Gretchen muses on the lack of understanding she once had shown for girls in this predicament. Now that she is pregnant also, though no one else knows as yet, she has learned compassion. Lisbeth's predictions about the other girl's lover make Gretchen more aware of her own plight, for Faust has abandoned her. Gretchen does not understand what drove her to sin, but insists to herself that her motives were pure.

Commentary
Originally in her idyllic affair with Faust, Gretchen had acted naturally and without submitting to the inhibitions of convention, following what one critic has called, "the divine right of emotion." Her only justification for her actions had been subjective. Now she is beginning to accept society's standards again, is regaining the conventional absolute distinctions between right and wrong, and will soon become a victim of the destructive forces set loose by a sense of guilt.

A SHRINE IN THE RAMPARTS

Summary
At a shrine of the Mater Dolorosa located in a niche in the city wall, Gretchen makes an offering of flowers and seeks consolation for her sorrows. Gretchen's prayer reveals the full extent of her anguish. She pleads for divine mercy, crying:

Save me from shame and death in one!
Ah, bow down,
Thou of the woeful crown,
Thy gracious face on me undone.

Commentary

Several months have gone by and Faust has deserted Gretchen. The vague premonitions of impending downfall that she felt in the last scene have now become more acute. Confused and frightened by the things she has experienced, Gretchen instinctively seeks solace from the "Mother of Sorrows." In a symbolic sense Gretchen is now a "mother of sorrows" herself, since she bears Faust's child within her.

NIGHT

Summary

Gretchen's brother Valentine, a soldier, stands in the street outside her house. He relates how his sister's unsullied reputation was once a source of pride and happiness for him. Now he has heard rumors about her and sadly realizes that her innocence has been lost.

Valentine's love for Gretchen is sincere, but his attitude is cruel and unimaginative. He is waiting at her doorway with hopes of catching her lover and getting revenge. Suddenly he sees two figures, Faust and Mephistopheles, advancing up the dark street. Valentine steps back into the shadows, hoping that this will be his chance.

Beneath Gretchen's window Mephistopheles sings a song that mocks her misery. Faust seems to have no feelings left for the poor girl and is interested only in satisfying his carnal appetites again. He asks Mephistopheles to get more jewels because he does not want to call on Gretchen empty handed.

Valentine steps forward, smashes Mephisto's lute, and challenges Faust. The two men draw their swords. Mephistopheles assists Faust in the fight and Valentine is mortally wounded. The noise wakes the neighbors and a crowd gathers, but Faust and Mephistopheles manage to escape.

Gretchen comes out and discovers to her horror that the dying man is her brother. She tries to comfort him, but with his last words Valentine insults his agonized sister and predicts a sordid future for her.

Commentary

Valentine serves as a representative of conventional morality. He demonstrates its intolerance, brutality, and inability, from Goethe's point of view, to deal compassionately with real human problems. Nonetheless, Valentine's personal inadequacies are not bad enough to justify his murder. Until this scene it has been possible to sympathize with Faust and to view him as an innocent victim of Mephisto's guile, or to ignore his immorality because of the empathy one feels for his dilemma. But now Faust is at his lowest ebb—he has no sympathy for the girl whom he seduced and deserted, he speaks of Gretchen as if she were a common prostitute, despite the love he once claimed to feel for her and her continued love for him, and he participates in a senseless and cowardly murder. From this point on the reader has an objective picture of Faust's evil side and will be better able to understand the moral crisis he faces on the Walpurgis Night and in Gretchen's prison cell.

CATHEDRAL NAVE

Summary

The heartbroken Gretchen attends a service at the cathedral to find forgiveness for her sins and solace for her almost unbearable suffering. The church is crowded, but she is alone, except for an Evil Spirit who lurks nearby and reproaches her. Whispering in her ear, the Spirit enumerates her transgressions—she is pregnant, Valentine is dead because of her, and her mother is dead also, killed by the sleeping potion which Gretchen gave her.

The Spirit's cruel taunts destroy Gretchen's remaining hopes for mercy and her misery increases. The emotional intensity of the scene is heightened by the alternation between the choir chanting the powerful Latin Hymn *Dies Irae* ("The Day of Wrath") and the hissing accusations of the Evil Spirit. At last Gretchen reaches the limit of her endurance and faints.

Commentary

Gretchen is unable to benefit from the comforting influence of religion because she is conscious of her guilt and fears damnation. In Goethe's view, conventional religion is too limited and inflexible to be able to solace the unhappy sinner. The Church does not understand God or human nature; thus it cannot help Gretchen or forgive her sins. Gretchen is indeed guilty in a legalistic sense, but her remorse is genuine and there were extenuating circumstances behind each of her crimes, even though this does not absolve her of personal responsibility. The Spirit that torments Gretchen takes none of this into consideration. It makes accusations that are grounded in facts, but it presents a wholly negative interpretation of God's mercy and withholds all possibility of forgiveness from the penitent. That is why Goethe has made it into an "evil" Spirit.

WALPURGIS NIGHT

Summary

It has been nearly a year since Valentine's death and Faust has again abandoned Gretchen. Now it is Walpurgis Night (April 30th), the time of the annual gathering of witches and spirits at the top of the Brocken in the Harz Mountains (located in central Germany) to celebrate a satanic orgy. The mountain top is covered with swarms of demons dancing and singing. The tension rises to a mad crescendo of evil as Mephisto guides Faust through his fiendish assembly, introducing him to all the infernal spirits of medieval legend, and inducing him to participate in their rites. While coupled in an erotic dance with a young female witch, Faust suddenly notices a mouse coming out of his partner's mouth. The shock of this causes him to remember Gretchen. He has a vision of her in chains, becomes distressed, and starts to wander away. Mephistopheles immediately springs into action. He gives a fanciful interpretation of the vision and tries to distract Faust by leading him to a theatre on the mountainside.

Commentary

Faust has been brought to the Walpurgis celebration to complete his degradation and make permanent his lapse from morality. This episode can be interpreted symbolically as the descent into Hell promised in the "Prelude in the Theatre." The atmosphere of the scene is one of evil, black magic, and fantastic confusion. The witches and demons whom Faust encounters are incarnations of all the many facets of evil. Their characterizations or satanic functions mirror many earlier incidents in the poem and bring home a bitter lesson to Faust about the true nature of his "new life." Here on the mountain Faust is made to face the awful reality of his own degeneration, but at the last moment his moral sensibility makes a final effort to assert itself. He remembers Gretchen and the love for her which was his first real participation in life.

WALPURGIS NIGHT'S DREAM
OR THE GOLDEN WEDDING OF OBERON AND TITANIA
A LYRICAL INTERMEZZO

Commentary

The play which Faust and Mephistopheles attend has no connection with the rest of the tragedy. It is made up of a series of satiric four-line verses directed against some of Goethe's contemporaries, and is of little interest to those who are not specialists in the history of the period. The poems of the play are recited by a succession of mythological figures, like Oberon, Titania, and Ariel, and various strange individuals whose names have symbolic or satirical meanings.

This poem was originally written by Goethe as a separate piece. He inserted it here because it served as well as anything else for an interlude and also expressed his contempt for artistic convention. To an extent the poem also illustrates the great influence which the works of Shakespeare had on Goethe.

DESOLATE DAY, IN OPEN COUNTRY

Summary

Faust knows now that Gretchen is in prison and asks Mephistopheles to help free her. The devil refuses. He says there is no need to be concerned since she is not the first girl to be punished for her sins. Faust becomes infuriated and harangues Mephisto:

Dog! Loathsome monster!...Not the first, you say...It pierces me to my marrow and core, the torment of this one girl—and you grin calmly at the fate of thousands!

Mephistopheles sneers that humans are always like this. They join forces with the devil but have not the courage or will power to endure the consequences of their decision. He also reminds Faust of his own responsibility for Gretchen's misfortunes. Mephisto says:

Now we're already back at our wit's end—the point where your human intelligence snaps. Why do you enter our company, if you can't follow it through?... Did we force ourselves on you— or you on us? I cannot undo the avenger's bonds, his bolts I cannot open. Save her! Who was it who plunged her into ruin? I or you?

Faust continues to insist that Mephistopheles rescue Gretchen. In his despair he shouts wild threats at the devil. Mephisto tries to sway him by pointing out that there would be great danger in any rescue attempt because avenging spirits linger at the place of Valentine's death to punish Faust, the murderer. But Faust is no longer concerned with his own welfare and persists. Finally Mephistopheles relents. He agrees to do all he can, but adds that he does not have unlimited power in matters of this sort.

Commentary

This is the only scene of the tragedy in prose. The violent shift in style makes a sharp contrast with the luxuriant lyrical poetry of the preceding scene to emphasize Faust's rediscovery of his moral responsibilities, incomplete as this is, and his return to the world of reality. Faust is still not fully aware of Mephisto's evil nature, since he calls upon him to help in the rescue of Gretchen, and this request reveals that he is still dependent on Mephisto and thus still a potential victim of the devil's powers of dehumanization. Faust's newly discovered moral fervor seems genuine, but he does not acknowledge his own guilt for Gretchen's misfortune. This scene is an affirmation of the power of love rather than morality, but it suggests the underlying relationship of the two principles and thus is not inconsistent with Faust's definition of God earlier in the poem and the conclusion of Part Two.

NIGHT, OPEN COUNTRY

Summary

Faust and Mephistopheles, mounted on magic black horses, gallop wildly past the gallows outside the town on their way to rescue Gretchen. The night is dark and threatening. Spirits prowl through the air.

Commentary

This scene of only five lines is the shortest in the tragedy.

PRISON

Summary

Assisted by Mephistopheles, Faust makes his way to Gretchen's cell. When he enters, Faust finds that she has been driven insane by her imprisonment and sense of guilt. Gretchen does not remember him and huddles fearfully in the corner of the cell, thinking he is the hangman come to execute her for having drowned her baby. Gretchen pleads with Faust to spare her life and begs permission to hold her infant once more.

Faust is grief-stricken by this discovery. He cries out in despair. Suddenly Gretchen regains her senses and recognizes him. She joyously leaps up and her chains fall off. Faust and Gretchen embrace. Now that her lover has returned, Gretchen is no longer afraid and feels confident that everything will be well.

Faust tries to hurry Gretchen out of the cell before morning light, but she rejects his offer of escape. She knows she cannot evade punishment for her crimes and foresees no peace except that of the grave. Faust unsuccessfully tries to change her mind.

As dawn breaks Mephistopheles enters the cell and warns Faust to come along. Gretchen recognizes the devil and fears he has come for her. She prays for divine mercy:

Judgment of God! I have given myself to Thee!

O Father, save me! I am thine!

Mephistopheles tells Faust to come at once or share Gretchen's doom, for, he says, "she is condemned!" But a voice from Heaven interjects, "Redeemed!" Once again Mephisto summons Faust and they depart together. The scene closes with Gretchen's voice faintly calling after her loved one.

Commentary

The scene is particularly praised by critics for its poignant portrayal of Gretchen's madness. Gretchen's restoration to sanity when she sees Faust illustrates the regenerative power of love. Her refusal to escape is based on her acknowledgment of responsibility for her acts and her acceptance of God's law. She has a simple and clear-cut conception of right and wrong which is incomprehensible to the still inwardly doubting Faust. Gretchen is granted salvation by God's grace (the voice from Heaven) because her crimes were the result of inexperience and her motives were never sinful or impure. Gretchen was led into sin by following her instincts, but in Goethe's thought it is part of being human to err. One is redeemed in the end if his conscience learns to know the difference between good and evil, rejects sinfulness, and repents. Gretchen's final words, "Heinrich! I shudder to look at you," express her horror at the ungodly, negativistic life Faust has chosen by maintaining his association with Mephisto, rather than any change in her feelings for him. Her final cries are an effort to make him abandon the devil and throw himself into the merciful arms of the Lord.

This is the end of the first part of the tragedy, a portion of a larger work but at the same time complete in itself. So far Mephisto has lost his wager with the Lord and failed to secure Faust's soul. God's faith in man has been upheld by Faust's moral renewal on the Walpurgis Night and his final though misguided effort to do a good deed. Despite his flirtation with sensuality and evil, Faust's love for Gretchen had developed into something more than lust. In addition, he has realized that the total abnegation of reason is repugnant to human nature. While he has not yet redeemed himself, these decisive changes in his outlook seem to justify the Lord's belief in the innate goodness of mankind.

Faust, however, has still not found happiness or fulfillment in life, and is not sufficiently purged of sinfulness to terminate his alliance with the devil. In his next to last speech Faust says, "I wish I had never been born!" showing his continued alienation, heightened now by the slight experience he has had with love and true spirituality. At this point, though, Faust is unable to apply his new knowledge to himself and still hopes to satisfy the craving of his empty soul through temporal achievements brought about with the devil's help. Thus, the resolution of Faust's struggle with his soul is in doubt, but a passionate and moving love story has come to a tragic end. At its close Faust seems at last to be on the right path. Gretchen's salvation and her loving concern for him right up to the moment of her death are lessons which will make a permanent impression on him. Faust knows now that he cannot find himself through uninhibited sensuality, but he must taste all the world has to offer before he learns that only in God lies human fulfilment. The relationship of the events in Part Two to those in Part One is not as close as might be expected, due to the long time interval between their composition by Goethe, but nonetheless the strand of Faust's adventures is taken up and carried to its ultimate philosophical conclusion in the remaining sections of the poem.

SUMMARIES AND COMMENTARIES: PART II

The second part of *Faust* is much longer than the first and contains many complicated allegorical elements. Because less emphasis is usually given to Part Two in classroom study and to avoid unnecessary confusion, this section of the treatment is briefer than the first. It concentrates on the main details of the plot and the broad philosophical themes of this part of the story.

ACT I

PLEASING LANDSCAPE

At twilight Faust rests in a flowery meadow where he tries to fall asleep. A choir of spirits led by Ariel sings to him. When Faust awakens he feels refreshed and ready to continue his adventures.

Commentary

Most striking about the beginning of Part Two is the complete change of mood from the final scene of Part One. It appears as if the past has been obliterated and Faust has retained in his memory no continuity of experience from which to draw upon to increase his self-knowledge or moral sensibility. At the same time the choir's song expresses the power of Nature to cleanse and renew even the most tormented soul. Faust seems inspired by a faint glimpse of the eternal truths he is seeking. He realizes now that man cannot grasp the ultimate directly and must find it in a context suited to his limited human perceptions. Faust will continue his efforts to satisfy his ambition, but on a scale more in proportion to his abilities. In addition, he will no longer seek fulfilment in sensual passion.

IMPERIAL PALACE

Mephistopheles appears at the Emperor's court in the guise of a jester. Various officials report to their sovereign about the government's financial crisis and related problems. The new jester suggests that the Emperor make use of the kingdom's hidden resources by mining the gold buried beneath the land, and also makes vague hints that the issuance of paper money would ease the situation. The court officials are confused by these suggestions and distrust Mephisto, but everyone admits that he seems to be competent and worldly. The Emperor ends the meeting and announces a great carnival to celebrate Ash Wednesday, the beginning of Lent.

Commentary

This scene has been shown by some critics to be an inversion of the "Prologue in Heaven" of Part One; the Emperor represents the Lord, the court officials the archangels, although they complain instead of offer praise, and Mephisto continues to play the role of an outsider, although here he supports the established order rather than condemns it. In this scene the devil continues to exemplify the spirit of mundane and physical things, as is implied in the advice he offers the Emperor. The reaction of the Emperor and his courtiers to Mephisto's suggestion shows the basic frivolity and emptiness of those concerned only with things of this world. This impression will be strengthened in the next few scenes. The portrayal of the weak, self-indulgent Emperor and his flighty court has been thought by some scholars to be a picture of the corruption of the Holy Roman Empire immediately before its collapse. Whether or not this is so, the scene is certainly a vivid picture of incompetent governments in general.

SPACIOUS HALL

Everything is prepared for the Lenten carnival. A herald announces its start, pointing out the differences between this affair, which will be in the Italian mode, and the typical Germanic festival.

Commentary

The herald's contrast alludes to the differences between the Gothic first part and the Classical second part of *Faust*.

A pageant now takes place in which many allegorical figures representing the different degrees of worldliness and many aspects of human experience appear. Faust is among them, disguised as the god of wealth. He demonstrates his magical skill to the Emperor and convinces him of the soundness of Mephisto's new financial scheme. The Emperor gives him permission to implement it.

Most of the figures in the pageant are drawn from Greek mythology, signifying the emphasis on Classical thought that will be maintained throughout much of Part Two. There is also a suggestion, from the predominance of artists and poets, that there is a close connection between the evolution of art and the evolution of the human spirit. The Boy-Charioteer who drives Faust is the personified spirit of poetry — a selfless source of beauty and inspiration — and seems to mirror one side of Faust's personality. The main sources of imagery in this scene — fire and gold — refer to the dangerous elements within and beneath society. Neither of them is basically bad, but both can be misused to the detriment of mankind. This scene has been read by some scholars as an allegory of the French Revolution, but its full meaning is looser and more generalized. It warns that society can be destroyed by the very things that also ensure its existence.

PLEASURE GARDEN

The next morning the Emperor and his courtiers gather. Faust and Mephisto are among them. The previous impression of decadence is reinforced in the conversations which now take place. It is revealed that the Emperor, with hardly any conception of the significance of his act, has accepted the advice about paper money based on the potential underground resources of his kingdom. The country has been flooded with the new currency and everyone is pleased by what appears to be prosperity.

A DARK GALLERY

Faust and Mephistopheles converse privately. The Emperor has asked Faust to invoke the spirits of Paris and Helen of Troy, but Faust needs the help of Mephisto to fulfil this request.

The devil is unable to offer any assistance. He suggests that Faust visit the "Eternal Mothers," mysterious spirits who are the source of all life and live in a grotto deep in the earth. Faust is suspicious of this advice, but Mephisto assures him that only by groping in emptiness and reaching through limitless space will he find what he seeks. Faust says he is not afraid and will search even in the Void to find the All. Mephisto gives him a magical jeweled key and instructions for finding the Mothers. He describes their abode and tells Faust how to behave there. After Faust goes out, Mephisto expresses his doubt about whether the mission will be successful.

Commentary

This is the first time in Part Two that Faust and Mephisto are alone together. Mephisto's role in this scene indicates that he no longer exercises the active influence over Faust that he had in Part One, for Faust's visit to the Mothers will be his first independent enterprise since he began his association with the devil. The superficiality of Christianity is suggested by Mephisto's inability to accompany Faust and his lack of power over Classical spirits, for he is a Christian devil. A religion which is unable to comprehend such basic elements of life, this implies, is not an adequate one. The Mothers are cosmic forces who symbolize the mystical essence of life which existed before man was ever created and which made his creation possible. They are the source of all form and being and it is important, to understand Goethe's philosophical thought, to note that they are feminine spirits. This femininity symbolizes the constant creative and generative force of the universe by virtue of which man and Nature exist, and which is reflected in all human and natural phenomena.

STATE ROOMS

The Emperor and his courtiers have gathered in a brightly lit chamber to see Paris and Helen. While waiting for Faust to complete his preparations, the ladies badger Mephisto for advice about cosmetics and love potions. The mood of the scene is light and cheerful.

BARONIAL HALL

Everyone moves to a dimly-lit Gothic hall where Faust will present his mythological spectacle. Mephisto offers to act as prompter and makes many sardonic comments throughout the scene. By magic Faust makes a Greek temple appear, then Paris and Helen are seen in the foreground. Most of the courtiers are unimpressed and make caustic remarks about their looks, but Faust is overwhelmed by Helen's beauty. When he tries to take her away from Paris, however, he is knocked down by a burst of thunder and falls unconscious. Mephisto lifts Faust up and carries him out of the room.

Commentary

The audience is too superficial to appreciate the classical ideals represented by Paris and Helen, but Faust sees in them the archetypes of human perfection. His attempt to seize Helen symbolizes the effort to join ancient and modern together to achieve a perfect synthesis of the universe's finest elements. His failure indicates the difficulty of grasping the mystery of life and blending such disparate factors by a single act of will. Space and time cannot so easily be conquered, Faust has learned.

ACT II

NARROW GOTHIC CHAMBER

This is the room which was Faust's study in Part One. Mephisto brings him here and puts him, still unconscious, on the bed. Wearing Faust's academic gown, Mephisto summons Nicodemus, the new famulus who has replaced Wagner. Wagner, in turn, has replaced Faust at the university. Mephisto asks the servant to call his master.

Meanwhile, a baccalaureus (graduate) enters. It is the freshman whom Mephisto teased in Part One. Now he has completed his studies and has a proud, complacent attitude about his knowledge and understanding. He still thinks Mephisto is a professor and engages in an argument with him. He praises his own academic stature and insults Mephisto. After the graduate leaves, Mephisto comments that he is still quite young, and one has to be old to understand the devil.

Commentary

The return to the scenes of Part One indicates that Faust is still far from his goals and is now about to start on an entirely different means of attaining them. Mephisto's final words imply that true insight can be the result only of experience and experimentation. The baccalaureus is Goethe's caricature of a new intellectual trend in his day which he felt carried pragmatism and faith in human omnipotence to dangerous lengths. The graduate's inability to recognize the devil is an example of the inherent limitations and artificiality of his kind of knowledge.

LABORATORY

In a nearby laboratory Wagner is hard at work. He tells Mephisto, who has joined him, that he is about to create a human being. After some manipulations, a tiny humanoid figure appears in the bottle Wagner is tending. It is Homonculus (*i.e.* "little man").

The tiny figure begins an animated conversation with Mephisto and Wagner. Seeing Faust on the bed in the next room, Homonculus floats to his side and eavesdrops on his dreams. He suggests that Faust should not be awakened in his present state of mind. Instead they should take him to Greece to participate in the Classical Walpurgis Night. Mephisto has never heard of this event and asks what it is. Homonculus explains that the Classical spirits are the only true ones and describes the differences between the gloomy northern witch's fete to which Mephisto is accustomed and the joyous warm southern festival. Mephisto is dubious, but finally accepts the invitation when Homonculus tells him about the erotic pleasures he can enjoy with the Thessalian witches who will also be there.

Mephisto lifts up Faust's unconscious body and goes out with Homonculus. They leave Wagner behind, telling him to continue his studies and predicting that someday perhaps he will find fame and virtue.

Commentary
Wagner's creation is the high point of conventional scholarly attainment; it bears the semblance of life but is not real flesh and blood. Homonculus is an archetypal figure, representing the vital life spirit in man and Nature. He is driven by an intense desire to find the secret of existence so that he can become truly alive. In some ways Homonculus is a miniature Faust, but their goals are different: Faust is trying to overcome his physical nature and find peace on a spiritual level, while Homonculus hopes to find fulfilment through an enhanced physical existence. Homonculus also seems to be a personification of Intellect, and is always conscious of his limitations because he possesses none of the emotions that lead real human beings into false impressions or aspirations.

Wagner is left behind because he has already fulfilled his noblest function – the creation of Homonculus. In other words, learning is valuable but not sufficient in itself. It must be abandoned for other means when no longer useful in the struggle to comprehend the ultimate.

CLASSICAL WALPURGIS NIGHT: *Pharsalian Fields, By the Upper Peneus, By the Lower Peneus, By the Upper Peneus (II), Rocky Caves of the Aegean*

Commentary
This series of connected scenes begins on the plain in Greece

where the spirits of mythology have gathered for their annual festival on the eve of August 9th (the day of the battle of Pharsalus in which Caesar defeated Pompey), but the action takes place in several other locations also. A profusion of historical and mythical characters appear in a dreamlike sequence of events. There are many references to a wide variety of philosophical and metaphysical ideas, on both didactic and allegorical levels. For the sake of brevity and clarity these scenes will not be summarized. Instead their main themes and events will be pointed out.

There are three interconnected strands of action in the Classical Walpurgis Night — Faust searching for his idealized vision of Helen, Homonculus searching for the way to become a real human being, and Mephistopheles looking for erotic adventures. The three characters move in and out of the action, as they separate and then rejoin each other at various points. Their adventures develop independently, but the experiences of each mirror the quest and aspirations of the others. The things that take place and the mystical figures who appear can be interpreted on various allegorical levels, but in general are related to the poem's exploration of ways to end Faust's alienation and to form a synthesis of the Romantic and Classical ideals.

At the end, despite many diversions, Faust is no longer trying to escape from reality. He retains his determination, now more enlightened and mature, to find Helen. Homonculus has discovered that the ocean is the ultimate source of all life. He throws himself into the water, among the sea gods and nymphs, where he is transformed into a potent life spirit with the prospect eventually of developing real manhood through Nature's evolutionary scheme. Mephisto is forced to face the enormous disparities between his Germanic Christian outlook and the Greek view of life. He finally finds amorous satisfaction only among the most repulsive and ugly spirits.

In all these scenes Goethe demonstrates his high regard for the free and courageous Greek spirit, and the harmonious Classical outlook on life. In addition, there are philosophical examinations of various beliefs about the origin of life in which Goethe supports a theory of gradual evolution that on a physical level reflects Faust's slow moral evolution. In effect Goethe uses these scenes to conduct a scientific and theological survey of the universe. Many of the incidents and characters also mirror earlier happenings in the poem or foreshadow coming ones. They provide deeper insights into the meaning and function of the episodes and the overall purpose of the second section of *Faust*.

ACT III

BEFORE THE PALACE OF MENELAUS IN SPARTA

The scene has changed to the kingdom of Sparta, shortly after the Trojan War. Helen enters with a chorus of captive Trojan women while Menelaus and the Greek troops remain on the beach to celebrate their victory and safe return home after the capture of Troy. The women express their fears about the future.

Mephistopheles enters, disguised as Phorkyas, an ugly hag. She reviles Helen and sadistically says that Menelaus plans to kill her and the others. The women become terrified, but Mephisto-Phorkyas assures them that there is a way to save themselves. Nearby, she continues, is the castle of a powerful northern lord whose armies have conquered much of the surrounding country while the Greeks were away at Troy. This barbarian chieftain (Faust) will surely protect them.

The women are unable to decide what to do, but the sound of approaching soldiers hastens their decision. They ask Phorkyas to take them to Faust.

Commentary

In many ways Act III resembles a Greek tragedy; Greek metrical forms and a chorus are used, and the development of the plot follows the Classical formula. The story seems intended to reconcile the Classical and Romantic ideals in a new synthesis — the Modern. This concept is at variance with Goethe's own view as expressed in other parts of the poem which were written at different periods in his life. The initial antagonism between Helen and Mephisto symbolizes the innate hostility between beauty and ugliness, or between idealism and evil.

INNER COURTYARD OF A CASTLE

Mephisto-Phorkyas instantaneously transports Helen and the women to Faust's medieval castle. The Gothic setting is in sharp contrast to the Classical one of the last scene. The movement from Sparta to the castle seems to have transcended Time, for it is now the Middle Ages and Faust appears as a Germanic knight.

Faust greets Helen with warmth and flattery. He calms the fears she and the women feel, and shows his trust in Helen by giving her the responsibility for the prisoner Lynceus. There is some elaborate medieval pageantry, organized by Mephisto, which successfully diverts the women and they soon feel at ease. Faust begins to woo Helen in earnest, much in the manner of a medieval troubador. He declares himself her vassal and pledges his undying love. Up to this point Helen's speeches have all been unrhymed, in the Greek manner. Now Faust teaches her how to rhyme and they join together in a love duet, while the chorus praises their union.

Suddenly Mephisto-Phorkyas warns that the army of Menelaus is coming. Faust assembles his soldiers and sends them to meet the enemy, speaking proudly of German military prowess. He goes on at length in praise of the glories of Greece's Golden Age, then urges Helen to flee with him to Arcadia, where they will find bliss and freedom together.

Commentary

Faust's role as a northern conqueror symbolizes the destruction of Greek civilization by barbarism, followed by the desire of the conquerors to possess the classical serenity and beauty of the earlier culture, here personified by Helen. Lynceus represents the disorganized wanderlust and lawlessness of the northerners which can be quelled by submission to Greek principles of order and restraint; thus his fate is determined by Helen. The marriage of Faust and Helen will combine Germanic energy and vitality with Greek moderation and sensitivity. It is a poetic representation of the rediscovery and absorption of Classical culture by the northern peoples during the Renaissance, and a prophecy of a new cultural synthesis which will merge the best of the two earlier civilizations to form a new and better one. The legendary Eden of Arcadia to which Faust and Helen go is a physical image of the youth of humanity. In Arcadia there are no established rules or conventions, and life can begin afresh. It is the only place where Faust and Helen can find the freedom in which to combine and give birth to their new principle of civilization.

ARCADIA

The women of the chorus lie at rest in a peaceful green meadow. Phorkyas enters and reports to them about the wondrous things that have just taken place in the secluded bower where the lovers Faust and Helen have hidden themselves. A son, Euphorion, has been born to them. The lad is beautiful, alert, energetic, artistic. Already he is able to talk and move about freely. A strange aura surrounds his head and sweet music emanates from the cave around him.

Helen, Faust, and Euphorion come out. The boy promises that his existence will make their love more intense. They express their tender affection for each other. Suddenly Euphorion is filled with a wild desire to fling off all earthly shackles and soar high into the heavens. He is unable to restrain his passion and begins to pursue the maidens of the chorus. He embraces one, but the girl vanishes in a burst of flame.

Next Euphorion tries to climb a tall cliff in an effort to reach the greatest possible heights and survey the entire world. He does not heed the warnings of the chorus or his parents that such a rash attempt to grasp the ultimate so early in life will only result in his destruction. Danger, he replies, is a necessary and exhilarating part of life. Euphorion reaches the top of the cliff and hurls himself off, in an ecstasy of Romantic enthusiasm. For a moment he remains suspended in air, then falls to his death. His body disappears, but his clothing and lyre remain on the ground.

Euphorion's parents and the chorus lament his untimely end. The boy's voice is heard calling his mother to join him. Helen sadly bids Faust farewell, saying that happiness and beauty can never permanently be combined. She vanishes, leaving her veil behind.

Phorkyas tells Faust to keep the garment as a memento and inspiration. The heartbroken Faust is carried off in a cloud. Phorkyas reveals herself to be Mephisto in disguise and predicts that he will soon meet Faust again.

Commentary

Euphorion is patterned after the English poet Byron, whose work blended Classic and Romantic themes, and whose temperament was unrestrained and adventurous in the "faustian" sense — ever striving to attain new experiences and greater heights of understanding. He was much admired by Goethe. The characterization also bears a similarity to the Boy-Charioteer of Act I. Euphorion's passionate aspirations and early death are meant to show the doom caused by excessive enthusiasm and extremes of violence and rebelliousness; in short, the inability to adjust to the requirements of real life. His death and Helen's disappearance convey the message that the two ideals, Romanticism and the Classical heritage, are integral parts of life, but are not in themselves sufficient for one to live by. The tangible remains left behind, the lyre and the veil, are reminders that for proper adjustment one must retain his belief in these ideals, but something more is required also. The final lyrics of the chorus assert the immortality of poetry, and affirm the value of life and creativity. They express Goethe's conception of the universe as a fluid whole which embraces all aspects of being.

ACT IV

MOUNTAIN HEIGHTS

Faust still has a vague image of Helen in his mind as he gazes about at the jagged mountains among which he finds himself. Mephisto enters and engages in a lecture on the origin of mountains with which Faust disagrees. Mephisto tries to tempt Faust with another offer of a life filled with pleasure and glory, but Faust does not accept. He has another sort of project in mind—a scheme for the reclamation of land from the sea. Such a battle against the forces of Nature is the only fit project for him to engage in, Faust says.

Mephisto claims to have known all along that Faust would suggest this plan. He tells Faust that a serious crisis was caused in the Empire by their earlier prank of inducing the Emperor to issue vast amounts of worthless paper money. Now the Emperor has been forced into a war to defend his throne and is encamped nearby with his army. Mephisto suggests that they aid the Emperor in this war, in return for which they can ask a gift of coastal lands for Faust to experiment with.

Faust protests that war is a wasteful pastime, and adds that he has no knowledge of military matters. Mephisto invokes the Three Mighty Men who fought with David and the Israelites against the Philistines. He assures Faust that with the help of these ancient heroes and his magic they will be successful. They set off for the Emperor's camp.

Commentary

The discussion on the origin of mountains is based on geological theories current in Goethe's time, but also illustrates the theme of order arising out of chaos, which is the symbolic meaning of Faust's land reclamation project. In this scene Faust tells Mephisto that he has learned that activity is man's "natural element." His intense desire to reclaim the useless lands that are submerged beneath the sea is based on a moral aversion to inactivity and sterility. This new plan of Faust's is an important confirmation of God's optimistic view of human nature in the "Prologue in Heaven" and reflects a significant change in his outlook.

At this point it may seem like a moral regression for Faust to accept Mephisto's offer of assistance, but since Mephisto's magical aid in the war will be intended to get land for this worthwhile project, it can also be related to the theme of order from chaos and illustrates the principle that even destructive forces can be harnessed for constructive ends. The most important point of this scene is that as a result of his uplifting experiences in Greece and his exposure to noble ideals, Faust has developed a more mature and vigorous moral sense. He is resolved to enter into a struggle with Nature itself to assert the dominance of human order over unrestrained chaos.

MOUNTAIN FOOTHILLS

The Emperor and his officers are in their headquarters discussing their dangerous position. Just as the Emperor turns the command of the army over to a more competent aide, Faust enters the royal tent and offers his assistance. He promises to help win the battle with the aid of his friends. The offer is accepted, the battle is fought, and the Emperor's forces are victorious. Mephisto and his magic play an important part in winning the victory.

Commentary

Faust's wise assignments during the battle of the Three Mighty Men, who represent Youth, Maturity, and Old Age, shows that all human talents are useful if well organized. The victory is won with the aid of Mephisto's magic, by virtue of which Nature is made to fight alongside the Emperor's army. This symbolizes Goethe's belief in the natural vitality of the Germanic peoples, and again asserts the beneficial uses to which destructive or neutral forces can be put by wise and systematic planning.

THE RIVAL EMPEROR'S TENT

After the battle the Emperor's troops carry off booty from the defeated enemy's camp. The Emperor and his courtiers enter his former rival's tent, and the sovereign distributes rewards to his loyal followers. The Emperor and the Archbishop argue about the morality of accepting diabolical help in the battle and the size of the share of loot to which the Church is entitled. The Emperor is forced to submit to the prelate's greedy demands because of the Church's great power. Afterwards he rewards Faust by giving him a large strip of coastal land, most of which is under water, and which everyone considers worthless.

Commentary

This scene reiterates Goethe's low opinion of the established Church, which has already been noted in the Commentary to Part One. The Emperor's indiscriminate rewarding of his courtiers and his neglect of his kingdom's real problems emphasizes the decadence of his Empire and any other human institution that is not organized according to sound and harmonious moral principles. In payment for his services, the Emperor gives Faust a large strip of what he thinks is worthless land. This is an additional demonstration of the Emperor's lack of imagination and good sense. It also serves to call attention to Faust's courage and dedication in attempting to reclaim the land for human use.

ACT V

OPEN COUNTRY

Faust's project, though not yet completed, has been successful. Philemon and Baucis, an old couple who live in the area, tell a wandering stranger about Faust's amazing achievements. It is also revealed that Faust is determined to own all the land in the region. They have refused to sell him the little cottage where they have spent their lives together, although he has offered them a great estate in exchange. The wanderer leaves and the two old people go to pray.

Commentary

Faust's great project, an achievement that is of widespread and permanent value to mankind, is seen through the eyes of a simple peasant couple. Their view shows that Faust's new world of power and prosperity possesses elements that menace the peaceful and humble way of life that they have enjoyed for so long. This may be an effect of Faust's continued reliance on Mephisto's demonic help. The couple's prayer in the chapel to the "old God" is a symbolic expression of resistance to Faust's new regime. The names Philemon and Baucis evoke an idyllic old Greek lengend in which a couple with the same names offered hospitality to Zeus and Hermes when the gods were travelling through the earth incognito. It is an ironic portent of events to come, but also definitively establishes the old people's virtue and innocence.

PALACE

Faust, now more than one hundred years old, broods in his palace garden about his failure to acquire the old couple's house and orchard. Mephisto and the Three Mighty Men return from a pirating expedition and land at the new port that Faust has built. They report the success of their voyage to him. He orders them to evict Philemon and Baucis from their cottage and secure the property for him.

Commentary

Faust is beginning to feel uncertain about his relationship with Mephisto and about the wisdom of having unleashed the evil forces which he allowed the devil to put to work in his behalf to help complete the project. Now they are slipping out of his control and are misusing the fruits of his labor, as is shown by the piratical expeditions that sail from his newly built port. Mephisto's reference to Biblical parallels to Faust's desire for the cottage, indicates the devil's belief that great human achievements cannot be accomplished without the unjust use of power, but this is not a fair interpretation of the feelings that are bothering Faust. The innocent and peaceful lives of Philemon and Baucis make him feel guilty and uneasy. Faust's comment that their cottage is situated on high, "original" ground, *i.e.* land not created by his drainage project, and his annoyance when he hears the bells from the chapel where they are praying, shows that he resents the natural life enjoyed by Philemon and Baucis because he is unable to participate in it. He believes foolishly that the possession of their land will satisfy his moral craving and bring him the peace he desires.

DEEP NIGHT

Faust learns to his sorrow that Mephisto and the Three Mighty Men have carried out his orders with more violence than he intended. Philemon and Baucis and their wanderer friend have been killed, and the house and orchard which Faust coveted have been burned. Faust is overcome by remorse and anger at this miscarriage of his plans. Left alone, he begins to feel strange premonitions.

Commentary

Faust had earlier justified to himself his plan to evict the old couple from their home by the rationalization that he would give them another house at a different location. Now he is genuinely sorry for what has happened and realizes that he is completely responsible for their deaths, even though this had not been the intent of the orders he gave Mephisto. This is the first time that Faust has taken on himself the full blame for the evil consequences of his acts and is a major step in his personal moral development.

MIDNIGHT

Immediately afterwards, while alone in his room, Faust is accosted by four grey hags who have risen from the smoke of the burning cottage. They are Want, Debt, Distress, and Care. The first three cannot reach him, but he is unable to resist Care, who warns him of the coming of her brother Death. In his conversation with Care, Faust tells her that he cannot become free until he releases himself from his dependence on Mephisto's magic power. He also says that he has learned that man should be concerned only with what is legitimately attainable in human life and should not seek after impossible things. Care tells Faust that man is unable to find peace in life, but she is unable to frighten him. In a final effort to weaken his resolution she breathes on him and makes him blind, but Faust remains determined to complete his great project in the short time left before his death.

Commentary

Faust has been rapidly coming to a state of moral regeneration as a result of meditations on his experiences caused by the needless deaths of Philemon and Baucis. Care's visit was an unsuccessful effort to deflect him from such thoughts. Faust's loss of sight does not alter his resolution to complete his task because he is now concerned only with spiritual and not material or physical things. He has at last rejected his constant obsession about his own destiny, and by so doing has begun to find himself through service to others and active leadership in humanity's struggle to build a better world.

THE GREAT OUTER-COURT OF THE PALACE

A gang of Lemures (a species of monkey, but also a name for a type of ghost) under the supervision of Mephistopheles works at digging Faust's grave. The blind Faust comes out and overhears the sound of their shovels. He thinks that they are continuing the work on his project. Faust is filled with a proud vision of the prosperity and happiness of the people who will someday inhabit the reclaimed lands. He is self-reliant and confident despite his impending death as he describes the utopian future he visualizes. As he speaks he utters the words of the bargain made in Part One, "Stay, thou art so fair," but he intends them in relation to the future in which he sees the fruition of his dreams and work and not to the present moment. After saying these last words Faust collapses dead in the arms of the Lemures, who lay him on the ground beside the grave. Mephisto has ignored the context of Faust's statement and complacently assumes that he has won Faust's soul.

Commentary

Mephisto is concerned only with the terms of the pact in a strict legalistic sense and does not realize that the most significant factor is that Faust's soul has never been surrendered to him. Faust's victory over Care has resulted in a personal reformation that will, in the eyes of God, outweigh all the years he lived in moral error. The deaths of Gretchen, Euphorion, Philemon, and Baucis have taught Faust the duty of self-surrender. Just before his own death he finally discovered that which he was seeking—the meaning of his relationship with the rest of humanity, past, present, and future, and the joy of participation in the continuous constructive activity that permeates the universe.

BURIAL SCENE

While the Lemures bury Faust, Mephisto and a horde of devils wait to take his soul into custody. Suddenly the heavens open and a host of angels appear. They strew the grave with rose petals and the air is filled with the sound of their singing. Mephisto argues with them as they descend to the grave, but to no avail. Chanting a hymn about the healing truth of Love and the bliss that awaits purified souls in communion with the "All-in-All," the angels take Faust's body in their arms and carry it up to Heaven.

Mephisto realizes that he has been defeated, and that his scheme to win Faust's soul has failed because of his own mishandling. He attributes his defeat to his failure to take into account the power of Love and the strange ways in which it manifests itself.

Commentary

The hymn sung by the angels explains that souls who have purged themselves of foreign elements and are in harmony with God and their fellow creatures, and with the Love that motivates the entire universe, are entitled to receive God's grace.

MOUNTAIN-GORGES, FOREST, CLIFF, WILDERNESS

A chorus of holy men, among whom are Pater Ecstaticus, Pater Profundis, and Pater Seraphicus, sing the praises of Heaven. A host of angels enters, bearing the immortal remains of Faust. Other angelic choirs join in the singing. They are joined by the spirits of children who died in innocence at birth, and by three famous penitant women from the Bible, Magna Peccatrix, Mulier Samaritana, and Maria Aegyptica, who prepare the way for the entrance of Una Poenitentium, once called Gretchen. Doctor Marianus chants the praises of the Blessed Virgin, the Queen of Heaven. The Penitent who was formerly Gretchen expresses her ecstasy that Faust has been saved. The Mater Gloriosa calls upon Gretchen and Faust to rise to the higher sphere. Doctor Marianus prostrates himself in adoration of the Virgin and the salvation which her grace brings. The scene closes as a Mystical Chorus chants a hymn which says that all things are symbols of the great Eternal Reality and that through love the spirit of Eternal Womanhood leads mankind to Truth and Salvation.

Commentary

Although there are many elements of Catholic religious symbolism in this scene, they were adopted by Goethe only because he saw in them a means to give tangible expression to his beliefs, and do not demonstrate his adherence to orthodox Christianity.

The three holy fathers in the first chorus represent three saints who manifested in their lives different aspects of Faust's longing for oneness with the universe. The spirits of the children who died at birth achieved salvation because of their experience, whereas Faust has been saved as a result of the heightened knowledge and insight gained through great experience. The presence of all these figures in the place to which Faust's soul is brought, indicates that striving for union with the ultimate is part of the essential character of all life, and is the basis from which immortality arises.

The angels who bring in Faust's soul reveal that he has not yet attained Salvation. Now that he has been liberated from sin, however, he will commence his purification and will free himself from the remaining traces of his earthly existence. He will be reborn, in a sense, like the spirits of the innocent children, and with them will rise to the higher levels of Salvation. Doctor Marianus is the leader of the community of holy men, and on earth was a teacher of the doctrine and meaning of the Blessed Virgin. The three penitent women pray to the Virgin in behalf of Gretchen, just as the children are praying for Faust, and Gretchen is praying for Faust. This indicates that Salvation is most surely gained by altruistic concern for others, which is also the message of Faust's great project in behalf of humanity.

All the inhabitants of Heaven seem joined together in a single harmonious adoration of the central glory represented by the Virgin, and all are in a state of motion in which the universal law of action is fulfilled. The striving which characterized Faust's life will be continued, but in another sphere and another form. He will be led and helped in his new journey toward beatitude by Gretchen, just as she helped him in Part One to participate in life's joys for the first time, and together they will reach a new summit of bliss in adoration and union with the spirit of the cosmos.

In the drama's final lines, the Mystical Chorus explains that all things are merely symbols of the eternal verity, that the earthly reflects the heavenly, and that in Heaven the unattainable becomes possible for the souls of the blessed. The Eternal Womanhood which is the spirit of the Mater Gloriosa is a symbol of the divine love and forgiveness that nurtures all man's acts and accomplishments and which inspires his spiritual development, and the creative principle that gives meaning and function to all elements of the universe.

The poetic expression of these metaphysical ideas in the final scene sums up the philosophical meaning of Goethe's powerful drama. It indicates that Faust has been admitted to Heaven because of his positive spiritual attitude and his constant striving, rather than any moral evaluation and weighing of his life. The drama has also demonstrated the delusions and tragedies that are caused by living in association with evil, negation, and frustration, through Faust's unhappy experiences while under the influence of Mephistopheles. The final message of *Faust* is that life's purpose is to live; that is, only through acceptance of life and continued effort to maintain life is one able to find immortality. Faust was victorious over Mephisto because, despite his errors and frustrations, he never lost his faith in life's essence and continued, in the face of adversity, to search for something higher than himself which alone could give his existence meaning.

THE PRINCIPAL CHARACTERS

Faust

Faust is a learned German scholar who, at the beginning of the poem, is disillusioned and demoralized by his inability to discover life's true meaning. Despite his worldly accomplishments he is assailed by frustration because the traditional and conventional modes of thought that he has mastered cannot help him to discern a coherent purpose or form behind all the numerous and varied phenomena of life and nature. In all his adventures in both parts of the poem Faust is driven by the need to perceive, without the aid of revelation, a rational order as the framework of the world in which he lives. Because of this desire and its effect on his outlook, Faust's philosophical dilemma has been held by many to typify the alienation of man in the modern world.

In the poem, Faust is intended by Goethe to represent all mankind. He possesses all the qualities of human ability and motivation, and is, in effect, an archetypal "everyman" figure. All Faust's virtues and faults, his strengths and weaknesses, are magnified so that his adventures and moral development are presented on a scale that is larger than life. This gives his story a stature and dignity equal to its cosmic theme, and makes Faust's life a mirror of human existence which all men may learn from. Although he is granted salvation at the end of the poem, Faust is a great tragic hero. His tragedy has been described as that of "titanism," for he tries to step beyond the limitations of humanity to seek that which is not given to mankind to know or experience. Because of this his career is a constant series of disappointments and frustrations, but Faust never loses heart and continues the struggle. Ultimately he comes to understand the meaning of life and is received into Heaven, a conclusion that is meant to be an inspiration to all those who read the poem.

Mephistopheles

Goethe's Mephisto is very different from the crude devil of medieval legend and the original Faust story. He is a cultivated, witty, and cynical exponent of materialism and nihilism, and preaches a sophisticated doctrine of philosophical negation. Mephisto's most outstanding characteristic is skepticism; the inability to believe in anything. Ironically, although Mephisto represents evil, he can also be an unconscious force for good. This is first indicated by his presence at the side of God in the "Prologue in Heaven," which implies that evil is an accepted and natural part of God's universal system. This view is emphasized by Mephisto's relationship with Faust. Through his unrelenting efforts to corrupt and destroy the protagonist, Mephisto forces him to react with positive action, and is thus the agent of his ultimate salvation.

Mephisto's specific observations about humanity and the universe are usually right, because it is easy for him in his role as a "cosmic outsider" to discern real faults in the established system. At the same time, however, his vision is narrow and his total outlook is wrong. As a result he never fully understands Faust, makes inadequate plans for the seduction of his victim, and is finally defeated by Love, a force which he never recognized or comprehended.

On another level Mephisto represents the negative elements in Faust's own personality. This is why the devil and his intended victim are able to remain so close throughout both parts of the poem, and why, at certain points, like the Walpurgis Night in Part One where Faust's evil side is dominant, Mephisto is able to come so close to winning him. Mephisto fails, however, because he cannot understand or appreciate the positive sides of Faust's character (or human nature in general), and does not attribute any powers of resistance or resilience to Faust in the struggle for his soul.

Gretchen

Gretchen is a simple, innocent, and pious maiden who develops into a figure of genuine tragic stature. She is essentially pure and innocent, but becomes a willing victim of Faust's seduction due to loneliness, inexperience, resentment of her mother's strictness, and an idealistic naïveté that leads her to assume that Faust's love will be as permanent and unselfish as her own. In a sense her crimes are the result of her innocence, although this does not negate her own responsibility for her downfall. Gretchen has an innate religious sense, and one critic has called her the only true Christian in the poem. This is why she is able to accept her punishment at the end of Part One, and also explains her intuitive aversion to Mephisto and her insight that Faust's plan for escape would be morally unbearable. Gretchen is admitted to Heaven at the close of Part One because, despite her acts, she was never motivated by evil intentions and had acted according to her natural instincts. Although in Goethe's view, positive action is better than negative action, nonetheless humans are basically creative and good, and action is better than non-action, so this entitled Gretchen to an opportunity to find salvation.

Gretchen appears again in the final scene of Part Two as Una Poenitentium, a penitent woman. While Faust's earthly adventures have continued, she has purged herself of sin and has progressed toward the attainment of ultimate Salvation. Her final entrance to Paradise is dependent on the aid of Love, which for Gretchen is represented by Faust. She welcomes him into Heaven because the highest and purest fulfilment of both of them can only be achieved together. At the end of Part One Gretchen's refusal to leave the prison prevented Faust from becoming absolutely dependent on Mephisto's power, and thus made his ultimate salvation possible.

At the end of Part Two her sacrifice is rewarded by the joy of guiding Faust to the highest level of Paradise and, with the aid of his Love, herself rising to the highest sphere.

SPECIAL PROBLEMS

THE RELATIONSHIP OF THE TWO PARTS OF FAUST

Goethe himself once described the differences between the two sections of his poem by saying:

> The first part is almost entirely subjective; it proceeded entirely from a perplexed, impassioned individual, and his semi-darkness is probably highly pleasing to mankind. But, in the second part, there is scarcely anything of the subjective; here is seen a higher, broader, clearer, more passionless world, and he who has not looked about him and had some experience, will not know what to make of it.

The two parts of the poem are essential elements of a single whole, but their relationship is an indirect and metaphorical one. They present alternative views of the human yearning for truth and fulfilment by exploring different aspects of this same problem. Part One is concerned mainly with highly personal experience, while Part Two treats society as a whole, and Faust develops from a single individual into a symbolic figure who represents the striving spirit of man in the modern world. This distinction between the two parts of the poem has been compared by some critics to the medieval philosophical conception of the microcosm and macrocosm; Part One is said to portray the "small world" of inner experience and Part Two the "great world" of social institutions, ideological systems and intellectual institutions. Thus, both sections mirror different aspects of the same philosophical theme.

The second part of *Faust* is less fragmentary than the first in structure, and adheres to the conventional dramatic organization of acts and scenes, but in fact it is far more disorganized and difficult to follow. In addition, it has many complicated and abstruse allegorical elements, often drawn from Classical mythology. There are many parallels between episodes and characters in the two parts, and comparison of these offers heightened insights into the poem's meaning. The Classical Walpurgis Night, for example, is a counterpart to the medieval one in the first part. It has often been pointed out, also, that the general tone of Part One is Gothic and Romantic, while that of Part Two is Classic and staid. Part One is often read as an individual and self-contained work, but this approach overemphasizes Gretchen's tragedy and hinders the reader from grasping the poem's full meaning. Only by studying the two sections of *Faust* in conjunction is it possible to fully appreciate what Goethe intended and to understand the philosophical message he was communicating.

THEATRICAL PRODUCTIONS OF FAUST

Although Goethe was an accomplished dramatist and wrote *Faust* in dramatic form, it is unlikely that he actually intended it to be presented on the stage. The work's full meaning and effect would be lost in a theatrical production since an understanding of *Faust* requires intensive study and rereading. In addition, it would take more than twenty hours to perform both parts of *Faust,* a period in which it would be impossible to maintain dramatic suspense and audience interest; and a total of 38 stage settings, six of which have multiple levels, are required.

Part One alone has been performed on several occasions and provided the basis for the libretto of Gounod's famous opera, *Faust.* As has been pointed out above, however, Part One is not an independent work and does not become clear unless presented in concert with Part Two. Although Part One is more stageworthy than Part Two, and requires fewer deletions for presentation on stage, even Goethe himself made important cuts in it when it was performed at the State Theatre in Weimar. There have been few attempts at production of Part Two, and generally in these only fragments of the whole work, like the "Helena" tragedy of Act III, have been put on.

An accurate view of *Faust* sees it as "monumental drama," a work of epic proportions that must be compared with other works of the same stature and intensity, like Dante's *Divine Comedy* and

Milton's *Paradise Lost,* rather than with works that resemble it only superficially because of their dramatic form. It is worth noting, however, that *Faust* has many inherently "theatrical" qualities for it is permeated by dramatic action—the progressive development and dynamic maturation of its central character.

THE MAIN THEME OF FAUST— A METAPHYSICAL QUEST

Despite the complicated plot and the numerous philosophical and literary digressions, a single main theme is evident throughout both parts of *Faust* and provides a unifying structure for the entire work. This is Faust's dissatisfaction with the finite limits on man's potential—the driving force that motivates him in all his adventures as he strives to find a way to pass beyond the boundaries set on human experience and perception.

The whole poem is colored by this sense of dissatisfaction and frustrated striving although its character changes as the story progresses. At the beginning Faust is in a state of negative dissatisfaction, in which he contemplates suicide and willingly accepts the terms of a pact that would terminate his life at its highest point of achievement. Further on in the poem Faust's dissatisfaction becomes a positive dynamic force that leads him eventually to find a form of personal fulfilment, but his whole life is marked by disappointment since he does not achieve peace of mind before his death, except in an inspired vision of the future.

Closely related to this theme is another one that is first established in the conversation between the Lord and Mephistopheles in the "Prologue in Heaven," and which is indirectly referred to at other points in the poem. The Lord acknowledges to Mephisto that it is natural for man to fall into error, but asserts that despite this he remains able to make moral distinctions. Thus the issue at stake in the wager made by God and the devil is whether Faust, as a representative of all mankind, will continue to be able to perceive the difference between good and evil, regardless of temptation and personal sinfulness. In the Lord's view of human nature, it is admitted that man is imperfect and that his ability is limited, but it is also assumed that human imperfection is not absolute and that man's potential for good can be cultivated. In this sense Faust's dissatisfaction and striving may be interpreted as an unconscious manifestation of man's potential to improve himself, even though Faust is frequently misguided by his obsessive efforts to rise beyond man's natural sphere. It is because Faust does retain his sense of right and wrong, and because his eyes are constantly focused on a vision of something higher than himself, which is ultimately the cause of his frustrated despair, that he is finally rewarded by entrance into Heaven.

Considered in this philosophical context, Faust's many adventures all communicate the message that to find happiness man must learn to conquer the lower elements of his nature and live constructively within the framework imposed on him. The concluding scenes of the drama and God's statements in the "Prologue" illustrate that good may arise out of evil, but they do not advocate that evil should be sought after as a means for finding the good. The moral doctrine that Goethe puts forward in *Faust* teaches that the essential feature of all existence and the law that governs the universe is one of untiring, purposeful, and positive effort, and that man can find his place in life only through striving to participate in this vast cosmic movement, although of necessity in terms appropriate to his human capabilities.

Faust's life has its tragic aspects, for his career is marked by a long series of crimes and frustrated illusions and he dies without ever having found complete personal satisfaction, but one recent critic has called Goethe's work "a poem of supreme optimism." This is because the story has a positive and confident conclusion which holds out the inspiring hope that men can find personal gratification in fruitful activity and acceptance of the laws that govern the universe. Faust's long, hard path to Salvation is not intended as an example for others to follow. His experience reveals the pitfalls and false turns that are dangers along the road and is meant to encourage readers in finding their own way to harmony with the cosmic order. The hymn of the Mystical Chorus in the final scene of the drama crystallizes this theme that human fulfilment is the result of communion with the spirit of creativity and action that permeates all life when it says, "Eternal Womanhood/Leads us on high."

FAUST AND ROMANTICISM

The Romantic Movement in Europe, which began in the later years of the 18th century, came to dominate literature and thought during the first part of the 19th century. This movement was characterized by the intense assertion of freedom and imagination, by the glorification of individualism and the virtue of untamed nature, and by a melancholy and sentimental oversensibility. Typical Romantic poets in English literature include Wordsworth, Byron, and Shelley.

An extreme form of this movement known as *Sturm und Drang* ("Storm and Stress") existed in Germany for several decades and found expression in a great outburst of literary activity. It was marked by a general mood of rebellion against convention and constraint of all kinds, by impetuosity and a strong belief in the validity of natural emotions and feelings. While still a young man Goethe was hailed as the leader of this movement after the publication of his novel, *The Sorrows of Young Werther,* in 1774.

Many aspects of the style and content of *Faust,* particularly those sections of it which existed in the earliest versions like the *Urfaust* of 1773, seem influenced by the Romantic outlook. Mostly in Part One, these include certain of Faust's expressions of suffering, the wild setting of scenes like "Forest and Cavern," Faust's definition of God, and the attitude regarding the divine forgiveness of Gretchen because of her obedience to her natural instincts. As Goethe's philosophical outlook developed, however, he passed beyond the confines of Romanticism to a broader and more comprehensive understanding of life. His mature view of the benefits and defects of Romanticism is best illustrated in the Euphorion episode in Act III of Part Two. Familiarity with the Romantic Movement is an important factor in understanding *Faust,* but to fully appreciate Goethe's poem it is necessary to approach it unemcumbered by the ideology of any particular school of thought.

68

SUGGESTIONS FOR FURTHER READING

Ancelet-Hustache, Jeanne. *Goethe*. New York, 1960 (paperback).

Atkins, Stuart. *Goethe's Faust: A Literary Analysis*. Cambridge, Mass., 1958.

Butler, E. M. *The Fortunes of Faust*. Cambridge, Eng., 1952.

Enright, Dennis J. *Commentary on Goethe's Faust*. Norfolk, Conn., 1949.

Fairley, Barker. *A Study of Goethe*. New York, 1961 (paperback).

Gillies, Alexander. *Goethe's Faust: An Interpretation*. Oxford, 1957.

Hatfield, Henry. *Goethe: A Critical Introduction*. New York, 1963 (paperback).

Santayana, George. *Three Philosophical Poets*. New York, 1960 (paperback).

Schweitzer, Albert. *Goethe*. Boston, 1948 (paperback).

Vietor, Karl. *Goethe the Poet*. Cambridge, Mass., 1949.

_____. *Goethe the Thinker*. Cambridge, Mass., 1950.

Wilkinson, E. M., and L. A. Willoughby. *Goethe, Poet and Thinker*. London, 1962.

SAMPLE EXAMINATION QUESTIONS

1. What is the purpose and meaning of the "Prelude in the Theatre"?

2. Discuss the meaning of the "Prologue in Heaven" and its similarity to the Biblical Book of Job.

3. In what ways does Goethe's Mephisto differ from traditional portrayals of the devil? What philosophical principle does he represent? What is his function in the divine plan and in regard to Faust's ultimate attainment of salvation?

4. Discuss the characterization of Faust and the spiritual dilemma that causes his despair at the beginning of the poem. In what ways is his role that of an archetypal symbolic figure? Why is he willing to associate himself with Mephistopheles? What prevents him from committing suicide?

5. Analyze Faust's religious beliefs as they are explained by him to Gretchen. Do Faust's ideas on this subject reflect those of Goethe?

6. What is the attitude toward the Church and institutionalized religion that Goethe reveals in both parts of Faust? Cite scenes that support your answer.

7. Discuss the characterization and function of Gretchen. Why is she a tragic figure? What responsibility does she have for her own downfall? Why is she received into Heaven at the end of Part One?

8. What is the symbolic meaning of the "Walpurgis Night" scene? What change in Faust's outlook becomes evident in this scene?

9. Is the "Walpurgis Night's Dream" episode related to the rest of the drama? What, if anything, is its function? Why is the scene that follows it written in prose?

10. Why is Faust unwilling to separate himself from Mephistopheles in the Prison scene at the end of Part One? Why does he refuse Gretchen's advice to ask for God's mercy?

11. What are the terms of the pact between Mephisto and Faust? What is the significance of the change in the original wording that Faust makes? What does he really have at stake?

12. Do Goethe's doctrines about sin, salvation, and the nature of the universe as presented in *Faust* conform to orthodox Christian theology? What use does Goethe make of Christian symbolism in *Faust?*

13. Discuss the relationship between the two parts of *Faust*. In what ways do they differ? In what ways do they serve a similar and interconnected purpose?

14. Discuss the functions of Wagner, Martha, and Valentine.

15. Discuss the function and meaning of Homonculus. What is the symbolic meaning of his creation by Wagner? What role does he play in the "Classical Walpurgis Night"?

16. Discuss the use of allegory and Classical mythology in Part Two, citing scenes in which this use is most prominent.

17. Act III of Part Two, the "Helena," is often treated by critics as an independent unit within the larger drama. Discuss its style, the meaning of Faust's love for Helen, and its philosophical message concerning the synthesis of Classical and Romantic culture.

18. Discuss the characterization of Euphorion. What does his birth symbolize and what is the meaning of his strange and premature death? What English poet does he resemble?

19. What is the symbolic meaning of Faust's land reclamation project? Why does it reflect an important change in his moral outlook?

20. Why does Faust assist the Emperor in the war? Who are the Three Mighty Men and what is the significance of Mephisto's use of magic in the battle?

21. Why does Faust crave the cottage of Philemon and Baucis? Why is he sorry after their deaths? Why is he visited by the spirit representing Care?

22. Does Faust undergo any kind of moral rejuvenation or change immediately before his death? Does he fulfil the terms of his pact with Mephisto?

23. What is the meaning of Faust's acceptance into Heaven? Why did Mephisto fail to win Faust's soul? What is the doctrine of "Eternal Womanhood" and who is Una Poenitentium?

24. Is *Faust* suitable for theatrical production? In what ways does it differ from the usual play? In what ways is it a tragedy, despite its happy ending?

25. Compare Christopher Marlowe's treatment of the Faust legend with that of Goethe.

26. In what ways does Faust change during the course of the drama? In what ways, if any, does he remain the same?

27. Part One of *Faust* is often treated as a work complete in itself. What misconceptions about Goethe's philosophical views and the ultimate ends of the main characters can this result in?

28. Discuss Goethe's life and his place in the history of German literature.

29. Identify: Microcosm, Macrocosm, Nicodemus, Arcadia, Doctor Marianus, Mater Gloriosa, Earth-Spirit, Harz Mountains, Pharsalus, Lisbeth, Phorkyas, Mater Dolorosa.

NOTES

THE METAMORPHOSIS
AND OTHER STORIES

NOTES

including
- *Life and Background*
- *Commentaries on the Stories*
- *Understanding Kafka*
- *Kafka's Jewish Influence*
- *Kafka—a "Religious" Writer?*
- *Kafka and Existentialism*
- *Review Questions*
- *Selected Bibliography*

by
Herberth Czermak, M.A.
Instructor
Amerika Institut, Vienna

Cliffs Notes

INCORPORATED

LINCOLN, NEBRASKA 68501

Editor	Consulting Editor
Gary Carey, M.A.	*James L. Roberts, Ph.D.*
University of Colorado	*Department of English*
	University of Nebraska

ISBN 0-8220-0700-2
© Copyright 1973
by
C. K. Hillegass
All Rights Reserved
Printed in U.S.A.

1990 Printing

Cliffs Notes, Inc.   Lincoln, Nebraska

CONTENTS

LIFE AND BACKGROUND 5

COMMENTARIES ON THE STORIES 12

"The Metamorphosis" 12
"The Judgment" 23
"A Hunger Artist" 33
"A Country Doctor" 39
"In the Penal Colony" 45
"The Hunter Gracchus" 53
"The Burrow" 57
"Investigations of a Dog" 62
"A Report to an Academy" 66
"The Great Wall of China" 69
"Josephine the Singer, or the Mouse Folk" 75

UNDERSTANDING KAFKA 78

KAFKA'S JEWISH INFLUENCE 83

KAFKA–A "RELIGIOUS" WRITER? 85

KAFKA AND EXISTENTIALISM 89

REVIEW QUESTIONS 94

SELECTED BIBLIOGRAPHY 96

Kafka's Stories Notes

LIFE AND BACKGROUND

Born in Prague in 1883, Franz Kafka is today considered the most important prose writer of the so-called Prague Circle, a loosely knit group of German-Jewish writers who contributed to the culturally fertile soil of Prague during the 1880s until after World War I. Yet from the Czech point of view, Kafka was German, and from the German point of view he was, above all, Jewish. In short, Kafka shared the fate of much of Western Jewry— people who were largely emancipated from their specifically Jewish ways and yet not fully assimilated into the culture of the countries where they lived. Although Kafka became extremely interested in Jewish culture after meeting a troupe of Yiddish actors in 1911, and although he began to study Hebrew shortly after that, it was not until late in his life that he became deeply interested in his heritage. His close relationship with Dora Dymant, his steady and understanding companion of his last years, contributed considerably toward this development. But even if Kafka had not been Jewish, it is hard to see how his artistic and religious sensitivity could have remained untouched by the ancient Jewish traditions of Prague which reached back to the city's tenth-century origin.

In addition to Kafka's German, Czech, and Jewish heritages, there was also the Austrian element into which Kafka had been born and in which he had been brought up. Prague was the major second capital of the Austrian Empire (after Vienna) since the early sixteenth century, and although Kafka was no friend of Austrian politics, it is important to emphasize this Austrian component of life in Prague because Kafka has too often been called a Czech writer—especially in America. Kafka's name is also grouped too often with German writers, which is accurate only in the sense that he belongs to the German-speaking world. Apart from that, however, it is about as meaningful as considering Faulkner an English novelist.

For his recurring theme of human alienation, Kafka is deeply indebted to Prague and his situation there as a social outcast, a victim of the friction between Czechs and Germans, Jews and non-Jews. To understand Kafka, it is important to realize that in Prague the atmosphere of medieval mysticism and Jewish orthodoxy lingered until after World War II, when the Communist regime began getting rid of most of its remnants. To this day, however, Kafka's tiny flat in Alchemists' Lane behind the towering Hradschin Castle is a major attraction for those in search of traces of Kafka. The haunting mood of Prague's narrow, cobblestoned streets, its slanted roofs, and its myriad backyards comes alive in the surreal settings of Kafka's stories. His simple, sober, and yet dense language is traced to the fact that in Prague the German language had been exposed to manifold Slavic influences for centuries and was virtually cut off from the mainstream language as spoken and written in Germany and Austria. Prague was a linguistic island as far as German was concerned, and while the Czech population of Prague doubled within the last two decades of the nineteenth century, the percentage of German Jews sank to a mere seven percent. The result was that Kafka actually wrote in a language which was on the verge of developing its own characteristics. This absence of any gap between the spoken and written word in his language is probably the secret behind the enormous appeal of his language, whose deceptive simplicity comes across in every decent translation.

Kafka's family situation was a reflection of his being a German-speaking Jew in a predominantly Slavic environment. The great socio-economic and educational differences between his father, Hermann Kafka, and his mother, Julie Löwy, were at the root of this complex situation. Kafka's father's whole life was shaped by his desperate and eventually successful attempt to break out of his poor Czech milieu and become accepted in the prestigious environment of German Prague; his mother, however, came from a wealthy German-Jewish bourgeois family. Throughout his lifetime, Franz Kafka could never extricate himself from the terrible friction between his parents which was caused, for the most part, by his tyrannical father. Kafka's only strong, positive ties with his family were with his favorite sister,

Ottla, who let him stay at her home and later helped him break off his relationship with Felice, his first fiancée. To one extent or another, all of Kafka's works bear the unmistakable imprint of the nerve-wracking struggle between his humility and hyper-sensitivity (his mother's heritage) and the crudity and super-ficiality of his father, who looked at his son's writing with indifference and, at times, with contempt. This total lack of un-derstanding and the absence of any home life worthy the name (young Franz was virtually brought up by a nurse) caused the boy's early seriousness and anxiety. As late as 1919, five years before his death, this lifelong trauma manifested itself in his *Letter to His Father* (almost a hundred pages, but never actually delivered), in which Kafka passionately accuses his father of intimidation and brutality. Although it will not do to reduce the complex art of Franz Kafka to its autobiographical elements, the significance of these elements in his work is indeed striking. His story "The Judgment" seems especially to be the direct re-sult of his deep-seated fear of his father.

Kafka is the classical painter of the estrangement of modern man, although he is never its apostle. As early as 1905, in his "Description of a Fight," Kafka already denied man's ability to obtain certainty through sensory perception and intellectual ef-fort because, according to him, these methods inevitably distort the nature of the Absolute by forcing it into their prefabricated structures. The resulting skepticism, of which he himself was to become the tragic victim, was the basis of his conviction that none of our fleeting impressions and accidental associations have a fixed counterpart in a "real" and stable world. There is no clear-cut boundary between reality and the realm of dreams, and if one of his characters appears to have found such a boundary, it quickly turns out that he has set it up merely as something to cling to in the face of chaos. The "real" world of phenomena de-velops its own logic and leaves Kafka's characters yearning for a firm metaphysical anchor which they never quite grasp.

At no time did Kafka seek refuge from his culturally and socially alienated situation by joining literary or social circles — something many of his fellow writers did. He remained an outcast, suffering from the consequences of his partly self-imposed seclusion, and yet welcoming it for the sake of literary productivity. Anxious although he was to use his positions, as well as his engagements to Felice Bauer and Julie Wohryzek, as a means to gain recognition for his writing, his life story is, nevertheless, one long struggle against his feelings of guilt and inferiority.

The one person who could and did help him was Max Brod, whom he met in 1902 and who was to become not only his editor but also an intimate friend. The numerous letters which Kafka wrote to him are a moving testimony of their mutual appreciation. Because of Brod's encouragement, Kafka began to read his first literary efforts to small private audiences long before he was recognized as a significant writer. With Brod, Kafka traveled to Italy, Weimar (where Goethe and Schiller had written), and Paris; later, Brod introduced him into the literary circles of Prague. In short, Brod helped Kafka to fend off an increasingly threatening self-isolation. Most significantly for posterity, it was Brod who, contrary to Kafka's express request, did not burn the manuscripts which Kafka left behind; instead, he became their enthusiastic editor.

If Kafka had a strong inclination to isolate himself, this does not mean he was indifferent to what was going on around him. Especially in the years until 1912, Kafka familiarized himself with some of the far-reaching new ideas of the day. At a friend's house, he attended lectures and discussions on Einstein's theory of relativity, Planck's quantum theory, and Freud's psychoanalytical experiments. He was also interested in politics, especially the nationalistic aspirations of the Czechs in the Austrian Empire. In his function as a lawyer at the Workers' Insurance Company, he was confronted daily with the social situation of workers, and toward the end of World War I, he even composed a brochure on the plight of the proletariat. This is, in part, proof that Franz Kafka was not the melancholy dreamer of nightmares, isolated in his ivory tower in Prague—a view still commonly held today.

It was at Max Brod's home that Kafka met Felice Bauer in 1912. This encounter plunged him into a frustrating relationship for many years, oscillating between engagements and periods of complete withdrawal. "The Judgment" (1912) is a document of this encounter. Having literally poured it out in one long sitting, Kafka came to regard it as an illustration of how one should always write; it was the subject of his first public reading. At that time, Kafka was already filling a detailed diary, full of reflections and parables as a means of self-analysis. The same year, 1912, he wrote "The Metamorphosis," one of the most haunting treatments of human alienation, and most of the fragmentary novel *Amerika*. According to his own conviction, his literary productivity reached a peak at precisely the time when his insecurity and anxiety over whether or not to marry Felice reached a climax. For the first time, the deep-seated conflict between his yearning for the simple life of a married man and his determination not to succumb to it became critical.

More and more, Kafka's writing began to deal with *Angst* (anxiety, anguish), probably because of the sustained anxiety induced by his domineering father and by the problem of whether or not to break away from his bachelorhood existence. Toward the end of "The Judgment," and in "In the Penal Colony," as well as in *The Trial* and *The Castle*, the father figure assumes the mysterious qualities of an ineffable god. Suffering, punishment, judgment, trial—all these are manifestations of Kafka's rigorous, ethical mind. The philosophy of Franz Brentano, to which he was exposed at the university, intensified his interest in these themes. The essence of this philosophy is that since emotions and concepts cannot sufficiently explain moral action, personal judgment alone must determine it; thorough self-analysis is the only prerequisite for such a total autonomy of personal judgment, a view which Kafka came to exercise almost to the point of self-destruction.

Kafka's fascination with these themes received new impetus when he began to read the Danish philosopher Sören Kierkegaard in 1913. As radical a skeptic as Kafka and equally religious by temperament, Kierkegaard envisages man as caught in the dilemma of wanting to comprehend Divinity with the altogether inadequate tools of rationality. Since God's transcendence is absolute for him, Kierkegaard sees no way of solving this dilemma except by abandoning intellectual pursuit and venturing a "leap into faith." Kafka's plea for man to "enter into the law," stated most explicitly in the parable "Before the Law" (in *The Trial*), deals with this dilemma. The difference is that Kierkegaard is cornered by the overwhelming presence of God forcing him to make decisions. In Kafka's parable, his hero wants to enter the first gate of the palace — that is, "the law" — but he dies because he does not exert sufficient will to enter and leaves all possible decisions to the gatekeeper; Kafka's searching man has no divine guidance to show him the way, and the situation he faces is one of total uncertainty and despair. Antithetically, Kierkegaard's radical skepticism results in faith.

Kafka and Kierkegaard have been called existentialists, and though this label has some merits, it should nevertheless be used very carefully. Both men were fascinated by the theme of moral integrity in the face of freedom of choice and were convinced that man lives meaningfully only to the extent which he realizes himself. In this connection, it is interesting to know that Kafka felt close to Kierkegaard because of the latter's lifelong unresolved relationship to his fiancée. The problem dominated Kierkegaard's life and work as much as Kafka's life and work was dominated by his relationships with Felice Bauer (to whom he was engaged twice — in 1914 and 1917), Julie Wohryzek (engaged in 1919), and Milena Jesenska (1920-22).

Perhaps more than any other story, Kafka's "In the Penal Colony" (1914) reflects his reaction to the outbreak of World War I, a feeling of sheer horror as well as disgust with the politicians in power. The result was a renewed fascination with Schopenhauer and Dostoevsky, whose extolment of physical pain finds expression in a variety of ways. Near this same time, Kafka began working on *The Trial*, about which he remarked that its ghastly thoughts devoured him in much the same way as did his thoughts about Felice. The novel is an elaborate and heavily autobiographical fantasy of punishment: on the eve of his thirty-first birthday, Joseph K. is executed; on the evening of his own thirty-first birthday, Kafka decided to travel to Berlin to break off his first engagement with Felice. Symptomatically for Kafka, this novel remained fragmentary—as did his other two, *Amerika* and *The Castle*. "A Report to an Academy" and the fragmentary "The Hunter Gracchus" followed, and in 1919 several stories were published under the title *A Country Doctor*. The title story is a symbolic description of modern man living outside a binding universal order and brought to death by sensuality and the aimlessness of the forces working within him. This volume contains perhaps Kafka's best parable on the nature of absurdity, "The Imperial Message." It is a terrifying description of how important messages, ordered at the top level to save men at the bottom, never stand a chance of getting through the manifold obstacles of bureaucracy. "The Imperial Message" is an interesting reversal of "Before the Law," where the lowly searcher never even gets beyond the first gate (the lowest obstacle) in his attempt to proceed to higher insights. In both cases, the human need to communicate is frustrated, and the inevitable result is alienation and subsequent death.

These stories were written during a time when Kafka, engaged once again to Felice, was finding a measure of stability again. Although he was determined this time to give up his insurance position and to use his time writing, he soon realized that this effort was an escape, as had been his (rejected) application to be drafted into the army. Kafka was to remain much like the roving hunter Gracchus, burdened with the knowledge that he could not gain inner poise by drowning the fundamental questions of existence in the comforts of married life.

In 1917 Kafka was stricken with tuberculosis, an illness which he was convinced was only the physical manifestation of his disturbed inner condition. For years he had fought hopeless battles for and against marriage (he had a son with Grete Bloch, a friend of Felice's, but never knew about him); during this time, he continually sought to justify his suffering by writing. Now he gave up. "The world—Felice is its representative—and my innermost self have torn apart my body in unresolvable opposition," he wrote in his diary. His suffering was alleviated by the fact that he could spend many months in the country, either in sanatoriums or with his favorite sister, Ottla. These months brought with them a new freedom from his work as a lawyer and, for the second time, from Felice.

In 1922, Kafka wrote "A Hunger Artist," "Investigations of a Dog," and most of his third novel, *The Castle*. Highly autobiographical like all of his works, the hero of "A Hunger Artist" starves himself because he cannot find the spiritual food he requires. The investigations of the chief dog in the story of the same name reflect Kafka's own literary attempts to impart at least a notion of the universal to his readers. In *The Castle*, K. becomes entangled in the snares of a castle's "celestial" hierarchy as hopelessly as does Joseph K. in the "terrestrial" bureaucracy of *The Trial*. All these stories originated in the years 1921 and 1922, years when Kafka lived under the strong influence of Milena Jesenska, to whom he owed his renewed strength to write. Although in many respects different from him (she was gentile, unhappily married, and much younger), the extremely sensitive Milena could justly claim "to have known his anxiety before having known Kafka himself," as she put it. Forever afraid of any deeper involvement with Milena, Kafka eventually stopped seeing her. That he gave her his diaries and several manuscripts, however, is proof of his deep commitment to her.

COMMENTARIES

"THE METAMORPHOSIS"
(DIE VERWANDLUNG)

Kafka wrote "The Metamorphosis" at the end of 1912, soon after he finished "The Judgment," and it is worth noting that the two stories have much in common: a businessman and bachelor like Georg Bendemann of "The Judgment," Gregor Samsa is confronted with an absurd fate in the form of a "gigantic insect," while Georg is confronted by absurdity in the person of his father. Also both men are guilty: like Georg in "The Judgment," Gregor Samsa (note the similarity of first names) is guilty of having cut himself off from his true self — long before his actual metamorphosis — and, to the extent he has done so, he is excluded from his family. His situation of intensifying anxiety, already an unalterable fact at his awakening, corresponds to Georg's after his sentence. More so than Georg, however, who comes to accept his judgment, out of proportion though it may be, Gregor is a puzzled victim brought before the Absolute — here in the form of the chief clerk — which forever recedes into the background. This element of receding, an important theme in Kafka's works, intensifies the gap between the hero and the unknown source of his condemnation. Thus the reader finds himself confronted with Gregor's horrible fate and is left in doubt about the source of Gregor's doom and the existence of enough personal guilt to warrant such a harsh verdict. The selection of an ordinary individual as victim heightens the impact of the absurd. Gregor is not an enchanted prince in a fairy tale, yearning for deliverance from his animal state; instead, he is a rather average salesman who awakens and finds himself transformed into an insect.

In a sense, Gregor is the archetype of many of Kafka's male characters: he is a man reluctant to act, fearful of possible mishaps, rather prone to exaggerated contemplation, and given to juvenile, surrogate dealings with sex. For example, he uses his whole body to anxiously guard the magazine clipping of a lady in a fur cape; this is a good illustration of his pitiful preoccupation with sex. Though it would be unfair to blame him for procrastinating, for not getting out of bed on the first morning of his metamorphosis, we have every reason to assume that he has procrastinated long before this — especially in regard to a decision about his unbearable situation at work. Gregor has also put off sending his sister to the conservatory, although he promised to do so. He craves love and understanding, but his prolonged inactivity gradually leads him to feel ever more indifferent about everything. It is through all his failures to act, then, rather than from specific irresponsible actions he commits, that Gregor is guilty. The price his guilt exacts is that of agonizing loneliness.

Plays on words and obvious similarities of names point to the story's highly autobiographical character. The arrangement of the vowels in *Samsa* is the same as in *Kafka*. More significantly yet, *samsja* means "being alone" in Czech. (In this connection, it is noteworthy that in "Wedding Preparations in the Country," an earlier use of the metamorphosis motif, the hero's name is *Raban*. The same arrangement of the vowel *a* prevails, and there is also another play on words: *Rabe* is German for *raven*, the Czech word for which is *kavka*; the raven, by the way, was the business emblem of Kafka's father.)

It is easy to view Gregor as an autobiographical study of Kafka himself. Gregor's father, his mother, and his sister also have their parallels with Kafka's family. Gregor feels that he has to appease his father, who "approaches with a grim face" toward him, and it is his father's bombardment with apples that causes his death. The two women, on the other hand, have the best of intentions—his mother pleading for her son's life, believing that Gregor's state is only some sort of temporary sickness; she even wants to leave the furniture in his room the way it is "so that when he comes back to us he will find everything as it was and will be able to forget what has happened all the more easily." And Grete, so eager to understand and help her brother at first, soon changes; she does not want to forgo her "normal" life and is the first one to demand the insect's removal. These people simply do not understand, and the reason they do not understand is that they are habitually too "preoccupied with their immediate troubles."

Gregor's situation in his family is that of Kafka within his own family: he had a tyrannical father who hated or, at best, ignored his son's writing; a well-meaning mother, who was not strong enough to cope with her husband's brutality; and a sister, Ottla, whom Kafka felt very close to. Shortly after completing "The Metamorphosis," Kafka wrote in his diary: "I am living with my family, the dearest people, and yet I am more estranged from them than from a stranger."

Returning to the subject of Gregor, what strikes one most immediately is the fact that although he is outwardly equipped with all the features of an insect, he reacts like a human being. Gregor never identifies himself with an insect. It is important to realize, therefore, that Gregor's metamorphosis actually takes place in his "uneasy dreams," which is something altogether different than saying it is the result of the lingering impact of these dreams. An interpretation often advanced categorizes Gregor's metamorphosis as an attempt at escaping his deep-seated conflict between his true self and the untenable situation at the company. He begs the chief clerk for precisely that situation which has caused him to be so unhappy; he implores him to help him maintain his position and, while doing so, completely forgets that he is a grotesquerie standing in front of the chief clerk.

What bothers Gregor most about his situation at the company is that there is no human dimension in what he is doing: "All the casual acquaintances never become intimate friends." If it were not for his parents' debt to his chief, whom—typical of Kafka's predilection for the anonymity of top echelons—we never hear about in concrete terms, Gregor would have quit working long ago. As will be shown later, he would have had every reason to do so. As it turns out, he was, and still is, too weak. Even now in his helpless condition, he continues to think of his life as a salesman in "normal" terms; he plans the day ahead as if he could start it like every other day, and he is upset only because of his clumsiness.

Although one might expect such a horrible fate to cause a maximum of intellectual and emotional disturbance in a human being—and Gregor remains one inwardly until his death—he stays surprisingly calm. His father shows the same incongruous behavior when confronted with Gregor's fate; he acts as if this fate were something to be expected from his son. The maid treats him like a curious pet, and the three lodgers are amused, rather than appalled, by the sight of the insect. The reason for the astounding behavior of all these people is found in their incapacity to comprehend disaster. This incapacity, in turn, is a concomitant symptom of their limitless indifference toward everything happening to Gregor. Because they have maintained a higher degree of sensitivity, the women in Gregor's family respond differently at first, Gregor's mother even resorting to a fainting spell to escape having to identify the insect with her son.

Gregor's unbelievably stayed reaction to his horrible fate shows Kafka, the master painter of the grotesque, at his best. In paragraphs bristling with the most meticulous descriptions of the absurd, Kafka achieves the utmost in gallows humor and irony. Gregor's crawling up and down the wall, his delighting in dirt, and the fact that he "takes food only as a pastime"—all these are described in detail and presented as normal; at the same time, however, on the morning of his metamorphosis, Gregor "catches at some kind of irrational hope" that nobody will open the door. The comical effect of this reversal of the normal and the irrational is then further heightened by the servant girl's opening the door as usual.

Let us return to Gregor's conflict. His professional and social considerations are stronger than his desire to quit working for his company. In fact, he even toys with the idea of sleeping and forgetting "all this nonsense." This "nonsense" refers to his transformation, which he does not want to accept because he sees it only as something interfering with his daily routine. His insect appearance must not be real because it does not suit Gregor the businessman. By ignoring or negating his state, he can, of course, in no way eliminate it. The contrary seems to be the case: the more he wants to ignore it, the more horrible its features become; finally he has to shut his eyes "to keep from seeing his struggling legs."

As a representative of the run-of-the-mill mentality of modern man, Gregor is frustrated by his totally commercialized existence and yet does nothing about it, other than try to escape by new calculations along purely commercial lines. He vows that once he has sufficient money, he will quit, and yet he has no idea what he will do. He does not really know his innermost self, which is surrounded by an abyss of emptiness. This is why Kafka draws this "innermost self" as something strange and threatening to Gregor's commercialized existence.

The insect is Gregor's "innermost self." It refuses to be further subjected to the miserable life Gregor has led in his concern for money. At last it has intruded into Gregor's life and it is not going to be chased away like a ghost. Having emerged under the cover of night, as also happens in "A Country Doctor," this "self" seeks a confrontation with the other parts of Gregor Samsa. Time and time again, Kafka pictures the alienated "inner self" of his heroes in the form of animals — for instance, in "Investigations of a Dog," "The Burrow," and "A Report to an Academy." Sometimes, too, Kafka uses absurd authorities of law to represent man's suppressed and estranged "self," as in *The Trial.* In this connection, it is valuable to compare the opening scenes of this novel and our story: Joseph K. was taken by surprise immediately on awakening, just as Gregor is here. Both men were seized in the morning, during the short period of consciousness between sleep and the beginning of one's daily routine. Joseph, too, did not hear the alarm, and he, like Gregor, was taken prisoner. Both men try to shake off their fate by acting as if it did not really exist, but, in both instances, the apparent delusion turns out to be terrifying reality.

The insect represents all the dimensions of Gregor's existence which elude description because they transcend rational and empirical categories. This is why Kafka was so adamant about not having the insect reproduced in any conventional manner when the story was published. He wrote his publisher that it would be wrong to draw the likeness of the insect on the book cover because any literal representation would be meaningless. Gregor — after his metamorphosis — can be depicted only to the extent he can see and grasp himself — hence not at all or merely by implication. Here, as in *The Trial,* the world is commensurate with the hero's concept of it. The agreement which Kafka and his publisher finally reached permitted illustrating the scene at the beginning of the third part where Gregor, "lying in the darkness of his room, invisible to his family, could see them all at the lamp-lit table and listen to their talk" through the living room door.

It has been said that the story draws its title not from Gregor's metamorphosis, which is already an established fact at the beginning, but from the change which the members of his family — especially Grete — undergo as his fate fulfills itself. Indeed, in contrast to Gregor's deterioration and ultimate death, Grete's fortunes and those of her family are steadily improving. In fact, it is through her eventually negative reaction to Gregor's misfortune that Grete finds a degree of self-assurance. Her father, also as a result of Gregor's incapacitating transformation, becomes active once more and seemingly younger after years of letting his son take care of the family.

Of all the members of the family, Grete plays perhaps the most significant role in Gregor's life because with her "alone had he remained intimate." He sleeps with his face toward her room, he once promised to send her to the conservatory, and he suffers more from the emotional wounds she inflicts upon him than from the apples which his father throws at him — fatal and symbolic bullets of perniciousness though they are. There is some evidence that his relationship with Grete has strong incestual overtones, as will be shown later. This aspect of the story is also highly autobiographical. Such lines as "he would never let her out of his room, at least not as long as he lived" and "he would then raise himself to her shoulder and kiss her on the neck" certainly appear in this light. Interestingly enough, Kafka wrote in his diary in 1912 that "the love between brother and sister is but a re-enactment of the love between father and mother." Be this as it may, as soon as Grete turns against Gregor, he deteriorates rapidly. Once she convinces her family that they must get rid of the "idea that this is Gregor," they ignore him completely and eventually consult about disposing of *it*, not *him*.

The most terrible insight which the story conveys is that even the most beautiful relationships between individuals are based on delusions. No one knows what he or anybody else really is: Gregor's parents, for instance, have no idea of their son's serious conflict, much less of the extent of his sacrifice for them. As Kafka puts it, "His parents did not understand this so well." They have no idea that one's nature can be deformed by the continued degradation it suffers, but now that this deformation has taken on such horrible proportions they are puzzled and look at Gregor as something alien. Typically enough, "the words he uttered were no longer understandable." The concern they should have shown for him finds a perverted outlet in their pre-occupation with total strangers, the three lodgers who get an enormous amount of attention simply because of the rent they pay. Finally, it is only consistent with their way of thinking that Gregor's parents should do away with the insect: pretense alone makes the world go round. Put differently, truth and life are mutually exclusive.

Gregor, for example, is mistaken about his family. He has believed it was his duty to help them pay their debts and secure a financially carefree life, and he has done this by selling his soul to the company. The truth is that his father has far more money than Gregor knows about; also, he was not nearly as sick as he has made Gregor believe. Gregor's self-chosen sacrifice has been senseless. Worse than that, the more he has done for his family, the more "they had simply got used to it." Gregor's relationship with the members of his family, and also their deal-ings among each other, are determined solely by the contrived order they have set up for themselves. Their lives are based on ever-new compromises and calculations. In Gregor's "uneasy dreams," the compromises and calculations finally rupture and, from them, truth rises in the form of a "gigantic insect."

As the maid sweeps out the dead insect, the Samsas have arrived at the threshold of what looks like a bright future. The harmony between them seems to be the result of their common fate of being drawn together by the misfortune that befell them. This return of the family to a life unfettered by a tragedy like Gregor's has often been seen as proof of their hypocrisy, possibly foreshadowing the emergence of another "inner insect" from one of them. The danger of this view is that it tends to see Gregor's transformation only as a sort of psychological mech-anism, thus detracting from its uniqueness and absurdity. The basic question here is this: who is to call another person — in this case, the entire Samsa family — hypocritical simply because this other person has the strength (and perhaps brutality) necessary to overcome tragedy? Certainly not Kafka (See "A Hunger Artist").

It has been argued that the epilogue is poor because it stands as a cheerful counterpoint to the tragic and absurd metamorphosis of Gregor. No matter how natural and, therefore, justifiable the family's return to a "normal life" may be, so runs the argument, it cannot possibly make up for the horror of what has happened. We must ask ourselves, therefore, if Kafka intended this. Is it not exactly the naturalness of the family's reaction and their callousness accompanying this "healthy reaction" that emphasizes the absurdity of Gregor's fate?

The questions pertaining to Gregor's identity are central to the story. The narrator brings up this problem of identity when he asks: "Was he an animal, that music had such an effect upon him?" Since only humans respond to music in the way the insect responds to Grete's playing the violin, we realize that he is indeed part human. The violin playing is also a part of the countless allusions to Gregor's repressed sexual desires, particularly his longing for his sister. As Gregor lies in front of Grete and listens to her music, he has only her on his mind. The confusion of violin playing and player—and his inability to admit this to himself—are they part of Gregor's guilt? Did he originally want to send her to a conservatory as a kind of "messenger" to a spiritual realm? Does it mean that he, too, once wanted to become a musician? His utter loneliness illustrates the abyss into which all these questions lead. It is most clear that Gregor responds to the music only now that he is not the traveling salesman he used to be, even though he is, in part, an insect. Thus Gregor's "animal state" seems to be a precondition of his yearning for this "unknown food." This food may very well be physical—that is, sexual. The ambiguity about the nature of the food remains—as does the uncertainty about whether Gregor is experiencing only a relapse into the sphere of the animalistic or whether or not he has been lifted up to a higher plane. His identity cannot be established from his reactions because whenever Gregor is impaired as a human being, he reacts positively as an animal and vice versa. When the women in his family clean out his room, for instance, he resents this as a human being, not as an insect. By the same token, mention of his horrible appearance bothers the human element in him, whereas it is the animal in him that is hurt when he is ignored. The most plausible answer is that, although he is an insect, Gregor nevertheless transcends his animal condition, craving spiritual *and* sexual food. During his existence as a salesman, he certainly lacked both these aspects of life. ("A Hunger Artist" is the most haunting treatment of this theme of the spiritual nourishment which cannot be found on earth. Also, in "Investigations of a Dog," the central issue concerns making spiritual food available through music.) Man or animal: maybe the answer cannot be answered here or in any of Kafka's works. Despite their different interpretations, all of Kafka's animals—the insect here, as well as the horses in "A Country Doctor," and the ape in "A Report to an Academy"—have one thing in common: like Kafka's human beings, they have lost the place which divine creation originally assigned to them. Like all creatures, man or animal, Gregor has lost his identity without, however, becoming a true insect. Perhaps Gregor is best identified as belonging to the vast realm of the in-between. *His* (or *its*) agonizing anxiety reflects *his* (or *its*) fate of belonging nowhere.

As an insect, Gregor cannot communicate with his family, but he does try "to return to the human circle." Through Grete's music, he seems to accomplish this to an extent which permits him to die at peace with himself, "thinking of his family with tenderness and love." The pretense is at an end when he finally takes his spiritual (and sexual) component into account and does justice to it (them) by permitting himself to become attuned to Grete's playing (and to Grete herself).

Concerning the story's formal aspects, a few observations should be made. It is divided into three parts, each dealing with a different aspect of Gregor's attempt to break out of his imprisonment. The first one deals with his professional conflict, the second deals primarily with his reaction to the increasingly tense alienation within his family, and the last deals with Gregor's death or, expressed positively, his liberation. Throughout the story, Gregor's deteriorating condition is in direct contrast to his family's slow but steady metamorphosis from sheer horror to self-satisfaction. In a sense, the three parts correspond to the dramatic pattern of exposition, conflict, and denouement.

Within the story's three-part construction, Kafka also deals with the concept of time. Awakening from his "uneasy dreams," Gregor is fully conscious throughout the first part—that is, for one hour, beginning at half past six. His consciousness sets in too late, however, for his train left at five. A frequently used device in Kafka's works, the discrepancy between the time shown on the clock and the time as experienced by the hero symbolizes his alienation. This is why Gregor's sense of time begins to vanish in the second part, when he wakes up "out of a deep sleep, more like a swoon than a sleep." Typically, time is expressed in rather general terms, such as "twilight" or "long evening." There is no longer the regular routine of the first day; Gregor spends his time crawling up and down and around his room. Vague indications of time are reflected in such terms as "soon," "later," and "often," blurring the boundary lines between what used to be precisely measurable units of time. At one point in the story, the narrator tells us that "about a month" probably has elapsed; on another occasion, Gregor mentions that "the lack of all direct human speech for the past two months" has confused his mind. The lonely quality of Gregor's bachelor existence assumes ever more self-destructive features, of which he is fully aware.

Time being so related to movement, Gregor's increasing lack of direction and continuous crawling around in circles finally result in his total loss of a sense of time. When his mother and sister remove the furniture from his room in the second part of the story, he loses his "last guideline of direction." Paradoxically, "The Metamorphosis" is enacted outside the context of time, and because of this, time is always frightfully present. As Kafka put it in an aphorism, "It is only our concept of time which permits us to use the term 'The Last Judgment'; in reality, it is a permanent judgment."

Gregor is doomed without knowing the charges or the verdict, and all he can do is bow to a powerful Unknown. And this is all the reader can do. Following the narrator, he can view all angles of Gregor's torment. Not one person within the story can do that, Gregor included. They are all shut off from seeing any perspective other than their own. This is their curse. There is no textual evidence in the story which explicitly tells us the cause of Gregor's fate. But because we too suffer from the sense of aloneness that Gregor does and because Kafka calls on us to share Gregor's tribulations with him, we discover that his experiences are analogous to our own.

"THE JUDGMENT"
(DAS URTEIL)

There are two reasons why "The Judgment" is considered the most autobiographical of Kafka's stories. First, there are Kafka's own commentaries and entries in his diary. When he re-read the story, for instance, he noted that only *he* could penetrate to the core of the story which, much like a newborn child, "was covered with dirt and mucus as it came out of him"; he also commented in his diary that he wanted to write down all possible relationships within the story that were not clear to him when he originally wrote it. This is not surprising for a highly introverted writer like Kafka, but it does illustrate the enormous inner pressure under which he must have written "The Judgment." In this connection, it should also be remembered that he completed the story in one sitting, during a single night; he "carried his own weight on his back more than once that night," he said, commenting that one can really write only in this manner, "completely open spiritually and physically." Indeed, everything Kafka wrote before "The Judgment" seems unfinished by comparison.

Second, "The Judgment" is partly the result of Kafka's fateful meeting with Felice Bauer (later, his fiancée) in the home of his friend Max Brod, six weeks before the story's composition (see Life and Background). Georg Bendemann's judgment at the hand of his father is as inexorable as was that of Franz Kafka at the hand of Felice, who was to create a dilemma between his ideal of bachelorhood—to him, the necessary prerequisite for his writing—and that of a happy family life. Immediately after meeting Felice, he wrote that he was "doomed," and some time after finishing "The Judgment," he remarked that he was indirectly indebted to Felice for the story, but also that Georg dies because of Frieda. From then on, Kafka never really stopped incriminating himself because of his feeling that if he were married to Felice, he would betray his art.

The story's most paramount theme, that of Georg's bachelorhood, has its origin in Kafka's complex relationships with his fiancée and his father, but also in his perfectionist notions of what writing should be. More than once, Max Brod wrote that Kafka was steeped in a trance during the autumn of 1912. Kafka regarded art as "a form of prayer," wanted to have nothing to do with writing for aesthetic reasons, and continuously suffered from the realization that he could not ever close the gap between what he heard inside himself and what he actually wrote. It is the realization of his impotence in the face of an Absolute that accounts for his terse and fragmentary, yet immensely dynamic, style—which is more noticeable in "The Judgment" than in most of his other works. Leaving so much unsaid which, Kafka felt, eluded his grasp as a writer, this style excites the reader's imagination and consistently drives him to question and comment. Better than most of his stories, "The Judgment" reflects Kafka's haunted mind, which, taking perfection and intensity of experience as its goal, races through the plot.

Kafka's curse of being able to write only in seclusion is the seemy side of his devotion to writing as life's only reward. In this sense, Georg Bendemann, like other heroes of Kafka's stories, reflects the author's most basic personal problem—that of bachelorhood. Kafka attempted to escape the conflict by being as pure a writer as possible, and in order to accomplish this, he "embraced" bachelorhood. The result was that in his stories the bachelor became an archetype of absolute loneliness.

A random selection of entries in his diary demonstrates Kafka's indecision and anxiety with regard to Felice. In spite of several letters imploring her to forget him because he would only make her unhappy, he nevertheless kept up his correspondence with her. He wrote of his desire for complete solitude, and yet only two days later, he dreamed of "growth and sublimation of his existence through marriage." He devised a list of seven points for and against marriage, in which he assured himself that everything he had ever accomplished was the result of his bachelorhood. He hated everything not pertaining to literature; he also dreaded the mere thought of having to waste time on other people. Yet he yearned for "a modest measure of happiness" as a family man. One of his most tragic entries reads: "I love her as much as I can, but my love lies stifled beneath anxiety and self-incriminations." For five long years, until after his second engagement to Felice, he was caught in this dilemma. In the end, Kafka's bachelorhood exhausted itself in the repeated description of its own contradictions. The same is, of course, true of Georg Bendemann, who answers his fiancée's argument that he should never have become engaged at all, by saying: "Well, we are both to blame for that."

Kafka's explanation of the names of the story's couple also sheds light on the heavily autobiographical nature of "The Judgment." That Frieda Brandenfeld is Felice Bauer is rather obvious. Less obvious is that Georg and Bende have the same number of letters as do Franz and Kafka; also, the vowel *e* in Bende is repeated at precisely the same places as is the vowel *a* in Kafka. While the first half of Brandenfeld may stem from Kafka's association with Berlin, where Felice lived (Berlin is located in the county of Brandenburg), the second half of the name Brandenfeld has, according to Kafka, a deeper meaning for him: *Feld* (field) is a symbol of the sensuous, fertile married life which he could not realize for himself. In *The Trial*, by the way, Felice Bauer will appear thinly disguised as Fräulein Bürstner, also abbreviated F. B.

The opening scene, on Sunday morning, radiates Georg's contentment, which, as the story progresses, will give way to a mounting emotional instability. But now, at the "height of spring," everything is fine, and the bridge connects the monotonous city on his side of the river with the "tender green" of the hills on the other side. The bridge is still intact as the symbol of communication, which it will not be by the time he uses it to jump to his death. As is typical of the beginnings of Kafka's stories, the hero finds himself awakening from a dream, or at least in a dreamlike state.

The basis of the story's structure — Georg's musing about his friend and the letter he writes — takes up about a third of the story. The letter is striking in that the one item which made Georg sit down and write to his friend is mentioned only at the very end: his engagement. Before breaking the news to him, Georg writes about the marriages of uninteresting people merely to test his reaction. To his father, Georg confesses that he wrote to St. Petersburg only to prevent the possibility of his friend finding out about his engagement from somebody else. Even after Georg had made up his mind to tell his friend, he is careful not to describe Frieda in detail. All we hear is that she is well-to-do and that the absent friend will have a "genuine friend of the opposite sex" in her. The letter reveals more about Georg's reluctance than perhaps he wants to admit: his reluctance to describe life at home as it really is; his reluctance to follow through with his plan to make his friend come back ("How could one be sure that he would make a success of life at home?"); and his reluctance, above all, to view his engagement without any reservation and to write about it.

Frieda is the symbol of the sensual world and, in this sense, the representation of the "normal" life Kafka really desired but could not attain. Naturally she senses Georg's reluctance and ambiguity toward her and insists that the distant friend attend the wedding so that this bond of bachelorhood can be dissolved. In the light of this, Georg's assurance to his friend that he will get along beautifully with Frieda is wrong: she realizes the potential danger to their marriage, and he is equally aware of the temptation in the form of this bachelorhood relationship. Frieda gains control over Georg to the extent he loses contact with his friend, and after discussing his friend with her, Georg says to himself: "I can't cut myself to another pattern that might make a more suitable friend for him." She remains the stronger and he becomes attached to the life she represents.

Who, then, is this friend whose very existence is questioned by Georg's father at first? He is absent, nameless, single, lonely, and unsuccessful. The only thing positive we hear is that he obviously sympathizes with the uprisings in Russia so much that he wants to stay there despite the uncertain political situation. The combination of political and religious imagery in the scene at Kiev suggests Georg's idealistic view of his friend pursuing some cause and of Russia as the source of social salvation—or at least rejuvenation. During his last visit he already had a full beard resembling the kind Russian monks used to wear. (The turn of the century brought repeated uprisings in Russia, the worst one in 1905. It resulted in the relative freedom of the press and the right of free assembly. Soon after, however, Czar Nicholas II succeeded in suppressing open revolution and had several leaders—Lenin, Trotsky, and Stalin— deported to Siberia. For more about Kafka's political views, consult Understanding Kafka.)

Georg's treatment of his friend is slightly condescending in tone, especially the paragraph beginning with "What could one write to such a man?" It is also highly ambiguous. He condemns him, and yet he pities him; he considers persuading him to return, and yet is afraid of the responsibility connected with it. He keeps toying with the idea of letting his friend know about his flourishing business, and yet insists it would look peculiar if he did it now. Most significantly, it is only with great reluctancy and countless reservations that he finally decides to tell him about his engagement.

Perhaps the distant friend is best described in terms of what Georg lacks and vice versa. His friend's business once flourished but has gone downhill; Georg's business has boomed. The friend once tried to talk Georg into emigrating because success was promising "for precisely Georg's branch of trade"; Georg thought of persuading him to come back. His friend has almost no contacts in St. Petersburg and is "resigning himself to being a permanent bachelor"; Georg is engaged. The question remains unresolved as to what his business really is. It is not ordinary, not exactly geared to money-making, and it seems to require isolation. Is it perhaps Kafka's own "branch of trade" — writing?

When Georg sits down to write to his friend, it is as if he were writing to part of himself. It is as if this were Kafka's soliloquy, told to his writing-self, full of all the self-incriminations and tortures he went through during the time he wrote "The Judgment." Successful in business, willing to enter into marriage — yet shuddering at the mere thought of business and marriage — Georg represents the bourgeois element in Kafka, the part that would love to quit writing for good and become a family man. In this case, the distant friend is the "inner Kafka," escaping his father's world and trying to pursue his writing in solitude. He develops the "yellow skin" and the religious visions of self-imposed asceticism, not unlike the hero of "A Hunger Artist." Considered in this way, "The Judgment" is really a story about the unrelenting "inner Kafka," defending himself against Kafka, the human being with all his weaknesses, rooted in the sensuous world.

However, the friend is also more than Kafka's "inner self," more than his symbolic perfection and more than his watchful superego. The atmosphere with which Kafka surrounds him is deliberately metaphysical and mystical. Georg sees him "among the wreckage of his showcases," a failure, a victim, almost a martyr. Yet he does not forsake the country which has ruined him materially; he has saved his spiritual purity. If he died, this purity and idealism would also die. If Georg died, this would only be the end of the Bendemanns. The friend survives, comes to control and, eventually, condemn Georg in the person of his father.

The autobiographical significance of old Bendemann emerging as his son's judge is obvious. In most of Kafka's stories, though to varying degrees, an overpowering father figure plays a decisive role. Georg's father "kept him from developing any true activity of his own"; "My father is still a giant of a man"; "Georg shrank into a corner as far away as possible from his father"; these are a few of the clear allusions to Kafka's own father. Yet old Bendemann's authority dissolves and he collapses on his bed after driving his son out of the room. He is the despotic father figure, the executor of a quasi-divine will. This realization that the judgment of the father, as well as the self-execution of his son, are in no way evidence of a tragedy and are meaningful only within the context of this story is important. It is the best argument against the interpretation of "The Judgment" as an expressionist horror piece (1912 is usually listed as the beginning of the expressionist movement in anthologies).

Regardless of which view of old Bendemann one has, he is also a symbol of the enormous force behind Georg's life with which he cannot come to grips. Here, Kafka uses his childhood experiences to give us a parable of how everything we cannot handle in ourselves continues to grow, is projected into the outside world, gradually eludes our control, and eventually turns against us. In other words, the death sentence is the result of Georg's father fixation, the real cause of his overriding sense of guilt. It is not that Georg is innocent and does not deserve punishment for his inactivity; it is the exclusiveness with which he keeps staring at his father that draws him into the whirlpool of self-annihilation.

That Georg has a guilty conscience is evident. The way he dodges his father's inquiry about the friend by answering "You don't really look after yourself"; the way he has neglected his parents; the way he believes his father has lured him into a trap: all these are proof of his guilty conscience. One issue of the story lies in Georg's recognition that his father's words are essentially just and therefore unbearable. As a consequence, Georg accepts his sentence without complaining.

Old Bendemann is also the embodiment of absolute law to his son, and the many references to his negligent physical appearance point to Kafka's use of dirt as an aspect of legal authorities. (In *The Trial*, for instance, Joseph K. finds pornographic literature as he prowls through the office of the legal authorities.) Old Bendemann has the quality of a god of wrath who punishes Georg for his failure to live up to the ideal of his friend (the "inner self"), the ideal of art as a form of prayer, and bachelorhood as the means of attaining it. One advantage of stressing this quasi-divine aspect of old Bendemann is that his bewildering contradictions about the friend's existence lose their paradoxical quality and can simply be ascribed to his ineffability. The view of him as insane has the same effect. The trouble with this interpretation is that the only scene which might justify it, the scene in which the old man plays with the watch chain on Georg's breast, is not proof enough. To see Georg's suicide as the result of the decree of an insane mind would reduce "The Judgment" to an unnecessarily complex story; it would leave us with the view that contradictions and paradoxes are simply insane. Nothing could be further from the intention of Kafka, who once remarked that to understand something and to misunderstand the same thing do not necessarily exclude each other.

A more likely, though by no means wholly satisfactory, interpretation of the father's contradictions about the existence of the distant friend is that the friend gradually ceases to exist in Georg's mind after the latter has betrayed his ideals. As a result, his letters to St. Petersburg do not reach a real friend, but are mailed to what we may consider the relic of happy childhood days lingering in Georg's mind. In fact, the letter announcing his engagement—the height of betrayal in his friend's eyes—severs the last link between them. Does Georg not sense its fatefulness when he stares out the window after writing it? To the extent that Georg becomes unfaithful to his ideals, Georg's friend becomes old Bendemann's favorite. Triumphantly, the old man admits he has been in touch with the friend all along, and he grows from a weak man in his dotage to an overpowering authority for his son. Alone like Georg—he is a widower—the father becomes the friend's representative: not only is this term taken from the world of business in which old Bendemann has moved, but it also indicates the great importance of the friend in whose name he accuses and condemns his son. Georg, however, is unable to see this representation because he remains attached to the sensual, empirical world. Only for a split second does his father's enthusiasm for his friend dawn on him when "his words turned into deadly seriousness." Old Bendemann's assertion that the friend knows everything "a thousand times" better is an indication of his closeness to him, as well as a literal allusion to the friend's power.

The old man then, like the distant friend, is neither a human being nor a symbol, but he is both. He appears to be interested after Georg reveals to him that he has written to his friend, but more and more he takes on the quality of a last authority for Georg in a legal and moral sense. According to Kafka, what the old and the young Bendemann have in common is symbolized by the distant friend, from whom they emerge in opposition to each other.

Georg's condemnation has a psychological aspect to it which builds up throughout the story and reaches a climax with the accusation old Bendemann hurls at his son before sentencing him to death: "Till now you've known only about yourself!" Then there is the paradoxical pronouncement itself that Georg was "truly" a child but "more truly" a "devilish human being." Here we have two norms contrasted which cannot be reconciled on the empirical level. The juxtaposition of these two adverbs illustrates the futility of empirical logic in the face of the Absolute and its unfathomable judgment. This knowledge of absolute truth that Georg experiences as the highest commandment and as a binding decree, this realization that he has irretrievably lost his opportunity to live because he has betrayed his "inner self"—they drive him to suicide. He has roots in this life, and yet he has spent his days trying to shun responsibilities and to avoid clear-cut commitments. This is his guilt. Faced with death by drowning, he desperately seeks to recapture the Absolute he has forfeited. Reminiscent of "The Metamorphosis" and, especially, "A Hunger Artist," where longing for spiritual food is a paramount theme, the Absolute is symbolized here by the railings Georg grasps "as a starving man clutches food."

Georg's death by drowning may be seen as an attempt to return to the unity his mother used to hold the family and the distant friend together, as we conclude from the fact that the friend — purity, idealism — never returns after the death of Georg's mother. Her lingering presence is still powerful, however, and even old Bendemann admits it was she who gave him enough strength to establish rapport with the distant friend.

Whether or not the "unending steam of traffic" drowning out Georg's fall from the bridge also has sexual connotations is a minor point. (The German *verkehr* means both traffic and intercourse.) What counts is that traffic *is* a symbol for life here, if only in the sense of communication. In the form of a motor bus, life silences a suicide, illustrating that his death is of interest only to him. Taken literally or figuratively, life on any level remains inaccessible to Georg, who dies from alienation.

Beyond all autobiographical and psychological considerations, "The Judgment" deals with the complex interactions of good and evil. Representing the purity of his friend, old Bendemann condemns the power which has corrupted this purity in his son. However, even the execution of this condemnation seems to be a paradox because the suicide toward which the story builds becomes an execution. Here, as in the case of other contradictions in other stories, let us remember that, for Kafka, truth always reveals itself in paradoxes. This is why Georg, the victim, is also the executor of his judgment.

Probably the most serious paradox is the absolute incompatibility of Georg's guilt and his punishment. Particularly in view of his love for his parents, which is present throughout the story and is repeated in a prominent position at the end, the gravity of the sentence is incomprehensible. Nothing except Kafka's lifelong, deep-seated, and colossal fear of his unpredictable father can possibly account for its justification. It lifts the story's second half to the level of a surreal and therefore a rationally inexplicable nightmare. The incredibly terse and dense language stands in horrible contrast to the dominant themes of anxiety and doom in Georg's mad rush to his death.

"A HUNGER ARTIST"
(EIN HUNGERKÜNSTLER)

The first sentence of this story seems to leave no doubt about the story's realistic content: "During these last decades the interest in professional fasting has markedly diminished." First off, then, Kafka induces a consciousness of time by tempting the reader to inquire into the situation of hunger artists *before* the present decade. But the sober, pseudo-scientific language of this first sentence tends also to suppress the reader's awareness of the essential *oddness* of the profession of hunger artists. Thus we have only a vague sense of something unusual. The result of this tension between the quasi-historical investigation and the strangeness of its object is irony. Full of meaning, this irony is the bridge between the story's factual style of narration and its abstract content.

This differentiation between two levels of time also supports Kafka's main theme: alienation. It is here presented in terms of the continued confrontation of the hunger artist with his overseers and his audience. From the audience's "diminishing interest" in hunger artists, to its "absence of interest" at the end of the story, Kafka uncovers the mechanism that deepens this alienation. The more the story progresses, the clearer it becomes that this is a parable of the author's spiritual quest, as well as of his relationship with the insensitive world around him. Like all parables, it has a firm basis but is open to more than one interpretation. That it is told from the point of view not of the hero, but of an independent personage outside the plot, is not an argument against this statement. The point where the hero and the world outside his own lie anchored is the narrator's mind. Emotionally disengaged, the narrator's view is both ambiguous and absolute in its pronouncements. Is it Kafka, the teller of the story, viewing the fate of Kafka, the hunger artist?

There is no limit to the paradoxical situations the hunger artist is exposed to. He, whose nature it is to abstain from food, "the very thought of which gave him nausea," suffers from the superficiality and callousness of the overseers who suspect him of cheating and, worse yet, from the greed of the impresario who forces him to interrupt his fasting in order to eat. Most of all, he hates those overseers who want to give him the chance of refreshment, "which they believed he could obtain privately." He prefers being severely checked by the "butchers" among the overseers because, this way, he can prove his seriousness and integrity. These "butchers" belong to the realm of "raw chunks of meat" and the "stench of the menagerie," near which the cage with the artist is set up. They literally prove the validity of fasting to him, simply by existing. (A lifelong vegetarian, Kafka was, literally, the very opposite of a "butcher.") It is exactly through his starving that he tries to cope with them. He suffers in his cage, the symbol of his lack of freedom, but he prefers to starve for the eventual attainment of spiritual freedom rather than accept any of the pseudo-salvations of the realm of the "butchers" —that is, the world around him.

The overseers judge him by their own mediocrity and impotence and have no understanding of his professional code, which forbids him to swallow the least bit of food—were he ever to feel a need to do so (which is impossible in the context of this story). That his fasting may not be a virtue because it is the result of his nature rather than a self-sacrifice, is a different issue and certainly does not bother the overseers. As far as they are concerned, he remains virtuous (and insane which, in their value system, is the same) as long as he does not cheat, even though, as we have said, they do not expect him to live up to his vows. At times, the artist even takes to singing for as long as he can to show that he is not taking food secretly. The reaction of the overseers, however, is surprise at his skill to eat even while singing. Few passages in literature describe the fate of artists as solitary singers in the wilderness more dramatically. This is, of course, one of the tragedies of life: there is no way in which the morally superior can *prove* their truthfulness to anybody unwilling or unable to believe it. As Kafka puts it here: "The fasting was truly taxing and continuous. Only the artist himself could know that."

So wide is the gap of understanding between the hunger artist and the overseers that one of them will "tap his forehead" with his finger to signal that the artist is insane. The impresario, "his partner in an unparalleled career," actively exploits him. He arranges the hunger artist's life according to the whims of his audience and his own. When a spectator remarks that it is probably the lack of food that makes our hero look so melancholic, the impresario has nothing better to do but to apologize for the physical appearance of his performer, to praise his ambition and "self-denial," and to agree with the remark. This is too much for the artist to bear because it literally turns upside-down the cause and effect of his fasting. He is melancholic not because he does not eat, but because he is continuously tempted to abandon his fasting and to accept the very food he tries to evade. Sometimes he also reacts with outbursts of anger when the merits of his fasting are questioned or when a spectator tries to console him because he looks so thin. Here Kafka succeeds in driving to an extreme the paradox of the hunger artist subsisting on fasting. With it, he also achieves the purest form of irony.

The people—the overseers and the audience—have the feeling that something is wrong with the hunger artist. Being snared in the logic of their minds, however, they never see beyond one and the same suspicion: the artist must be cheating. This limitation of their vision keeps them from uncovering his real cheating —namely, that of making a virtue out of his "misery." "He alone knew what no other initiate knew: how easy it was to fast." This sentence is the key to understanding why the hunger artist is so dissatisfied with himself: he wants to live, and in the context of this paradoxical story the way to live is *not* to eat. His fasting is an art, though, and art requires to be acknowledged as achievement. It needs to be accepted as the ability to do something positive, whereas in the case of the hunger artist it turns out to be only a necessity, the surrogate for his inability to live on earthly food. Note especially his confession at the end of the story when he breaks down under the burden of his guilt. Ironically, he becomes fully aware of his guilt at precisely the instant when one of his overseers, moved by the sight of the dying artist, answers his confession ("I always wanted you to admire my fasting") by assuring him that he actually *has* admired him.

To Kafka, fasting is tantamount to being engaged in a spiritual battle against the enemies in this world. But to be thus engaged is his nature. In one of his fragments he says, "Others also fight, but I fight more than they. They fight like in a dream, but I stepped forward to fight consciously with all my might . . . why have I given up the multitude? Why am I target number one for the enemy? I don't know. Another life didn't seem to be worth living to me." And we might safely add, another life would not have been possible for him. In our story, the artist, barely able to utter his last words to the overseer, confesses that he, had he only found the food he liked, would have eaten it like anybody else. He does not transcend life by fasting, but he is fasting in order to survive. His fasting is not opposed to life; it merely makes it possible for him to bear it at all. If the hunger artist needs fasting to survive in the spiritual desert, Kafka needed his writing. In this sense, the story is a parable of the author's own lifelong spiritual quest.

Unlike the hunger artist, however, Kafka never thought of his art as a great achievement. The hunger artist does not merely exist and fast, but he also deliberately and consistently exhibits himself. His vanity leads him to ponder why he should be cheated of the fame he would get for breaking his own record by a "performance beyond human imagination." Kafka was the very opposite: he was overly harsh against himself when it came to judging his work. That his nature forced him to sacrifice his whole life, including three engagements, to writing—this fact he considered, above all, a curse. The hunger artist parades his fasting as a virtue, whereas Kafka was so convinced of the irrelevance of his art that he requested that his manuscripts be burned after his death. Or is Kafka's conviction perhaps only pride on a larger scale, the pride of an obsessed mind that takes absolute knowledge as its goal and suffers ever-new agonies because this knowledge is bound to remain fragmentary?

No doubt Kafka overstates the insensitivity and the lack of engagement of the overseers and the audience in the story. Yet we must not make the mistake of confusing his criticism with value judgment: nowhere does he consider the artist as superior because he is more "sensitive," and nowhere does he ridicule the audience or the overseers as despicable because they are callous, gullible, or even brutal. There is certainly more excitement connected with watching a panther than there is with staring at the solitary hunger artist. No doubt, also, panther-watchers are artistically less demanding and more likely to be fascinated by raw force. It was, nevertheless, *not* Kafka's intention to label panther-watching an inferior pastime. He, for one, suffered too much from the lack of the "panther" in himself to despise the animal. After all, the panther possesses, in a sense, freedom even though he is in a cage; his freedom is a freedom from consciousness — a state Kafka longed for. Too, the audience can hardly bear watching the "joy of life" and the "ardent passion" exuding from the beast. Kafka is simply pitting two equally justified forces against each other: the yearning for spiritual nourishment of the hunger artist against the elemental affirmation of life by the many. If Kafka condemns anybody, it is the hunger artist who should have pursued his vocation *away* from spectators and for its own sake. Not even the tremendous admiration of the audience for the hunger artist can, as long as it lasts, be said to be a success for him in Kafka's view because it is based on a serious misjudgment of the artist's intention.

Let us revert to the two opposing forces determining our lives, one pushing in the direction of spiritualization and beyond, the other one pulling back toward the animalistic sphere. In the interest of his own survival, man, according to Kafka, must not permit himself to be governed by either one of the two. If he did, he would find himself in a spiritual realm and thus become incapable of carrying on, or else he would relapse into a pre-human realm. In his diary, Kafka referred to these opposing forces as "the assault from above" and the one "from below." He explained his desire to escape from the world in terms of the "assault from above." All of Kafka's stories are permeated and deal with this opposition, but few show it as clearly as does "A Hunger Artist." The hero's loathing for regular food and his desire to fast to unprecedented perfection are the workings of this force and pull him from earthly life. The wild animals' and, especially, the panther's taking his place represent life-affirming forces. The audience moves between these two opposing forces, but it does not have the capability of either the hunger artist or the panther. Their fate is mere passivity.

The tight structure of the story neatly divides it into two parts, whose major difference may be discussed in terms of these two opposed forces. The first part reveals both forces at work within the hunger artist, the force driving him to fast and the elemental force sustaining his desire to survive. The drive to fast is stronger in the first part, and his art brings him success and even moments of enjoyment. In the second part—for all practical purposes beginning with the words "a few weeks later"— the artist fasts even though the audience stays away. The "assault from above" is gaining the upper hand and begins to mark him for destruction. Without an audience, he lacks the affirmation of his outward existence. As a result, the force counteracting his desire to fast is becoming increasingly weaker. This life-sustaining elemental force lies no longer within him but within the beasts next door. More and more, they are attracting the crowd, which now considers him only as an obstacle on their way to the stables. The crowd shifts their attention to whatever is most exciting at the moment and thus mills around the cage of the panther. That the artist's cage was placed so close to the animals "made it too easy for people to make their choice." At the end, when he has starved himself to death, the embodiment of sheer vitality appears as his principal enemy: the panther.

If we look at the two parts in terms of the relationship between the hunger artist's fasting and truth, we can say that the perversion of truth becomes greater the more his art is lowered to the level of show. The more successful his show is, the less true it is. Typically enough, the highpoint of his outward success, the fortieth day of fasting, beyond which he was not allowed to go by the impresario for commercial reasons, is also the point at which the hunger artist suffers defeat. As a "reward" for his fasting, he, whose sole desire it is to find spiritual food, is offered precisely the physical food he cannot eat. Here, as elsewhere in Kafka's works, the hero is tempted by women to abandon his goal: in "The Judgment," it is Frieda, in "A Country Doctor," it is Rosa, and in *The Trial,* it is Fräulein Bürstner and Leni. The impresario forces the food between the stubborn artist's lips while a military band drowns the scene in cheerful music and enthusiastic crowds swarm around the "flower-bedecked cage"; at the same time, the image of the circus, a frequent one in Kafka's works, reflects all the absurdities of this world. In the second part, when nobody cares for the hunger artist, he can live for his fasting. For his best performance, nobody forces a reward on him, and "no one, not even the hunger artist himself, knew what records he was already breaking." At his death, he is now at one with his nature and can finally ease his burden by confessing his lifelong guilt of having paraded his fasting as a virtue.

The sum total of truth (his art) and life are the same at all times, but one goes on at the expense of the other. By living, man gets in his own way as regards the fulfillment of his art, his search for truth. Expressed in terms of our story, it is true that *not* eating eventually takes the hunger artist's physical life, but from the debris of this life there flows forth a new, spiritualized life unknown to others. If the artist wants to find his truth, he must destroy himself. Suffering, here fasting, is the only possible way for man to redeem his true self. It is both the prerogative and curse of the hunger artist (and Kafka) that he is driven to follow this path to its inevitable conclusion.

The story of the man who lives on hunger contains the realization which Kafka consistently develops until the inherent paradox dissolves into two parts—the part of fasting and that of the elemental life force. Kafka may not make statements about something rational, but his paradoxes are highly rational statements.

"A COUNTRY DOCTOR"
(EIN LANDARZT)

Kafka used an unusual technique for telling his story of "A Country Doctor": he wrote in the first person, thereby imparting an exciting degree of immediacy to the story. The story is also exciting because of its fragmentary character—a symptom of

Kafka's searching mind, reflected here in an almost stammering rhythm. This effect is heightened by a lavish use of semicolons that chop up the already short and forceful sentences into even smaller units. An atmosphere of quasi-detached objectivity stands in almost eerie contrast to the story's dramatic impact and underlying miraculous character. Typical of Kafka, however, the language reflects the complete union between dream world and reality; in fact, the horses, ghostly embodiments of irrational forces, seem to drive, besides the doctor, even the author farther on. Kafka's recurring motif of the hunt (compare this story with "The Hunter Gracchus" and "The Burrow") has found expression in these galloping sentences, each seeming to chase the one before it.

The story begins in the past, switches to the present in the rape scene, reverts to the past, and finally shifts back to the present at the end, thus elevating the final catastrophe to the level of timelessness. At an even faster pace, images that share no logical connection with each other rush toward the story's last sentence: "A false alarm on the night bell once answered – it cannot be made good, not ever." Here is a good starting point for examining the story.

From the story's last sentence, it becomes evident that the whole story is the inevitable consequence of a single mistake. By following the call – a mere hallucination, a nightmare – the doctor triggers a long chain of disastrous events. His visit to the patient seems to be a visit into the bewildering depths of his own personality, for there is no actual ringing of the bell. The strange (and estranged) patient waiting for him does not really exist outside the doctor's imagination; he may be seen as part of the doctor's personality, playing a role comparable to that of the "distant friend" in "The Judgment" or the gigantic insect in "The Metamorphosis." "A fine wound is all I brought into the world," the patient complains, thereby suggesting that the doctor is his potential healer and belongs to him. During his entire journey, the doctor never leaves the vast regions of his unconscious, of which his patient is perhaps the darkest aspect.

In portraying this nightmare, Kafka has succeeded in portraying the situation of the man who wants to help but cannot. Kafka may well have seen himself and the whole profession of writers in the position of the country doctor: a man fighting against ignorance, selfishness and superstition, he remains exposed to "the frost of this most unhappy of ages." This is a diagnosis not only of a specific situation but also of the condition of our whole age. This is why the patient's question is not if the doctor will heal him or cure him, but if he will *save* him. "That's how the people act in my district; they always expect the impossible from the doctor," he says, explaining why he — or, on another plane, the writer — cannot be of any real help to the patient. He finds himself confronted with people whose consciousness is still attached to the realm of magic. They reveal this by stripping the doctor of his clothes and laying him in the bed alongside the patient. "The utterly simple" tune following this ritual reflects their primitivity, which would not hesitate to use the doctor as a scapegoat and kill him if his art should not work.

Although "In the Penal Colony," written two years earlier, is a better expression of Kafka's horror of World War I, there is much concern here for innocent scapegoats. The anxiety prevailing throughout this story also reflects Kafka's problems resulting from his second engagement to Felice Bauer and his deteriorating health. Shortly after his condition was diagnosed as tuberculosis, he wrote to Max Brod that he had predicted this disease himself and that his anticipation occurred in the wound of the sick boy in "A Country Doctor."

There are many more autobiographical elements, none of them "proving" anything in the strict sense of the word, but all of them shedding some additional light on the gloomy world of Kafka. The story is dedicated to his father, who ignored it completely. The misunderstanding between the physician and the patient is a reflection of the equally barren relationship between the old Kafka and the young Kafka. Knowing to what extremes Kafka tends to carry the art of name-giving, it is easy to see that the servant girl's name, Rose, is by no means accidental: "rose-red" is the color of the meticulously described wound, and the color *rose*, as well as the flower, is an age-old symbol of love in its manifold facets. There is no need to insist on one specific meaning of the word, if only because Kafka himself does not. The meaning is clear, considering that December 1917, the year after he wrote "A Country Doctor," brought Kafka's final separation from Felice, his "rose" in both senses of the word.

The groom represents Kafka's sometimes almost obsessive fear of a sexually superior rival. On this subject, he wrote that Felice did not stay alone and that someone else got close to her who did not have the problems which he, Kafka, had to face. In the story, the groom certainly gets to Rose easily, and if she says "no," she nevertheless runs into the house fully aware of her fate.

"If they misuse me for sacred reasons, I let that happen too," the doctor says. Yet his sacrifice would be senseless because it is beyond a physician's power to help an age spiritually out of kilter. It is out of kilter because, as everywhere in Kafka's work, people have lost their faith and have taken to living "outside the law," listening to the false prophets of unbridled technological progress and conformism. The boy does not trust the doctor, and his family displays the subservient and naïve behavior of the average patient. As the doctor puts it: "They have discarded their old beliefs; the minister sits at home, unraveling his vestments, one by one; but the doctor is supposed to be omnipotent." This is why the song of "O be joyful, all you patients — the doctor's laid in bed beside you!" is the "new but faulty song": the empirical and the transcendental realms are no longer one; the only way they meet is in the form of a clash leading to a "false alarm."

Only if we understand Kafka's notion of disease as resulting from seclusion can we begin to understand the country doctor. He is the subject and the object of his long quest or, expressed differently, the psychoanalyst of his own inner landscape (on another level, our whole secularized age) *and* the patient. And Kafka, though interested in Freud's teachings, regarded at least the therapeutical part of psychoanalysis as a hopeless error. According to Kafka, anxiety and concomitant alienation are the direct consequence of man's spiritual withering, and all psychoanalysis can possibly do is discover the myriad pieces of one's shattered universe.

Without his doing anything special, the doctor draws exactly the help he needs when he kicks the door of the pigsty. Like his whole trip, the sudden appearance of horses, groom, and gig bears the mark of the miraculous and the supernatural. Ever since Plato's *(Phaidros)* famous parable of the chariot being pulled by one white horse and one black horse, symbolizing the bright and the dark aspects of irrationality (rationality is in charge and tries to steer a middle course), horses have symbolized instincts and drives. The fact that they have come out of a pigsty here underscores their animalistic nature. Twice the doctor complains that his own horse died, and both times his remarks are accompanied by winter scenes, suggesting the barrenness of the (spiritual) wasteland around him.

Right away, the horses respond to the fiery "gee up" of the groom, who has already demonstrated his kinship with their world by calling them "brother" and "sister." The doctor also yells "gee up" at the end but, time being the correlative of experience, they will only crawl "slowly, like old men"; escaping from the patient and erring through the snowy wastes, the doctor has no experience by which to divide up time and, consequently, loses his orientation. The horses take over completely, at any rate, covering the distance to the patient's farm in an incredibly short period of time which, symbolically enough, is exactly the time it takes the groom to subdue Rose. Greatly adding to the story's dramatic impact, the doctor's night journey and Rose's rape are merged here on a logically inexplicable level.

"You never know what you're going to find in your house," Rose says, "and we both laughed." This line may be a clue. It is important that it is she who says this statement; she is better attuned to the realm of irrational forces than he, who spends most of his trip regretting that he has never noticed her, much less enjoyed her physically and spiritually. Now he realizes his negligence, but now it is too late because she has already been sacrificed to the groom. Her comment and their laughter at the sudden appearance of the horses reveal that these sensual and spiritual elements are present, but that they need to be brought out. On a literal level, this happens as they come out of the pigsty.

The closing picture of the fur coat trailing in the snow behind the doctor mirrors the helplessness of one who has been "betrayed." Traveling through endless wastes on his straying gig, the doctor is doomed to see the symbol of warmth and security without being able to reach it. Naked and cold and gone astray, the country doctor is the pitiful picture of disoriented mankind drifting over the treacherous landscape of its sick collective consciousness. And there is no end in sight because "he was used to that."

The question of the doctor's guilt provokes thoughts of uncertainty and ambiguity. As everywhere else in Kafka's work, the hero does not commit a crime or even a grave error. We are apt to get closer to the situation when we realize that he maneuvers himself, or permits himself to be maneuvered, into a state of mind which forces him to refrain from concrete decisions and commitments. In this sense, he becomes guilty of the classic existential sin—failing or refusing to become involved. By not taking his profession seriously and therefore lacking in responsibility, he forfeits his only chance of taking the decisive step from mere vegetating to conscious living. True, as a medical man he cannot be expected to save a patient whose sickness is, above all, of a spiritual nature. Yet he is guilty because he lacks the will to try his level best; he is afraid to act like a "world reformer" and pats himself on the shoulder for doing so much work for so little pay. Nor does he bother to view the wound as the result of the complex but undeniable interrelationship between physical and psychological factors of which Kafka himself was very much aware. Symptomatic of our age, the country doctor is the one-dimensional man who has lost a sense of participation, not only in the sphere of the sensual, but also in that of the spiritual.

Like the doctor himself, his "pack of patients" has stepped "outside the law" and into chaos. From there, they cannot help, the point being that they have lost the capability of doing that long ago. Whoever breaks out of Kafka's "human circle" alienates himself to the point of death. Kafka is most clear in this story: the impossibility of curing our age is his subject.

IN THE PENAL COLONY
(IN DER STRAFKOLONIE)

Schopenhauer and Dostoevsky are the two most likely spiritual mentors of this story. In his *Parerga und Paralipomena,* Schopenhauer suggested that it might be helpful to look at the world as a penal colony, and Dostoevsky, whom Kafka re-read in 1914, supplied Kafka with many punishment fantasies. It was especially Dostoevsky's preoccupation with the interaction between guilt, suffering, and redemption which fascinated Kafka. In this story, pain is a major precondition for comprehending one's sins: nobody can decipher the Designer's writing except he who has reached the halfway mark of his ordeal. Enlightenment "begins around the eyes. From there it radiates. A moment that might tempt one to get under the Harrow oneself." This is Kafka at his masochistic best. Yet there is also a philosophical meaning to this cult of pain. Insight and death go hand in hand, and transfiguration is the reward of those undergoing torture.

As for the punishment, or torture, however, even the simplicity and precision with which the remarkable "machine" operates cannot convince us that it is justifiable. Designed to imprint upon a condemned man's back the sin of which he is found guilty, it executes the sentence in the smoothest way possible. Everything is as simple as the "trial" preceding an execution, each cog fulfilling its proper function. But while the machine may enable the condemned person to "see" after the sixth hour, it does not offer him a chance to repent and to survive. He has neither the time nor the strength to do anything but continue suffering. Regardless of the gravity of his offense, capital punishment is the only possible verdict. As so often in Kafka's work, we are confronted with a punishment out of all proportion with the offense; in this case, the condemned man is supposed to fulfill the senseless duty of saluting in front of his captain's door every hour, thus missing the sleep he needs to serve as sentry during the day. The fundamental question is raised and remains unanswered: what logic does it take to condemn a man to death for a mere threat, particularly when he is described as a "stupid-looking creature"? At least, however, this story differs from "The Judgment," "The Metamorphosis," and "The Trial"; here, for instance, the source of the punishment and the charges are clear.

The torture machine is ever-present at the center of the story, the first sentence introducing it as "a remarkable piece of apparatus." Lifeless and fatal, the machine reduces the people around it to mere adjuncts who do not even have names of their own. Occupying an entire valley all by itself, it is a strange symbol, carrying out detailed instructions with utmost precision. It performs like the hand of some inexorable power, whose primitive nature is reflected in the stark landscape surrounding it and contrasted with civilization. In keeping with its commanding location, the machine is so high that the officer controlling it has to use a ladder to reach its upper parts. He who has helped construct the monster talks about its efficiency and intricacies with passion, yet it becomes clear that even this officer is the servant of his machine.

The secret of the machine lies in the mystery of the unusual order it sets up, sustains, and symbolizes. The nature of this order is so foreign to any conventional logic, including that of the New Commandant, that it must be assumed to serve a world beyond ours. The incident of the threatened captain is a good case in point: although he reports the incident to his superior, the latter takes it upon himself to sentence the man and put him in chains. He emphasizes that all this "was quite simple," proving that the machine and he belong to one and the same system, namely that of the Old Commandant, whose declared maxim was that "guilt is never to be doubted." This view reflects Kafka's conviction that man, merely by living with others and infringing upon their integrity, is bound to become guilty. Since nobody can claim innocence, it is senseless to collect evidence against an accused person. This argument is carried further in the scene in which the officer claims that to collect evidence against a condemned man would only cause confusion in his mind and that there is no need to explain the sentence; the condemned man will learn it best through his suffering. Unlike Georg in "The Judgment" or Joseph K. in *The Trial*, who both question the inhuman system persecuting them, however, the dull-witted condemned man in this story cannot do this.

The figure of the explorer is ambiguous. Hailing from Europe — that is, the civilized world beyond the sea surrounding the penal colony — he is on tour overseas to learn about foreign customs. Since he has been invited to attend this execution by the New Commandant, there is reason to assume he has been sent to pass judgment on this institution. Although as a guest he is determined to remain strictly neutral, he nevertheless has to admit to himself from the beginning that "the injustice of the procedure and the inhumanity of the execution were undeniable." Gradually, he becomes involved with the apparatus — for no other reason than that he alone is a foreigner and therefore *expected* to be neutral. He cannot be neutral; he condemns the institution of the apparatus, displaying the superiority of a man brought up in the spirit of democracy and liberalism.

The result of his condemnation of the apparatus is the collapse of the entire system on which the penal colony is based. Hurt and disappointed by the explorer's stand, the officer frees the prisoner with the ambiguous words "Then the time has come" and takes his place on the Bed of the apparatus himself. What happens is that the inhuman iron monster begins to collapse under the burden of the officer's self-sacrifice: "the machine was obviously going to pieces." What is more significant, the officer lying there with the big spike running through his forehead does not show the slightest trace of the transfiguration which every other dying man experienced under the grueling performance of the Harrow. This means that his self-sacrifice has been rejected by the forces controlling the machine. The words which he had the Designer write on his body, namely "Be Just," signify the end of that justice of which the officer has been the last defender.

It is difficult to imagine a more appropriate expression of the dehumanizing horror of World War I (at whose outbreak the story was written) than this symbol of self-destructive human ingenuity. Kafka succeeded beautifully with this machine; it combines all the brilliance of technological progress with the unspeakable primitivity of archaic, divine law.

The machine, of course, is also a symbol of the torture Kafka himself was exposed to as a writer. It is not exaggerated to compare the pain of creation with an execution; when he wrote, according to Kafka's own words, he experienced moments of transfiguration just like the condemned man here. Looking at the directions for the Designer, shown to him by the officer, the explorer cannot say much except that "all he could see was a labyrinth of lines crossing and recrossing each other, which covered the paper so thickly that it was difficult to discern the blank spaces between them." Prior to his self-execution, the officer shows the words designed to be imprinted on his own body to the explorer, who replies that he "can't make out these scripts." These are Kafka's allusions to his own writing — fascinating hieroglyphics and symbols of a horrible beauty that often bewildered even him. "Labyrinth" is certainly a most fitting name for the unknown regions through which Kafka's figures roam. All the explorer can do is admit that the writing is "very ingenious." What is self-evident and binding for the officer — that the inscription of the commandment violated by a man should be imprinted upon that man's body — remains unintelligible to the explorer, the outsider. This leads us to the story's other major theme, the officer's affiliation with the Old Commandant, whose "strength of conviction" he still shares.

The explorer is the product of a new system whose commandant, according to the officer, "shirks his duty" and is interested in such "trivial and ridiculous matters" as building harbors. He represents an enlightened and progressive system, which, however, does not meet Kafka's undivided acceptance as a meaningful alternative to the old system, as we shall see later.

The primitive order which the machine represents points to the dawn of civilization, which appears as a kind of Golden Age to the officer; he longs passionately for the restoration of a world dominated by a superhuman power. The outward perfection of the machine does not detract from its primitivity but heightens it through contrast, adding to it the dimension of the brutality of modern technology. Its destruction seems to stand as an indispensable prerequisite for any change toward a more rational and humanitarian system.

Change does not come easily, however, though the Old Commandant, uniting the functions of soldier, judge, mechanic, chemist and draughtsman, died some time ago (*Zeichner* is the German term for both "draughtsman" and "designer," thus indicating that the apparatus was, in effect, the Old Commandant's right hand). Though not the ruler of the colony, the officer carries on and defends the heritage of the Old Commandant against the new one. He is the "sole advocate" of the old method of execution, and he is thoroughly upset when the condemned man "befouls the machine like a pig-sty." As the embodiments of power in so many other Kafka stories recede from those who grope for an explanation of their irreversible fate—Klamm in *The Castle*, the legal authorities in *The Trial*, and the chief clerk in "The Metamorphosis"—so the New Commandant, like the old one before him, never appears on the scene personally. From the officer's fears, we gather that the New Commandant is a businessman rather than a supreme judge, that he does not care for the machine and the system it stands for, that he is eager to open the colony to international contacts and to grant it a hitherto unknown degree of liberal administration. In fact, the new regime is so open-minded that the officer takes it for granted that the visitor will be invited to participate in meetings on the future of the machine. Naturally, this strikes the officer as a further threat on the part of the New Commandant against traditional order.

As a result, the officer tries to coax the visitor into taking his side. In doing so, he talks himself into a frenzy, eventually assuming that the visitor has always approved of the old system anyway and only needs to choose the most appropriate language before the assembled administrators to tip the balance toward a revival of the old system. By trying to win the visitor over to his side, the officer clearly betrays the system he represents: without a single scruple, he sets the torture machine in motion whenever a condemned man was brought to him and never considered checking the evidence, much less exercising mercy. Yet he now asks for understanding and help. It is his downfall that the old system of absolute justice, which he represents, does not show human stirrings — even in his case. In keeping with its unbribable, clock-like mechanism, it condemns him to death. Now it is his turn to learn that, raised to the level of absoluteness, even such an ideal as justice becomes inhuman because it serves an abstract concept rather than human beings.

The officer's death, however, does not imply Kafka's wholehearted approval of the emerging new era. He keeps an ambivalent and ironical distance from the New Commandant and his reign. There is much change for the better on the island, as we have seen, but the "new, mild doctrine" has also brought with it much superficiality and degeneracy. Time and again, the officer complains about the great influence of ladies — even he himself "had tucked two fine ladies' handkerchiefs under the collar of his uniform"; these antics add a touch of the ludicrous to the new achievements. What Kafka is saying is that a certain measure of decadence seems to be inevitably a part of civilization and that the "modern" ideals of rationality and liberalism tend to give way too easily to considerations of utility and to the whims of the people.

To be sure, the explorer is interested in seeing the old system crumble. Yet he is extremely well-versed in abstaining from definite commitments, a trait which explains his reaction to the officer's description of the machine: "he already felt a dawning interest in the machine." Later on, when the apparatus is tried out, he completely forgets its deadly function and only complains that the noise of its wheels kept him from enjoying it all the more. When he finally realizes that the machine produces only horrendous results, he decides to make a compromise. Although opposing the system it serves, he is impressed by the officer's honest conviction. Not even when the latter places himself under the Harrow does the explorer lift a finger to stop the madness. Instead, he proclaims that he can "neither help nor hinder" the officer because "interference is always touchy."

The explorer shies away from committing himself because he has no binding standards. He expresses his disgust with the old system, but his humaneness is little more than a cover for his basic relativism. Especially at the end of the story, he reveals his true nature: already in the boat that is to take him to the steamer, he "lifted a heavy knotted rope from the floor boards, threatened the freed prisoner and the soldier guarding him with it and thus prevented them from leaping." His animosity is all the more surprising since he has played the decisive, though accidental, part in their liberation. It would therefore be only logical that he should show some concern for their future, should translate his theoretical condemnation of the old system into a concrete act of humaneness. By remaining unmoved, and therefore uncommitted, he displays cruelty which we may regard to be of a baser kind than the one shown by the Old Commandant, whom he condemned. Even the human element within the freed man does not really interest him. Reconsidering the story, we realize, as so often in Kafka's pieces, that the value judgment with which we may have identified ourselves in the course of our reading collapses under later evidence. In this case, evidence has accumulated that he who represents the "enlightened" ideals of tolerance and liberalism is not automatically superior to the Old Commandant and his admittedly outmoded and cruel system.

Kafka touches upon fundamental philosophical and political issues here. Ever since the time of the Greek political writer Polybius, human society has been confronted with the complex questions revolving around the apparently perennial alternation between tyranny and anarchy. From all evidence compiled over two thousand years, man, as a "political animal," has had to struggle to walk the thin tightrope between totalitarianism and the sometimes chaos which we have come to call democracy. Like a pendulum between two extremes, man's collective fate seems to swing back and forth between these two poles, symbolized in our story by the old and the new systems. On its way from one extreme to the other, the pendulum only briefly stays in the temperate zones — that is, democratic conditions are the result of a rather temporary constellation of forces. This is why the old system has had to give way to the new one, at least for the time being, but this is also why the Old Commandant will rise again when the new system will have worn itself out. Ultimately, neither system can last because neither can meet all of man's needs by itself.

On his way to the coastline, which is rather like an escape from the lingering spirit of the disintegrated machine, the explorer reaches the teahouse. It impresses him as being "a historic tradition of some kind." Upon his request, he is shown the grave of the Old Commandant, located under a stone plate. If there are indeed religious allusions in the story, they are most prominent here because the teahouse does resemble a holy place of some kind. The people gathered here are "humble creatures," wearing "full black beards" — Kafka's way of saying they are disciples of some quasi-religious mission. The inscription on the grave tells us that the Old Commandant's followers, now in the underground, will reconquer the colony after his resurrection and that they should be faithful and wait. Also, the explorer kneels down before the grave, and if he does so merely to be able to decipher the epitaph, he nevertheless goes through the motions of paying reverence in a religious manner.

Yet a total Christian interpretation is out of the question simply because the faith the old system rests on is one of sheer brutality. We have no reason whatever to assume that the predicted reconquering of the island will come about in a way other than through outright terror. This likelihood permits us to read the story, at least on one level, as a nightmarish vision of the annihilation camps of the Nazis. The story is religious only in the sense that the archaic system of the Old Commandant still prevails, though hardened into purely mechanical routine. Punishment by terror, which once meant purification and therefore was the focus of the colony's greatest festival, is considered nothing but a ridiculous remnant by the new regime. The machine still executes people (until it falls apart), but the motivation is gone and moral codes are imposed which lost their power when people lost faith in the divinity that once instituted them.

As in every one of Kafka's stories, a basic ambiguity remains, last but not least regarding Kafka's own feelings about it. While it is true that he condemned the old system for intellectual and humanitarian reasons, it is no less true that he lived with the uneasy awareness that the old system expresses a deep truth about human nature: suffering is part and parcel of man's nature, and the choice he has is not between accepting and rejecting it, but only between bestowing meaning to it or dragging it along as a stigma of the absurd.

THE HUNTER GRACCHUS
(DER JÄGER GRACCHUS)

Kafka's stories often deal with the power that either drives man beyond himself into the spiritual sphere or pulls him back into a primitive, this-worldly realm. (Compare the "assault from above" and the "assault from below" in "A Hunger Artist.") In several of his stories, he uses the symbol of the hunt to illustrate that wherever there is life there is also persecution and fighting. Nobody can escape it. A man may allow himself, it is true, to be driven in one direction by the hunt (as does the chief dog, for instance, in "Investigations of a Dog"), but having gone as far as he can, he will have to allow the hunt to drive him in the opposite direction and take him back if he wants to survive. Man remains the battleground of opposing forces, and this is why he roams the vague realms of life and death without being firmly anchored in either.

Few of Kafka's stories convey such a dense atmosphere of vagueness, remoteness, and dreamlike absurdity. This absurdity is intensified by the highly realistic description of Riva and the factual setting of the opening paragraphs, accenting a total lack of any common frame of reference between the townspeople of Riva and the newcomer. A touch of uncertainty and mysteriousness hovers over the story: the death ship glides into the harbor "as if" borne by "invisible means"; a man who is "probably dead" was "apparently" lying on a bier. Yet there can be no doubt about the "realness" of the story. To make this clear, Kafka has the hunter Gracchus remind us that, by contrast to the "real" world, "aboard ship, one is often victimized by stupid imaginations." In other words, the events taking place in Riva are not imagined by its inhabitants or by the hunter. In sober diction and short punctuated sentences, Kafka enumerates facts which, because of their almost meticulous factuality, stand in eerie contrast to the incredible occurrence itself.

Yet if the stranger's arrival is incredible, nobody really troubles about him or pays the least bit of attention to him. "Without any mark of surprise," the Burgomaster tells the visitor his name and profession, and the stranger's reply is equally calm. This contrast does not merely increase the impact of the story, but it also carries its own logic, in the sense that it reflects the impossibility of penetrating the story rationally.

It is of some interest that in a fragment belonging to the story, Kafka argues that Gracchus may be seen as an interpreter between earlier generations and those living today; he can transcend all limits of time and space ordinarily imposed upon a human being. Gracchus is capable of doing so because, as a dead person who is nevertheless "alive" in a certain sense, he has universal knowledge of everything that was and is. Comprised of both life and death during his travels in "earthly waters," Gracchus represents the totality of being, the universal elements of existence of all forms of being. This view is the only possible starting point for a logical explanation of how the hunter knows (or remembers) the Burgomaster's name. According to this explanation, the Burgomaster also participates in the timeless, universal quality of the hunter.

Who is the hunter Gracchus? Where is he coming from? We hear that he is "dead," and yet "in a certain sense" also alive. For hundreds of years he has sailed "earthly waters" ever since the day he fell into a ravine hunting chamois in the Black Forest. His barge was to take him to the realm of the dead, but it got off its course and has been aimlessly roaming the shadowy regions between life and death ever since.

While they know each other's names, the hunter and the Burgomaster know nothing of their respective worlds. Each is anxious to find out something but neither succeeds: the Burgomaster cannot even furnish the stranger with some desperately needed information about the town of Riva. This is, of course, a typical situation in a Kafka story: a complete lack of communication between people, or between worlds. The question arises: which world does the hunter represent? It is tempting to believe that the regions he comes from are a higher realm of reality, as opposed to the empirical world of Riva (which Kafka visited with his friend Brod in 1909). Once we analyze the hunter's world, however, it becomes clear that his world cannot be put into any fixed category. In fact, it is the most striking characteristic of the story of the hunter Gracchus that he no longer belongs anywhere, neither in a metaphysical realm nor in an empirical one. This was not always the case: he had been happy as a hunter, following his calling. He was happy even after he bled to death. Only long afterward did his mishap throw him into this predicament of total estrangement from any sense of belonging. We hear that it all began with a "wrong turn of the wheel" of his pilot and are immediately reminded of the "false alarm of the night bell once answered — it cannot be made good" again, the tragic insight of the country doctor doomed to roam through the snowy wastes.

Alienated and excluded from this world *and* the one beyond, the hunter Gracchus is at home everywhere and nowhere. Asked by the Burgomaster if he is not part of the "other world," he replies that he "is forever on the long staircase leading up to it." Typical of so many of Kafka's stories, this one begins with the hero's breaking away from a limited but clearly defined order. He once enjoyed living in this world, governed by a fixed set of rules, where people referred to him as "the great hunter." Now he who wanted nothing more than to live in the mountains must travel through all the lands of the earth and find no rest, even among the dead. All he knows is that no matter how hard he strives toward oblivion, he keeps regaining consciousness; he remains still "stranded forlornly in some earthly sea or other." The possibility of salvation does not exist, even under the best possible circumstances, because there is no way of communicating. Hence his frightening insight; to care is every bit as futile as not to care and "the thought of helping me is an illness."

As he so often does in his stories, Kafka drew on his own situation as a "hunter" here. The name Gracchus is derived from the Latin *graculus*, which means "raven," as does Kafka's name in Czech. Kafka repeatedly referred to himself as a "strange bird, aimlessly sailing about humans." Once upon a time it was possible to determine man's position in this world and the next one. As Gracchus puts it, commenting on his own death: "I can still recall happily stretching out on this pallet for the first time." Now he circles back and forth between spheres, and his apparently universal view of things is really that of Kafka, exploring all possible modes of thinking and living, dipping into each and staying with none.

As a result, the hunter Kafka was incapable of understanding the fixed order of earthly existence. He explained this failure in terms of a sudden lack of orientation, a distraction, "a wrong turn of the wheel." In his diary he referred to it as "self-forgetfulness," a lack of concentration, a "fatigue" which caused him to step out of the flow of time.

This lack of orientation and subsequent isolation, however, which permeates Gracchus' (Kafka's) life is not to be seen as something which one can explain autobiographically or psychoanalytically, as has too often been done in connection with Kafka's conflict with his father. The experience of such fundamental disorientation and isolation is rather the precondition for Kafka's uncompromising prodding into the complexities of human experience. That this human experience retreats even before his literary genius and permits only approximations is to be expected: language is by definition self-restrictive. What we term Gracchus' "totality of being" or his "transcendence of time and distance," for instance, we have therefore put in these terms simply because it defies any adequate description. This does not mean that "totality" and "transcendence" do not exist; the whole story illustrates that they do indeed exist. It is simply that to force Kafka's attempts to penetrate to the very core of the mystery of existence into a set of ready-made definitions would be tantamount to violating his intentions.

In this context, it is important to recall that Kafka himself has done everything, both in his stories and his commentaries on them, to qualify and even retract so-called clear-cut interpretations which he may have advanced or which others may have read into his writing. Naturally his stories are also interpretations and reflections, giving expression to manifold social, psychological, biographical, philosophical, and religious phenomena. But only up to a point. If interpreting were all he had had in mind, there would have been no need for him to leave his readers wondering about the answers to so many questions. The paradoxes and absurdities that abound in his works are the logical, because inevitable, expression of the fact that "reality" or "truth" on their highest level are indeed paradoxical and absurd when defined by our own limited comprehension.

THE BURROW
(DER BAU)

In terms of narrative method, Kafka writes from within the mind of the protagonist, and the introspective protagonist — through whose eyes we see the maze of the burrow — is the author himself. Any number of entries in his diary reveal the affinity of Kafka's existence with that of the animal, and in letters to his fiancée Milena, he even refers to himself as "the wood animal." But this animal is also man alone, man hunted and haunted, man confronted with powers that forever elude his control. And the burrow with its innermost sanctuary, the Castle Keep, is his painfully constructed bastion against the animosity of the world around him.

That the burrow's description so closely resembles that of an actual subterranean animal's hideout enhances its symbolic meaning and illustrates that it is really more complex than its outward appearance indicates. The "unique instrument" of the animal's forehead is a symbol of Kafka's (man's) passionate battle against the encroaching confusion of earthly existence, a battle he fought with "intense intellectual" rather than "physical" prowess. As he was to put it in his merciless, almost masochistic fashion: "I was glad when the blood came, for that was proof that the walls were beginning to harden. I richly paid for my Castle Keep."

What really is the burrow and against which inimical world is it intended? Let us view the animal's attempt to set up a shelter for itself in terms of a fight between mind and reality—that is, between man's effort to construct a rational world of his own making and the outside world dominated by irrational forces. It is against this incalculable world of irrational forces that he builds the burrow where he alone intends to be in charge. He believes his burrow will be superior to the reality of the outside because it is rational—which to him means perfect and entirely identical with its builder. (Compare this story with "A Hunger Artist" for another of Kafka's representations of the complete detachment of the outside world.) That his complete seclusion from the "real" world above results in an unhealthy preoccupation with it, is also the result of his failure to understand that everybody ultimately takes himself with him wherever he may flee to, thereby contaminating the imagined perfection of his new, artificial realm. For this reason, it is not exaggerated to call the burrow a solipsistic world.

The narrator's obsession with building a perfectly safe realm for himself dulls his mind to the decisive factor that, no matter how hard he tries to set up a self-sustaining world, this world will nevertheless depend on the outside for such basic necessities as air and food. The entrance, however, is not only the point of contact with the outside world supplying air and food: it is also the place where potential enemies can make their way inside. In other words, the impossibility of creating a perfect inner world goes hand in hand with the impossibility of shutting himself off completely. Hence the burrow will remain unsafe in the last analysis. The awareness of this imperfection drives him mad and, as a result, he will go on building and mending corridors as long as he lives. To live is to be afraid, and to be afraid is to be worried about defending oneself. The trouble is, as Kafka put it in one of his well-known aphorisms: "The hunting dogs are playing in the courtyard, but the hare will not escape them, no matter how fast it may be flying already through the woods."

The burrow is "another world" which affords new powers to him who descends into it from the world above. Time and again, it is praised as the sanctuary of tranquility and peace, sometimes even evoking associations of voluntary death. As in so many of Kafka's stories, the theme of hunting and being hunted figures prominently. In "The Hunter Gracchus," for example, this hunt makes the "wood animal" a battlefield of opposing forces—the "assault from above" and "the assault from below." Tranquility and the hunt, peace and annihilation—these are the opposite poles between which the narrator's life and our lives vascillate.

The entire story, it should be said, is dialectic in character. The burrow stands for the assumed safety of the animal's rational faculties, but it also stands for danger where "we will both blindly bare our claws and our teeth" when disaster strikes; the entrance symbolizes hope, but it is also the weak spot of his structure, through which the perils of the outside world threaten to leak in; and in spite of the owner's attempts at making himself independent of the outside world, he wants occasional contact with it because it exerts a certain fascination upon him. Outside "reality" even loses its horror for short periods of time for him, but he soon returns to his burrow, incapable of enjoying the freer mode of existence. Kafka has magnificently expressed the all-pervading law of movement and counter-movement here, a reflection of his own life embroiled in counter currents.

The description of the unknown and yet steadily approaching noise ranks among the most brilliant passages Kafka ever wrote. There are few pieces in which he caught the nightmare of his own anxiety-ridden existence in such fearfully dense diction. Comprising almost half of the story, beginning with his being awakened by an "inaudible whistling noise (the twilight zone of consciousness following sleep is most important in Kafka's stories), these passages are an ever-mounting frenzy of self-doubt, bottomless fear, and exhausted resignation. They seem to be one long scream, reflecting his own seismographic sensitivity to the tremendous, though partly still latent, upheavals of our age. At first, the builder of the burrow only talks about certain "small fry" that have dug their way into his domain, and what bothers him most at this point is that they have succeeded without his noticing them. Soon, however, the noise grows louder and keeps him on a steady alert. From everywhere within his burrow he can hear the whistling coming nearer and—this enervating thought completely overwhelms him—it may come "from some animal unknown to me." Battling his overwrought imagination, he begins to calm himself by imagining a swarm of harmless little animals. Once anxiety has made inroads into his badly shaken self, however, his agony is intensified. Reeling with visions of horror, he cannot keep the sound of the blood pounding through his veins distinct from the ubiquitous whistling any longer. Unable and even unwilling to trust his observations, he jumps to conclusions which he discards before he has even set out to carry them through. In a maddening escalation of frenzy, the invisible pursuers are holding ever more sway over him, alternately scaring him to death and lulling him into short respites of exhaustion. As everywhere in Kafka's world, it is precisely the elements of the unknown that cause his anxiety. (In fact, the psychological term anxiety (Angst in German) is generally used to describe feelings of being threatened that lack concrete, known reasons.) As sheer horror approaches, invisible and yet more and more audible, "the growing-louder is like a coming-nearer." Now he does not think of the source of his anxiety as a swarm of little animals any longer; it now begins to assume the looming proportions of "a single great beast." He goes into frantic last-minute attempts at fortifying his maze but, at the same time, he suffers from nagging self-incrimination because he has neglected to take defensive steps while there was still time. In fact, there had been plenty of time, for he was still young when he first heard the noise for the first time; as it happened, the danger subsided and, instead of taking this as a warning, he went on building his burrow as if nothing had happened. He begins to realize that rather than making him feel more secure, the burrow has weakened his ability to meet an assault successfully.

The most tragic realization in this story is that not even the best possible entrance or the best possible bulwark can save him, that "in all probability it would . . . rather betray" him. There is no direct correlation between the safety one desires, the efforts to achieve it that one goes through, and the realization of this safety. Or, expressed in terms of the story's main theme: in the face of advancing irrationality, man—relying on his rational powers—is doomed to failure. It is not enough to register the "scratching" of the enemy's claws, for whenever that happens "already you are lost." The irony is that there may be no objective threat at all, that the noise may be nothing but a projection of the dweller's own anxiety. He may have created a nightmare for himself, which of course does not make his agony any less harrowing. When we look at the story in this way, we realize that the whistling may well have been delusion, the result of his pathological preoccupation with himself.

On several occasions, Kafka referred to tuberculosis as being his "beast," and we may safely read the story on this level. Primarily, of course, it is a reflection of his own lifelong quest for security and salvation, as well as a sensitive diagnosis of an age which, while still deeming itself healthy and safe, was rapidly falling victim to the barbarities of twentieth-century political ideologies. "In the Penal Colony" comes to mind immediately, a nearly perfect portrayal of this "evil beast" at work. Quite in keeping with the intensity of its truthfulness to life, "The Burrow" has no end to indicate the termination of the drama described. Everything remains open and the battle rages on.

Whenever the hero of a Kafka story is also its narrator, we are faced with the question of who it is that he is actually telling the story to. To whom is it, for instance, that the dog in "Investigations of a Dog" tells about the research he has conducted all by himself and in which nobody else is interested? Or to whom is it that the ape talks in "A Report to an Academy"? This is part of Kafka's genius. The wide use of interior monologue designed to record the internal emotional experience of the animal on several levels of consciousness is most effective. Hence, also, the experience on the part of the reader as if the author did not exist, as if he were overhearing the animal's articulations of thought and feeling directly.

INVESTIGATIONS OF A DOG
(FORSCHUNGEN EINES HUNDES)

Like "The Burrow" and "Josephine the Singer," this story deals with an animal that finds itself in a world beyond the empirical one. Unlike Gregor Samsa in "The Metamorphosis," the animal is not abruptly torn out of a concrete situation and plunged into a conflict with the universal sphere; instead, it is encompassed by this sphere from the very outset. This immediate confrontation with the whole universe is a characteristic of the later Kafka and may serve as an indication of his own increasing aloofness from "real life" concerns. He, the investigating dog of the story, is not "different from any other dog," and yet he asks if it is possible for a creature to be "more unfortunate still" than he is.

Looking back on his investigations, the old dog admits he has always asked the most baffling questions rather than trying to adjust to the ways of his fellow dogs. The result is that his boundless thirst for knowledge has forced him out of his "social circle." The event which set him on this path was his encounter with seven dogs that turned out to be excellent musicians. Although that happened when he was young, he distinctly recalls being overwhelmed by their performance in spite of his attempts to keep his wits. Most significantly, the appearance of the seven dogs was really his doing, at least indirectly, because he had harbored a "vague desire" for such an event. It also follows from the text that the light into which the seven dogs stepped was by no means light in the empirical sense of the word. Both the music they played and the dazzling light were really conjured up by him whose "premonition of great things" had kept him blind and deaf. This explains why the music tears him away from his routine reflections and even robs him of his power of resistance.

The paradoxical nature of these remarkable dogs, the apparent "dumb senselessness of these creatures" which have "no relation whatever to the general life of the community," is an illustration of the inexplicable forces alive within man. Defying all clear-cut classification and behaving in a multitude of contradictory ways, these dogs are nevertheless most "real" in all their seemingly absurd "unrealness." As are the sciences of music and nutrition later on in the story, these beings — or imagined beings — are symbols of the futility of the dog's attempts at explaining empirically the reason of his existence. No wonder he thinks it possible that "the world was turned upside down." Again, the dilemma is Kafka's own: the insistence on the use of rational and empirical means beyond their legitimate range.

The music which the seven dogs play "appeared to come from all directions . . . blowing fanfares so close that they appeared far removed and almost inaudible." In his state of alienation, man is further removed from his innermost self than from anybody else. The ubiquitousness of this music seems to symbolize the totality of all things within which there are no barriers between the individual and the universal, between question and answer. Their refusal to answer any question strikes the chief dog to be "against the law"; in the sense that their music suspends the traditional order of things, this is correct. There can be no answer to any concrete question because this totality *is* the ultimate answer: the antithesis of question and answer, like every other one, recedes in one blaring sea of sound.

Kafka has attempted to describe this totality elsewhere. In *The Castle*, for instance, the protagonist K., as well as the people of the village where he performs his work, hears only indistinct murmuring over the telephone connecting them with the castle; this murmuring is said to sound as if it originated from countless individual voices merged into one single sound. Later on, K.

learns that this vague, drawn-out singing sound is all the people can rely on because all other "messages" are deceptive. It so happens that he learns this as he complains about the contradicting bits of information he gets from the castle officials. In other words, no single piece of information can amount to more than a fraction of the truth; also, our limited mind is necessarily partial and uncertain. In *The Trial*, Joseph K. does not understand the people talking to him in the courthouse; he merely hears a monotone noise permeating everything. It, too, remains open to a bewildering array of interpretations. "Truth," as Kafka put it, "lies in the chorus of the whole."

The annihilating quality of this music is, at the same time, the dog's safeguard for breaking out into freedom and toward a total view of things. His further investigations bear him out: at the end of the story, as he wants to die because he has not succeeded in leaving this "world of falsehood" for that of "truth," a strange hound appears to save him by chasing him away. He comes as a "hunter." (Compare this incident with "The Hunter Gracchus.") Exhausted and desperate, the chief dog does not understand and resists until he is again smitten by "irresistible" music. It threatens to destroy him, as did the music of the seven soaring dogs in his youth, but it enables him to "leave the place in splendid condition." As a puppy, he begged the seven dogs to "enlighten" him who "had roamed through darkness for a long time" and "yet knew almost nothing of the creativity of music." Now he detects a new life through the overpowering melody that "was moving toward only him." Now he has found "the law" of all creation in its application to himself. It is important to realize that it is only after his senses have been sharpened by fasting that he is rescued by the hound. "If it is attainable at all, the highest is attainable only through the greatest effort, and that among us is voluntary fasting."

The tragic realization remains, as it does elsewhere in Kafka, that this "law" and its liberating effect—here in the form of music—cannot be told." His speedy recovery and liberation is his own new reality. Even more tragic, however, this new state is also "delusive," not merely in the eyes of his fellow dogs, but also in his own mature judgment: "Certainly such freedom as is possible today is a wretched business."

The question of sustenance runs throughout the story until the investigating dog seeks to combine the science of music with that of nurture. When he asks himself if such a combination is possible, fully aware that he is moving in a "border region between sciences," he expresses Kafka's favorite theme of spiritual nourishment versus physical nourishment. In "The Metamorphosis," Gregor Samsa believes he has found his "unknown nourishment" in music, and the hunger artist sets his all-time record of fasting because he has not been able to find the right food to live on. Here, the dog has found out in earlier experiments that the earth does not merely supply all food by making it grow, but that it also calls down the food "from above." This is why he believes that not merely the indispensable task of working the soil is important, but also believes in "incantation, dance, and song," designed to attract food from "above." In other words, his concern is not with spiritual *or* physical food but with a synthesis of both.

This concern for the right food reflects Kafka's harsh criticism of traditional science as being preoccupied solely with working the soil. Though "to the best of my knowledge science ordains nothing else than this," the chief dog's investigations have shown time and again that "the people in all their ceremonies gaze upwards." Here Kafka criticizes both the scientific thinking that disregards the "upward gaze," as well as the quasi-religious stance which makes people "chant their incantations with their faces turned upwards . . . forgetting the ground." Despite his repeated professions to be a dog like all others, our chief dog differs from other members of his race in that his tremendous curiosity does not permit him to accept certain discrepancies. These pages show the dog (Kafka) pondering the fatal rupture between faith and reason (and between religion and science) that has run through our civilization since Descartes. To a large extent, the dog argues, a perverted science with a fixation on the measurable and statistical is to be blamed for the frightening success of so many pseudo-philosophies and surrogate religions in our time. By not taking into account man's need for food from "above," this notion of science has aided the confusion of minds.

Although the "theory of incantation by which food is called down" is a basic experience of all dogs, it is also an experience each one has to make himself. Therefore it eludes translation into the language of scientific proof. This is what Kafka means when he writes at the end of the story: "To me, the deeper cause of my lack of scientific abilities seems to be an instinct—and not at all a bad one. It is an instinct which has made me prize freedom higher than anything else—perhaps for a science superior than today's." Freedom is indeed the basis of the "science of man," even though its existence cannot be proven within the framework of conventional scientific methods. By deliberately risking his life, the investigating dog has shown that this freedom exists nevertheless.

A REPORT TO AN ACADEMY
(EIN BERICHT AN EINE AKADEMIE)

Wounded and captured by an expedition, a formerly "free" ape found himself aboard a boat headed for Europe. Confined in a tight cage, he realized for the first time that escape was impossible. Thus he decided to opt for something less than animal freedom—in fact, he didn't even require freedom. He simply wanted "a way out." For him, a "way out" required taking on as much as possible of the human world around him. This he did.

He succeeded in overcoming his animal existence to an astounding degree and, today, he is not really unhappy. Everything he learned he could not have achieved had he chosen to remain an ape, but: "One learns when one needs a way out." The seamy side of this statement is that the memories of his former life are becoming increasingly vaguer as the ape becomes adjusted to the world of man. As he takes on more characteristics of his human environment, he has trouble even comprehending the freedom of his past. It eludes his comprehension and even his power of description: the "direction" from where he came is really all he can tell his learned audience.

Yet, no matter how comfortable he may feel in the human world, the "gentle puff of air" tickling his heels reminds him, as it does every human being, of his lost freedom. (Cool breezes in Kafka's stories usually stand for freedom — sometimes too much freedom, causing man to lose his orientation.) The trouble is, however, that any regaining of this freedom could only come about at the expense of being a human being. To the narrator, the idea of being human and being free are mutually exclusive; maintaining a measure of each is therefore tantamount to being caught in the middle of two modes of existence.

This is exactly what has happened to him. He willingly shows his wound — this symbol of animal turned human — to visitors because "when the plain truth is in question, great minds discard the niceties of refinement." His development toward "humanness" is something he has aimed for, and yet it is a "forced career" he has never really wanted. His situation between two worlds is particularly tragic because he is actively involved in the human world during the day, in variety shows and lectures; by night, he sleeps with his half-trained chimpanzee mate. He cannot bear to see the chimpanzee by day, "because she has that insane look of the bewildered half-broken animal in her eye." He chose to turn human and has visible wounds and painful memories of a lost freedom, but she — still one hundred percent animal — is bound to go crazy among humans.

The narrator's position may be described as being between a past world in which he represented something he does not represent any more and a present world in which he represents something he *knows* he is not. This is why he begins his account with the words "I belong to the Gold Coast." His report deals almost solely with what he has experienced as a human being — which he is only in a more or less superficial way. His self-awareness was nonexistent when he was captured, and so he has to "depend on the evidence of others" when it comes to telling his audience about that part of his life. He apologizes for being in no position to supply any meaningful data on his former condition as an ape; his return to "apeishness" becomes more difficult proportionate to his development toward "humanness."

The language of this report bears the unmistakable marks of something artificially acquired. The enormous discrepancy between man and ape, as well as his attitude as an ape rather than that of a human being are quite evident, as, for example, when he casually boasts of having "emptied many a bottle of good red wine with the expedition leader" and when he jeers at such ridiculous human demonstrations of freedom as that acted out and applauded in the course of a circus trapeze act. Having achieved his goal to the degree which would guarantee his survival, he has learned how to participate in human society, even to be a great success in his performances. At the same time, it is important to realize that he remains a curiosity unable to bridge the gap between his two natures. Symbolic of his in-between situation, he thinks "with his belly." He belongs nowhere.

At no point in the ape's development in the direction of a human being is there any hint of a change for the superior. In fact, the story ends on a clear note of resignation that stands in sharp contrast to any belief in progress. There can be no advances without concomitant payments of freedom and life: "Even if my prowess and determination would be enough to get me back . . . I would have to peel every piece of skin from my body to squeeze through."

The story abounds in satire that sometimes borders on sarcasm, such as the description of the drunken ape accidentally gurgling "Hallo." The view is often held that Kafka permitted his ape to be raised to a level of "humanness" — a distorted one, to be sure — only to reveal the beast in man or, at least, the fact that man cannot attain his potential humanity in freedom. While not altogether wrong, this view does not do justice to Kafka, whose transformation stories are essentially parables of spiritual disorientation. In all of them, whether in "The Metamorphosis" or "Investigations of a Dog," the protagonist has not merely lost his sense of identity, but he has actually lost this identity itself. Whether the change is from man to animal or the other way around is beside the point: they all wind up in in-between situations. In all these instances, Kafka gives expression to this deepest of all human predicaments by using the essential "otherness" of man and animal.

THE GREAT WALL OF CHINA
(BEIM BAU DER CHINESISCHEN MAUER)

The discussion of the system employed in the construction of the wall takes up most of the story's first section. The way average workers react to the piecemeal system of building is contrasted with the way the sensitive workers react. This latter group would succumb to discouragement rather easily if they were to work far away from home, under difficult circumstances, without ever seeing their efforts come to fruition. It is only after they see finished sections of the wall that these sensitive workers go on performing with enthusiasm; being intellectuals and therefore more aware of the possible illusory nature of the whole project, they need continued reassurance of purposefulness. The piecemeal system was selected to give them this feeling of purposefulness (by having them marvel at finished sections) while permitting the high command to transfer the regular day laborers (who do not have this problem) to wherever they are needed. In its wisdom, the command has taken human nature of all kinds of workers into account by decreeing the piecemeal system.

In China, which Kafka uses as a symbol of the whole of mankind, people have been convinced of the meaningfulness of construction ever since architecture was raised to the level of the most important science. They are convinced because the workers have common plans and common goals. There is no chaos because no one is preoccupied with his own personal problems. The way for the individual to prevent chaos is by stepping out of his isolation, at least at certain intervals, and joining the great reservoir of mankind in a common ideal.

The narrator tells of a scholarly book which in the early days of the construction persuaded people to "join forces as far as possible for the accomplishment of a single aim." In those days, it was possible to achieve aims every bit as impressive as the building of the Tower of Babel although, "as regards divine approval," the Great Wall to be built is presented as a venture that, unlike the Tower of Babel, does bear the stamp of divine sanctioning. This book that the narrator cites says further that the Tower of Babel failed because its foundations were too weak, and that the "Great Wall alone would provide for the first time in the history of mankind a secure foundation for a new Tower of Babel."

The trouble is that the construction of a new skyscraper, be it ever so commendable an attempt on the part of mankind to fulfil its ancient dream of reaching the heavens, clearly goes beyond man's capabilities. This is why the new Tower of Babel remains something "nebulous." How can the wall be the foundation of this gigantic venture if it consists only of individual segments with numerous wide gaps not filled in? There is also justified doubt if the Great Wall will ever be finished. Kafka's comparison of the construction of the wall with that of the Tower of Babel has decidedly political overtones. In this connection, it is interesting to cite a passage from Dostoevsky's *Brothers Karamazov* (Part I, Chapter 5), with which Kafka was thoroughly familiar. There, in his criticism of political tyranny, Dostoevsky used the image of the Tower of Babel: "For Socialism is not only the labor question, or the question of the so-called fourth state, but above all an atheistic question, the question of the modern interpretation of atheism, the question of the Tower of Babel which is deliberately being erected without God, not for the sake of realizing heaven from earth, but for the sake of bringing heaven down to earth."

Fully aware though Kafka was of man's need for a common cause, he nevertheless shrank from endorsing any mass movement that enscribed the liquidation of the individual on its banners. His sensitivity to the emerging totalitarian ideologies of our century made him cautious and suspicious of "people with banners and scarfs waving." He detested and ridiculed their naïve belief in uncompromising solidarity for some version of perennial bliss on earth. His clear rejection of such ideologies is all the more remarkable because it demonstrates how well and consistently he could differentiate between totalitarian utopias on the one hand and the promise the Zionist dream held out to him on the other.

The greatest threat to which mankind is exposed comes from those fanatics who submit detailed blueprints for the wall and the new tower to be placed on top of it without having the right methods of construction. As the scholarly book explains, it is exactly this "nebulous" idea of a great common cause that appeals to people. Enthusiasm alone will not do, however. What makes the situation so much more difficult today is that almost everyone knows how to lay foundations well and the general yearning for a common cause has taken the form of yearning for *any* common cause. Naturally, the scholarly book is a great success with everyone now too: it gives people insight into their "essentially changeable, unstable" natures that "can endure no restraint" and will "tear everything to pieces" once it gets the chance to pool its energies. By revealing the counter forces to which people are exposed, Kafka has once again described his own situation — namely, that of a battle field. Two antagonistic forces are within him — the hunt that drives him beyond his limits and the forces chasing him back in the opposite direction, back to his concrete and earthbound existence. As he himself termed his anguish, he was continually torn by the "assault from above" and the "assault from below."

All we know about the nature of the command is that in its office, whose location remains unknown, "all human thoughts and desires were revolved, and counter to them all human aims and fulfilments. And through the window the reflected splendors of divine worlds fell on the hands of the leaders." These leaders represent the totality of human experience, and while they are far from divine themselves, they nevertheless reflect divine splendors. Like the officialdom in *The Trial* or in *The Castle*, the command may be seen as the symbol of man's spiritual world.

Remote, nebulous, and impersonal, it has probably existed from times immemorial. But it is also powerful and omniscient. And as in virtually all Kafka pieces, men rebel against an imperfect world created by a power which, they believe, could have done better. The human situation is aggravated because men have to assist in the expansion of this deficient world.

Any accusation leveled at the leadership is futile in the sense that we may say it is directed not at actual beings, but at man's world of imagination. This is why Kafka keeps warning us to try and comprehend things only up to a point. This message is clearly stated for us with the help of the parable of the river that floods the lands beyond its banks: as soon as man tries to transcend his limits — the "destiny" of the parable — he loses his direction. The thing to remember is that man's apparently innate temptation to attempt something beyond his limits is something the command has taken into account by ordering the piecemeal system of construction. As stated at the outset, the realization of the wall's imperfectability is something the workers could not cope with. Kafka has, of course, drawn his own lifelong battle here between his understanding "that the limits which my capacity for thought imposes upon me are narrow" and his unending, self-tormenting intellectual probing into the unanswerable questions of human existence.

Since work on the wall is completed (though large gaps will always remain) and since the narrator's "inquiry is purely historical," this probing continues. Doubt is expressed not merely as to the meaningfulness of the piecemeal system but also about the whole construction. Was the wall really intended to protect the land from northern nomads (Kafka's symbol of incalculable evil that might intrude anytime)? (Compare this with the threat of evil from the "outside world" of "The Burrow.") The mere mention of the nomads scares the children, it is true, but the enemies may very well be harmless fairy-tale creatures — again very much like the mysterious animal drilling away in "The Burrow." Surely the nomads are too far away to pose much of a threat. At any rate, the command's decision to have the wall built was *not* the result of this potential, if unlikely, threat because the decision is as old as the command itself. Man may mark certain points in time as beginnings and ends, but both the command and the building of the wall have been, and are, eternal. The decree to defend the territory against the nomads resulted from the wise realization of the command that men cannot survive without concrete tasks in a secured order of things or, to put it in Kafka's terms, "outside the law."

Empire is one of the most ambiguous institutions in China, as the narrator assures us at the beginning of the second part of the story in one of Kafka's characteristic efforts to dress the most profound questions in factual, quasi-scientific terms: the narrator knows a method whereby certain subjects may be "probed to the marrow" because he has studied the "comparative history of races." People do not even know the name of their ruler, and "Pekin itself is far stranger to the people in our village than the next world." Complete confusion prevails as to government guidelines and laws of everyday life, and any meaningful concept of time has been lost. As a result, dead emperors are venerated as if they were still alive and contemporary crimes are condoned because they are believed to have occurred in the distant past. Here Kafka has expressed a terrible insight about man, namely his tendency to turn his back on the problems of his own time and permit himself to be guided by the outmoded ways of thinking in bygone ages. Whole societies are fashioned after obsolete models, no matter how they terrorize people living now. The "law" of their own day remains hidden from them. This is their tragic fate.

The enormous distance between Pekin and the people of the south may also be seen as Kafka's illustration of Jewry outside history. It is a fact that Kafka chided Jews who deliberately forsook their own ways in order to try and become assimilated. If one reads the story on this level, China appears not only as the symbol of the universe but also as that of the Jews, scattered far from their spiritual center and yet, in a sense, held together by tradition.

If anyone should think that "in reality we have no Emperor because confusion abounds, he would not be far from the truth," the narrator says. Since the Emperor is immortal, however, at least as an institution, this means that man cannot know the institutions of the empire nor, as a result, abide by the laws it decrees. This is so not because the people have forsaken their Emperor: on the contrary, "there is hardly a more faithful people than ours." While one may read the story as dealing with the secularization of our age, the theme of the ambiguous relationship between the Emperor (God) and man is more paramount. Under no circumstances can the Emperor's message reach a specific individual because even the strongest and fastest messenger is bound to become lost in the infinite spaces between the imperial courts and the endless wastes beyond the palace gates. Only distorted fragments of a message may eventually trickle down to a subject, but even if this should happen, the message would arrive too late. Besides, the village people would not take any such messenger seriously and would probably kick him out anyway.

Nonetheless, the narrator says, we all "sit by our windows dreaming of such a messenger descending." A message would give direction and meaning. The situation resounds with all the melancholy of human longing for "law." The people, "insignificant shadows cringing in the most remote stretches before the imperial sun," stand no chance of making themselves heard at the distant court. It is partly beyond their capabilities to do so and partly due to circumstances they cannot change which keep them from succeeding. Yet subtly and consistently, an overtone of reproach is in motion which charges the people with not mustering up enough imagination and initiative when it comes to dealing with the cumbersome machinery of the state. As in the parable "Before the Law" in *The Trial*, where Joseph K. fails to act firmly on his own behalf against the clumsiness and callousness of a nebulous authority, Kafka attacks man's subservience before the state. The odds may be heavily against him and he may be aware of this, but he should nevertheless continue fighting. He must continue if he wants to secure a measure of dignity for himself in a basically hopeless and—which is worse—absurd situation.

This story is eminently "religious" in the broad sense of the term. Whether we interpret the empire to be a spiritual realm actually existing or whether we take it to be a figment of man's spiritually starved imagination, in both cases it serves to show human longing for meaningfulness. The empire's inaccessibility and the wall's imperfectability stand as convincing bits of evidence that man's desire and search for a fixed order must be thwarted unless he learns to employ the right means: it may be better, after all, to have old-fashioned believers than victims of "scientific investigations" into realms that must, of necessity, retreat before such probing. Kafka knows, as does the high command of the story, that people would lose the ground under their feet without some measure of hope anchored in the metaphysical. "Therefore I shall not continue probing these questions beyond this point."

JOSEPHINE THE SINGER, OR THE MOUSE FOLK
(JOSEPHINE DIE SÄNGERIN)

The story's double title is one of its striking outward features. Kafka attached special meaning to this, arguing that it expresses an equilibrium, a set of scales, the careful weighing between the evaluation of Josephine and the people around her. While the meaning of "singer" becomes clear, however, Kafka's decision to use the term "mouse folk" is perhaps not so clear. Apart from underlining the aspect of mass behavior of the people who adore Josephine, he could have wanted to depict the miserable situation of Jews scattered all over the world and yet, at the same time, their sense of community as an ethnically and religiously distinct group. More than any other story of Kafka's, this one reflects his growing interest in, and defense of, traditional Jewish ways — above all, his positive view of the orthodox and Zionist sense of community.

The enormous power Josephine wields over the people is all the more surprising because they "forgot how to sing long ago" (they do not cherish their traditional Jewish ways any more) and do not care about music. Even more surprising, they agree that Josephine's singing is not really any better than their own. We are quickly told, however, that if this should be so, it is true only in a strictly musical sense; the essential difference between her singing and that of everybody else is still there: she sings consciously, whereas the people "pipe without thinking of it, indeed without noticing it." In her piping (for this seems to be all it is), the people's main characteristic—that is, piping—becomes a conscious action.

Another aspect to Josephine's singing leads to the people's identifying with her art. Not only does each individual listen to her singing as if he were listening for a message, but her singing "resembles people's precarious existence amidst the chaos of a hostile world." Totally absorbed by this tumult, they have forgotten about their true existence and have stopped singing, a reference to the secularized Jewry which Kafka came to despise. Whenever they listen to Josephine, the populace retrieves something of their short childhood, symbolizing a carefree (because less conscious) existence.

The narrator, the "we" of the story, tells us that nobody would really care to listen to a highly trained singer in times of general hardship; in other words, aesthetic perfection cannot be the objective of art in times such as theirs. As Kafka puts it here, "May Josephine be spared from recognizing that the mere fact of . . . listening to her is proof that she is no singer." People flock to her performances precisely because her singing is *not* art in the traditional sense of the word, because "it is not so much a performance of songs as an assembly of people."

Josephine, however, does not share the public's opinion of her singing. She is convinced that she creates perfect music, that her singing is infinitely superior to that of the people around her, and that nobody really understands her. She is certain the people are in need of her much more than she is in need of them. She insists that her singing takes the most decisive place in their lives and that she should therefore be exempted from all routine work. This alone would guarantee her ability to attain the highest possible artistic standard at all times. She desires nothing short of a whole-hearted recognition of her art as unparalleled and eternal. This is exactly the limit, though, to which people will not go. Such boundless recognition would be possible only if Josephine really stood "outside the law." If this were the case, the freedom from daily chores which people would grant her would be proof that "they are smitten by her art, feel themselves unworthy of it, try to assuage the pity she awakens in them by making sacrifices for her; to the same extent that her art is beyond their comprehension, they would also regard her personality and her desires to lie beyond their jurisdiction."

Here the essence of Kafka's view of art emerges — the view, that is, which he held toward the end of his life. He wrote "Josephine the Singer" in March 1924, three months before his death, and "A Hunger Artist," which also deals with the antithetical nature of art, two years before. In both stories, the protagonist falls victim to the temptation of deeming himself among the "select few," and in both stories his conflict results from his assumption that his art is vastly superior to the forms of expression of the people around him. In both stories, his refusal and inability to feel at ease in the "vast, warm bed of the community" cause his eventual isolation and death, and in both stories, his claim to stand "beyond the law" is rejected by Kafka. Even Josephine, whose magic makes people forget their hardships, has to remain bound by the laws of human community. The reason for this is that her individual self is at the same time the self of the people who find themselves reflected in her singing: whatever she may sing is also being sung by them, and whatever vision of freedom she may create is also present in the people sharing her performances. In its most profound sense, art is never beyond the people.

One may even go so far as to argue that Kafka foresees the disappearance of art in the traditional sense and, more important yet, that he does not shed a tear for its essential disappearance. "Josephine is a small episode in the eternal history of our people, and the people will overcome losing her" is only one sentence among many that reflects this view. The story is Kafka's final pronouncement on that esoteric notion that art is likely to die because it insists on being nothing but art. Everything seeking absolute perfection must necessarily refrain from becoming contaminated with life. But everything fleeing communion with life because of life's countless imperfections must die. To be perfect is to be dead. On one level, the story of Josephine is probably the story of a Yiddish singer-actress whom Kafka met in Prague in 1911, and on a higher level, it is the story of the universal artist faced with the large (mouselike) audience of our time. On still another level, it is the story of the inevitable death of self-imposed seclusion.

Historically speaking, the story stands as an attack on the obstinate arrogance of official art as taught and propagated by the academies of the nineteenth and early twentieth centuries. Rarely had art been more hypocritical, with its insistence on "higher values" and quasi-religious "purity." It is not that art cannot have these higher values and have this religious meaningfulness; it is just that in the nineteenth and early twentieth centuries, it had long lost the metaphysical basis for such lofty claims.

Josephine's last words stand as Kafka's own last words about his life. The mere fact that he prepared the story for publication from his deathbed, while requesting that all his other pieces be burned, attests to the significance he attached to it: "Josephine . . . will happily submerge herself in the numberless masks of our heroes and soon, since we are no historians, will ascend to the heights of redemption and fall victim to oblivion like all her brothers."

UNDERSTANDING KAFKA

A major problem confronting readers of Kafka's short stories is to find a way through the increasingly dense thicket of interpretations. Among the many approaches one encounters is that of the autobiographical approach. This interpretation claims that Kafka's works are little more than reflections of his lifelong tension between bachelorhood and marriage or, on another level, between his skepticism and his religious nature. While it is probably true that few writers have ever been moved to exclaim, "My writing was about you [his father]. In it, I merely poured out the sorrow I could not sigh out at your breast" [*Letter to His Father*], it is nevertheless dangerous to regard the anxieties permeating his work solely in these terms. Kafka's disenchantment with and eventual hatred of his father were a stimulus to write, but they neither explain the fascination of his writing nor tell us why he wrote at all.

The psychological or psychoanalytical approach to Kafka largely ignores the content of his works and uses the "findings" of the diagnosis as the master key to puzzling out Kafka's world. We know Kafka was familiar with the teachings of Sigmund Freud (he says so explicitly in his diary, after he finished writing "The Judgment" in 1912) and that he tried to express his problems through symbols in the Freudian sense. One may therefore read Kafka with Freud's teachings in mind. As soon as this becomes more than one among many aids to understanding, however, one is likely to read not Kafka, but a text on applied psychoanalysis or Freudian symbology. Freud himself often pointed out that the analysis of artistic values is not within the scope of the analytical methods he taught.

There is the sociological interpretation, according to which Kafka's work is but a mirror of the historical-sociological situation in which he lived. For the critic arguing this way, the question is not what Kafka really says but the reasons why he supposedly said it. What the sociological and the psychological interpretations have in common is the false assumption that the discovery of the social or psychological sources of the artist's experience invalidate the meaning expressed by his art.

Within the sociological type of interpretation, one of the most popular methods of criticism judges Kafka's art by whether or not it has contributed anything toward the progress of society. Following the Marxist-Leninist dictum that art must function as a tool toward the realization of the classless society, this kind of interpretation is prevalent not merely in Communist countries, but also among the New Left critics this side of the Iron and Bamboo Curtains. Marxist criticism of Kafka has shifted back and forth between outright condemnation of Kafka's failing to draw the consequences of his own victimization by the bourgeoisie and between acclamations stressing the pro-proletarian fighting quality of his heroes. That Kafka was the propagator of the working class as *the* revolutionary class has been maintained not only by official Communist criticism, but also by Western "progressives." And it is true that Kafka did compose a pamphlet lamenting the plight of workers. Yet in a conversation with his friend Janouch, he spoke highly of the Russian Revolution, and he expressed his fear that its religious overtones might lead to a type of modern crusade with a terrifying toll of lives. Surely a writer of Kafka's caliber can describe the terror of a slowly emerging totalitarian regime (Nazi Germany) without being a precursor of communism, as Communist criticism as often claimed. One can also read *The Trial* as the story of Joseph K.'s victimization by the Nazis (three of Kafka's sisters died in a concentration camp); it is indeed one of the greatest tributes one can pay to Kafka today that he succeeded in painting the then still latent horror of Nazism so convincingly. But one must not neglect or ignore the fact that Kafka was, above all, a poet; and to be a poet means to give artistic expression to the many levels and nuances of our kaleidoscopic human condition. To see Kafka as a social or political revolutionary because his country doctor, for instance, or the land surveyor of *The Castle* seeks to change his fate through voluntary involvement rather than outside pressure is tantamount to distorting Kafka's universal quality in order to fit him into an ideological framework.

Closely connected with the quasi-religious quality of Marxist interpretations of Kafka's stories are the countless philosophical and religious attempts at deciphering the make-up of his world. They range from sophisticated theological argumentation all the way to pure speculation. Although Kafka's religious nature is a subject complex and controversial enough to warrant separate mention, the critics arguing along these lines are also incapable, as are their sociological and psychological colleagues, of considering Kafka simply as an artist. What they all have in common is the belief that Kafka's "real meaning" lies beyond his parables and symbols, and can therefore be better expressed in ways he himself avoided for one reason or another. The presumptuousness of this particular approach lies in the belief that the artist depends on the philosopher for a translation of his ambiguous modes of expression into logical, abstract terms. All this is not to dispute Kafka's philosophical-religious cast of mind and his preoccupation with the ultimate questions of human existence. It is just that he lived, thought, and wrote in images and not in "coded" conceptual structures. Kafka himself thought of his stories merely as *points of crystallization* of his problems: Bendemann, Samsa, Gracchus, the hunger artist, the country doctor, Josef K., and K. of *The Castle* — all these men are close intellectual and artistic relatives of Kafka, yet it will not do to reduce his deliberately open-ended images to a collection of data.

Interpretations are always a touchy matter and, in Kafka's case, perhaps more so than in others. The reason for this is that his works are 1) essentially outcries against the inexplicable laws that govern our lives; 2) portrayals of the human drama running its course on several loosely interwoven levels, thus imparting a universal quality to his work; and 3) very much imbued with his high degree of sensitivity which responded differently to similar situations at different times. Particularly this last aspect suggests incohesion and paradox to the mind which insists on prodding Kafka's stories to their oftentimes irrational core. Kafka's pictures stand, as Max Brod never tired of pointing out, not merely for themselves but also for something beyond themselves.

These difficulties have prompted many a scholar to claim that Kafka rarely thought of anything specific in his stories. From this view, it is but a short step to the relativistic attitude that every interpretation of Kafka is as good as every other one. To this, one may reply that "to think of nothing specific" is by no means the same thing as "to think of many things at the same time." Kafka's art is, most of all, capable of doing the latter to perfection. Paradoxical though it may seem at first, viewing Kafka's work from a number of vantage points is not an invitation to total relativism, but a certain guarantee that one will be aware of the many levels of his work.

Despite the many differences in approaching Kafka's writings, all of them must finally deal with a rather hermetically sealed-off world. Whatever Kafka expresses is a reflection of his own complex self amidst a concrete social and political constellation, but it is a reflection broken and distorted by the sharp edges of his analytical mind. Thus the people whom his heroes meet and whom we see through their eyes are not "real" in a psychological sense, not "true" in an empirical sense, and are not "natural" in a biological sense. Their one distinctive mark is that of being something *created*. Kafka once remarked to his friend Janouch, "I did not draw men. I told a story. These are pictures, only pictures." That he succeeded in endowing them with enough plausibility to raise them to the level of living symbols and parables is the secret of his art.

Kafka's stories should not tempt us to analyze them along the lines of fantasy versus reality. An unchangeable and alienated world unfolds before us, a world governed by its own laws and developing its own logic. This world is our world and yet it is not. "Its pictures and symbols are taken from our world of phenomena, but they also appear to belong somewhere else. We sense that we encounter people we know and situations we have lived through in our own everyday lives, and yet these people and situations appear somehow estranged. They are real and physical, and yet they are also grotesque and abstract. They use a sober language devoid of luster in order to assure meaningful communication among each other, and yet they fail, passing one another like boats in an impenetrable fog. Yet even this fog, the realm of the surreal (super-real), has something convincing about it. We therefore have the exciting feeling that Kafka's people say things of preeminent significance but that it is, at the same time, impossible for us to comprehend.

Finally, the reader seems to be left with two choices of how to "read" Kafka. One is to see Kafka's world as full of parables

and symbols, magnified and fantastically distorted (and therefore infinitely more real), a world confronting us with a dream
vision of our own condition. The other choice is to forego any
claim of even trying to understand his world and to expose oneself to its atmosphere of haunting anxiety, visionary bizarreness,
and—occasionally—faint promises of hope.

KAFKA'S JEWISH INFLUENCE

Prague was steeped in the atmosphere of Jewish learning
and writing until the social and political turmoil of the collapsing
Austrian Empire put an end to its traditional character. The first
Jews had come to Prague in the tenth century, and the earliest
written document about what the city looked like was by a
Jewish traveler. According to him, Prague was a cultural crossroads even then. Pulsating with life, the city produced many a
lingering myth during the subsequent centuries, and they, in
turn, added to its cultural fertility. The myth of the *golem* is
probably its most well known: *golem* ("clay" in Hebrew) was
the first chunk of inanimate matter that the famed Rabbi Loew,
known for his learnedness as well as his alchemistic pursuits,
supposedly awakened to actual life in the late sixteenth century.
This myth fathered a whole genre of literature written in the
haunting, semi-mystical atmosphere of Prague's Jewish ghetto.
It is this background, medieval originally, but with several layers
of subsequent cultural impulses superimposed on it, that pervades the world of Franz Kafka, supplying it with a very "real"
setting of what is generally and misleadingly known as "Kafkaesque unrealness."

One of the unresolved tensions that is characteristic of
Kafka's work occurs between his early (and growing) awareness
of his Jewish heritage and the realization that modern Central
European Jewry had become almost wholly assimilated. This
tension remained alive in him quite apart from his situation as a
prominent member of the Jewish-German intelligentsia of
Prague. The problem concerned him all the more directly

because his family clung to Jewish traditions only in a superficial way. Although perhaps of a more orthodox background than her husband—and therefore not quite so eager to attain total assimilation into gentile society—even Kafka's mother made no great effort to cherish Jewish ways. On one level, then, Kafka's animosity toward his father and his entire family may be explained by his mounting interest in his Jewish heritage which they did not share.

Kafka felt drawn to Jews who had maintained their cultural identity, among them the leader of a Yiddish acting group from Poland. He attended their performances in 1911, organized evenings of reading Yiddish literature, and was drawn into fierce arguments about this subject with his father, who despised traveling actors, as did the Jewish establishment of Prague. It was at that time that Kafka began to study Hebrew. As late as 1921, however, he still complained about having no firm knowledge of Jewish history and religion.

What fascinated Kafka about the various members of this group was their firmness of faith and their resistance to being absorbed into the culture of their gentile environment. There are numerous letters and diary entries which point to Kafka's awareness of the essential difference between Western and Eastern Jews concerning this matter. Kafka felt a great affinity with the chassidic tradition (*chassidic* means "pious" in Hebrew; it was an old conservative movement within Judaism which came to flower again in the eighteenth century in eastern Europe). Kafka admired very much their ardent, this-worldly faith, their veneration of ancestry, and their cherishing of native customs. He developed a powerful contempt for Jewish artists who, in his estimation, too willingly succumbed to assimilation and secularization.

Kafka was particularly interested in Zionism, the movement founded by Theodor Herzl (*The Jewish State*, 1890) to terminate the dissemination of Jews all over the world by promoting their settlement in Palestine. Zionism preached the ancient Jewish belief that the Messiah would arrive with the re-establishment of the Jewish state, and Kafka's desire for such a Jewish state and his willingness to emigrate should be noted. Kafka published in a Zionist magazine, planned several trips to Palestine (which never materialized because of his deteriorating health), and was most enthusiastic about the solidarity, the sense of community, and the simplicity of the new *kibbuzim*.

While it is true that Kafka's friend Max Brod influenced him in supporting the ideals of Zionism, it is incorrect to say that without Brod's influence Kafka would never have developed an interest in the movement. His Hebrew teacher Thieberger, a friend and student of Martin Buber, was also a major influence on Kafka. Thieberger emphasized Jewish responsibility for the whole world and believed that everybody is witness to everybody else. Oddly enough, Kafka's father's steady exhortations to "lead an active life" may have added to his growing esteem for the Jewish pioneer ideal. Another source of Kafka's growing interest in Jewish tradition was, of course, his sickness, the very sickness that kept him from carrying out his plans to emigrate to Palestine and live there as a simple artisan. The more Kafka became aware of his approaching end, the more he delved into the study of his identity. A year before his death, he started attending the Berlin Academy of Jewish Studies, and it was during that same year, 1923, that he met Dora Dymant, who was of chassidic background and further accented his search and love for his Jewish roots.

It is clear that Kafka's interest and love for the various aspects of Jewry are not merely an attempt on his part to make up for past omissions in this matter. They are, above all, the result of his religious concerns—"religious" in the wider sense of the word—that is, religious by temperament, religious in the sense of ceaselessly searching and longing for grace.

KAFKA—A "RELIGIOUS" WRITER?

To know Kafka is to grapple with this problem: was Kafka primarily a "religious" writer? The answer seems to depend on the views one brings to the reading of his stories rather than on even the best analyses. Because so much of Kafka's world remains ultimately inaccessible to us, any such labeling will reveal more about the reader than about Kafka or his works. He himself would most likely have refused to be forced into any such either/or proposition.

Perhaps one of the keys to this question is Kafka's confession that, to him, "writing is a form of prayer." Everything we know about him suggests that he probably could not have chosen any other form of expressing himself but writing. Considering the tremendous sacrifices he made to his writing, it is only fair to say that he would have abandoned his art had he felt the need to get his ideas across in some philosophical or theological system. At the same time, one feels that what Kafka wanted to convey actually transcended literature and that, inside, art alone must have seemed shallow to him — or at least inadequate when measured against the gigantic task he set for himself — that is, inching his way toward at least approximations of the nature of truth. Each of Kafka's lines is charged with multiple meanings of allusions, daydreams, illusions and reflections — all indicating a realm whose "realness" we are convinced of, but whose nature Kafka could not quite grasp with his art. He remained tragically aware of this discrepancy throughout his life.

This does not contradict the opinion that Kafka was a "philosopher groping for a form rather than a novelist groping for a theme." "Philosopher" refers here to a temperament, a cast of mind, rather than to a man's systematic, abstract school of thought. Whatever one may think of Kafka's success or failure in explaining his world, there is no doubt that he always deals with the profoundest themes of man's fate. The irrational and the horrible are never introduced for the sake of literary effect; on the contrary, they are introduced to express a depth of reality. And if there is one hallmark of Kafka's prose, it is the complete lack of any contrived language or artificial structure.

Essentially, Kafka desired to "extinguish his self" by writing, as he himself put it. In terms of craftsmanship, this means that much of his writing is too unorganized, open-ended, and obscure. Even allowing for the fact that he was concerned with a realm into which only symbols and parables can shed some light (rather than, say, metaphors and similes which would have tied his stories to the more concrete and definitive), it is doubtful whether Kafka can be called an "accomplished writer" in the sense that Thomas Mann, for instance, can.

Kafka was, then, a major writer, but not a good "craftsman." And he was a major thinker and seer in the sense that he registered, reflected, and even warned against the sickness of a whole age when contemporaries with a less acute consciousness still felt secure.

The question of Kafka's being a religious writer has been going on for decades, but has often been meaningless because of the failure of critics or readers to explain what they mean by "religious." It is essential to differentiate between those who call Kafka and Kafka's works religious in the wider sense of the term — that is, religious by temperament or mentality — and those who assert that his stories reflect Kafka as a believer in the traditional Judaic-Christian sense of the word. Of this latter group, his lifelong friend and editor Max Brod was the first and probably most influential. A considerable number of critics and readers have followed Brod's "religious" interpretations — particularly, Edwin Muir, Kafka's principal English translator. However, for some time now, Kafka criticism has not investigated the "religious" aspect. This is so partly because the psychoanalytical approach and the sociological approach have been more popular and fashionable (especially in the United States), and also because critics and biographers have proven beyond doubt that Brod committed certain errors while editing and commenting on Kafka. While the original attitude toward Brod was one of absolute reverence (after all, he saw Kafka daily for over twenty years, listened to his friend's stories, and advised him on changes), the consensus of opinion has more recently been that, although we owe him a great deal as far as Kafka and his work are concerned, he was a poor researcher. He was simply too self-conscious about his close friendship with Kafka and therefore too subjective: he would never admit the obviously neurotic streak in Kafka's personality. While we may trust Brod when he claims that Kafka's aphorisms are much more optimistic and life-asserting than his fiction, it is difficult to consider Kafka primarily as a believer in the "indestructible core of the universe" or more pronouncedly Jewish-Christian tenets. His famous remark, striking the characteristic tone of self-pity, "Sometimes I feel I understand the Fall of Man better than anyone," is more to the point. We have no reason to doubt Brod's judgment about Kafka's personally charming, calm, and even humorous ways. It is that in Kafka's fiction, calmness is too often overshadowed by fear and anxiety, and the rare touches of humor are little more than convulsions of what in German is known as *Galgenhumor* ("gallows humor") — that is, the frantic giggle before one's execution.

In summary, one can argue in circles about Kafka's work being "religious," but one thing is clear: Kafka's stories inevitably concern the desperate attempts of people to do right. And as noted elsewhere, Kafka and his protagonists are identical to an amazing extent. This means that the main characters who try to do right but are continuously baffled, thwarted, and confused as to what it really means to do right are also Kafka himself. Viewed in this way, Kafka becomes a religious writer *par excellence:* he and his protagonists are classical examples of the man in whose value system the sense of duty and of responsibility and the inevitability of moral commandments have survived the particular and traditional code of a religious system — hence Kafka's yearning for a frame of reference which would impart meaning to his distinct sense of "shalt" and "shalt not." If one takes this all-permeating desire for salvation as the main criterion for Kafka's "religiousness" rather than the grace of faith which he never found, how could anyone *not* see Kafka as a major religious writer? "He was God-drunk," a critic wrote, "but in his intoxication his subtle and powerful intellect did not stop working."

KAFKA AND EXISTENTIALISM

Kafka's stories suggest meanings which are accessible only after several readings. If their endings, or lack of endings, seem to make sense at all, they will not do so immediately and not in unequivocal language. The reason for this is that the stories offer a wide variety of possible meanings without confirming any particular one of them. This, in turn, is the result of Kafka's view — which he shares with many twentieth-century writers — that his own self is a parcel of perennially interacting forces lacking a stable core; if he should attain an approximation of objectivity, this can come about only by describing the world in symbolic language and from a number of different vantage points. Thus a total view must inevitably remain inaccessible to him. Such a universe about which nothing can be said that cannot at the same time — and just as plausibly — be contradicted has a certain ironic quality about it — ironic in the sense that each possible viewpoint becomes relativized. Yet the overriding response one has is one of tragedy rather than irony as one watches Kafka's heroes trying to piece together the debris of their universe.

Kafka's world is essentially chaotic, and this is why it is impossible to derive a specific philosophical or religious code from it — even one acknowledging chaos and paradox as does much existential thought. Only the events themselves can reveal the basic absurdity of things. To reduce Kafka's symbols to their "real" meanings and to pigeonhole his world-view as some "ism" or other is to obscure his writing with just the kind of meaningless experience from which he liberated himself through his art.

Expressionism is one of the literary movements frequently mentioned in connection with Kafka, possibly because its vogue in literature coincided with Kafka's mature writing, between 1912 and his death in 1924. Of course, Kafka does have certain characteristics in common with expressionists, such as his criticism of the blindly scientific-technological world-view, for instance. However, if we consider what he thought of some of the leading expressionists of his day, he certainly cannot be associated with the movement: he repeatedly confessed that the works of the expressionists made him sad; of a series of illustrations by Kokoschka, one of the most distinguished representatives of the movement, Kafka said: "I don't understand. To me, it merely proves the painter's inner chaos." What he rejected in expressionism is the overstatement of feeling and the seeming lack of craftsmanship. While Kafka was perhaps not the great craftsman in the sense that Flaubert was, he admired this faculty in others. In terms of content, Kafka was highly skeptical and even inimical toward the expressionist demand for the "new man." This moralistic-didactic sledgehammer method repulsed him.

Kafka's relationship with existentialism is much more complex, mainly because the label "existentialist" by itself is rather meaningless. Dostoevsky, Nietzsche, and Kierkegaard all have a certain existentialist dimension in their writings, as do Camus, Sartre, Jaspers and Heidegger, with whose works the term existentialism has been more or less equated since World War II. These various people have rather little in common concerning their religious, philosophical, or political views, but they nevertheless share certain characteristic tenets present in Kafka.

Kafka certainly remained fascinated and overwhelmed by the major theme of all varieties of existentialist thinking, namely the difficulty of responsible commitment in the face of an absurd universe. Deprived of all metaphysical guidelines, a man is nevertheless obligated to act morally in a world where death renders everything meaningless. He alone must determine what constitutes a moral action although he can never foresee the consequences of his actions. As a result, he comes to regard his total freedom of choice as a curse. The guilt of existentialist heroes, as of Kafka's, lies in their failure to choose and to commit themselves in the face of too many possibilities — none of which appears more legitimate or worthwhile than any other one. Like Camus' Sisyphus, who is doomed to hauling a rock uphill only to watch it roll down the other side, they find themselves faced with the fate of trying to wring a measure of dignity for themselves in an absurd world. Unlike Sisyphus, however, Kafka's heroes remain drifters in the unlikely landscape they have helped create. Ulrich in Musil's *The Man Without Quality* and Mersault in Camus' *The Stranger*—these men are really contemporaries of Kafka's "heroes," drifters in a world devoid of metaphysical anchoring and suffering from the demons of absurdity and alienation. And in this sense, they are all modern-day relatives of that great hesitator Hamlet, the victim of his exaggerated consciousness and overly rigorous conscience.

The absurdity which Kafka portrays in his nightmarish stories was, to him, the quintessence of the whole human condition. The utter incompatibility of the "divine law" and the human law, and Kafka's inability to solve the discrepancy are the roots of the sense of estrangement from which his protagonists suffer. No matter how hard Kafka's heroes strive to come to terms with the universe, they are hopelessly caught, not only in a mechanism of their own contriving, but also in a network of accidents and incidents, the least of which may lead to the gravest consequences. Absurdity results in estrangement, and to the extent that Kafka deals with this basic calamity, he deals with an eminently existentialist theme.

Kafka's protagonists are lonely because they are caught midway between a notion of good and evil, whose scope they cannot determine and whose contradiction they cannot resolve. Deprived of any common reference and impaled upon their own limited vision of "the law," they cease to be heard, much less understood, by the world around them. They are isolated to the point where meaningful communication fails them. When the typical Kafka hero, confronted with a question as to his identity, cannot give a clear-cut answer, Kafka does more than indicate difficulties of verbal expression: he says that his hero stands between two worlds—between a vanished one to which he once belonged and between a present world to which he does not belong. This is consistent with Kafka's world, which consists not of clearly delineated opposites, but of an endless series of possibilities. These are never more than temporary expressions, never quite conveying what they really ought to convey—hence the temporary, fragmentary quality of Kafka's stories. In the sense that Kafka is aware of the limitations which language imposes upon him and tests the limits of literature, he is a "modern" writer. In the sense that he does not destroy the grammatical, syntactical, and semantic components of his texts, he remains traditional. Kafka has refrained from such destructive aspirations because he is interested in tracing the human reasoning process in great detail up to the point where it fails. He remains indebted to the empirical approach and is at his best when he depicts his protagonists desperately trying to comprehend the world by following the "normal" way.

Because they cannot make themselves heard, much less understood, Kafka's protagonists are involved in adventures which no one else knows about. The reader tends to have the feeling that he is privy to the protagonist's fate and, therefore, finds it rather easy to identify with him. Since there is usually nobody else within the story to whom the protagonist can communicate his fate, he tends to reflect on his own problems over and over again. This solipsistic quality Kafka shares with many an existential writer, although existentialist terminology has come to refer to it as "self-realization."

Kafka was thoroughly familiar with the writings of Kierkegaard and Dostoevsky, and it pays to ponder the similarities and differences between their respective views. The most obvious similarity between Kafka and Kierkegaard, their complex relationships with their respective fiancées and their failures to marry, also points up an essential difference between them. When Kafka talks of bachelorhood and a hermit's existence, he sees these as negative. Kierkegaard, on the other hand, was an enthusiastic bachelor who saw a divine commandment in his renunciation of women. For Kafka, bachelorhood was a symbol of alienation from communal happiness, and he thought of all individualism in this manner. This makes him a poor existentialist.

Unlike Kierkegaard, who mastered his anguish through a deliberate "leap into faith," leaving behind all intellectual speculation, Kafka and his heroes never succeed in conquering this basic anguish: Kafka remained bound by his powerful, probing intellect, trying to solve things rationally and empirically. Kafka does not conceive of the transcendental universe he seeks to describe in its paradoxical and noncommunicable terms; instead, he sets to describing it rationally and, therefore, inadequately. It is as if he were forced to explain something which he himself does not understand—nor is really supposed to understand. Kafka was not the type who could *will* the act of belief. Nor was he a man of flesh and bones who could venture the decisive step toward action and the "totality of experience," as did Camus, for instance, who fought in the French Underground against the Nazi terror. Kafka never really went beyond accepting this world in a way that remains outside of any specific religion. He tended to oppose Kierkegaard's transcendental mysticism, although it might be too harsh to argue that he gave up all faith in the "indestructible nature" of the universe, as he called it. Perhaps this is what Kafka means when he says, "One cannot say that we are lacking faith. The simple fact in itself that we live is inexhaustible in its value of faith."

In the case of Dostoevsky, the parallels with Kafka include merciless consciousness and the rigorous conscience issuing from it. Just as characters in Dostoevsky's works live in rooms anonymous and unadorned, for example, so the walls of the hunger artist's cage, the animal's maze, and Gregor Samsa's bedroom are nothing but the narrow, inexorable and perpetual prison walls of their respective consciences. The most tragic awakening in Kafka's stories is always that of consciousness and conscience. Kafka surpasses Dostoevsky in this respect because that which is represented as dramatic relation—between, say, Raskolnikov and Porfiry in *Crime and Punishment*— becomes the desperate monologue of a soul in Kafka's pieces.

Kafka's philosophical basis, then, is an open system: it is one of human experiences about the world and not so much the particular *Weltanschauung* of a thinker. Kafka's protagonists confront a secularized diety whose only visible aspects are mysterious and anonymous. Yet despite being continually faced with the essential absurdity of all their experiences, these men nevertheless do not cease trying to puzzle them out. To this end, Kafka uses his writing as a code of the transcendental, a language of the unknown. It is important to understand that this code is not an escape from reality, but the exact opposite — the instrument through which he seeks to comprehend the world in its totality — without ever being able to say to what extent he may have succeeded.

REVIEW QUESTIONS

1. What did Kafka try to express through the metamorphosis of Gregor Samsa?

2. Is Samsa partly to blame for having incurred his fate?

3. Samsa's metamorphosis goes hand in hand with a description of the world around him as he sees it in his new state. Give some specific illustrations of this.

4. The subject of the "earthly nourishment" and the "heavenly nourishment" plays a decisive role in several of Kafka's short stories. Which are the stories and how does Kafka deal with this subject in each of them?

5. In your view, does Kafka consider the hunger artist as one whose art is too advanced and too pure for the crude audience to appreciate, or does he finally call the hunger artist an arrogant show-off who does not have stamina enough to survive?

6. "A Country Doctor" has generally been said to contain the most clearly surreal elements of all of Kafka's stories. Do you agree with this view and, if so, what in specific would you say is typical of Kafka's surreal dream world?

7. In which sense is "A Country Doctor" the analysis of the spiritual disease of our age?

8. Explain why "The Judgment" is commonly regarded as the clearest reflection of Kafka's complex relationship with his father.

9. Discuss the differences between the reigns of the Old Commandant and the New Commandant in "The Penal Colony."

10. What do the two commandants symbolize in a religious and/or political sense? Do you have the impression that Kafka favors one of the two against the other and, if so, how would you support your viewpoint?

11. What are the chief elements of "The Hunter Gracchus" that make this story such a perfect parable of human alienation as it results from the loss of orientation?

12. Discuss the idea behind the "piecemeal technique" of construction as employed by the workers on the great wall of China.

13. What are the political ideas of "The Great Wall of China"?

14. Discuss the fate of the ape and his mate in "A Report to an Academy" in terms of his relative success and contentment versus her failure to achieve these.

15. What is the central theme of "Josephine the Singer"? Compare it to the same theme in "A Hunger Artist."

16. Explain why symbols and parables are better suited to deal with Kafka's main themes than are metaphors and similes.

17. What are the traits in Kafka's thinking that one could label "existentialist"?

18. Why is it irrelevant and meaningless to approach Kafka's writings with the attitude of explaining them rationally?

19. Why is the use of the term "Kafkaesque" dangerous for a serious and meaningful appraisal of Kafka?

20. Discuss whether or not Kafka may be called a religious writer.

SELECTED BIBLIOGRAPHY

BROD, MAX. *Über Franz Kafka*. Frankfurt, Heidelberg: Fischer, 1966. This volume was the first to contain Brod's three important pieces on Kafka. For over twenty years Brod saw his friend daily and discussed his work with him. Because of Brod, four-fifths of Kafka's work was not burned, as Kafka had requested it to be.

EMRICH, WILHELM. *Franz Kafka*. Frankfurt: Athenaeum Verlag, 1958. Dealing with a cross section of Kafka's work, the author argues that an autonomous logic prevails in Kafka's world of images. The book, which even Politzer lists as having most influenced his own *Parable and Paradox*, is permeated by an atmosphere of intimate contact with Western philosophical-religious tradition. The excellent bibliography warrants mention.

FLORES, ANGEL, ed. *The Kafka Problem*. New York: New Directions, 1946. A collection of essays on various philosophical, literary, and biographical aspects. Themes of special interest for a further study of Kafka are given preference over interpretations of individual pieces, although the two main novels figure prominently.

FLORES, ANGEL, and SWANDER, HOMER, eds. *Franz Kafka Today*. Madison: University of Wisconsin Press, 1958. The three parts deal with specific stories, the novels, and diaries and letters, respectively. Of special value is a complete bibliography of all of Kafka's works that have appeared in English and a complete bibliography of secondary material.

GRAY, RONALD, ed. *Kafka: A Collection of Critical Essays*. Englewood Cliffs, New Jersey: Prentice-Hall, 1962. The volume contains fourteen critical and interpretive essays from a wide variety of writers and critics. It attempts to do justice to the reading of Kafka by presenting his work from many different viewpoints, some of them strongly disagreeing with most Kafka criticism.

HELLER, ERICH. *The Disinherited Mind*. Cambridge, England: Bowes and Bowes, 1952. The tenor of the essay "The World of Franz Kafka" (the other two deal with other aspects of modern literature) is that Kafka, although fully aware of his own sickness and the sickness of the age, could at no point even begin to extricate himself from his personal tragedies. He would not and could not venture the "leap into faith" and can under no circumstances be called a believer.

JANOUCH, GUSTAV. *Gesprache mit Kafka* (Conversations with Kafka). Frankfurt: Fischer, 1951. Janouch, who met Kafka in 1920, participated in several translations of Kafka's work into Czech. The volume is a collection of letters, notes, diary entries, and personal memories. The material is therefore rather personal in character, expressing Kafka's views in the form of parables, aphorisms, and anecdotes.

KAFKA, FRANZ. *Letter to His Father*. New York: Schocken, 1966.

———. *Selected Short Stories*. New York: Modern Library, 1952.

POLITZER, HEINZ. *Franz Kafka: Parable and Paradox*. Cornell University Press, 1962. Politzer's Austrian-Jewish background and his friendship with Kafka were largely responsible for his undertaking the task, together with Brod, of editing Kafka's *Collected Works*. Foremost in this volume, which was started in the early thirties as his thesis, is the concern with Kafka's work as a literary document. The emphasis is on the three novel fragments.

REIMANN, PAUL, ed. *Franz Kafka aus Prager Sicht.* (Franz Kafka Viewed from Prague) Prague: Voltaire, 1966. This collection of lectures delivered at the now famous Kafka Symposium of 1963 marked a turning point in the Communist appraisal of Kafka. For the first time, the relevance of his work was admitted for Socialist countries as well. In the meantime, this cautious new approach has been completely reversed, especially since the Warsaw Pact Invasion of August, 1968. Once more, Kafka's work is regarded as decadent and irrelevant for Socialist societies. Since all contributions are by noted Communist critics and politicians – many of whom emigrated to the West after Dubcek's fall – the emphasis is on such concepts as realism, alienation, and the function of art in a Socialist society.

WAGENBACH, KLAUS. *Franz Kafka in Selbstzeugnissen und Bilddokumenten.* (Franz Kafka: Testimonials and Picture Documents of Himself) Reinbek bei Hamburg: Rowohlt, 1964. Largely biographical, this study shows the diverse personal, political, and literary influences shaping and changing Kafka's views.

NOTES

NOTES

NOTES

NOTES

NOTES

NOTES

STEPPENWOLF
& SIDDHARTHA

NOTES

including
- *Life and Background*
- *Introductions to* Steppenwolf *and* Siddhartha
- *Lists of Characters*
- *Critical Commentaries*
- *Character Analyses*
- *Review Questions*
- *Selected Bibliography*

by
Carolyn Roberts Welch, M.A.
Associate Professor of English
Quinsigamond Community College

INCORPORATED
LINCOLN, NEBRASKA 68501

Editor

Gary Carey, M.A.
University of Colorado

Consulting Editor

James L. Roberts, Ph.D.
Department of English
University of Nebraska

ISBN 0-8220-1224-3
© Copyright 1988
by
C. K. Hillegass
All Rights Reserved
Printed in U.S.A.

1990 Printing

Cliffs Notes, Inc.   Lincoln, Nebraska

CONTENTS

LIFE AND BACKGROUND 5

INTRODUCTION TO "STEPPENWOLF" 10

LIST OF CHARACTERS 12

CRITICAL COMMENTARIES 14

    Preface 14
    "For Madmen Only" 22
    Treatise on the Steppenwolf 27
    Continuation of Haller's Records 32

CHARACTER ANALYSES 52

    Harry Haller 52
    The Nephew 53
    The Aunt 54
    The Peddler 54
    Hermine 54
    Pablo 55

REVIEW QUESTIONS 55

INTRODUCTION TO "SIDDHARTHA" 57

LIST OF CHARACTERS 58

CRITICAL COMMENTARIES 60

    The Brahmin's Son 60

With the Samunas 62

Gotama 63

Awakening 65

Kamala 66

Amongst the People 68

Sansara 69

By the River 70

The Ferryman 71

The Son 73

OM 74

Govinda 75

CHARACTER ANALYSES 77

Siddhartha 77

Kamala 77

Govinda 78

REVIEW QUESTIONS 78

SELECTED BIBLIOGRAPHY 80

Life and Background

Even though Hermann Hesse belongs to German literature because of his language and culture, his background is quite unlike that of most German authors. This is due in part to the fact that Hesse had missionary parents and grandparents, and is due in part, also, to the fact that his mother and father were, respectively, of southern German plus French-Swiss stock and northern German plus Slavic stock. Born in the Black Forest town of Calw in the German grand duchy of Württemberg in 1877, Hesse was, paradoxically, reared in the severe austerity of Pietist German Protestantism and yet, at the same time, was suffused in the languages, lore, and mysticism of the Far East. The interaction of these elements influenced Hesse's entire life.

To understand *Siddhartha* and *Steppenwolf,* one should continually be aware of the process of synthesis, a mental process of reconciling dualities of antithetical elements. Hesse became aware of this process of unifying opposites during his period of psychoanalysis under Dr. Joseph Bernhard Lang and Lang's mentor, Dr. Carl Gustav Jung. We can see this process at work in his psychoanalytic and post-psychoanalytic literature (including *Siddhartha* and *Steppenwolf*), in which the theme of self-quest by resolving chaotic polar opposites appears.

Hermann Hesse's long lifetime (1877-1962) spanned the rise of the post-Bismarkian military-industrial complex, the rise of fanatical right-wing extremism, two traumatic world wars, the plague of Nazism which sent his wife's family to extermination, and the Cold War. Hesse deplored industrialism, right-wing nationalism, and war, and, for these reasons, he left Germany to live in the seclusion of Switzerland from 1912 to his death in 1962.

Hesse's works are difficult, different, and unlike most of the works of Western writers. But Hesse was different, even from the beginning. His father, Johannes Hesse, was a Pietist missionary who renounced his Russian citizenship to become a Swiss citizen and pursue the theological studies at the Basel Mission Society. Like his father, Hermann Hesse was also to renounce his own citizenship—in his case German, which he held from 1891 to 1923—when he resumed his Swiss citizenship and became naturalized. Both of Hesse's parents had very close contact, through their missionary work, with India and the Far East. His mother was, in fact, born in India, and his grandmother was remembered for her striking collection of Eastern garb, artifacts, and religious objects. Hermann's grandfather was a highly renowned missionary and a veritable walking encyclopedia of Eastern lore and languages. He served as a missionary to the East for thirty years and his home exuded the flavors of Indian, Buddhist, and Mohammedian ceremonies, Oriental songs, and unusual stories and folklore.

Among the significant impressions and experiences of Hesse's early years were those associated with formal education and educational institutions, particularly those in 1892 at the Protestant Theological Seminary at Maulbronn. Hesse's life in school was turbulent. He hated school and was truant and delinquent upon more than one occasion. During his school days, he became conscious of two antithetical worlds—one, the world of mediocrity upheld by the authoritarian establishment of the school system; the other, the world of greatness and genius that this very same establishment supposedly represented. Already we can see the dichotomy of the mundane bourgeois world and the world of the Immortals. It is in *Under the Wheel* (1906) that Hesse depicts his vivid memories of unhappy school days in a story concerning a student's processes of mental exhaustion and suicide for which the school system is held blameworthy. After a period of school truancy and delinquency at Maulbronn and at Constance, Hesse worked in a bookstore as an apprentice in Esslingen for only three days and then assisted his father in the Calw publishing house until 1895. He began his career in poetry during the four-year period in Tübingen from 1895 to 1899, during which he held a conventional apprenticeship in the Heckenhauer Bookshop. *Romantic Songs* was published in 1899.

Between 1899 and 1903, Hesse spent time in Calw and Gaienhofen, but spent his busiest years of this period in Basel. These
years are marked by *An Hour Beyond Midnight* (1899) and *Hermann Lauscher* (1901) which, like the bulk of Hesse's early
works, bear out the German Romantic tradition of lingering
melancholy, gentle fantasy, and lyrical beauty. In 1902, Hesse's
mother died, and in 1903, he had quit the book business entirely
and was devoting his full energies to writing.

The 1904-12 period was a prolific one, during which his
writing style hardened into realism. This period was largely
spent in Gaienhofen, and it was during this time that Hesse had
his first literary success in the novel *Peter Camenzind* (1904), for
which he received his first award. It was in 1904, also, that Hesse
married Maria Bernouelli and settled with her on Lake Constance. The year 1905 heralded Hesse's founding of the liberal
weekly periodical *März*, which he edited and to which he contributed liberal material until 1912. Other works of the 1904-12
period include *Under the Wheel* (1906); volumes of short stories,
including *In This World* and *Neighbors* (1907, 1909); the novel
Gertrude (1910); and a volume of poetry in 1911. During 1911
and 1912, Hesse's long interest in the East resulted in his traveling to India in search of peace and timelessness beyond the world
of Western man. He conveyed this mystical vision in two later
works, *Siddhartha* (1922) and *The Journey to the East* (1931);
interestingly, his memoirs of the trip, *From India* (1913), contain
a sense of disillusionment, a feeling that India was already too
Westernized. Some critics feel that Hesse had begun to doubt
the validity of missionary work, believing that it was Western
man's attempt to do away with Eastern gods.

The period between 1912 and 1919 was a grim period in
Hesse's life for it included a succession of psychoanalytic sessions. This was the period during which he made Switzerland his
permanent home, living in Bern from 1912 until 1919, when he
moved to Montagnola, where he lived for the rest of his life. The
primary causes of this period's grimness were his father's death
(1916), the long illness of his youngest son, his wife's insanity
(note Haller's wife in *Steppenwolf*), and the outbreak of World

War I (1914). Hesse was exempted from active combat duty due to his poor eyesight, but he was assigned to the German embassy at Bern to work on behalf of German prisoners of war. It was during these war years that Hesse's pacifism became emphatically articulate and politically committed. As a result of his anti-war articles, some of which are profoundly beautiful, the right-wing press excoriated Hesse and labeled him a traitor. The fever of nationalism was so rampant that many of his subscribers refused to buy or sell his work. The materials of this period include a variety of short stories, poems, and a significant series of articles for German prisoners of war in the newspaper *Deutsche Internierten Zeitung*. The horror with which Hesse viewed World War I cannot be underestimated and the amount of his anti-war material is quite large. Anti-war activities included his co-editorship of the pacifist periodical *Vivos Voco* and his directorship of the bi-weekly *Sunday Courier for German Prisoners of War*. Notable are his "Friends, Do Not Speak in These Tones!" (1914), the title of which alludes to one of Schiller's poems. It was the impact of these events between 1912 and 1919, especially the war, which drew Hesse to consultations with Dr. Lang and Dr. Jung, two men who were to have a profound synthesizing effect on his mind and art. The works which came as a result of this period of psychoanalysis were considerably more introspective than any of Hesse's previous publications. Works of this period include *Rosshalde* (1914), *Demian* (1919), the beginnings of *Siddhartha*, and a collection of three essays, *In Sight of Chaos* (1919). Hesse, indeed, had his own glimpse into chaos while undergoing psychoanalysis, and the essays in *In Sight of Chaos* dealt with the theme of antithetical God/Satanism in man and the idea that irrational depravity lurks beneath the surface of man, collectively as well as individually. Hesse forecast that these irrational forces would rise to the surface and beget the criminality which would beset not only Germany, but mankind as a whole. The outstanding essays in this collection influenced T. S. Eliot's *Waste Land* (1922), and several references to Hesse appear in Eliot's notes. The most brilliant essay of the three is "The Brothers Karamazov, or the Downfall of Europe."

The years from 1919 to 1962 encompass the time from which Hesse became a naturalized Swiss citizen (1923, also the year of his divorce from his first wife) to the time of his death on August 9, 1962. From 1919 on, he lived in the same secluded villa on the edge of Montagnola in the Ticino valley into which he invited very few visitors. During this time, Hesse embarked on, as it were, a period of self-quest, using certain theories of Jung. The idea of self-quest (through synthesis) begins in *Demian* and continues through a number of Bildungsroman-type, semi-autobiographical novels; this is the period of *Klein and Wagner* (1920); *Klingsor's Last Summer* (1920); the literary experiment dealing with self-exorcism, *Steppenwolf* (1927); *Crisis* (1928), the verse counterpart to *Steppenwolf; Narcissus and Goldmund* (1930); and *The Journey to the East* (1931). In 1924, Hesse married Ruth Wenger, and after his divorce from her, he married Ninon Ausländer with whom he lived until his death.

After 1931, Hesse's literary output diminished. It was, however, during this time that he wrote a major volume of poetry, published in 1942, completed a new edition of *Steppenwolf*, containing his own introduction, and spent a decade preparing the masterpiece which accounted largely for his winning the Nobel Prize for Literature in 1946, *The Glass Bead Game* (1943). This period also included *War and Peace* (1946), a volume of essays; and *Letters* (1951), a collection of correspondences. During World War II, while Hesse was writing for Will Vesper's *Neue Litteratur,* he was again reviled by Germany's right-wing press. Hesse, however, was not dealt with as severely as was Thomas Mann, whose books were officially burned and who escaped to the United States; Hesse was discounted as merely a "victim of Jewish psychoanalysis" and was not granted paper or other materials for publishing. Hesse's wife's family was not so lucky; they were murdered in the extermination camps by the Nazis. The bitterness and shock that resulted remained with Hesse for the rest of his life.

Steppenwolf Notes

INTRODUCTION

Steppenwolf, published in 1927, is an offbeat but decorous little novel. At times, it is structurally reminiscent of Goethe's *Sorrows of Young Werther* in its use of the notebook device; in places, it is philosophically reminiscent of *Siddhartha*, although it is more ambivalent in conception and, unlike *Siddhartha*, it has an unresolved ending. What Hesse created in *Steppenwolf* was a novel in which the text departed increasingly from reality into fantasy, without intrusions in the narrative announcing the protagonist's traversing the boundary between these disparate worlds. Reality and fantasy are unobtrusively fused into one another by an accumulation of motifs which are forcefully recapitulated in the Magic Theater sequence.

Harry Haller's notes are presented as recorded internal monologue, spontaneous inner autobiography showing the chaotic and schizophrenic qualities of Haller's fantasies. The wolf of the steppes, *der Steppenwolf*, represents the dark, suppressed, rebellious side of Haller's personality. It lies dormant at times, but frequently stalks and threatens Haller's inclination toward bourgeois life and tastes. Haller's records present both Haller's inclination toward the ordered world and the Steppenwolf's inclination toward rebelliousness, art, and flights into imagination. His vision of art, which reaches its highest form in music, is that of art as an end in itself—the Kantian ideal of art for art's sake, which runs exactly counter to the Bürger's ideals of practicality and technical progress. This is not all that Haller's records reveal, however. They progress and finally end problematically—that is, the resolution concerns not just a split personality, but a multiple personality. To Hesse, this was the human condition of not just Harry Haller, but of twentieth-century man. The notes of Haller depart increasingly from reality as they progress, reflecting a syndrome of dissolution as Hesse and Haller partake of their own glimpses into personal and collective chaos. We should not, however, regard *Steppenwolf* as just a *roman à clef*, an exact parallel to the author's life. Rather, we should regard it as a creative work in its own right despite its heavy overlay of autobiography.

The bulk of the accumulating images in *Steppenwolf* are basically Jungian, as are the processes of self-realization and the approach toward equilibrium. Yet *Steppenwolf*, it should be pointed out, presents only an *approach* toward equilibrium. The ending of the novel, despite its promise of impending stabilization for Haller, is unlike the ending of *Siddhartha* in that it is unresolved and technically dissonant.

The technique of *Steppenwolf* places heavy demands upon a translator because the work is a kind of experiment in atonality, in unresolved dissonance. The work has been said to be symphonic in form, which indeed it is; but the mark of such innovative composers as Arnold Schönberg (Austrian, 1874-1951) and Alban Berg (Austrian, 1885-1935) has been unmistakably left on *Steppenwolf*. Schönberg abandoned tonality completely in his "Three Piano Pieces" (Op. 11) of 1908, and had devised the atonal twelve-tone scale by 1915. Shortly thereafter, Alban Berg composed a startlingly dissonant opera, *Wozzeck* (produced in Berlin in 1925), which contains striking combinations of symphonic form and radical atonality.

As far as the novel is concerned, we should note that its technique of verbal and syntactical dissonance rises when departures into unreality are made. The book begins in an unobtrusive realistic style, in keeping with events in the early parts of the book. As the novel progresses, however, and as the departures from reality become more frequent and striking, the prose technique changes accordingly. It becomes more symbolic and the first-person narrative of Haller eventually approximates a stream-of-consciousness technique in the Magic Theater sequence. The first hints at a departure from reality come when Haller discovers a previously unnoticed, visionary gate in a churchyard wall; he imagines that he sees fleeting

12

iridescent letters above the gate, advertising entertainments for madmen.

Further departure from reality becomes apparent in Haller's dream of Goethe, laughing. The final sequence of unreality concerns Hermine's and Pablo's attempts to cure Haller by means of mirrors (the "trifling suicide," the extinguishing of the will in Schopenhaurean terms; the ego in Jungian terms) and the subsequent fragmentation and potential synthesis of Haller's thousandfold personality in the psychoanalytic shock therapy of the Magic Theater sequence. Of primary significance, of course, is the "golden thread" or "golden trace" which draws Haller to Mozart. As we explore the novel, we should be particularly conscious of the interplay of elements derived from Arthur Schopenhauer's *The World as Will and Idea* (1818), including his concepts of will, intellect, individuation and Nirvana. If we couple Schopenhauer's thought with Jung's, bearing in mind the influence upon each of Eastern mysticism, we may then find a critical basis on which to build an understanding of what possibly makes Haller "tick." The polarity of will and intellect plus the Nietzschean theory of man's being driven by a will to power and perfection is basic to much of the art and literature of Germany's twentieth century.

LIST OF CHARACTERS

Harry Haller

The disillusioned protagonist who, according to the nephew, has left behind a collection of notes embodying the *Weltschmerz* of the twentieth-century artist-type.

The Nephew

To some people, he may seem to be the perpetrator of a publishing hoax, but, to others, he is a young businessman whose affinity to the phantom-like Haller draws him to salvage and interpret the bizarre, abandoned manuscript.

The Aunt

A kindly, maternal embodiment of the positive values of the pre-decadent, nineteenth-century middle class. She accepts Haller and elicits interesting philosophical responses from him which are recorded in the manuscript.

The Peddler

An eerie encounter between Haller and the peddler, which is recorded in the manuscript, anticipates the first departure from reality and portends the Magic Theater sequence.

Hermine

Psychologically, this character from the commercial, worldly realm functions as Haller's "double," the reverse of his disciplined and contemplative self. As his Jungian "anima," or female self, she serves as his mentor in the realm of illusion and gives him the perspective to apprehend a reality transcending the illusory.

Maria

An attractive young girl who is Hermine's disciple in the realm of illusion; she attempts to teach love as a kind of art.

Pablo

The guru of the world of commercial jazz and of voyages into artificially induced fantasy; he is the leader of a corrupt realm but extends to Haller a firsthand awareness of the duality of mind and matter through the Magic Theater. His polarity with the Mozart consciousness heightens Haller's awareness of Mozart's transcendence.

Erica

A friend of Haller's; her picture is prominently displayed in his apartment, and she and Haller frequently quarrel.

The Professor

A complacent, right-wing extremist who hates Jews and Communists.

Attorney-General Loering

A visionary bureaucrat who lacks conscience and rationalizes his having been responsible for men's deaths by stating that it was his duty as a public prosecutor.

Gustav

He returns to join Haller in destroying the products of the military-industrial complex. Unlike the attorney-general, he kills for pleasure.

CRITICAL COMMENTARIES

PREFACE

This section of the novel serves the important function of placing all that follows into proper perspective, and the instrument through which this is accomplished is the retrospective, first-person narrative of the landlady's nephew. We are given certain crucial pieces of information in this section which make Haller's manuscript intelligible to us. Much, of course, is left to the reader for conjecture—but we at least learn of the nephew's familiarity with Greek classicism which gives some degree of probability for his attraction to the classical ideals so embraced in Haller's recorded moments of transfiguration. Despite the nephew's middle-class milieu and seeming preoccupation with "business," he is well read and inclined toward cultural entertainments. He comes upon Haller's manuscript by accident; he tells us about his encounters with Haller, his impression of Haller's background and tastes, and about Haller's collection of notes. And all we know about the nephew is what he tells us himself, with the exception of a few references within the manuscript.

We learn that Haller's book collection included many works from Germany's eighteenth century; and we learn, too, that Haller admired Goethe—so, we can probably assume that Haller was familiar with such philosophers of that era as Arthur Schopenhauer and Immanuel Kant. The reasons for his probable familiarity with these minds goes far beyond the mere consistency of a library, however. Schopenhauer presented his concepts of will and intellect in his *The World as Will and Idea,* and Kant is famous for what is known as the "transcendental aesthetic" in his dictum on art for art's sake in *The Critique of Pure Reason.* Harry Haller's idealism concerning artistic form, his inner division and torment relating to the collective activity or "will" of his age, and the agonizing insight of "intellect" remind us of Schopenhauer and Kant. Such clues about Haller, plus the heavily introspective quality of the nephew, help to place much of the novel in perspective. The reader, however, has to place much of it in perspective himself because a demand similar to Haller's in synthesizing is also placed upon us. We must undergo the process of synthesis as we undergo psychoanalysis ourselves with Haller. Haller, in a sense, is a martyr (the nephew calls him a "true Christian martyr") because he suffers hell and deliverance—of which we, the readers, symbolically partake. And he undergoes an exorcism of the evil of a whole segment of society in what he leaves behind; his records are his exorcism. The nephew conscientiously picks them up and prepares them for all men, particularly the more than literate middle-class intelligensia, to read and follow so that all of society may be saved.

Steppenwolf is the only instance in Hesse where we find a lengthy formal introduction in a novel, and it is his only work in which he used a contemporary setting. As previously noted, this is not a strict *roman à clef,* but the unnamed cultural metropolis is probably either Basel or Zürich.

In placing the body of the work in perspective, the indispensable prologue traces the development of a bond between

Haller and his complementary double, the landlady's nephew, who was at first skeptical and guarded toward the strangely bohemian and alien Haller. He, however, became so inextricably and fraternally bound to Haller that he had plaguing dreams and memories of him, long after Haller's ten-months stay at the house. As their acquaintance developed, we learn, the nephew grew to appreciate Haller's apparent intellectuality and, therefore, ultimately salvaged what appeared to be the genuine manuscript of a tormented potential genius, a manuscript that ordinary men would have dismissed as the aberrant scribblings of a deranged man. The nephew finds the notes to be of so much significance to men of his time that he plans to publish them.

A basic issue in this novel is a pervasive one in twentieth-century German literature: the middle-class view of illness and health in terms of the respective absence or presence of will as a life force. Intellect is frequently associated with what would seem to be illness — and yet it is these estranged beings who have the true vision of the inner sickness of the times, a sickness rooted to that very will which the Bürgers associate with the ambition and activity which amasses fortunes and builds empires.

Harry Haller, in some ways, bears a resemblance to Raskolnikov in Dostoevski's *Crime and Punishment*. Note the similarity between their untidy attic apartments; note also that each is an idealist; in addition, neither Raskolnikov nor Haller can reconcile himself with the Nietzschean vision of a world in which the powerful feel justified in unleashing their will. In addition, both Raskolnikov and Haller have a propensity toward murder, but Haller's is directed inward, against himself. His inability to attain the peace of the masters of music and poetry is rooted in the fact that his self is so divided that all he can achieve artistically are some lines of poetry and some anti-establishment newspaper articles. His divine "golden thread" which has endowed him with his responsiveness to genius is also a curse, for because of his ability to respond, he can also see his own inadequacy. Some critics might indict Haller for being a n'er-do-well who is also a fraud, but Haller seems conscious of this himself: he is sufficiently contaminated by will as to be incapable of the arduous duties of enterprise. He is not only in an individual limbo, but he is representative of a collective one as well, and is so polarized that he can calmly imagine his committing suicide.

The twentieth century will never produce a Bach, a Handel, a Mozart, or a Goethe because, according to Haller, will has so contaminated the Kantian ideal of art for art's sake that music has become the projection of a frenzied, chaotic, destructive national consciousness. The classical ideals of self-discipline — balance and simplicity in idealized form — have been crushed by the magnitude and tangled dissonance of modernity. As Haller could be called a fraud, so could all of the twentieth-century intelligensia who aspire to artistic achievement. The times that produced the Immortals is, according to Haller, gone forever.

Haller, however, is seemingly unique in that he can recognize the contaminant from which the disease ensues, and thus proceeds through a kind of self-hypnosis with a diagnosis and prognosis, which are negative unless the ego can be extinguished for the ideal. Haller is a tormented creature who hungers for the unity of pure, balanced form which emerges from pure intellect. He thrashes about with his mercurial, ever-shifting personality, his acts being frequently contradictory. He seems bohemian and yet he eagerly pays his rent in advance and complies with the rules of the house. He shrinks from the routine of notifying the local police of his new residence and yet he is magnetically drawn to the sights and smells of middle-class housekeeping.

Once the details of Haller's arrival and personal appearance are completed, focus is placed on the bond which forms between Haller and the nephew. For the latter, Haller represents the dark allurement of a world very different from that of men bound to duty and responsibility; Haller's world of literary and artistic things is considered impractical and strangely Eastern to the Bürger mentality. The nephew initially becomes so curious and taken by Haller that he goes beyond his middle-class prejudices and indulges in a bit of snooping through the stranger's apartment — before he has even been invited to Haller's apartment.

The bond between Haller and the nephew, which forms a large part of the perspective of the book, is further revealed in the prologue during the nephew's reminiscences of three specific encounters with Haller. The first of these evening encounters happened near the end of Haller's stay when he and the nephew had become rather friendly to one another. Attracted by Haller's intellectuality and sensitivity, he recalls Haller's attitude toward the pseudo-intelligensia: a withering glance, flashed in a confiding way to the nephew during a boring public lecture. The glance is memorable to the nephew for its being a signal of Haller's recognition of the triteness and shallowness of twentieth-century academe and the public's ignorance of the speaker's fraudulent, pompous tricks.

Shortly after Haller's arrival, the nephew immediately recognizes the fact that Haller is suffering from some strange malady—spleen, perhaps, but he readily senses that this is an outgrowth of Haller's superior mentality, "a profusion of gifts and powers that had not attained to harmony." These gifts and powers include his artistic idealism and intellect—irreconcilable with contemporary values. Because Haller might well have considered himself a fraud in a society of frauds, unable to embrace the ideal in a world where artistic joy is but a fleeting thing, he views himself with contempt and thus practices self-hate.

The nephew surmises that Haller was probably brought up in an austere German family; he thinks that Haller's family probably believed that individuality was wrong and that one was made to feel guilty for exhibiting marked individuality. Haller, however, was not broken. Currently, his idea of misery is the thought of his ever working in an office, a place where one feels the pressures of the competitive world of will and enterprise, and he is agonized by society's complacency in spiritual and artistic matters. We have arrived at a crucial part of the book when the nephew reflects on Haller's self-hate: ". . . self-hate is really the same thing as sheer egoism, and ultimately breeds the same cruel isolation and despair." Haller is conscious of his own hopeless exigencies and of those of the world around him. He knows that if he can attain the permanent nirvana of art, embodied in the Immortals, then this consciousness of self-limitation will disappear; likewise, he will be rid of his ego-obsessed self-hate and the frustration of feeling himself just a quasi-bourgeois fraud who indirectly aids and abets such enemies to idealism and art as Germany's right-wing establishment. The antidote for Haller's self-hate is a detachment which includes humor. As Vasudeva and the river smile and sublimely laugh for Siddhartha, so will Goethe and Mozart smile and laugh for Haller. As "OM" is Siddhartha's sacred key to self-realization and the absolving of one's ego, so Mozart enlivens Haller's intellect, his "thread of gold"; Mozart and his disciplined music, it should be noted, had much the same significance for Hesse: they represented the most perfect and eternal elements of form.

Haller's apartment contains many belongings which remind one of Hesse as well as give insight into Haller. Mention has already been made of the volumes in Haller's personal library, but we should consider other objects as well. Hesse was fascinated by southern Europe, particularly Italy, and one notices a picture of a southern landscape on Haller's wall. Hesse enjoyed water coloring as a pastime, producing numerous pastoral paintings (perhaps an influence from the East); Haller also paints water colors. Hesse was as un-Germanic in his artistic tastes as he was in his language studies, and we can see Hesse's taste reflected in Haller's interest in Italian Renaissance painting and Eastern sculpture.

Of the various encounters involving Haller which the nephew recalls, he particularly remembers their first lengthy conversation; during it, Haller revealed, despite his estrangement, his basic attraction to middle-class things. The nephew recalls their meeting one another on the stairs and he brings our attention to some poignant remarks made by Haller regarding the little household commonplaces along the stairwell and the downstairs hallway. The reason this particular section of the prologue is important is because it suggests Haller's fascination with experiences not directed by the conscious will. Such experiences have the power to transfigure a man and are frequently associated with memories of childhood. Of these sensory memories, smells seem to have a special effect on Haller, lifting him from unwilled, involuntary memory into a state of ecstasy. The fragrance of potted plants in the fastidiously polished hallway evokes a childlike, idealized vision of Bürger life, and Haller periodically tries to retrieve and expand this part of his past by sitting now and then and inhaling the smells of turpentine and flowers. He tries to recapture the original sensations of the past as the floral fragrances evoke memories of his mother. Then he invites the nephew into his apartment for the first time and reads some passages from his favorite works of literature.

The nephew recalls an evening when they separately attended a concert during which the nephew scrutinized Haller's facial reactions as Haller responded to the varied program of music; he was obviously fascinated by the disciplined neoclassical forms of Friedemann Bach, but he seemed barely to hear the somewhat dissonant modernity of "Variations and Fugue on a Theme by Mozart" by Max Reger, the controversial German composer, one of the forerunners of the more radically atonal composers of our century.

Another evening involving Haller which the nephew recalls vividly is one which seemed to mark the beginning of Haller's extreme turmoil in the latter part of his stay, the period during which he began to spend entire days in his room while he was writing his manuscript. On the particular evening in question, a woman with whom Haller had planned to spend an evening's outing arrived at the house. However, less than an hour after their departure, Haller returned alone, terribly dejected. Successive encounters between Haller and this woman ended in violent arguments and depression. One might note a parallel to Haller's distress in Hesse's own life; each had a wife who became insane. Contact with Erica might have aggravated Haller's already frayed nerves and may have triggered old memories, thus partially inducing his state of mind during the writing of the manuscript. Indeed, Haller's deeply probing manuscript is more than the mere product of marital difficulties, and already it has been pointed out that this novel is not merely a *roman à clef*, but certain incidents might bear significance as manifestations of a divided personality.

As the nephew reflects on the fantasies and quasi-fictional elements of Haller's records, he makes the keen observation that these fantasies are not mere fabrications, but are symbolically founded in the matrix of deep personal truths: ". . . the deeply lived spiritual events which he has attempted to express by giving them the form of tangible experiences." The suggestion is made by the narrator after his remarks on the manuscript that there is a possibility that Haller committed suicide, but he dismisses this idea as probably inaccurate because he feels that the manuscript served as a catharsis (or in the case of this "true Christian martyr," an exorcism) for Haller.

The nephew's final statements concerning Haller's manuscript reveal that, despite his middle-class background, he has a genuine appreciation and understanding of the manuscript. He sees it as a document of the times; he believes that Haller's "soul sickness" is not merely the aberration of a single individual, but the sickness of Haller's generation. Further, he believes that the sickness does not afflict only the weak and the worthless, but particularly those who are the strongest in spirit and richest in artistic gifts.

The manuscript, then, is an attempt to manifest schizophrenia — not just tell about it. Like the twentieth century, with its polarity of the will against the classical and literary Western heritage of intellect, the manuscript is a journey through Hell, a plunge into the abyss of the collective soul of man. The nephew then finishes by recalling that Haller told him once that every epoch has its own characteristic will, even the murky Dark Ages. Even the very worst, least enlightened epochs had their own separate identities, but the twentieth century embodies, instead, an unresolved clash of new and old: it is a terrifying age of transition in which the absolutes of the past overlap with the non-rational uncertainties of the future. The result is an irrevocable, destructive conflict. The narrator remarks that there are times when a whole generation is so caught between two epochs that two life styles emerge. The consequence is that the generation loses all power to understand itself. We are reminded that a generation earlier Friedrich Nietzsche postulated his theory of the *Übermensch* and of will as a positive force in what he regarded as a world contaminated by the slave morality of the weak. In a world where the absolutes of morality, philosophy, and religion seem to fail in answering man's great questions concerning truth, we see manifestations of the Nietzschean will and its problematical aspects in a superman-oriented, supernationalistic Germany.

"FOR MADMEN ONLY"

Haller has given his volume of memoirs a very apt title, a title bearing tremendous irony because it suggests that in order to comprehend truth, one must expand one's consciousness to a degree which the average, "normal" citizen would label insanity. According to Hesse, twentieth-century man's quest for truth cannot be resolved on rational grounds by absolutes. The deepest truths do not come by one's conscious will because most of our psyche lies in the unconscious; revelations come only in fleeting, flickering moments of unwilled spontaneity. In this segment, the reader can observe a kind of parallel between Arthur Schopenhauer's mystical conception of Nirvana (or nothingness) and Jung's conception of the collective unconscious. Nirvana and the unconscious are non-rational states, bordering on madness, according to some critics, and are important in understanding the title of Haller's records.

This section, which follows the prologue and ends just prior to the Magic Theater sequence, forms a second portion of the novel even though the work is not divided formally into chapters. It is told in relatively conventional prose and some readers might dispute the conventionality of the style because of certain unannounced departures from reality, but these are, for the most part, only occasional and the plot line is still paramount.

In the prologue, we were presented with the nephew's (possibly a potential Haller-type himself) view of Haller. In the sequence immediately preceding the treatise, we have the Steppenwolf's own interpretation of his problematical self. Basically, the Haller-type is established as a lost or misplaced bourgeois, what some people refer to as a "bourgeois manqué."

This solitary, internally polarized creature calls himself a "wolf of the steppes," the steppes being the alien domain to which such divided personalities are exiled by self and society. Haller has, voluntarily, cut himself off from those transitory things from which ordinary men derive their pleasure. These ordinary men are incapable of fathoming eternity, for they have not been endowed with the "golden thread" which would give them the capacity for insight and awareness. This golden thread is an endowment exclusive to those who appear sick by bourgeois standards. It is the anguish of unattainability which curses the artistic Steppenwolf-type; common men are spared from continual anguish because in them there is no battle between will and intellect. The bourgeois are not bothered by the twentieth century's artistic sterility; they are preoccupied by the active life of enterprise of which the will is the vital factor and time the godhead. To them, creativity is impractical, irrational, and almost malevolent because it subordinates time and interferes with duty and responsibility.

As Haller realizes how thoroughly he is rooted in the middle class, he lapses into a state bordering on psychic depression for he is aware of so much fraud within the bourgeois intelligensia. Yet he has a tender respect for the middle-class houses of his reveries while at the same time he professes abhorrence for bourgeois standards. He seems almost free as an artistic spirit, yet he is still bound to the bourgeoisie because he is dependent upon it financially and he is aesthetically stifled by it. Haller has fleeting moments of joy and release, yet too often he is bound by the time-obsessed, ego-inflated Bürger mentality, a basic twentieth-century predicament, according to Hesse, of the artist.

As Haller walks down the foggy city streets, morbidly contemplating the valuelessness of his existence, he lapses into a reverie of his youth when the mysterious Hoffmannesque atmosphere of evenings with a Gothic quality inspired him to write poetry. He reflects regretfully that the present is devoid of any sense of aesthetic awakening except upon very rare occasions. Haller misses the mundane pleasures of the will-imbued active life of the teeming bourgeoisie, but he has other pleasures: he has psychic antennae which give him the capacity to respond to things forever lost to the bourgeoisie, an ability to see "God at work." This intuitive experience grasps essences and defies the will.

Haller recalls a specific concert of "old" music—that is, Baroque music—music superior to modern music which seems embued with the spirit of the Nietzschean *Übermensch,* the orchestrated frenzy of the Germanic nationalistic ego. Haller is able to recapture the memory of this concert of Baroque music with its elegant neoclassical balance and dignity. Its golden thread lies in its purity of disciplined form, and thus its liberation from ego contamination, for classical self-discipline has almost the effect of meditation in extinguishing the aberrations of ego and idiosyncrasy. Even the sculpture of the Greeks, perhaps the very purest root of the classical tradition in art, was idealized form—not mere portraiture of passing individuals in a solid medium. The golden thread of this superb old music draws the evocation of it into an actual present and it penetrates Haller's soul.

Haller recalls other instances of direct firsthand experience with the golden thread—instances of a sublimely transcendent and yet almost torturous, transient quality. One such experience took place while he was reading poetry; another took place in the presence of his beloved. It seems that Haller's non-rationally founded, unwilled response to ultimate harmony never ceases to fascinate the nephew, despite the nephew's seeming obsession with technology and progress. It is this golden thread whose "beams" enliven Haller's intellect in a world of unchanneled will that sustains him, and it is through it that he can perceive essences beyond the ordinary world.

As Haller continues to stroll, he feels within himself a fleeting and alluring quality similar to that of the golden thread—but this time it is peculiar and bizarre. It is a vision of letters vaguely resembling an electric sign, announcing upcoming entertainments. The vision fascinates Haller because it is an involuntary experience, an experience not elicited by the conscious will; it taps the wellspring of intellect, a mental faculty beyond the reaches of ordinary men. Likewise, the entertainments themselves are not the domain of ordinary men; they are not for those whom the world thinks are "normal." These entertainments are specifically "not for everybody." This experience is the first departure from reality in the book. When Haller looks at the advertisements for the Magic Theater, the last line reads "Not for Everybody"; but when he turns to look again, the words have changed to the bizarre "For Madmen Only." Some might believe that these visions are merely a result of the various pain relievers to which Haller seems to be addicted, but their significance lies in that they serve to distinguish Haller from other men and to emphasize his fascination for that which lies submerged in the subconscious, evoked only in moments when the conscious will is suspended. Haller is fascinated by the lure of the chaotic and the dissolute; it is in his encounters with these elements that he will find the hope of resolution through exorcism.

After experiencing the mysterious letters and their eerie reflection on the black sheen of the street, Haller takes refuge in a familiar old tavern which has remained unchanged in more than a quarter of a century. Haller observes the clientele, some of which could be possible Steppenwolf-types. Contemplating the reverie-invoking atmosphere of the place, his mind wanders; a succession of forgotten piano notes returns to him, generating memories of paintings, literature, and history. All of this seemingly chaotic jumble culminates with his being reminded of the golden thread and Mozart. Hesse himself associated Mozart with the essence of beauty; Mozart's name served as a kind of cipher, signaling the onset of that ecstasy which often accompanies creative intellect. Haller is now somewhat regenerated, lifted from his feelings of suffering: "The golden trail was blazed and I was reminded of the eternal, and of Mozart, and the stars. . . . I could breathe once more and live and face existence."

Haller continues his solitary walk down the cold, damp street. He is subsequently confronted with echoes of the antithesis of the Mozart ideal—the alluring pulse of hot, commercial jazz emanating from a cheap dance hall. This music embodies a sense of abandon and a pretense of sentiment, two elements which are musical counterparts to Nietzschean phenomena and will perversion — an artless, syncopated materialism. The sensual, rhythmic cacophony of the jazz seems to embody the forces of dehumanized will and collective negation. Nevertheless, despite Haller's scorn for its raucous brassiness, the primitive aggressiveness of jazz holds an appeal for him. Due to the middle-class standards which have been inherited by Haller, he tends at first to shy away from this forbidden music. He has not yet had the chance to experience it firsthand and must be guided into an understanding of jazz by Hermine, just as Dante was guided through Hell by Virgil. He must be able, through firsthand encounter, to observe and live through the aggregations of the fad-oriented jazz band so that he can see the seriousness of man's obsessions with such things and see the humor of it as well. Once Haller gains some objectivity and the ability to observe this musical notation of an age, then he will be able to understand the humor in it, a humor much like that which is evoked today by "pop" or "op" art.

Haller prefers the raw artlessness of this jazz, however, to contemporary academic music. He senses a pretentious dissolution in the academic tastes of the day, a sense of disease and violence which harbors the perverse forces of anarchy and annihilation. In music, this corrosive extremism is epitomized in the frantically chromatic and hugely orchestrated excesses of the interminable, unresolved melodic lines of Richard Wagner. Jazz of even the most commercial ilk is overt, according to Haller, whereas contemporary serious music embodies sinister forces, disguising rather than releasing its cryptic notation of potential eruption into chaos.

Returning to the mysterious wall, Haller looks hopefully for the mirage-like door. It is not there, but his attention is absorbed by a signbearing peddler. After being requested to allow Haller to read his placard, he turns around and Haller again sees fleeting letters reeling about in random fashion:

Anarchist Evening Entertainment
Magic Theater
Entrance Not For Everybody

Haller is intensely fascinated by this almost hallucinogenic vision, for it promises a reality beyond will or phenomena. Upon Haller's inquiry about these "entertainments," the peddler begins to walk wearily away and, upon Haller's pursuit, gives Haller a little booklet and disappears.

Overwrought with fatigue and arriving back at his landlady's house, Haller draws out the little book to examine it. He sees to his astonishment that is a treatise on the Steppenwolf. As we read through this next section, much of the material about Haller's multiple personality will be reviewed for us. But the treatise is important because it helps explain further Haller's golden thread. Past ages which are forever lost chronologically become, for exhilarating, fleeting moments, an essential reality which transcends time and defies rational analysis. Even though the classical age of Mozart and Goethe has chronologically gone by, its divine presence—through its music—suspends time and affirms a kind of life beyond the temporal realm.

TREATISE ON THE STEPPENWOLF

Before actually reading the treatise, some readers might expect it to be somewhat dull due to its length and its essay form, which departs from the novel's narrative. It may also come a little unexpectedly, although several distinguished modern novelists (Proust, Joyce, Mann) dealing with the predicament of the artist allow analytical essays to appear in their works. The essay vaguely resembles a Pietist tract, bringing an element of mysticism to the material on the Steppenwolf's inspirations and self-realization. Some translators use the word "tractate" instead of "treatise" due to its closeness to *tractat* in the original German. Hesse was familiar with such tracts because his father's Calw publishing house circulated many of them for missionaries and their converts.

Basically, the treatise postulates and elaborates upon two types of Steppenwolves. This is done because a Steppenwolf is so precariously balanced between two worlds that he may go in either direction — the direction of will or the direction of intellect. A Steppenwolf is a man whose rare talents and vision set him apart from everyday people. If he veers toward will, a Steppenwolf could become a great entrepreneur, inventor, or engineer. However, if he veers toward intellect, a Steppenwolf is not so fortunate because pure art is impossible in our time and the Steppenwolf's life will never be fulfilled. The will-Steppenwolf can respond to flux and change and make his mission one for progress. Yet because he does not hover midway in torment, he is not a true Steppenwolf in the sense that Haller is one.

Harry Haller is a Steppenwolf in the truest sense, and any fulfillment that comes within his reach is only fleeting, the lot of artist types. There is also a dichotomy of God/Satanism which plagues the artist's soul — a postulation reminiscent of that made by the French poet Charles Baudelaire. Nevertheless, despite the artist-Steppenwolf's doom to intense torment, he is endowed with a capacity for intense joy beyond the furthest reaches of the world of phenomena. An artist on a par with the Immortals could, likewise, transmit this joy to others through the radiant permanence of his creations. Even though an artist-Steppenwolf cannot attain to pure intellect because of the vast will-contamination by the twentieth century, vestiges of intellect yet untrammeled by will give such an individual the ability to apprehend permanence and eternity.

Among the artist-Steppenwolf's strange ways are his solitary nocturnal walks and his propensity toward suicide. At the root of the latter is his ego, ". . . an extremely dangerous, dubious and doomed germ of nature." This concern for the negative qualities of the ego is part of the Jungian influence which implies that the ego is a projection of the corrupt "anima" (associated with *Natur*) of the personality. The influence of Arthur Schopenhauer is present, also, in the references to individuation and its association with guilt. Much of Schopenhauer's material on individuation is drawn from the Eastern mystics' concept of the transmigration of souls. This cycle of reincarnative birth-death, or metempsychosis is directly related to the ordeal of sansara (associated with dissolution, guilt, and chaos) through which one must pass to return to Asia, the Eternal Mother, the beginning of things. Nirvana, the Eastern concept of salvation, is the converse of individuation — a depersonalizing process involving a psychic *tabula rasa* on which eternal essences can be imprinted. Cultures, according to this theory, must also undergo this process. The dissolution and demise of one culture gives rise to the beginning of a new culture. Hesse's idea of a new culture, a pure culture in which there are no wars and where a perfect synthesis of will and intellect exists, is explored in a utopian novel set in the twenty-fourth century, *The Glass Bead Game (Magister Ludi)*, for which the author won the Nobel Prize in 1946.

The treatise which Haller reads is suffused with mysticism and, we realize, has strong echoes of *Siddhartha*. For example, consider the section of *Siddhartha* in which the protagonist has just left the city, obsessed with the transitory quality of the illusion-filled life style and hanging on the precipice of suicide: ". . . suicides present themselves as those who are overtaken by the sense of guilt inherent in individuals, those souls that find the aim of life not in the perfecting and molding of the self, but in liberating themselves by going back to the mother, back to God, back to the all." This is basically what is involved in Nirvana, the extinguishing or surrendering of the ego. The treatise concludes its remarks on suicide by deprecating the act as shabby; suicide displays the most extreme sort of ego for it is an act of will. Suicide affirms the supremacy of will and the surrender to the chaotic, dissolute forces of negation. Man can overcome this world of illusory phenomena not by suicide but by meditation, an ascendency of intellect which apprehends eternity — suspending time, affirming life, and denying death. Albert Camus was to write in "The Myth of Sisyphus" in 1943, sixteen years after *Steppenwolf*: "It is nobler and finer to be conquered by life than to fall by one's own hand."

The treatise then examines Haller's relationship with the bourgeoisie, a class to which he seems alien and yet to which he is magnetically drawn. He does not wish to envisage himself as a system-man, and yet, to a large extent, he is one. Some might think of this haunting man-wolf creature as a kind of semi-animal, but he has qualities that are more human than most people. It is his outward appearance which repulses middle-class men (as does Gregor Samsa's changed appearance in Kafka's "The Metamorphosis"). Within Haller are standards of decency as high as those of any middle-class man. In fact, he abhors any crime of violence more than ordinary men because of his intellect's hyperconsciousness of respectable society's war-mongering super-patriotism.

As the excursus on the bourgeoisie continues, the men of this class are described as people who avoid conspicuous, readily observable extremes, but who, in a more sinister way, embrace the most extreme of extremes — that is, they place the will above all else. Steppenwolves, in contrast, have a sense that makes them superior to the majority of sheep-like people. If the Steppenwolf's ability to project and if his extraordinary spirit are channeled into personal drive and ambition, he becomes a will-Steppenwolf who contributes to the system and strengthens it. These men stand out from ordinary men because of their individuality. In the artist-Steppenwolf, intellect holds the will in check, and the introspective man becomes aware of the guilt inherent in individuation. He cannot reconcile himself to the change and flux of our times in which the will thrives. Because the contrast in the artist-Steppenwolf's personality is so pronounced, he is conscious "that all extreme individuation turns against itself intent upon its own destruction." He devotes his life to meditation of pure essence although the creation of original, pure art is fruitless in the twentieth century. He aspires to the realm of the Immortals rather than to personal success. Those other Steppenwolves who remain in the ambitious circles of the middle class devote their gifts to technical progress, wealth, and national security. Yet there is also hope for these will-Steppenwolf men through humor.

Even though he may submerge himself in his work, a Steppenwolf is never really depolarized. But as the Immortals can temporarily extinguish polarity in the artist type, humor holds hope for the type in which will is dominant. This "kingdom of humor" is central to the novel because artist types can find it also, upon visitation by the Immortals. Even though this humor is somewhat bourgeois in quality, the bourgeois do not really understand it. For instance, a bourgeois of today with no problematical Steppenwolfian quality would not understand what is humorous in large posters of Coke bottles and Campbell soup cans. Only Steppenwolves can grasp the ultimate comedy and affirmation inherent in cosmic humor, and it is this which depolarizes them. Humor is central to the novel because it resembles meditation; inherent in humor is the observing and resolving of chaos by rising above it, and the subsequent detachment from it through the transcendence of inner synthesis. This meditative process requires self-examination; one "must look deeply into the chaos of one's soul and plumb its depths."

A sequence occurs which prefigures the end of the book, with the references to mirrors and Haller's impending self-examination. The split personality of the precariously balanced man-wolf will either explode and completely scatter, or it will "come to terms in the dawning light of humor." Inherent in the process of synthesis and the cosmic vision is an ability to see objectively all levels of the world and of consciousness, as in a looking glass.

The treatise continues to its conclusion with an explanation that the Steppenwolf's self is not split into only two parts but into a thousand fragments, and that the oscillations of his life are likewise between thousands of poles. Thus, to regard the thousandfold chaos of the ego as twofold is a delusion. Some of the material that follows at this point is again reminiscent of *Siddhartha*. The comment is made that the ancient poets of India did not deal with the individual ego or the individual hero, but dealt instead with "whole reels of individualities in a series of incarnations." Likewise, in modern poetry, poets (artist-Steppenwolves) deal with the "manifold activity of soul" and with their characters as "the various facets and aspects of a higher unity . . . of the poet's soul." Hesse alludes to Faust, suggesting that he, like the Steppenwolf, is imbued with the delusion of the twofold personality. Man, to attain inner harmony and peace, must confront the illusion of a single, unified personality. Here one can observe a Jungian influence, and a contrast between the West and the East ensues. Hesse admired the wisdom and sense of permanence of the East and considered the West's progress-oriented influence as a corruption and a defilement.

The ability to strip one's ego bare, to surrender the ego (as taught in the East) brings immortality. Mozart, Haller's favorite of the Immortals, attained his immortality by transcending his sansara-like existence and attaining the essence of form by his immense powers of "surrender and suffering." The process of surrendering the ego and of subsequent synthesis is likened to a kind of Nirvana. One cannot regain lost innocence and hope to become once again as a little child by attempting to go backward chronologically or through psychic regressions. Synthesis can be attained only by passing forward first through the realm of chaos. Rather than attempting to narrow and simplify the soul, men must draw in the whole world and go through the painful ordeal of expanding the soul. One should consider the Buddhist method of attempting to escape all that is imbued with birth and subsequent time and death; as the Buddhist attempts to escape Maya, the realm of illusion, through meditation, likewise the Steppenwolf must give himself to "expansion of the soul until it is able once more to embrace the All."

Like Haller's solitary reflections, the Treatise on the Steppenwolf is a mirror of all those men who are caught in the delicate balance between going the way of will or the way of intellect. These men are the Steppenwolves of whom the Steppenwolf-Haller is but one who goes falteringly in the direction of intellect.

CONTINUATION OF HALLER'S RECORDS

Following the Treatise on the Steppenwolf comes its poetic counterpart, a poem that Haller has written (actually one of

Hesse's *Crisis* poems). This section pursues Haller's "asceticism of the intellect" and his concern with death, bringing the predicament back to Haller's wife's insanity and the job he lost. Haller feels that he cannot avoid his self-destruction from his multiple personality "unless molten in the fire of a renewed self-knowledge, he underwent a change and passed over to a self, new and undisguised."

On the raw wintry morning following the encounter with the peddler, Haller goes to bed, firm in his resolve to eventually do himself in. He reads and rereads the treatise, as well as constantly recalling the memory of the churchyard wall, realizing that the two are strangely interconnected. The announcement of the Magic Theater entertainment, with its fleeting, illuminated letters, marks the first significant departure from reality; it "promised much that was hinted at in the treatise, and the voices of that strange world aroused my curiosity."

When Haller returns to the site of the announcement, he discovers a funeral procession. The cemetery seems steamlined and gadgety, and the whole funeral sequence reeks with the odor of depersonalized modernity and efficiency. The ceremony seems to be a hollow performance, embodying a sterile, death-like hypocrisy. It even seems, in a macabre way, comic because of its "vultures" and "functionaries." Haller suddenly sees someone whom he thinks he recognizes; it is the peddler, but he is of little help. Haller is told to go to the Black Eagle.

Now Haller is at an all-time low, almost paralyzed with emptiness and despair; and, despite his disgust for the professor's sense of self-importance, he is actually pleased to come across an acquaintance. Haller accepts the professor's dinner invitation, contemplating with reservations the required courtesy and small talk. At home before the dinner, Haller reads some of his beloved eighteenth-century literature; later, while he is shaving, his thoughts return to the funeral sequence. He contemplates modern civilization in terms of the symbolic cemetery, "a cemetery where Jesus Christ and Socrates, Mozart and Haydn, Dante and Goethe were but the indecipherable names on moldering stones." Whether or not Haller's cutting himself with the razor is entirely coincidental is a matter for the reader's reflection for Haller is deeply depressed, has contemplated suicide and, in his state of depression, the thought of visiting the professor becomes almost unbearable. The professor is pretentious, self-satisfied, and naive, besides being a rabid supporter of right-wing causes.

From the first moments after Haller's arrival at the professor's house to the visit's abrupt ending, all goes completely wrong. Immediately upon arrival, Haller's glance falls upon a sentimentalized etching of Goethe which is so unlike Goethe that it seems to "shriek" at Haller (Franz Kafka made the shriek a stock motif). In the engraving, Goethe looks more like a bourgeois "success" than a tempermental artist. This incident of the engraving embodies Haller's own crisis, the conflict of his "selves." Haller's antagonism is no doubt aggravated by his consciousness of his own Bürger background.

When the professor rails interminably about the journalist Haller, whom he ironically alludes to as his guest's namesake and calls him a traitor, we should realize that this is similar to the type of reviling Hesse himself received for his articles and columns during World War I. His writings were also blacklisted in 1943 by the Third Reich. Like Hesse himself, Haller is conscious of Germany's war guilt, is critical of the Kaiser and other leaders, but is not anti-German. He is merely critical of the direction his country has taken in the twentieth century. We can almost hear Hesse himself as Haller discloses that he is the Harry Haller who wrote the article, terminating his visit with a declaration that "it would be better for our country and the world in general, if at least the few people who were capable of thought stood for reason and the love of peace instead of heading wildly with a blind obsession for a new war."

After the visit with the professor, Haller resolves to commit suicide, but he first takes to the streets. Despite his resolve to return to his room, he dreads going back and so he roams the streets for hours. He finally finds his way to the Black Eagle in an unfamiliar part of the city. Here he will meet Hermine, who will alternately draw forth all of Haller's levels of consciousness.

Haller's encounter with Hermine marks the beginning of an apprenticeship sequence (similar to Goethe's *Wilhelm Meister*). Hermine tells Haller that, even though he is an intellectual, he has a great deal to learn — specifically, the simple pleasures of life, such as ballroom dancing, which she offers to teach him. He tells her of his life and of his experience in the professor's house, and she listens. She suggests to him that she has a special role in his life similar to that of a looking glass. She then gives him advice which is similar to that in the treatise: "If you had sense, you would laugh at the artist and the professor — laugh and be done with it." At this point, Hermine is rather like an Oedipal mother figure as she implores Haller to close his eyes and get some sleep; as he does her bidding, he closes his eyes as a child with its mother. His dream of Goethe is significant because Hesse is departing again from reality.

Haller's dream begins in a vestibule of Goethe's house where Haller has been waiting for an interview with the master. Here, a symbol with deep mythological roots as an archetype appears. It is a scorpion, noted for its strange beauty as well as for its ferocious sting. As a Jungian archetype, it symbolizes characteristics associated with women. This particular scorpion has been attempting to crawl up Haller's leg, and he has feared to reach for it. Allusion is made to the tempestuous German "Storm and Stress" poet Gottfried August Bürger (1747-94) who addressed lyric poems to a seductive mistress named Molly. Haller seems aware that there is some kind of connection between the scorpion and Molly. Then, as he considers the possibility of its being some kind of messenger from Molly, he thinks simultaneously that its name might be Vulpius. Christiane Vulpius (1765-1816) was the wife of Goethe who was, at one time, his mistress, and the name "Vulpius" relates the mythical symbol and the allurements of women.

When Goethe appears, he resembles the pretentious bourgeois of the professor's engraving rather than the artist-poet that

Haller has always envisioned. After considerable altercation, Goethe alludes to Mozart's *Magic Flute*, suggesting that it "preaches optimism and faith." Haller professes his love for *The Magic Flute* and for Mozart, its composer, asserting that, unlike Goethe, Mozart did not live to see his works regarded as monuments of creativity.

The dream image of the eighty-two-year-old Goethe tells of his conquest of life over death and, when he does so, he loses his pompous appearance and begins to bear a sublime resemblance to Mozart. The air fills itself with songs of Goethe, Mozart, and Schubert. Then Goethe reiterates the central theme of the book, as do the treatise and Hermine: "You take old Goethe much too seriously . . . we Immortals do not like things to be taken seriously. We like joking. Seriousness . . . is an accident of time. . . . In eternity, however, there is no time; eternity is a mere moment, just long enough for a joke." Goethe has even learned to dance, avoiding the obsessive idealism which has been Haller's problem. Haller asks if Molly is there, and Goethe gleefully hands Haller a jewel box containing a miniature lady's leg. This little replica becomes suddenly associated with the scorpion for, as Haller reaches for it, it seems fearfully animated. The dream ends chillingly with an aged Goethe laughing.

After the dream, Hermine tells him that she has had the same discouraging experience with saints' pictures as Haller had with Goethe's. Hermine subsequently becomes philosophical in her remarks, unusual for women of her calling. When asked if she is religious, she replies that one must be released from the concept and the demands of time and money before one can become truly religious—and this has not happened to her yet. She repeats one of the main themes of the novel: "You can't be religious in earnest and at the same time live in actual things and still take them seriously, time and money . . . and all that."

Haller's conversation with his "alter ego" has brought him to a euphoric state of relaxation. He falls asleep fully dressed and awakens several hours later refreshed and, soon after, we have a highly poignant (and often under-emphasized) conversation between Haller and his landlady. Haller's inhibitions have lifted and the time is perfect for a friendly, jocular conversation. The aunt prepares tea and, as they converse, she learns much about the normally taciturn Haller, without actually posing personal questions. She is not shocked by Haller's nocturnal absence; in fact, she finds her tenant's solitary, quiet ways agreeable. The conversation turns to the nephew and, for the first time, we are told about him from Haller's point of view. The nephew's hobby is tinkering with radios, and Haller is able to joke about this. This develops into a conversation of rare depth as Haller reflects on the nephew's fascination with scientific accomplishments. He comments that even the greatest scientific minds of the contemporary West have not grasped what the sages of India knew in ancient times — that is, the "omnipresence of all forces and facts." The wisdom of the East is permanent; the wisdom of the West is transitory. The ancients of the East were aware of the "unreality of time," which science has not yet comprehended. Haller, however, suggests that, one day, the past will be able to be retrieved and transmitted like the electronic impulses of a broadcast. Not only does the present float around us, but the past does also: "All that ever happened in the past could be recorded and played back likewise." This entire conversation proves that Haller has learned something from the dream rendezvous with Goethe; he can laugh at the impermanence embodied in the nephew's toy. The radio motif will be reintroduced near the end of the novel in the "radio music of life" sequence that includes a portrait of Mozart, laughing.

Anticipating his dinner date with Hermine, Haller reveals the positive effect she has had on him: "What I longed for in my despair was life and resolution, action and reaction, impulse and impetus." Later that evening, Hermine will become, in Jungian terms, Haller's "anima" or "shadow" in the form of a sexually ambiguous hermaphrodite. She vaguely reminds Harry of an old-time school friend named Hermann, and the composite of masculine/feminine can be easily observed in the names Hermann/Hermine. We also know that "Harry" is a diminutive of "Hermann," and so the observation can also be made that

38

Harry/Hermann/Hermine are one composite personality. (The sequence involving the reminiscence of a boyhood friend in a woman's presence is akin to Castorp's recollection of the sexually ambiguous Pribislav Hippe in Clavdia Chauchat's presence in Thomas Mann's *Magic Mountain*.) The idea of the female "anima" here symbolizes the inclination toward dissolution and corruption inherent in *Natur;* the male "animus" symbolizes the realms of the mind and spirit inherent in *Geist*. It is at this point of self-recognition that Haller guesses Hermine's name.

The nucleus of the Haller-Hermine relationship is further solidified when she tells Haller of her role as a mirror: ". . . the reason why I please you and mean so much to you is because I am a kind of looking glass for you, because there's something in me that answers you and understands you." Haller is quite correct when he answers that she is his opposite, that she has all he lacks. Shortly afterward, a premonition of a future departure from reality ensues when Hermine indicates that Haller will carry out certain orders, that he will carry out her command and kill her. This prefigures Haller's "killing" his "other self" embodied in the image of Hermine in the picture world of Pablo's Magic Theater. This often misunderstood event symbolizes the only partially successful attempt at extinguishing Haller's conscious ego and his necessity for attaining the undestructive, gleeful perception of the Immortals.

Events proceed rapidly now: the following day, Haller finds Hermine curiously looking at a right-wing newspaper containing excoriating references to Haller as "a noxious insect and a man who disowned his native land." Haller is, above all, disturbed by the prospect of another war, "the next war that draws nearer and nearer, and it will be a good deal more horrible than the last." After several pages of anti-war material, Hermine takes Harry, as it were, under her wing. They purchase a record player, take it to Harry's apartment, and practice the fox trot. On the following day, Harry is to dance in public for the first time. Here Haller is introduced to Pablo, for whom he instantly feels the antagonism of jealousy in Hermine's presence — not a lover's jealousy, Haller says, but a "subtler jealousy." Haller is also antagonistic toward Pablo because he is the polar opposite of Mozart, Haller's idol.

Hesse is readying us for this transformation: Haller will have to undergo the process of expanding his soul, and he will have to reconcile himself with the jazz world in order to effect "the disintegration of the personality"; this will be a painful process. Currently, Haller is undergoing deep self-examination under the tutelage of Hermine; he is "given over bit by bit to self-criticism and at every point is found wanting." His Bürger beliefs are no longer strong. He, nevertheless, still has reservations about what he considers "slumming" in dance halls, and his opinion of Pablo is still negative. We learn in this section of Pablo's drug habits and what he thinks about music. For Pablo, music is an immediate, nonverbal experience; for Haller, music is a spiritually transcendent and thereby permanent experience.

Much inner turmoil ensues; suffering and happiness come simultaneously—as, for example, when Haller finds Maria in his room after an organ recital of Buxtehude, Pachelbel, Bach, and Haydn, which induced reveries of the past. Here is Hesse's literary counterpart of atonality. The reader is wrenched from one stratum to another—from the realm of religious music to the realm of Maria. During a walk immediately following the recital, Haller comes to the realization that much of Germany's heritage has rested in the irrational emotionality of its music (the collective "anima" or *Natur* of the collective German personality). Rather than turning to the mind or reason (*Geist*) in which he (and Hesse) have faith, Germany is turning to dissolution, to dreams of a "speech without words that utters the inexpressible and gives form to the formless." This embodies the chaos, the process of decadence and decay, elements that were never "passed home to reality."

According to Hesse, modern music (from Brahms and culminating in Wagner), with its spirit of anarchy, will ultimately give way to the corroded irrationality that is but a hair's breadth from the Nazi mystique. It is this state of confusion that is lessened upon encountering Maria, who has been sent by

Hermine. Maria is a variation on the character of Kamala in *Siddhartha*, teaching the art of love to the intellectual ascetic.

On the following day, Haller finds out that he is to participate in the upcoming Fancy Dress Ball, a kind of masked ball that serves as Hesse's counterpart to Goethe's Walpurgis Nacht sequence in *Faust*. After a series of reflections and musings on love, Haller encounters all three members of the offbeat coterie, learning of and rejecting many of their weird secrets. He finds Maria in many ways a joy, but he finds Pablo's amorality repugnant. Ambiguity of gender is repeated in Hermine's oblique references to her relationship with Maria.

Preceding the Fancy Dress Ball, a feeling of heavy anticipation prevails. Hermine is to become a kind of Mephistopheles, and the sequence begins with Haller's remark that what he is looking for is not ordinary happiness or contentment, but a kind of "spiritual food." Haller is cognizant of the fact that sensual pleasures do not last. As in Cervantes' *Don Quixote*, Haller's quest here is for the unattainable, and he feels disenchanted because of the immense gulf between the ideal and the real. At this point, Hermine makes a remark that is memorable for its philosophical depth: "Time and the world, money and power belong to the small people, the shallow people. To the rest, the real men, belongs nothing . . . but death" and "eternity . . . the kingdom on the other side of time and appearances . . . for that reason . . . we long for death." This is what the Immortals (Steppenwolf-types who have attained equilibrium) live for. Here Hermine transcends her profession and reminds us of Socrates in Plato's *Phaedo*, in which the true philosopher is presented as the man who tends his soul, cultivating his awareness of reality by engaging in a constant process of dying (attaining "ideals," "forms," or "essences"). Like Plato's philosopher, Hesse's Immortals live for eternity. Hermine also suggests that, among the saints, many were sinners first. She remarks that we must err "before we reach home. And we have no one to guide us. Our only guide is our homesickness." Hermine's comments about spiritual rebirth remind us of Sonya's remarks in *Crime and Punishment* concerning the miracle of Lazarus. When Haller leaves, he becomes ever more conscious of the similiarity between his mind and Hermine's—that her mind is but a side of his and that her thoughts are his also.

Hermine does more than just teach Haller to dance; she has recovered for him "the sacred sense of beyond, of timelessness, of a world which had an eternal value and the substance of which was divine." The dream of Goethe laughing returns to Haller and he feels for the first time that he understands it. The laughter is light and clear; it penetrates eternity and time and it includes a return to innocence.

The philosophical dialogue with Hermine remains in Haller's mind for a long time; even as he goes to meet Maria once again, he continues to reflect on the Immortals "living their life in timeless space." His mind settles around compositions of Bach and Mozart, whose artistic permanence suspends time, giving a feeling of time frozen in space. Suddenly Haller hears the laughter of the Immortals and he hurriedly writes down a poem ("The Immortals"). Later, however, his mood changes when he becomes conscious of a dread of death—a dread, however, that is already conscious of its being a surrender and a release.

The final section of *Steppenwolf,* which includes the Magic Theater sequence, begins with the events leading up to and including the Masked Ball. Haller has taken leave of Maria and has slept; upon awakening, he suddenly remembers the festivities of the upcoming evening while shaving. No doubt, the fact that Haller is shaving and looking in a mirror is significant because he is soon to be directed toward self-recognition. On his way to the ball, Haller stops at the Steel Helmet, well-remembered and unchanged for twenty-five years, and he has reveries of the pain and beauty of the past. He then lapses into visions of modern man, with his predilection for automobiles and war. Haller's being in a nearly dreamlike state is the author's way of preparing us for the interlude of unreality which follows shortly. On the way to the Globe Rooms, where the Masked Ball is to be held, Haller sees part of a film extravaganza of the Old Testament in which Moses resembles portraits of the rugged, white-bearded Walt Whitman. Another level shift takes place when Haller is reminded of some G. F. Handel vocal music (probably the English language oratorio of 1738, *Israel in Egypt*).

When Haller arrives at the ball, the motif of the cloakroom is introduced and much is made of the care with which Haller puts away his claim ticket. In a short while, he will not be able to find the ticket and, when given one, he will observe bizarre lettering on it much like that on the churchyard wall. Also, Haller will be instructed by Pablo, upon entering the Magic Theater, to leave his personality in the cloakroom. Now, however, we notice that Haller joins the members of the party; he enters a basement decorated much like Dante's Hell, through which he must make an ultimate ascent. The ascent is to approximate structurally the stages of Haller's process of synthesis wherein the mundane and the spiritual levels of consciousness are resolved. During the ball, Haller must surrender his conscious ego and take the (inward) path to attain the perception of the Immortals, a fine madness attainable by artists only. The admission fee is his supposedly rational, bourgeois, ego-oriented "mind."

When Haller thrusts himself back toward the basement labeled "Hell," he recognizes Maria, who tells him that Hermine is in "Hell" and that she has summoned her. When Haller sees Hermine, she is again in ambiguous clothing and resembles Harry's former school friend, Hermann. She is, seemingly, a hermaphrodite. She dances with girls, but other things are odd too: "Everything was fanciful and symbolic." At this point, as Haller lapses into a kind of incipient stupor, we are presented with one of the most important symbols in this novel—that is, Jung's idea of equilibrium and the ancient Hindu and Buddhist archetypal symbol of the All, the symbol of the lotus blossom. Dr. Jung's symbol of self-recognition was that of the mandala, the four-petaled lotus flower, and it is for this reason that we can assume that Hesse intended for the rest of the novel to contain many ideas of Jungian psychoanalysis. In antiquity, the lotus, a a symbol of the *Upanishads,* was within the heart, wherein abided Brahman or All. To know Brahman, however, one must experience the "Tat Twam Asi" (That Art Thou), Brahma dwelling within the lotus of the heart. Only in this way can man escape sorrow and death and become one with the essence of the All. Hesse and Jung were both exponents of Eastern mysticism, and, in his own way, Haller approaches a kind of Nirvana in nearly achieving unity with the Immortals. The Magic Theater sequence could be stated as being symbolic psychoanalysis in offbeat garb. The camaraderie of Pablo and Hermine represents archetypes of Haller's consciousness. At the advent of the Magic Theater sequence, Haller contemplates a peculiar bond with Pablo's psyche: "Was it not perhaps I who made him speak, who spoke from within him?"

The stimulation and excitement of the Masked Ball increases to near delirium; Haller speaks of "the intoxication of a general festivity, the mysterious merging of the personality in the mass, the mystic union of joy." The potential for overcoming inhibitions is suggested, an essential element of psychoanalysis. Images begin to liquify, much like the images in Siddhartha's river, reminding us of the primal sea; Haller says that his personality was dissolved in the intoxication of the festivity like salt in water. His exhilaration reaches new heights as he reflects on his feeling of release and on his loss of the sense of time.

As Haller has many selves, his "other self" likewise has many selves. Hermine disappears from his sight and reappears as a Pierrette whom he is to recognize as part of his other self. The feverish pace of the ball accelerates and culminates with Haller's meeting Pablo as the place resounds with music. Haller hears a superhuman laugh and Pablo invites him to a realm beyond time, for madmen only, for the price of his mind. Harry is escorted upstairs, making an ascent, to "a stratum of reality . . . rarefied in the extreme." As he mounts this staircase, symbolically to the cosmic realm, possible resolution is hinted at.

Pablo now assumes the role of a guru for Haller. He reveals that Haller has a longing to forsake this world and to penetrate a reality more native to him—a world beyond time. Pablo tells Haller that it is his soul that he seeks, but that only within exists "that other reality" for which he longs. The object of the upcoming voyage is to externalize Haller's fantasies. This "trip," to use the modern vernacular, is partially initiated by drugs, but it is important to bear in mind, drugs notwithstanding, that this expansion is only a yielding of what is already within the subject's soul. Haller has already had a pondering, idealistic mentality marred by psychic hyperactivity.

The structurally and psychologically significant mirror motif reaches its culmination as Pablo shows Haller a hand mirror; within, Haller sees the frightened eyes of a Steppenwolf. The journey then begins and Haller finds himself in a corridor full of doors, significant already as symbols. Earlier, Hermine had been thought of as a "door," and it is through opening the doors that Haller will be projected into externalized fantasy. Motifs previously introduced in the novel are also recapitulated here. Jungian psychoanalysis is presented here in a strange guise, but its essence of negating the ego is, nevertheless, present. The guru Pablo announces that what Haller wants is to be relieved of his so-called "personality" which is to be left in the cloakroom. He also suggests that the aim of the Theater is to teach Haller how to laugh, remarking that true humor begins when one ceases to take himself seriously. Much of this, of course, echoes the ideas of the Goethe dream and Hermine's remarks about it. More significantly, this is the final enactment of the treatise. This is another departure from ordinary reality. Haller is to cast aside the "spectacles" of his conscious ego, his projected self-image. He stands now before a full-length mirror which is evidently faceted, for he is apparently to see his reflection when it "fell to pieces." Here, he is prepared for catching a glimpse into the chaos of the schizophrenic soul of modern man. All sorts of Haller-creatures run helter-skelter, one young boy figure emerging running toward a door labeled "All Girls Are Yours. One Quarter in the Slot." The imaginary figure then appears to fall headfirst into the slot, and Pablo at once disappears, leaving Haller to his own resources.

At this point, the radically surrealistic Magic Theater sequence begins. It serves the dual function of being both a recapitulation of previously introduced leitmotifs and as an exorcism recounted in semi-retrospect in Haller's diary. Like the cubist painter or the atonic composer, the surrealistic novelist dissects his subject into a myriad of chaotic pieces and hints that its inner reality may be grasped through synthesis into a new harmonious whole. We might refer to the recounting of the Magic Theater as being in "semi-retrospect" because the material at the end of Haller's abandoned manuscript was probably written about the same time he left it behind. His leaving no doubt resulted from his being able to approach self-recognition because of these recollections and his synthesizing of experiences.

As far as the Magic Theater sequence is concerned, it is more valuable to be able to examine its symbols and images in terms of Jung's analytical psychology than it is to attempt to summarize it. Basically, the Magic Theater marks the culmination of Hermine's and Pablo's efforts at breaking down the ingrained inhibitions and suppressed aggressions of the man-wolf. Hermine and Pablo have been gradually eliciting complementary parts of Haller's personality; in the upcoming fantasies, they are integral parts (along with Pablo's polar opposite, Mozart) of Haller's personality. More significantly, the fantasies represent the schizophrenic selves within collective man, all of whose parts are seemingly irreconcilable and mutually exclusive. Through Harry Haller's expanded consciousness, we look closely at that sickness of the times that the nephew alluded to in the prologue.

That Haller's neurosis is more Jungian than Freudian is evident because Haller's symptoms include marital strife, domestic dislocation, the war, and a general sense of disenchantment rather than the problem of sexuality *rooted in childhood*. The Magic Theater is therapeutic because its function is to draw the symbolism of dream visions and fantasies to the surface so that the psychic forces of the deepest levels of the unconscious may be examined and constructively integrated within the conscious through a synthesizing process. Because Jungian psychoanalysis is forward-oriented rather than oriented backwards around root causes, self-recognition becomes its aim as a constructive goal.

In resolving the individual personal consciousness or ego with the collective unconscious, man's conscious self may complement his ancestral soul. For Haller, the artist's collective ancestral soul is suffused in that beatific laughter that peals at the pettiness of ego consciousness, and Haller's "trip" comes very close to being disastrous because his jealousy allows him to become deadly serious and desecrate his vision of Hermine and Pablo together. Hermine represents the mundane, illusory side of Haller's self which he unfortunately cannot view with enough classical detachment to laugh off, as Mozart might. The paranoic side of Haller's ego is shown by the bizarre mutation of the chess pieces into the form of a knife which he will use in "killing" the image of his alter ego. By not fully attaining the perception of the Immortals, and by not being able to laugh spontaneously, he stains the "stage" of his soul with blood, and he checkmates himself in the dark corner of his neurosis. His contact with that fine madness of Mozart and Goethe is caught only in fleeting moments when touched either by the golden thread or by Baroque and Classical music.

Regarding certain specifics of the Magic Theater itself, Haller has found himself in a corridor full of doors beyond which various parts of the twentieth-century personality may be examined psychoanalytically as, as it were, mental sideshows. Of the numerous choices, Haller enters only five, by which the following announcements appear:

"Jolly Hunting — Great Hunt in Automobiles"
"Guidance in the Building Up of the Personality"
"Marvelous Training of the Steppenwolf"
"All Girls Are Yours"
"How One Kills for Love"

The first of the sideshows is perhaps the most interesting because it depicts a violent enactment of inner hostilities and aggressions while impugning the contemporary military-industrial "machine complex." The paramount element of this sideshow is the "war between men and machines," of which the machines not only include cars but also political "machine-like" bureaucrats. Men are the victims of these runaway machines which pollute the air with anarchy. Haller reflects that this war, despite its ferocity, lacks real direction and that this is one of the most terrifying things about it ("Everyone . . . strove to prepare the way for a general destruction of this iron-cast civilization of ours."). In a way, it depicts the fall of Western man, and Haller joins in, hurling all his suppressed violence against the machine-oriented establishment.

Of prime importance in this section is the symbolism of the wheels of the upturned bureaucrat's car. The wheel is an arche-typal symbol dating back beyond early Hindu and Buddhist symbolism. In Eastern mythology through Hinduism and Bud-dhism, it generally represents the realm of Maya which is associ-ated with illusion and spiritual death. Also important is the fact that the car, an upturned wreck with its wheels wildly spinning in the air, is a Ford — the very embodiment of mass production. As Haller and Gustav examine the wreckage, allusion is made to the "Tat Twam Asi" of the Hindu *Chandogya-Upanishad* which concerns itself with the nature and subjective analysis of the self. The innermost being of universal nature, Brahman, and our innermost self, Atman, are one — "That Art Thou" (Tat Twam Asi).

The car containing Attorney-General Loering, the unques-tioning public prosecutor, appears and is subsequently pre-vailed upon. Loering is a man of duty who justifies his role of passing sentences upon unfortunates by stating that it is his duty. In this sense, he resembles Kafka's legal bureaucrats who are oblivious to the sinister forces they represent. Significantly, Haller reflects that what seems to be the best rational order can lead to the worst oppression of all, and that war will end only if men can become more like the artist and the madman, and less like the machine-made article.

As Haller enters the doorway labeled "Guidance in the Building Up of the Personality," his multifaceted personality takes the form of pieces resembling chess pieces. Here, the process of re-integrating one's split personality, an integral part of the artist's "fine madness," is presented as a process of synthesizing the chess pieces into new, resolved wholes. This is what the building up of the personality means. For example, he is told: ". . . anyone whose soul has fallen to pieces . . . can rearrange these pieces of a previous self in what order he pleases, and so attain to an endless multiplicity of moves in the game of life."

Haller enters a door marked "Marvelous Training of the Steppenwolf" in which the man and the wolf are alternately dominating one another. Eventually, Haller has the taste of blood in his mouth. This is a particularly hellish sideshow and it concludes with Haller recalling the world war.

"All Girls Are Yours" presents a succession of flashing images of all the girls Haller has ever known in his life. He recalls Rosa Kreisler, in particular, in a setting much like Hesse's own Calw. Much of the sequence is similar in style and content to the pre-Romantic "Storm and Stress" literature.

The sideshow "How One Kills for Love" begins with a recollection of Hermine's having told Haller that he would "kill" her for love. Haller's "pieces" of his personality suddenly become a knife. In anguish, he runs about looking again for the chess master, but he suddenly sees a horrifying image of his tired, world-weary self in a full-length mirror. This uncreative, worldly self longs for death and, suddenly, strains from Mozart's opera Don Giovanni can be heard. It is the music that accompanies the approach of the white stone statue of the Commandant as this ghostly figure comes to deliver the unrepentant Don Giovanni to the demons of Hell for his murder. Ice-cold laughter rings out, "out of a world unknown to men, a world beyond all suffering, and born of the divine of divine humor." Then Mozart appears and Haller follows him into a dark compartment where the composer tells him that they are in the final act of Don Giovanni. Leporello, Don Giovanni's lackey and accomplice in murder, appears before us on his knees before the vengeful stone figure. Leporello is a kind of alter ego for Don Giovanni, who has allowed his worse self to control his actions.

Remarks are made about the decadence of composers after Mozart (Franz Schubert, Hugo Wolf, Frederick Chopin, and Ludwig von Beethoven) to the effect that there is something sinister and irrational lurking beneath the music of post-classicism, "beautiful as it may be . . . something rhapsodical about it, something of disintegration."

Then Mozart and Haller look to the images of more recent and even more decadent composers, such as Johannes Brahms and Richard Wagner. Mozart, who epitomized the lean clarity of classicism, regards the compositions of the late Romantics to bear excesses in orchestration and emotionality, "a fault of their time." Mozart impugns Haller and his vocation of writing by suggesting that Haller's work is merely plagiarized trivia. Haller, furious, grabs Mozart's queue which extends to such fantastic lengths that it resembles a comet with Haller still holding onto it as he flies into the furthest reaches of rarefied space. He lapses into a trance of icy gaiety in this realm of the beyond, after which he seems to lose consciousness altogether.

There is a break in the text at this point, and we now embark on Haller's gradual recovery to consciousness. Haller is fretful and suffering, his mind churning in the after-effects of intoxicants and strenuous mental exercise. One can observe, however, that certain bourgeois inhibitions have broken down for Haller, but that he still feels bound by time. There is still something awaiting Haller: he is to open a final door and, because he is nearly conscious, he will be vulnerable prey to his ego when his jealousy is aroused by the vision of Pablo with Hermine. Haller uses the knife on his other self, his "anima," which must be overcome, not destroyed. Pablo then leaves and smiles, knowing that Haller has fallen into the ego trap.

Suddenly, music can again be heard, and Mozart enters the compartment. He adroitly repairs a radio and tunes in a Munich broadcast of Handel's "Concerto Grosso in F Major," considered one of the finest of the Baroque master's compositions. The signal reception is quite distorted, which places a creative demand upon the listener to let his imagination compensate for the technical difficulties. Haller finds the broadcast to be sheer cacophony, not seeing that these emissions are merely a very imperfect copy of an indestructible original which is eternal. When Haller refers to the radio as a final weapon "in the war of extermination against art," Mozart merely laughs because he knows that the essence of the masterpiece transcends any radio transmission of it. Mozart directs Haller to the essence of Handel, imploring him to let the inspiration of Handel penetrate his "restless heart" and give it peace. The radio, he says, cannot destroy the original spirit of the music. Then Mozart makes his culminating remarks on the radio music of life, remarking that we must laugh rather than destroy, and that Haller attempted to destroy Hermine rather than laugh.

Memorable are Mozart's comments likening the mundane world and ego consciousness to a radio. The mundane life is a temporal projection of a higher reality, but it comes through like a poor signal in the Magic Theater. When Mozart remarks on Haller's desecration of the picture world of the Magic Theater, and says that killing Hermine was actually her own idea, Haller realizes that whatever was *her* idea was actually *his* as well. He recalls his former awareness of her role as his double, his shadow. Mozart laughs when Haller seems to realize the truth about himself. He also laughs at Haller's desire for self-punishment. In a way, Mozart's remark that humor is always "gallows humor" is almost a corollary to Miguel Unamuno's postulation of "the tragic sense of life" as a way to immunity from the events of this life which is, in turn, rooted to a longing for immortality. Interestingly, Hesse's work was so alluring to the Spanish-speaking world that it went into translation in the Romance languages (and even the Oriental languages) before it was translated into English.

At the end of this novel, a sign flashes before Haller's eyes which reads "Haller's Execution." His execution, however, is not what ordinary men would think of as a usual execution. Rather, it is an execution administered by the "madmen," the Immortals. Haller is sentenced to eternal life, and he is to be the object of the Immortals' endless laughter. Haller has misused the

Magic Theater, besmirching it with everyday reality; "he confounded our beautiful picture gallery with so-called reality."

Haller must listen to more of the "radio music of life" so that he can see the seemingly real in proper perspective as but a poor reflection of the ideal. Mozart here plays the role of the psychiatrist trying to orient the patient's mind in a forward, constructive direction, giving him an immediate goal ("listen to the cursed radio music of life . . . reverence the spirit behind it . . . laugh at its distortions"). Mozart suddenly mutates into his polar opposite, Pablo, who also comments on Haller's negative act of destruction in the picture world. The image of Hermine then takes the form of a tiny chess figure; and Pablo, the master of the game of personality building, puts it away in his pocket for next time. *Steppenwolf* has an unresolved but positive ending, for we are given to feel that there will be a "next time" — then Haller will have surely improved at this game. The game, with its little pieces, is a symbol for the path within, the glimpse into chaos which is the way to ultimate equilibrium.

From the standpoint of technique, this novel, which began in a basically realistic technique, has become radically surrealistic with its seemingly random succession of leitmotifs and allusions in the Magic Theater, which in turn presents an examination of the self from all sides and angles. This dissonant technique is consistent with the level-shifts and departures from ordinary reality in the story.

Above all, we must remember that what we read after the prologue in *Steppenwolf* is what Haller himself wrote and included and abandoned, hopefully along with his ego. As Haller's mental life increases in intensity toward the end of his stay at the landlady's house, his lattermost notes not only reflect this increased inner intensity, but they follow upon the heels of firsthand experience so closely that the experiences they relate have not as yet attained the distance in time perspective that would make them lend themselves to detached recounting. As a result, the cool realism of Haller's early memoirs gives way in the concluding ones to a surrealistic stream-of-consciousness.

CHARACTER ANALYSES

HARRY HALLER

Through Harry Haller's first-person narrative, we have some-what of an autobiographical projection of Hesse at the age of forty-eight. Haller feels that the different facets of his multiple man-wolf (will/intellect) personality will never complement one another, but will conflict with one another to the point of destruc-tion, so he seriously entertains the idea of a shaving mishap on his fiftieth birthday to end it all. "Harry" is a nickname for Hermann, and it is no accident that Haller's initials are H. H. Likewise, it is not mere coincidence that Haller has sciatica, wears eyeglasses, has a library much like Hesse's grandfather's, and has anti-establishment ideas. Haller dislikes modern urban life as did Hesse, is politically committed against Germany's right-wing politics, and has premonitions of Germany's prepara-tions for the next war. We must note, also, that Haller's musical tastes lean toward those masters of supremely balanced form whose work predates the idea of *will* as a collective, positive Germanic force. Haller loves music which is uncontaminated by the manifestations of will in torrential, dissonant frenzy. Haller craves community with that corporate realm of Immortals who embody pure, self-disciplined intellect — Bach, Handel, and Mozart.

Haller, however, is not a musician; he is a writer — a creator of only subsidiary stature — and is aware that neither he nor any other men of his time can attain the stature of the Immortals. Writing fragments of less than great poetry and occasional es-says falls far short of the Kantian idealism of art for art's sake; thus Haller, with his middle-class background of which he is so wearily conscious, no doubt feels himself to be an ego-centered, will-imbued fraud like other twentieth-century men. Haller, however, is at least aware of his predicament — so much so that he alternates between Bürger and madman, becoming a vivid em-bodiment of the collective schizophrenia that he sees in

Germany. He is a victim of his own self-hate; his manuscript is his exorcism.

We learn, also, that a certain amount of Haller's psychological trouble can be rooted to his wife's insanity, which resulted in his leaving home as a kind of "non-person" — stripped of identity and manhood, according to bourgeois standards. Haller's agony lies in his divided self. He is part bourgeois in that he was brought up with middle-class values, is inclined at times toward orderliness and tidiness, and has tremendous feelings of guilt. He pays his taxes and owns corporate industrial securities, deriving his income from their dividends. But Haller is also part "wolf." His life style is essentially bohemian and he is resentful of the military-industrial complex which Germany has become. He is transfigured not by will but by intellect, by the ideal of eternal perfection which he believes exists in classical art, music particularly.

THE NEPHEW

The landlady's nephew has studied Greek and seems to have a consciousness of classical ideals which gives him the capacity to respond to the positive vein of Haller's manuscript. He is of Bürger stock, and his consuming hobby is tinkering with radios (the "wireless"). Even though his initial reaction to Haller is one of repugnance (a typical reaction of the supposedly healthy bourgeois toward those souls who appear to be sick), he grows progressively more interested in what seems to lie beneath the surface of Haller. After he salvages Haller's manuscript, he realizes that what lies beneath the surface of Haller, the individual, is what lies beneath the surface of twentieth-century man collectively. The nephew has the projection and insight to recognize that Haller's manuscript is a document of the abruptly changing times. As a bourgeois, the nephew also possesses that germ of will which gives him an interest in scientific advances. But he is also endowed with enough intellect to give him the capacity to respond positively to the seemingly irrational manuscript. The nephew and Haller complement one another because each is, in his own way, a divided personality, and each is strangely drawn toward the other's dominant world. Each becomes, in a sense, the other's "double."

THE AUNT

Some readers might be tempted to dismiss Haller's landlady as a typical "dear old lady" of the Bürger class. Indeed, she is a staunchly middle-class woman; she is a proud Bürger, dutifully keeping her house fastidiously tidy, as would any respectable lady of her station. There is, however, another side of the landlady's personality. She seems not to possess any of the negative attributes of the middle class. She is not meddlesome or gossipy. She seems to accept Haller's eccentricities and, rather than reacting with alarm, seems to like Haller. She is even mentioned in Haller's manuscript as inviting him to join her for tea, during which an interesting conversation ensues about the nephew's scientific bent and his love for the wireless.

THE PEDDLER

This street vendor hands Haller a little manual entitled "Treatise on the Steppenwolf." Harry reports seeing the peddler shortly after his vision of the sign "Magic Theater: Entrance Not For Everybody; For Madmen Only." The peddler also carries a sign about which Haller wants to inquire, but rather than answering Haller's inquiry about the advertisement, the peddler hands Haller the little handbook. Several days later, Haller sees the signbearer again and tries to inquire about the Magic Theater entertainments, but perhaps because Haller winks at him, he misunderstands and directs Haller to the notorious Black Eagle dance hall.

HERMINE

The name "Hermine" is a feminine form of "Hermann," and this peculiarly offbeat woman of the night is Haller's symbolic "double" or "anima" or "alter ego." Haller takes on a kind of apprenticeship under Hermine, who has rescued Haller in his night of despair, and they eventually engage in some unusual philosophical discussions. This philosophical and spiritual inclination in a woman of Hermine's calling seems to be a Dostoevskian influence, reminiscent particularly of Sonya in *Crime and Punishment*. Hermine tries to relieve Harry of his social awkwardness by teaching him how to dance and by exposing him to jazz. As the novel progresses, Hermine takes on different symbolic guises. At the Fancy Dress Ball, Hermine emerges as a hermaphrodite. Her ambiguity of gender gives her the appearance of a certain Hermann, a childhood friend of Harry's. Then she appears as a masked Pierrette. Finally, Hermine becomes part of the picture world reflected in Pablo's Magic Theater, and she symbolizes Haller's egotistical possessiveness of her. Haller attempts to destroy her because of a jealousy that proves that he has still not overcome polarity and egocentricity.

PABLO

Pablo is the dark, languid, saxophone-playing jazz musician who is the symbolic polar opposite to Mozart. He is thoroughly amoral and sensual. He is a creature of feeling and not of intellect. He resorts to drugs and is so non-verbal that, upon Haller's request to discuss music seriously with him, he withdraws, declaring that music is to be played—not discussed. It is Pablo's Magic Theater, however, that forms the nucleus of the Haller manuscript. It is Pablo's little mirror and his apparently faceted larger mirror that reflects with kaleidoscopic effect all the facets of the thousand-fold personality and all levels of consciousness.

REVIEW QUESTIONS

1. Discuss the parallels between Goethe's *Faust* and Hesse's *Steppenwolf*.

2. Relate Harry Haller's predicament in a bourgeois, urban milieu to his idealism.

3. Discuss the narrative points of view and the level shifts in *Steppenwolf*.

4. Discuss trends in post-classical and contemporary music as signs of decadence and decay as viewed by Haller's higher self.

5. Discuss the structural significance of the Treatise, the Goethe dream, and the Magic Theater.

6. Examine the nephew as an observer of Haller.

7. Discuss what the Mozart figure meant by referring to "radio music" in relation to the "life" of ordinary reality in the Magic Theater when he spoke of the "radio music of life" in distinguishing the real and the ideal.

8. In terms of the attainment of the deepest truths through what might appear to be insanity to ordinary men, discuss the meaning of the word "madmen."

9. Examine the polarities of Pablo/Mozart and of Hermine/Harry in terms of the many selves of Harry, and suggest how this is a microcosm of modern man.

10. Examine the role of Haller's manuscript as an enactment of Haller's fantasies, and suggest how the whole novel is, likewise, Hesse's enactment of Jungian visions and fantasies.

11. Compare and contrast, in terms of Oriental influence and in terms of the process of synthesis, *Siddhartha* and *Steppenwolf*.

12. How does Hermann Hesse's work fit into the perspective of twentieth-century surrealism?

Siddhartha Notes

INTRODUCTION

This novel is one of Hesse's finest and, certainly, is the finest product of Hesse's so-called psychoanalytic period. Begun in 1919, with its first section (through "Awakening") dedicated to the pacifist author Romain Rolland, the book's composition spanned nearly three years. The second section (through "By the River") was written during 1919-20, and the rest was completed eighteen months later. The entire work is loosely based on the life of Gotama Buddha. It also, however, bears a relationship to Hesse's own life for, like Siddhartha, Hesse decided to choose another career than that which his father suggested. Siddhartha left the strict bonds of his Brahmin father to seek his own salvation; Hesse left the strict bonds of his Pietist-Lutheran father to become a writer. Pietists, like Calvinists, believed that man is basically evil and thereby placed heavy emphasis on austere disciplinarianism. Likewise, Siddhartha's father was persistently performing ablutions at the river.

As for a similarity between the lives of Hesse's Siddhartha and the actual Buddha, we may observe that as a child, Siddhartha, like Buddha, was an outstanding pupil and athlete. He also left his wife and unborn son for the life of an ascetic, as did Buddha. Moreover, Buddha reportedly practiced yoga and meditated by the side of a river for six months. Also, as Siddhartha's most important decision comes to him under a mango tree, the most important decisions of the Buddha come to him in what are reported to be three visions under a Bo tree. In each case, it was beneath a tree by a river that the vision of all previous existences emerged in a revelation of the simultaneity of all things. Thus both men, by attaining Nirvana, were liberated from the vicious circle of metempsychosis and thereby attained salvation.

The Christian influence on *Siddhartha* may not be immediately obvious, but it is, nevertheless, unmistakable. To attain salvation, Siddhartha must once again regain his innocence, becoming once again as a little child before entering the Gates of Heaven. Herein lies the perfect resolution of the novel.

LIST OF CHARACTERS

Siddhartha

The protagonist of the novel, his life is vaguely based on that of Gotama Buddha (563?-483? B.C.), born Prince Siddhartha Gotama. Siddhartha is the personal name and means "he who is on the right road" or "he who has achieved his goal." Gotama is the clan name, and Buddha, which means "to know," is the title which his followers, who regarded him as almost a kind of god, gave to him.

Govinda

Siddhartha's dearest friend and confidant. He is Siddhartha's follower, his "shadow."

The Samanas

Three impoverished, emaciated ascetics who believe that temporal life is but an illusion; they practice extreme self-denial and meditation. Siddhartha and Govinda remain with the Samanas for three years.

Gotama Buddha

The "Illustrious," the "Enlightened," the "Sakyamuni" who achieved Nirvana, the supreme goal of Buddhism. "Sakyamuni" means the "Sage of the Sakyas" and is a title given to the Buddha by those outside of his clan. Nirvana is a form of salvation from the process of rebirth (which is the result of desire) by the extinguishing of desire. What the Buddhist seeks to avoid is separation from the whole of life, the unity of existence. The life-death-rebirth cycle, rooted in the concept of the transmigration of souls, separates man from the whole and is thereby associated with evil. The Buddhist endeavors to extinguish desire and thereby suspend this cycle. The process of passing from one form of existence to another is suppressed by high aspiration, purity of life, and the elimination of the ego. The resulting suspension of the rebirth cycle is accompanied by a state in which man ceases to exist and, instead of becoming, he attains Being. Thought is the highest faculty of man and meditation holds a prominent place in the final steps of his deliverance. Buddha is nearly always depicted as sitting with his legs crossed and his feet facing upwards, the posture of meditation he had assumed under the Bo tree when he achieved enlightenment. The Buddha, although not a god, embodies the ideal of what any man may become; Buddhism seeks to vitalize this ideal in the minds of believers.

Kamala

The courtesan from the city who claims that she is capable of dispensing and teaching love as an art, but who appears later among the followers of Buddha. In the city, Kamala is the embodiment of sensual desire, the polar opposite of Nirvana. She brings Siddhartha his son eleven years later; later still, she dies of snakebite.

Kamaswami

The rich merchant for whom Siddhartha worked in the city. His name means "master of the material world."

Vasudeva

The ferryman who takes Siddhartha across the river and with whom Siddhartha is later to live and work. Vasudeva is serene and enlightened and tells Siddhartha what the river can teach. Siddhartha eventually succeeds Vasudeva as the ferryman. Vasudeva is another name for Krishna, who is the teacher of Arjuna (the principal hero of the *Bhagavad-Gita*) and a human incarnation of Vishnu, a Hindu deity.

CRITICAL COMMENTARIES

THE BRAHMIN'S SON

The novel begins with a brief retrospective glance at Siddhartha's Brahmin (priestly Hindu caste) family background, his upbringing, and the innocence and tranquility of his childhood. We are promptly aligned with Siddhartha at the threshold of young manhood and simultaneously observe the orthodox Brahmin father of Siddhartha who, with his son, performs the rite of ablution at the river. Later, as we meet Govinda, Siddhartha's boyhood friend and close comrade, we feel them to be so close intellectually and fraternally that they are almost one.

In spite of the admiration and adoration which Siddhartha receives from his family and friends, his soul is perpetually restless and fraught with disquieting dreams. Unable to find inner peace, Siddhartha initiates his search for Atman. He knows that Atman, the individual spirit or Self, is within him and is inclined toward Brahman (the supreme universal Soul), and he strives to find his own way to experience Atman. Siddhartha is troubled by the fact that nobody—not the wisest teachers, or his father, or the holy songs—can lead him to the discovery of Self. Teachers and scripture have yielded only second-hand learning, not the first-hand experience from which knowledge emanates. Siddhartha suggests that his father, like himself, must not be actually experiencing Atman, for he continually performs ablutions to absolve himself of spiritual impurity and guilt. (The individual soul will not merge with the all-perfect Being unless the individual soul is cleansed of guilt.)

Up to this point, the passage of time has been vague and barely perceptible, but we are suddenly made conscious of a specific evening. It is important to note that this time pattern continues throughout *Siddhartha:* years pass imperceptibly; then, a day and a half or two days will suddenly emerge as strikingly distinct. Now, the Samanas are briefly described, and on this specific evening, Siddhartha breaks the news to Govinda that he has decided to free himself from his predetermined Hindu caste and plans to leave his father to join the Samanas. After standing on his feet all night in defiant endurance and upon receiving reluctant consent from his father, Siddhartha leaves home at daybreak. The father alludes to his own spiritual disquietude as Siddhartha departs, and he asks his son to teach bliss to him should he find it in the forest among the Samanas. Govinda's shadow then appears and he joins Siddhartha.

We have now been introduced to two important motifs—the river and the shadow. The river is introduced as a cleansing agent, and Govinda, who will part ways with Siddhartha and again rejoin him, is Siddhartha's shadow. Among the important themes of the book is the father-son theme, which will be reestablished at the end of the novel with Siddhartha's defiant, prodigal son leaving him. Also introduced in this section is Hesse's unique handling of time through compressing longer time periods and unexpectedly expanding shorter time periods. The syllable "OM," the sacred syllable of the Hindu yoga breathing exercise, is introduced and we become aware that concentration on the word—and abstraction from all mundane things—will enhance unity with Brahman and will suspend the concept of time.

Another of the important considerations in this section is this: for Siddhartha, Atman is all-perfect. The god Prajapati is not nearly so important to Siddhartha because Prajapati was created. Siddhartha concedes more attributes of deity to Atman, for a created god, like anything else created, emanates from something else and is thereby not a first cause. But Siddhartha is not able to evoke Atman at will. Atman is discovered only after the ego is negated and the conscious and the unconscious are resolved through synthesis. References to the Hindu scriptures, the *Vedas* (specifically the *Rig Veda*) and the *Chandogya-Upanishads,* are made but they do not satisfy Siddhartha because they do not show him the way, even though they contain learned material. In short, it is becoming evident already that Siddhartha is a rebel; he must think for himself. He is not a ready-made disciple.

WITH THE SAMANAS

It is in this sequence that Siddhartha and Govinda attempt to gain salvation through asceticism. Using as a premise the ascetic idea that the sensual world is transitory and illusory, Siddhartha attempts to void his self and thus void with it all the torments of the senses. He resolves that if he can let the self die, then something deeper than the self will surface — that is, Being. Siddhartha, however, finds the process of trying to void the self a vicious circle because even though the ascetic meditation of which the aim is emptying the self involves the assuming of different forms, it inevitably leads him back to self again. All the paths leading away from self eventually lead back to it and are particularly tormenting because, like the life cycle, they are imbued with a sense of time. Thus Siddhartha regards this as just another form of escapism, in this case through self-denial, just as drinking is escapism through self-indulgence. Even though Govinda states that he is still learning, Siddhartha asserts that he himself is far from knowledge and wisdom.

After the imperceptible passage of three years with the Samanas, Siddhartha resolves to leave them. Not only does Siddhartha again object to discipleship and assert the impossibility of learning things second-hand, he asserts that learning impedes knowledge. Govinda is, of course, troubled by Siddhartha's lecture. At this point, we learn of the arrival of Gotama Buddha, who has conquered sorrow and brought the cycle of rebirth to a standstill. He has attained Nirvana; he remembers former lives and will never return to the cycle. Govinda enjoins Siddhartha to go and hear the teachings of Buddha. Siddhartha is amazed that Govinda (heretofore always Siddhartha's shadow) is initiating a course of action, and since Siddhartha desires to go, they both decide to leave the Samanas. Here we have another time expansion, a kind of enlargement of a particular day when a specific allusion is made to "the same day," and Siddhartha draws the angry Samana teacher into the same hypnotic spell that the teacher himself had taught.

Important in this section is the fact that living among the ascetics dissatisfies Siddhartha for the same reason that Brahminism never really satisfied his father. As the rules and rituals of the Brahmin priests did not provide knowledge through experience, likewise the Samana rules and ascetic observances do not either. Instead, they are merely a kind of escapism. Supremely important is the fact of Gotama Buddha's having attained Nirvana, transcending and suspending the transmigratory life cycle and the agony of time.

GOTAMA

In this sequence, Siddhartha goes with Govinda to hear the teachings of Buddha, and Govinda remains with Buddha to become his disciple. Siddhartha, however, feels that everyone must find his own way to salvation and, hence, does not remain. The "Gotama" sequence begins with Buddha's taking alms in the town of Savathi and his abiding in the Jetavana grove.

Reference is made to a specific night when a lady tells Siddhartha and Govinda that they may sleep among the pilgrims. By daybreak, the town is swarming with the followers of Gotama Buddha, and Siddhartha and Govinda see him for the first time. Despite his commonplace appearance and traditional yellow monk's garb, he stands out because he radiates inner peace. It is during this day that we learn of Siddhartha's affinity to Buddha and his complete love for him for possessing truth, knowledge, and peace. However, we learn that despite his attraction toward Buddha, Siddhartha is adamant in his disinterest in teachings.

That evening, Buddha preaches before the crowd that there is salvation from pain and suffering for those who follow the prescribed course of Buddhism—that is, the Four Noble Truths —of which the fourth involves the taking of the Eightfold Path. Govinda volunteers to join the Buddhist pilgrims and hopes that Siddhartha will also join. Siddhartha, however, declines, and the impending separation of the two boyhood friends brings tears to their eyes. After their fraternal embrace and Govinda's taking the monk's habit, Siddhartha wanders through the grove and meets Gotama. They engage in a deep conversation in which Siddhartha extols Gotama's doctrine of understanding the world as a complete, unbroken, eternal chain, linked together by cause and effect. It is in this conversation that Siddhartha points out that the doctrine of salvation is neither shown nor proven. Gotama concedes the flaw in logic but asserts that his message is not for the intellectually curious, but that he seeks only to teach salvation. Siddhartha again voices the central idea of the novel: he reminds the Buddha that the process of enlightenment which he underwent is unteachable, that there is no way of communicating first-hand experience to disciples. One can find the secret of self-realization only by going one's own way. Siddhartha, speaking only for himself and not for the other pilgrims, tells of his resolve to leave all doctrines and all teachers behind and to reach his goal alone. As they part, the smile of the Buddha remains in Siddhartha's mind, and he associates it with a man who has conquered his self. And even though Siddhartha feels that he has lost his friend Govinda to Buddha, he feels that he has gained something from Buddha—the inspiration of direct, firsthand contact with the Illustrious One, which further strengthens his resolve to conquer self. Yet Siddhartha again rejects formal doctrine for the same reason as before: enlightenment defies structured doctrine and transcends the teaching process.

The formal doctrine of Buddhist salvation is briefly as follows: it includes a system of which the keys are alluded to in the text—that is, the Four Noble Truths and the Eightfold Path. The Four Noble Truths include (1) the existence of pain, (2) pain's cause being desire or attachment, (3) the possibility of enduring pain by suppressing desire, and (4) the Eightfold Path to salvation. This path involves right faith, right life, right language, right purpose, right practice, right effort, right thinking, and right meditation. The link between this system and salvation lies in a "chain of causation," which is based on the cause-effect relationship between desire and pain. The root cause of pain is birth (which arises from desire), for the consequence of birth is exposure to time, illness, and death. Birth is but one point in the transmigration of souls inherent in the life cycle.

Of the important motifs of the novel, the one which is introduced in the "Gotama" sequence is that of the smile. It is evoked
from self-realization and will appear again in the final section
of the novel.

AWAKENING

This brief sequence portends a basic turning point in the
novel and signals the end of Part I. The mood of this sequence
is one of great loneliness, for Siddhartha is beyond the point of
being able to return home again, and now he has parted ways
with Govinda. He reflects that he has left his former life behind
him and has now matured from youth to manhood. He again contemplates the limitations of teachers and reflects that among the
things that they cannot teach is the matter of the self. The tone
approaches despair as Siddhartha seeks to rid himself of self, or
at least to try to flee from self. He sees that there is nothing about
which he knows less than his self. He reflects that his lack of
knowledge of his self grew out of fear and the desire to flee, and
that in his search for Atman he became lost. He feels an awakening and asserts that he will no longer try to escape from Siddhartha. He believes now that he can slough off his search for
Atman, his asceticism, and the scriptures. He resolves to learn
the secret of Siddhartha from himself.

At this point, all the world around Siddhartha exudes the
colorations of sensual beauty, and he is at the brink of the theory
that reality is in the world itself, the sensual world. He feels that
he has suddenly awakened. Then an icy chill comes over him as
he realizes that he is completely alone. Having shed the old skin
of meditation, he realizes now that he is not the Brahmin's son
any more. Realizing that he belongs to no family or peer group
whatever, he falls into a spasm of despair, while at the same time
he feels more firmly himself than ever. As Siddhartha experiences
the pangs of this awakening, he resolves to never again "walk
backwards."

This "Awakening" sequence terminates Part I and prefigures Siddhartha's crossing the river to enter into the sensual world of the city with the beautiful courtesan Kamala. The metaphorically rich imagery of a snake molting its old skin anticipates a later appearance of this popular Indian motif.

KAMALA

Unlike Part I, the second part of this novel was written with extreme difficulty. Part I, Hesse said, flowed in a potent burst of creative energy, but this creative energy seemed suddenly to run dry; Hesse didn't know how to continue his story or how to end it, so he put the manuscript away for about eighteen months. One would never guess, however, that Hesse had problems with this section. It begins with a superb lyric passage extolling the wonders of the tangible world. Its descriptions of nature have a lulling, trancelike quality, swirling with color and suggestion. The prose is almost biblical, awesome and spellbinding. And beneath the prose, we discern the familiar Hesse theme of *Natur/Geist*—the temporal realm and the spiritual realm residing on opposite sides of reality—the temporal world on this side of reality and the permanent world on the other side. Now we will learn about the impact of Siddhartha's three years with the Samanas. Despite the allurements of the sensual world of *Natur,* Samana life has so conditioned Siddhartha that he will be capable of realizing the nature/spirit dichotomy. Siddhartha's inner voice, though neglected, is never quite extinguished.

The "Kamala" sequence, like previous sequences, seems to hover for some time in expository prose, undelineated in definite time, and then suddenly Hesse zooms in for a close-up of a particular day and a half, beginning with a night and continuing through the next day. The events of this particular night and the following day are extremely important in the development of the rest of the novel because they are heavy with symbols and motifs that are used in later sections of the novel. For example, Siddhartha sleeps in a ferryman's hut; the ferryman will be the key figure in Siddhartha's self-resolution and synthesis. Also, the dream which Siddhartha has in the hut is not only full of Jungian symbolism, but it is also the vehicle by which the worlds of sense and spirit are united. Govinda, Siddhartha's shadow (the Jungian other self), appears in that dream as not only Siddhartha's shadow, but also as a hermaphrodite—that is, a symbol of the "anima" (the weak, sensually oriented, female component of the total personality). There is also the symbolism of the beginning of life, of oneness, in the maternal images associated with the female element in the dream. The sense of the flow of life and of oneness can also be associated symbolically with the ferryman's hut, perhaps itself a womb symbol because it will be the ferryman who will be instrumental in Siddhartha's union with the river, a symbol of beginning and of life.

The day after Siddhartha has his dream is significant because it is during this time that Siddhartha meets the ferryman and hears his remarks about one's being able to "learn" from the river. The river, of course, is an archetypal symbol, and here it is the symbolic boundary between the two worlds of sense and spirit. Siddhartha regards his meeting the ferryman as a mere accident, but the ferryman's comments about Siddhartha's destiny to return eventually are structurally and philosophically important. One of the secrets of the river that the ferryman has learned, and one which Siddhartha will finally learn, is that all things eventually return. Like primal waters, everything is imbued with the quality of recurrence. There is no death. There is no time. The river is timeless, ever-changing and yet changeless. Siddhartha, however, is too involved in pursuing the education of his senses to fathom the significance of his conversation with the ferryman and so he dismisses him as, for the present, merely a likeable, Govinda-like person.

After having passed the river and the ferryman, Siddhartha finally has his first glimpse of Kamala in the late afternoon. He resolves to shed his beggar's appearance, fearing that Kamala would scorn him. The night passes and on the following day, Siddhartha manipulates his meeting with Kamala, who recalls Siddhartha's deferential bow of the previous afternoon. Siddhartha beseeches Kamala to be his teacher, and we see Kamala's utterly materialistic values in her demand that Siddhartha have fine clothes and shoes. When the question arises as to what Siddhartha can do to earn a living, he can only remember the virtues of thinking, waiting, and fasting which he learned as a Samana. Shortly, however, it is discovered that he can read and write, whereupon he is considered valuable enough to become the partner of the rich merchant Kamaswami. It is even suggested in Kamala's remarks that Siddhartha might be qualified to succeed Kamaswami, for a remark is made about the rich merchant's advanced age. The observant reader, however, can sense that he is not the man whose place Siddhartha will take. In this city, Siddhartha will no more learn love from Kamala's teaching than would he have learned truth from the Hindus' or Buddhists' or Samanas' teachings. But Siddhartha will never quite lose those arts which he learned as a Samana. It will be by way of the conditioning inherent in thinking, waiting, and fasting that he will attain the capacity to attain his goal. Siddhartha, of course, means "he who attains his goal."

AMONGST THE PEOPLE

This second sequence of Part II develops Siddhartha's acquaintance with Kamala and introduces Siddhartha to Kamaswami. Significant is the meaning inherent in names, beginning with "Kama"; Kama is the Hindu god of lustful love and desire. The word "swami" designates Kamaswami as a master—in this case, the master of the hedonistic, worldly realm.

We can begin to see the conditioning of the Samanas surfacing when Siddhartha takes an indifferent attitude toward business, possessions, and worldly people. Siddhartha can sense that he is different from these worldly "child-people," but he finds this distinction between himself and them problematical. Siddhartha's spiritual background has only partially enlightened him for he has not yet found peace, and he comes to envy these ordinary, unintellectual people. Kamala, nevertheless, is attracted to Siddhartha because of his detachment, this refuge which she feels that only the two of them have. Likewise,

Kamala's detachment will also become problematical for it will be discovered that love cannot be dispensed as an art. The most significant event of this section is Siddhartha's mentioning Gotama Buddha to Kamala for the first time. To Siddhartha, Buddha exemplifies the kind of man who possesses a special guide and wisdom within himself. This conversation is of particular significance because it prefigures Kamala's future destiny. The eventual coming of Kamala's future son is also signaled at this point. The sequence ends with a verbal exchange on the subject of love, significant because an inability to love will be the source of both Kamala's and Siddhartha's despair.

SANSARA

We plumb the depths of the world of illusion in the sequence entitled "Sansara." Sansara, the polar opposite of Nirvana, is identified in the Buddhist system with illusion, spiritual death, and ultimate despair. Many years pass during this sequence that takes place in the city, and the fine poetic image of the potter's wheel symbolizes Siddhartha's spiritual awareness grinding to a halt. Siddhartha has abandoned his soul for a life that will become a barren, sterile waste for him, and because Siddhartha is an intellectual, ennui and soul sickness set in. Siddhartha becomes obsessively acquisitive and yet, at heart, he is contemptuous of wealth; again, then, he is part of a vicious circle. In this temporal, hedonistic world of the city, time is the devourer of all things. Herein lies the root of Siddhartha's suffering; all that is imbued with the element of time is doomed to death.

Also in the "Sansara" sequence, we again experience one of Hesse's close-ups — in this instance, Siddhartha is reminded of a peculiar dream on a certain evening. Siddhartha, so thoroughly conditioned by his life with the Samanas, is utterly unfulfilled by the superficiality of life with the child-people. He reflects on the elements of time and aging, retires after midnight, and puts in a night of complete personal misery. It is only at dawn that he sleeps at all, at which time he has the dream of which he seems to have been reminded the evening before. It is a highly symbolic dream in which a primal element of nature is the key symbol. He dreams of Kamala's little pet bird, symbolic of Siddhartha's spiritual self which he now believes to be dead. He reflects upon the desert of his soul and resolves that because his life among the child-people is a slow, corrosive death, he must leave the city that night. The sterile life of the city has become a prison for his soul as the cage is a prison for the little songbird.

BY THE RIVER

As we embark upon this sequence, we must realize that Siddhartha is now in his forties and that he has spent a little over twenty years in the city. Time rushes by in this novel very much like a current beneath the time close-ups. Plot progression seemingly takes place only when we zoom in on isolated days and nights, yet the story unfolds continually and unrelentingly. The sense of undercurrent becomes even more awesome in the sequences involving Siddhartha at the river with Vasudeva. We learn what Siddhartha is to learn: the river subsumes all time, all creation, all destruction. It is timeless and transcendent. Here, Vasudeva's prophecy of roughly twenty years earlier is fulfilled: everything does indeed return, even Siddhartha. Vasudeva will conquer his antithesis (Kamaswami) and we are gradually prepared for Siddhartha's succeeding Vasudeva. Upon Siddhartha's initial return to the river, prior to the actual encounter with Vasudeva, he begins his self-restoration. He hears the Brahmins' sacred syllable for the unity of all being—OM—as it wells up from his soul and forms a bond with the water. The transcendent OM of the river lulls Siddhartha into a trancelike sleep from which he later awakens, refreshed and face-to-face with Govinda. Siddhartha and the Buddhist monk Govinda have a talk, from which a basic revelation emerges: the cause of Siddhartha's soul sickness is an inability to love. The syllable OM had awakened this revelation within Siddhartha's soul and seeing Govinda has brought it to the surface. Siddhartha then regains his lost innocence and smiles.

With Siddhartha's spiritual restoration, already time begins to dissolve, to fall away. Large parts of this sequence are devoted to solitary reflection in which Siddhartha realizes that it is not the bird of his innermost soul that has died, but his conscious, grasping egotistical self. The process of synthesis is an agonizing process, an ordeal of sansara and self-realization, of individuation, from which resolution and equilibrium are to come forth. As Siddhartha reflects on salvation, he is also aware that his inner voice is still there. He is a newly awakened, innocent and childlike Siddhartha, endowed now with the capacity to love the flowing waters of the river. The river is the agent through which Siddhartha will plumb the depths of his consciousness—a kind of psychoanalysis, as it were.

THE FERRYMAN

Vasudeva, the quiet ferryman whose name is derived from one of the names of Krishna, and which basically means "he in whom all things abide and who abides in all," is an unforgettable character. In Siddhartha's decision to stay by the river, he recalls the ferryman and resolves that his new life will begin again with the ferryman. Siddhartha's inner synthesis will be effected through a resolution of permanence and transience — and it is Vasudeva, as well as Siddhartha's own inner voice, which affirms that the river will prove to be the agent of Siddhartha's fulfillment. As Siddhartha requests that Vasudeva take him across, Siddhartha is completely absorbed by the tranquil human presence of the ferryman, as earlier he had been by that of Gotama Buddha.

The key to learning from the river, according to Vasudeva, is *listening*. We will discover, however, that before Vasudeva's knowledge can be of any significance to Siddhartha, it must be tempered with love. What Siddhartha learns from Vasudeva is an affirmation of life and a sense of harmony with nature.

After Vasudeva tells Siddhartha that the river has spoken to him, he tells Siddhartha that he will learn two things from the river. Already he has learned one of these: to strive downwards like a stone. Vasudeva cannot tell Siddhartha what the other thing to be learned will be, for it is a form of intuitive experience which defies verbalization. Vasudeva then tells Siddhartha about the job of ferryman, his task being to take people across the river and to give them directions once they get across. Symbolically, his task is to show men the way to salvation. He can only show the way, however. Men must attain salvation themselves. The conversation continues through the evening and into the night and, at its end, the narrative lapses into indefinite time.

One of the outstanding conversations of the entire novel occurs when Siddhartha asks Vasudeva about time. The ferryman tells him of the transcendent timelessness of the river, which brings Siddhartha to the realization that life is also a river and that past, present, and future are all one. Childhood, adulthood, and old age are separated only by shadows, not by reality. This, basically, is Siddhartha's Nirvana. This mystical union with simultaneity, with Brahma, forms the nucleus of the book. The conversation then culminates with Siddhartha's equating time with suffering, another basic idea of the book. We are reminded that the river embodies all creation, all layers of consciousness: it is the collective unconscious of man's ancestral soul in its ten thousand voices, and the eternal OM brings them to the surface of our consciousness simultaneously. The two ferrymen, Vasudeva and Siddhartha, become as brothers, united by the sacred river.

Years pass and we come to learn that Gotama Buddha is on the threshold of eternal salvation and his Buddhist followers are gathering to their teacher for the last time. Siddhartha recalls the living presence of the Buddha which has awed him so much, and he feels a strong bond with him.

The montage narrative again zooms into a definite time sequence as we observe the day when Kamala and her eleven-year-old son come to see Buddha. The observant reader somehow knows now that Kamala has been attracted to the life of the Buddhist monks, for she made a direct inquiry about Gotama when Siddhartha was taking leave of the city. The father-son motif is soon to be re-established, and we are to realize that the boy is one of the child-people. We are, however, given little hints that this boy will eventually seek his own goals despite his current recalcitrance. The most substantial hint lies in the fact that the boy is called "little Siddhartha."

After the events of the day, Siddhartha has another of his visions of the mystical transcendence of the river and of its transcendence of time, experiencing again the simultaneity and unity of all life. The next morning, as preparations are made for Kamala's pyre, Siddhartha's hopes are directed toward his son.

THE SON

As this sequence begins, the action occurs on no particular day or any particular time of day; we are simply given a report of the father-son relationship. The sadness of the events which follow are sublimely tempered by the wisdom and kindness of the old Vasudeva. Despite Siddhartha's efforts to win the love and respect of his son, the son is more drawn to the enticements of the city, the milieu of his mother, than to the spiritual leanings of his stranger-father. Vasudeva reminds Siddhartha that, like his father, the boy will have to rebel, that he too must run away and learn things for himself.

Earlier the ferryman told Siddhartha that he would soon be learning something that he could not verbalize, and Siddhartha now realizes what it is as he looks into his son's face. The child's face evokes the memory of Kamala when she and Siddhartha told each other that they were incapable of love, and that it was this that separated them from ordinary people. Because of the anguish of this memory, Siddhartha realizes that he not only loves the river, but that — like ordinary men — he loves another person — the essence of Kamala in little Siddhartha.

The time comes when Siddhartha must accept little Siddhartha's departure. Little Siddhartha runs away bitterly from his father, returns late in the evening, and departs across the symbolic river with Siddhartha and Vasudeva following — not, as

Vasudeva warns, to catch him, but to observe him and to retrieve the boat. Vasudeva's laughter concerning the boy's departure is not the cruel laugh of ridicule, but a sublime laugh embodying Vasudeva's knowledge of the boy's way—that is, his destiny, meaning that all things return. Siddhartha wants to spare his son from the grueling ordeal of sansara, but Vasudeva knows that this is impossible. Siddhartha has a sudden visionary glimpse of the city and sees that Kamala converted her pleasure garden into a refuge for Buddhist monks. His mind returns to the early days when he first saw the rich Kamala from outside, when he was a poor Samana; recalling the processes of life and death, he remembers the syllable OM, symbolized by the caged songbird. The sense of loss because of his son's abrupt departure lingers in Siddhartha like a deep wound. For the first time, Siddhartha has direct, firsthand experience with the pain of love.

OM

This sequence begins with the wound motif and traces Siddhartha's recovery from the sickness he felt because of his son. Its primary material concerns the sense of simultaneity and unity within Siddhartha, expressed by the river's utterance of OM. It ends with Siddhartha's succeeding Vasudeva as the ferryman of the river.

Still suffering from his wound, Siddhartha hears the sublime laugh of the river. He sees his face reflected in the river and he recognizes his father in it, thereby effecting a unity with his father, who also experienced Siddhartha's "wound." Siddhartha's solitary meditation beside the river is broken by a compelling desire to go to Vasudeva, to confess his wound and its source to Vasudeva, and to disclose his guilt feelings. Vasudeva, the sublime listener whose very presence is transcendent, becomes like the river itself; Siddhartha's baring his soul to him has the effect of bathing his wound in the river. Vasudeva tells Siddhartha that, even though he has heard the ten thousand voices of the river and its laugh, he will hear yet something more from it. Siddhartha then sees many pictures and hears a voice of sorrow in the river. As he watches and listens, the text moves into a beautiful lyric passage embodying the liquid, eternal feel of the river itself. Siddhartha now feels that he has completely mastered the art of listening as he listens further and hears the voices of the river coalesce into perfection: OM. Following this experience, he sees Vasudeva's smile and realizes that his wound has healed.

GOVINDA

As this sequence begins, Govinda has arrived to cross the river, meeting Siddhartha, who is now an old man. Siddhartha's eyes smile as did Vasudeva's many years earlier. A superlative dialogue between them follows in which Siddhartha declares that in order to find one's goal, one must be free. The goal, Nirvana, is so elusive as to defy formulation, and too much seeking on the *conscious* level can make fulfillment impossible. Govinda knows that Siddhartha has found his own way and realizes that he did it without the formal system of Buddhist doctrine. As the Buddha tried long ago, Siddhartha now tries to express how he found his way, but verbalization cannot create or invoke the intuitive, transcendent experience for Govinda. As Siddhartha invites Govinda to stay with him in his hut for the night, we come to another close-up time sequence.

On the following morning, after Govinda asks Siddhartha about any doctrine which he might have, Siddhartha tries to explain how he attained inner peace from Vasudeva and the river rather than from teachers. He then draws the distinction between knowledge and wisdom, remarking that wisdom cannot be imparted from one man to another. Knowledge may be acquired from teachers, but wisdom must come from direct experience. Siddhartha then offers his thoughts on truth, suggesting that if an attempt is made at putting truth into words, something is always inherently missing. Verbalization eliminates that other side of a truth which defies verbalization. All that is thought and expressed verbally is, in fact, only a half-truth. Also, in every truth which is complete, not only does the truth which appears exist, but its antithesis also inherently exists.

This section reveals that not only Samana life left its mark on Siddhartha, but that his brief contact with the Buddha left its mark also. Buddhist doctrine is predicated on the antithetical elements of Nirvana and sansara; all truth possesses these two opposites — the truth side and the illusion side, all things being imbued with salvation and suffering. The speech concludes in a final excursis on time: if time is not real, then the line between this world and eternity is also not real. Siddhartha uses the example of a stone and suggests that because it is but one part of the whole cycle of life and thereby has transmigratory potential, it is consequently not just a stone but at once God and Buddha. We come back to the idea that all things return — that the stone has been all else and will again become all else.

Words, however, are not endowed with transmigratory potential. Thoughts, which are also mere verbalizations, are not so endowed either. After once again extolling Vasudeva, Siddhartha concludes his discourse by declaring that love is the most important thing in the world. We can sense that he feels that Gotama Buddha also embraced love — despite his verbalizations to the contrary, and Siddhartha projects this contradiction as just cause for being distrustful of words. He extols Gotama, but Govinda admits that he still has not found peace. Govinda has a sudden, transcendent, verbally inexpressible experience in the awesome presence of Siddhartha, much like that which Siddhartha had in the presence of Vasudeva years earlier.

When Siddhartha summons Govinda to kiss him on the forehead, Govinda feels as if he is touching eternity, a kind of mystical transference from Siddhartha, and he sees in Siddhartha's beatific smile a continuous stream of thousands of faces much like those Siddhartha saw many years earlier in the river. Like Siddhartha, Govinda attains Nirvana, reaching the depths of the ancestral soul of man, the Jungian collective unconscious.

CHARACTER ANALYSES

SIDDHARTHA

The preeminent factor in a study of Hesse's Hindu protagonist is his growth from the impatience and impetuosity of youth and young adulthood to the fulfilled wisdom of age. Despite the fact that Siddhartha leaves his father, the influence of his Brahmin upbringing stays with him, for the goal of his life is the attainment of Nirvana. It is merely the means to the end with which he disagrees with his father and also with the Samanas, Gotama Buddha, and the Buddha-follower Govinda. The growth pattern of Siddhartha's entire life consists of several phases of conditioning which are necessary to attain a perfect unity with the Absolute. Siddhartha must experience Brahman spontaneously and without artificial preparation in order to transcend time and gain Nirvana. In all stages of his life, Siddhartha must, as his name suggests, "seek his own goal" in an untutored, unassisted first-hand quest. His traversing the river into the city is, likewise, an integral phase of the quest. The transparency of this illusory world only becomes apparent to Siddhartha after he has had the chance to experience this time-bound world directly. The despair which follows prepares us for the final realization of a middle-aged Siddhartha: pursuing the way of the sense deity, Kama, will lead to nothingness. Vasudeva completes Siddhartha's entry into his final stage of self-realization by *not* attempting to teach or indoctrinate, but by showing Siddhartha that the inexplicable ways of the river promise revelation.

KAMALA

We first encounter this attractive courtesan upon Siddhartha's arrival in the city of child-people; she is the "queen" of the Hindu art of love. Then, as life in the city becomes transparently illusory for her, as it did for Siddhartha, she seems to realize that love cannot be dispensed secondhand, as an art form.

There is a subtle pause in the role of Kamala in the plot after we follow Siddhartha out of the city, but it is strongly hinted that she will reappear later as a changed person. She emerges finally as a Buddhist and we learn that she transcended the "art" of love by directly experiencing it with Siddhartha. Her being carried off from this world in Vasudeva's hunt bears symbolic significance to her transformation.

GOVINDA

The primary significance of Govinda in the novel as a secondary character is his attaining Nirvana, a growth similar to Siddhartha's, but delayed somewhat because of his function as Siddhartha's "shadow." Govinda is slower to realize that Nirvana does not come after years of study and learning; in contrast, Siddhartha seems already to know this when Govinda joins Gotama Buddha. Their parting at that strategic point serves to reinforce the importance of direct, firsthand experience when they reunite at the river. Govinda has come the way of Siddhartha, but on his own — not as a disciple or as a follower of Siddhartha. Govinda's attaining the transcendent beatific smile and union with the river of life is, therefore, his own. Most important, he has accomplished this in the only way one can — independently.

REVIEW QUESTIONS

1. How does Siddhartha's life with the Samanas condition him for his process of self-recognition?

2. What is the function of the river and of Vasudeva in this novel?

3. Discuss the father-son theme.

4. Examine the process of synthesis as it relates to Hesse's contact with Jungianism and relate its thematic influence in a selected novel.

5. Examine Hesse's treatment of time lapses in this novel, focusing on the close-up technique for extending short spans of time, and the "telephoto" effect for foreshortening long spans of time.

6. Siddhartha and Buddha both eventually attain Nirvana. However, the way that each achieves it is different. Explain the difference, relating this to the reason for Siddhartha's not following the Buddha.

7. What is the function of Kamala in the novel?

Selected Bibliography

BAUMER, FRANZ. *Hermann Hesse*. New York: Frederick Ungar Publishing Company, 1969. This work originally appeared in Berlin in 1959, remaining untranslated into English for ten years. It is a delightfully readable little book and presents a vivid study of the contemplative and solitary Hermann and Ninon Hesse of the Ticine years.

BOULBY, MARK. *Hermann Hesse: His Mind and Art*. Ithaca, New York: Cornell University Press, 1968. This is a very detailed study of the imagery, language, and intricate motif patterns in Hesse's novels and poems. It is a study of form; hence, its focus and emphasis goes beyond facts and biography.

FIELD, GEORGE WALLIS. *Hermann Hesse*. New York: Twayne Publishers, Inc., 1970. This book is a comprehensive and detailed study of the novels of Hesse, augmented by biographical and factual information.

FREEDMAN, RALPH. *The Lyrical Novel*. Princeton: Princeton University Press, 1962. Now in a paperback edition, this book centers its focus on novelists whose works deal with autobiographical revelation and poetic depths rather than conventional plot. Various sections are devoted to, besides Hesse, Andre Gide and Virginia Woolf.

MILECK, JOSEPH. *Hermann Hesse and His Critics*. New York: AMS Press, Inc., 1966. This is one of the finest academic studies of Hesse in English, containing a detailed and authoritative biographical section, a bibliography of works on Hesse in many languages, and commentaries on the major books, monographs, and articles. This book may be difficult for some undergraduates because some of its quotations and references remain in the original German.

ROSE, ERNST. *Faith from the Abyss: Hermann Hesse's Way from Romanticism to Modernity.* New York: New York University Press, 1965. This highly readable volume is now in paperback, and it presents poignant and useful biographical information relating it to the changes in the author's many works. It correlates Hesse's major works to corresponding periods in his life and his state of mind at those times.

SERRANO, MIGUEL. *C. G. Jung and Hermann Hesse: A Record of Two Friendships.* New York: Schoken Books, 1968. This book, now in paperback, presents intimate insight on the two men from the viewpoint of a member of the Spanish-speaking world, an ambassador from Chile. The photographs are valuable.

ZELLER, BERNHARD. *Portrait of Hesse.* New York: Herder and Herder, 1971. This paperback contains numerous photographs which do not appear in any other biography of Hesse. Its style is refreshing.

ZIOLKOWSKI, THEODORE. *The Novels of Hermann Hesse: A Study in Theme and Structure.* Princeton: Princeton University Press, 1965. This superlative academic study is the best full-length, English-language study of Hesse's work. It is comprehensive, of unusual depth, and thorough in detail, yet it is not heavy or dull reading. Ziolkowski's influence on Hesse scholarship is extensive, many of the original and highly relevant concepts and phrases bearing the unmistakable conciseness which is Ziolkowski's mark.

NOTES

NOTES

NOTES

NOTES

NOTES

NOTES

NOTES

THE TRIAL

NOTES

including
- *Life and Background*
- *Critical Commentaries*
- *On K.'s Guilt, the Court, and the Law*
- *The Neurotic Element in Kafka's Art*
- *Structure and Order of Chapters*
- *Composition and Reception*
- *Understanding Kafka*
- *Kafka's Jewish Influence*
- *Kafka—A "Religious" Writer?*
- *Kafka and Existentialism*
- *Selected Bibliography*

by
Herberth Czermak, M.A.
Instructor
Amerika Institut, Vienna

INCORPORATED

LINCOLN, NEBRASKA   68501

Editor

Gary Carey, M.A.
University of Colorado

Consulting Editor

James L. Roberts, Ph.D.
Department of English
University of Nebraska

ISBN 0-8220-1304-5
© Copyright 1976
by
C. K. Hillegass
All Rights Reserved
Printed in U.S.A.

Cliffs Notes, Inc.   Lincoln, Nebraska

CONTENTS

LIFE AND BACKGROUND 5

LIST OF CHARACTERS 10

CRITICAL COMMENTARIES 12
    Chapter 1 12
    Chapter 2 16
    Chapter 3 18
    Chapter 4 19
    Chapter 5 20
    Chapter 6 21
    Chapter 7 22
    Chapter 8 25
    Chapter 9 27
    Chapter 10 31

ON K.'S GUILT, THE COURT, AND THE LAW 34

THE NEUROTIC ELEMENT IN KAFKA'S ART 35

STRUCTURE AND ORDER OF CHAPTERS 38

COMPOSITION AND RECEPTION 40

UNDERSTANDING KAFKA 43

KAFKA'S JEWISH INFLUENCE 46

KAFKA—A "RELIGIOUS" WRITER? 48

KAFKA AND EXISTENTIALISM 50

SELECTED BIBLIOGRAPHY 54

The Trial Notes

LIFE AND BACKGROUND

Born in Prague in 1883, Franz Kafka is today considered the most important prose writer of the so-called Prague Circle, a loosely knit group of German-Jewish writers who contributed to the culturally fertile soil of Prague during the 1880s until after World War I. Yet from the Czech point of view, Kafka was German, and from the German point of view he was, above all, Jewish. In short, Kafka shared the fate of much of Western Jewry — people who were largely emancipated from their specifically Jewish ways and yet not fully assimilated into the culture of the countries where they lived. Although Kafka became extremely interested in Jewish culture after meeting a troupe of Yiddish actors in 1911, and although he began to study Hebrew shortly after that, it was not until late in his life that he became deeply interested in his heritage. His close relationship with Dora Dymant, his steady and understanding companion of his last years, contributed considerably toward this development. But even if Kafka had not been Jewish, it is hard to see how his artistic and religious sensitivity could have remained untouched by the ancient Jewish traditions of Prague which reached back to the city's tenth-century origin.

In addition to Kafka's German, Czech, and Jewish heritages, there was also the Austrian element into which Kafka had been born and in which he had been brought up. Prague was the major second capital of the Austrian Empire (after Vienna) since the early sixteenth century, and although Kafka was no friend of Austrian politics, it is important to emphasize this Austrian component of life in Prague because Kafka has too often been called a Czech writer — especially in America. Kafka's name is also grouped too often with German writers, which is accurate only in the sense that he belongs to the German-speaking world. Apart from that, however, it is about as meaningful as considering Faulkner an English novelist.

For his recurring theme of human alienation, Kafka is deeply indebted to Prague and his situation there as a social outcast, a victim of the friction between Czechs and Germans, Jews and non-Jews. To understand Kafka, it is important to realize that in Prague the atmosphere of medieval mysticism and Jewish orthodoxy lingered until after World War II, when the Communist regime began getting rid of most of its remnants. To this day, however, Kafka's tiny flat in Alchemists' Lane behind the towering Hradschin Castle is a major attraction for those in search of traces of Kafka. The haunting mood of Prague's narrow, cobblestoned streets, its slanted roofs, and its myriad backyards comes alive in the surreal settings of Kafka's stories. His simple, sober, and yet dense language is traced to the fact that in Prague the German language had been exposed to manifold Slavic influences for centuries and was virtually cut off from the mainstream language as spoken and written in Germany and Austria. Prague was a linguistic island as far as German was concerned, and while the Czech population of Prague doubled within the last two decades of the nineteenth century, the percentage of German Jews sank to a mere seven percent. The result was that Kafka actually wrote in a language which was on the verge of developing its own characteristics. This absence of any gap between the spoken and written word in his language is probably the secret behind the enormous appeal of his language, whose deceptive simplicity comes across in every decent translation.

Kafka's family situation was a reflection of his being a German-speaking Jew in a predominantly Slavic environment. The great socio-economic and educational differences between his father, Hermann Kafka, and his mother, Julie Löwy, were at the root of this complex situation. Kafka's father's whole life was shaped by his desperate and eventually successful attempt to break out of his poor Czech milieu and become accepted in the prestigious environment of German Prague; his mother, however, came from a wealthy German-Jewish bourgeois family. Throughout his lifetime, Franz Kafka could never extricate himself from the terrible friction between his parents which was caused, for the most part, by his tyrannical father. Kafka's only strong, positive ties with his family were with his favorite sister, Ottla, who let him stay at her home and later helped him break off his relationship with Felice, his first fiancée. To one extent or another, all of Kafka's works bear the unmistakable imprint of the nerve-wracking struggle between his humility and hypersensitivity (his mother's heritage) and the crudity and superficiality of his father, who looked at his son's writing with indifference and, at times, with contempt. This total lack of understanding and the absence of any home life worthy the name (young Franz was virtually brought up by a nurse) caused the boy's early seriousness and anxiety. As late as 1919, five years before his death, this lifelong trauma manifested itself in his *Letter to His Father* (almost a hundred pages, but never actually delivered), in which Kafka passionately accuses his father of intimidation and brutality. Although it will not do to reduce the complex art of Franz Kafka to its autobiographical elements, the significance of these elements in his work is indeed striking. His story "The Judgment" seems especially to be the direct result of his deep-seated fear of his father.

Kafka is the classical painter of the estrangement of modern man, although he is never its apostle. As early as 1905, in his "Description of a Fight," Kafka already denied man's ability to obtain certainty through sensory perception and intellectual effort because, according to him, these methods inevitably distort the nature of the Absolute by forcing it into their prefabricated structures. The resulting skepticism, of which he himself was to become the tragic victim, was the basis of his conviction that none of our fleeting impressions and accidental associations have a fixed counterpart in a "real" and stable world. There is no clear-cut boundary between reality and the realm of dreams, and if one of his characters appears to have found such a boundary, it quickly turns out that he has set it up merely as something to cling to in the face of chaos. The "real" world of phenomena develops its own logic and leaves Kafka's characters yearning for a firm metaphysical anchor which they never quite grasp.

At no time did Kafka seek refuge from his culturally and socially alienated situation by joining literary or social circles — something many of his fellow writers did. He remained an outcast, suffering from the consequences of his partly self-imposed seclusion, and yet welcoming it for the sake of literary productivity. Anxious although he was to use his positions, as well as his engagements to Felice Bauer and Julie Wohryzek, as a means to gain recognition for his writing, his life story is, nevertheless, one long struggle against his feelings of guilt and inferiority.

The one person who could and did help him was Max Brod, whom he met in 1902 and who was to become not only his editor but also an intimate friend. The numerous letters which Kafka wrote to him are a moving testimony of their mutual appreciation. Because of Brod's encouragement, Kafka began to read his first literary efforts to small private audiences long before he was recognized as a significant writer. With Brod, Kafka traveled to Italy, Weimar (where Goethe and Schiller had written), and Paris; later, Brod introduced him into the literary circles of Prague. In short, Brod helped Kafka to fend off an increasingly threatening self-isolation. Most significantly for posterity, it was Brod who, contrary to Kafka's express request, did not burn the manuscripts which Kafka left behind; instead, he became their enthusiastic editor.

If Kafka had a strong inclination to isolate himself, this does not mean he was indifferent to what was going on around him. Especially in the years until 1912, Kafka familiarized himself with some of the far-reaching new ideas of the day. At a friend's house, he attended lectures and discussions on Einstein's theory of relativity, Planck's quantum theory, and Freud's psychoanalytical experiments. He was also interested in politics, especially the nationalistic aspirations of the Czechs in the Austrian Empire. In his function as a lawyer at the Workers' Insurance Company, he was confronted daily with the social situation of workers, and toward the end of World War I, he even composed a brochure on the plight of the proletariat. This is, in part, proof that Franz Kafka was not the melancholy dreamer of nightmares, isolated in his ivory tower in Prague — a view still commonly held today.

It was at Max Brod's home that Kafka met Felice Bauer in 1912. This encounter plunged him into a frustrating relationship for many years, oscillating between engagements and periods of complete withdrawal. "The Judgment" (1912) is a document of this encounter. Having literally poured it out in one long sitting, Kafka came to regard it as an illustration of how one should always write; it was the subject of his first public reading. At that time, Kafka was already filling a detailed diary, full of reflections and parables as a means of self-analysis. The same year, 1912, he wrote "The Metamorphosis," one of the most haunting treatments of human alienation, and most of the fragmentary novel *Amerika*. According to his own conviction, his literary productivity reached a peak at precisely the time when his insecurity and anxiety over whether or not to marry Felice reached a climax. For the first time, the deep-seated conflict between his yearning for the simple life of a married man and his determination not to succumb to it became critical.

More and more, Kafka's writing began to deal with *Angst* (anxiety, anguish), probably because of the sustained anxiety induced by his domineering father and by the problem of whether or not to break away from his bachelorhood existence. Toward the end of "The Judgment," and in "In the Penal Colony," as well as in *The Trial* and *The Castle,* the father figure assumes the mysterious qualities of an ineffable god. Suffering, punishment, judgment, trial – all these are manifestations of Kafka's rigorous, ethical mind. The philosophy of Franz Brentano, to which he was exposed at the university, intensified his interest in these themes. The essence of this philosophy is that since emotions and concepts cannot sufficiently explain moral action, personal judgment alone must determine it; thorough self-analysis is the only prerequisite for such a total autonomy of personal judgment, a view which Kafka came to exercise almost to the point of self-destruction.

Kafka's fascination with these themes received new impetus when he began to read the Danish philosopher Sören Kierkegaard in 1913. As radical a skeptic as Kafka and equally religious by temperament, Kierkegaard envisages man as caught in the dilemma of wanting to comprehend Divinity with the altogether inadequate tools of rationality. Since God's transcendence is absolute for him, Kierkegaard sees no way of solving this dilemma except by abandoning intellectual pursuit and venturing a "leap into faith." Kafka's plea for man to "enter into the law," stated most explicitly in the parable "Before the Law" (in *The Trial*), deals with this dilemma. The difference is that Kierkegaard is cornered by the overwhelming presence of God forcing him to make decisions. In Kafka's parable, his hero wants to enter the first gate of the palace – that is, "the law" – but he dies because he does not exert sufficient will to enter and leaves all possible decisions to the gatekeeper; Kafka's searching man has no divine guidance to show him the way, and the situation he faces is one of total uncertainty and despair. Antithetically, Kierkegaard's radical skepticism results in faith.

Kafka and Kierkegaard have been called existentialists, and though this label has some merits, it should nevertheless be used very carefully. Both men were fascinated by the theme of moral integrity in the face of freedom of choice and were convinced that man lives meaningfully only to the extent which he realizes himself. In this connection, it is interesting to know that Kafka felt close to Kierkegaard because of the latter's lifelong unresolved relationship to his fiancée. The problem dominated Kierkegaard's life and work as much as Kafka's life and work was dominated by his relationships with Felice Bauer (to whom he was engaged twice – in 1914 and 1917), Julie Wohryzek (engaged in 1919), and Milena Jesenska (1920-22).

Perhaps more than any other story, Kafka's "In the Penal Colony" (1914) reflects his reaction to the outbreak of World War I, a feeling of sheer horror as well as disgust with the politicians in power. The result was a renewed fascination with Schopenhauer and Dostoevsky, whose extolment of physical pain finds expression in a variety of ways. Near this same time, Kafka began working on *The Trial,* about which he remarked that its ghastly thoughts devoured him in much the same way as did his thoughts about Felice. The novel is an elaborate and heavily autobiographical fantasy of punishment: on the eve of his thirty-first birthday, Joseph K. is executed; on the evening of his own thirty-first birthday, Kafka decided to travel to Berlin to break off his first engagement with Felice. Symptomatically for Kafka, this novel remained fragmentary – as did his other two, *Amerika* and *The Castle.* "A Report to an Academy" and the fragmentary "The Hunter Gracchus" followed, and in 1919 several stories were published under the title *A Country Doctor.* The title story is a symbolic description of modern man living outside a binding universal order and brought to death by sensuality and the aimlessness of the forces working within him. This volume contains perhaps Kafka's best parable on the nature of absurdity, "The Imperial Message." It is a terrifying description of how important messages, ordered at the top level to save men at the bottom, never stand a chance of getting through the manifold obstacles of bureaucracy. "The Imperial Message" is an interesting reversal of "Before the Law," where the lowly searcher never even gets beyond the first gate (the lowest obstacle) in his attempt to proceed to higher insights. In both cases, the human need to communicate is frustrated, and the inevitable result is alienation and subsequent death.

These stories were written during a time when Kafka, engaged once again to Felice, was finding a measure of stability again. Although he was determined this time to give up his insurance position and to use his time writing, he soon realized that this effort was an escape, as had been his (rejected) application to be drafted into the army. Kafka was to remain much like the roving hunter Gracchus, burdened with the knowledge that he could not gain inner poise by drowning the fundamental questions of existence in the comforts of married life.

In 1917 Kafka was stricken with tuberculosis, an illness which he was convinced was only the physical manifestation of his disturbed inner condition. For years he had fought hopeless battles for and against marriage (he had a son with Grete Bloch, a friend of Felice's, but never knew about him); during this time, he continually sought to justify his suffering by writing. Now he gave up. "The world — Felice is its representative — and my innermost self have torn apart my body in unresolvable opposition," he wrote in his diary. His suffering was alleviated by the fact that he could spend many months in the country, either in sanatoriums or with his favorite sister, Ottla. These months brought with them a new freedom from his work as a lawyer and, for the second time, from Felice.

In 1922, Kafka wrote "A Hunger Artist," "Investigations of a Dog," and most of his third novel, *The Castle*. Highly autobiographical like all of his works, the hero of "A Hunger Artist" starves himself because he cannot find the spiritual food he requires. The investigations of the chief dog in the story of the same name reflect Kafka's own literary attempts to impart at least a notion of the universal to his readers. In *The Castle*, K. becomes entangled in the snares of a castle's "celestial" hierarchy as hopelessly as does Joseph K. in the "terrestrial" bureaucracy of *The Trial*. All these stories originated in the years 1921 and 1922, years when Kafka lived under the strong influence of Milena Jesenska, to whom he owed his renewed strength to write. Although in many respects different from him (she was gentile, unhappily married, and much younger), the extremely sensitive Milena could justly claim "to have known his anxiety before having known Kafka himself," as she put it. Forever afraid of any deeper involvement with Milena, Kafka eventually stopped seeing her. That he gave her his diaries and several manuscripts, however, is proof of his deep commitment to her.

LIST OF CHARACTERS

Anna

The maid who should have brought K.'s coffee the morning of his arrest.

Assistant Manager

K.'s superior at the Bank who becomes his adversary when the manufacturer complains about K.'s treatment of him.

Bertold

The student lover of the usher's wife. He is a symbol of the corruption of the Court's hierarchy, himself a pyramid-climber.

Block

A tradesman and client of Huld's, whose submissiveness before Huld causes K. to want to dismiss the lawyer.

Fräulein Bürstner

A boarder at Frau Grubach's, where K. lives. K.'s arrest takes place in her room. His desire for her and her refusal to deal with him put her in a unique position among the women he meets.

Elsa

K.'s girl friend at the time he meets Leni. She does not appear in the novel.

Erna

K.'s cousin who informs her father, K.'s Uncle Karl, of the trial.

Examining Magistrate

The indifferent and corrupt judge presiding at K.'s first interrogation.

Frau Grubach

The elderly lady who owns the boarding house where K. lives and is arrested.

Hasterer

A lawyer friend of K.'s, whom he wants to telephone during his arrest. He does not appear in the novel.

Dr. Huld

A key figure in K.'s case. His name means "grace" or "meekness" in German. Through inefficiency, sickness (or perverted religiousness), he prevents K.'s case from getting a fair trial. He stands for the ambiguity of the Court.

Inspector

He conducts K.'s arrest with Willem and Franz.

Uncle Karl

Worried about K.'s trial because of the shame it brings over the family, he introduces him to his friend Dr. Huld.

Kaminer, Kullich, and Rabensteiner

K.'s three colleagues from the Bank whom the Inspector brings along to the arrest. Their presence demonstrates the inseparability of K.'s case from his Bank life.

Captain Lanz

Frau Grubach's nephew, K.'s neighbor.

Leni

The servant and mistress of Dr. Huld, she reflects the corrupt atmosphere of the Court. She pretends to love K., but tries to seduce him to make him subservient to Huld.

Manufacturer

One of the countless mediators. He tells K. about Titorelli, who already knows about his case.

Fräulein Montag

Fräulein Bürstner's friend who is moving in with her. She functions as her roommate's mediator with K.

Priest

He tells K. the parable "Before the Law" in the cathedral and discusses its meaning with him.

Titorelli

The painter whom K. tracks down in his efforts to find outside help. He is the only one to tell K. about the nature of the Court he is up against and about his hopeless case. As the Court painter, he has some knowledge of K.'s case.

Whipper

He executes the ancient law that "punishment is just as just as it is inevitable" on the warders.

Willem and Franz

The warders who arrest K.

CRITICAL COMMENTARIES

Chapter 1

If we look at the novel in terms of its opening sentence, we see that this sentence contains nothing but unproven assumptions: "Someone must have traduced Joseph K., for without having done anything wrong he was arrested one fine morning." Until the end of the book this atmosphere of ambivalence, temporariness, and possible deception is reflected in Kafka's language. Slander, which perhaps comes to mind when we focus on the word "traduced," is not likely to be the reason for K.'s arrest because he remains at large. The trouble is we will not know the reason at the end of the story either, though one warder's remark that "K. claims to be innocent and doesn't even know the Law" gives us a certain hint. Yet no legal charges are leveled and no verdict is passed. The trial takes place before an invisible Court without ever getting off the ground, at least in the conventional sense of the phrase.

All this leads one to think of the novel's title in terms of the connotations of the German original. "Prozess" is cognate with the English "process," and Kafka uses it interchangeably with "Verfahren" ("procedure"), which in turn has definite undertones of "entanglement." In other words, we are not necessarily dealing with a trial but perhaps a lifelong "process" of some kind. After all, everybody and everything belongs to the Court, as we are told time and again.

Certainly the timing of K.'s arrest, whatever its meaning, the morning of his thirtieth birthday, is well chosen: birthdays, especially one marking off a decade, tend to cause some soul-searching. Block, the tradesman, is also to be arrested shortly after the death of his wife—that is, at a moment when the routine of his life suffers a decisive break. At any rate, K. is caught by surprise and is in no way prepared to fend off the characters arresting him. If he were at the Bank, where he is thoroughly familiar with every detail, nothing of the kind would happen to him. He admits that much to Frau Grubach during the evening following his arrest: he regrets he did not have the presence of mind to ignore the unexpected events of that morning (for example, Anna did not bring his coffee)—in short, he did not act "reasonably." As in so many of his other pieces, Kafka shows his hero waking up and being unprepared. ("The Metamorphosis," for instance). It is Kafka's way of saying that K.'s arrest is not a dream but inescapable reality.

The invisible Court jealously guards the "highest Law," whose content remains as inaccessible as its top level judges. How it operates on the low levels is beautifully shown in the arrest scene: two obnoxious warders, who do not even know their superiors, much less anything about his case, are sent to arrest K. They are not even eager to apprehend him; they merely claim to do their job. But quite the contrary, by waiting for K. to ring the breakfast bell, they let him take the initiative. In other words, K., by ringing for his breakfast, is actually ringing for his arrest. This, by the way, is a major argument against the interpretation of the novel as essentially a political satire or even a symbolic account of the totalitarian mind: neither the Gestapo nor the Soviet K.G.B. have been known to leave the details of arrest up to their victims. Anyway, the warder lets K.'s question about his identity go unanswered, as if nothing unusual had happened, and casually asks whether K. has rung the bell.

The problem of whether K. could do anything to alter his fate will be dealt with elsewhere. If we accept the line of interpretation that he becomes guilty because he mishandles his trial, then we will have to look at this arrest scene more carefully because it is here that things already begin to take their fateful course. K. commits his first, though on first glance perhaps negligible, mistake: rather than pushing for an immediate clarification of the strange occurrences surrounding his arrest, K. acknowledges the warder's insolent question ("Did you ring?") by referring to Anna and the breakfast she is supposed to bring. K. is trying to convince himself that he is merely gaining time to observe the intruder to detect his intentions. In reality, he has already accepted his appearance and assault. His insistence that the stranger introduce himself before any more questioning is only a desperate attempt on K.'s part to suppress the gravity of what has happened and cannot be reversed. Toward the end of this scene, the two warders reveal that they have been sent merely to "observe your reactions." If K.'s guilt is predetermined for any reason, does it make sense that the invisible Court tries to prod the "reactions" of someone already firmly in its grip? No wonder this sentence has been used to back up the interpretation of K.'s guilt, resulting solely from his wrong handling of his case.

All one has to do in order to show the built-in ambiguity of this central issue is to see the warders as part of K.'s own personality, as some sort of ever-watchful superego. Their observing mission assumes a very different meaning because the simplistic opposition "Court versus K." is considerably modified. There are several lines about how close the warders feel toward K., and at the end the executioners also accompany K. to the quarry like a "unity."

There are more instances of people watching K. or K. feeling watched: before he is even arrested, a woman is "peering at him with a curiosity unusual even for her," and a bit later the same "inquisitiveness" is mentioned. During his arrest several people are "enjoying the spectacle," and the Titorelli scene in Chapter 7 is full of peeping girls. All these instances of observing, feeling observed, or actually being observed reflect Kafka's own neurotic self-analysis and his deep-felt need to get at every aspect of everything in order to arrive at a bearable degree of certainty (for an example of his self-analysis, see the pros and cons about marriage in his diary or read the stories "The Burrow" or "A Hunger Artist").

K. will never be able to extricate himself from his acknowledgment of his arrest. It is precisely his strange arrest that causes him to feel attracted to the Court; the warders also admit that the Court feels attracted by guilt and that this is the reason they have been sent out. This mutual attraction prevails throughout the story, yet there is also the possibility that it, too, is a lie. Certainly it is remarkable that the Inspector himself says the warders may have told K. a lot of nonsense about the arrest and their role in it.

In an obvious parallel to Gregor Samsa's futile attempt in "The Metamorphosis" to separate the extraordinariness of his insect personality from his daily life, K. also seeks to separate his daily routine at the Bank from the events surrounding his arrest. His three colleagues from the Bank, whom the Inspector has brought along to faciliate K.'s unobtrusive return to his office, show that such a separation is impossible. In fact, K. refers to them as a "Court of Inquiry" during his re-enactment of his arrest later on in Fräulein Bürstner's room. This inseparability is exactly what his uncle means when he says, "to have a case like this means to have already lost it." It has to be this way, for if we accept any real guilt (beyond that purely tactical one of mishandling his trial) on K.'s part, it has been brought about exactly by the way he has lived as a carefree bachelor-businessman. At any rate, by desperately trying to keep the arrest away from his consciousness (conscience), he tries to keep the metaphysical sphere from interfering with his daily life. If something is to make sense to him, it must appear in the familiar form of his material world.

He is guilty because he has completely buried his moral sensitivity under his job at the Bank. He cannot deal with things, including his case, in terms other than those he uses at the Bank: "The trial was nothing but a big business deal, the kind he has managed successfully many times for the Bank." He never begins to comprehend the fundamentally different nature of this case against him; he only comes to accept certain facts about it later on. He cannot even think of guilt unless it is put in clear-cut legal terms and definitions to him. Neither Samsa nor K. can imagine that their guilt consists precisely of their ignorance of the Law beyond its known bourgeois codification.

K.'s encounter with Fräulein Bürstner is important because she is the first of the three women he meets. They represent the three possibilities vis-à-vis the Court: to stand outside of it, like Fräulein Bürstner; to live in conflict with it, like the usher's wife; and to be its slave, like Leni. As a result of his inability to understand his own case, K. cannot establish any meaningful contact with Fräulein Bürstner beyond that of sexual desire and subsequent deprivation. (In some areas of Germany, "bürsten" is a slang expression for sexual intercourse). The description of K. as "chasing over her face with his tongue like a thirsty animal, then kissing her violently on her neck, right on the throat, before resting his lips there" speaks for itself. (The scene between Frieda and K. in *The Castle* is similar even to details; it is patterned, in turn, after the seduction scene in "The Stoker" chapter of *Amerika*). It is important to see that in this assault scene, K. desperately tries to drown himself in sensuality in order to forget his situation. He craves something no woman can possibly supply—oblivion from his suppressed guilt feelings. And these he has from the outset, for in spite of his put-on defiance, he senses he has been summoned before this strange Court to justify his life. He is not even all that taken aback by his arrest, as he says to the Inspector. The assault scene conveys a pattern typical of Kafka, the conflict between pairs of opposites, the continuous ebb and flow between desire and tranquillity, movement and standstill.

It is Fräulein Bürstner's function to distract K. from his case simply by being around him. When she asks him how his arrest was he replies, "terrible," and the narrator continues that he "did not even think about it now that he was moved by her sight." Her other function — and she is the only woman who does so — is to turn him away after their first encounter, thereby trying to direct his attention back to his own case. At the end, K. will think of this when her image appears again and will accept his fate because he realizes he has not taken her advice seriously. That the Inspector conducts his first questioning in her room is evidence for the role she plays in his case.

Chapter 2

The opening of the second chapter is ample proof that *The Trial* cannot be read literally as a reflection of political tyranny or even as a satire of such a system. There has never been a police state which made sure a defendant is rested before his interrogation, nor has there ever been one that has left it up to its victims to choose the time of their arrest. "If K. had no objections," he is to appear on a Sunday, not necessarily every Sunday, but so that his case can be quickly concluded. As if to prove this point, the authorities do not even specify the time K. is to appear and, as it turns out, give him only a vague description of the place he is to go to. (One might note that this is a specific suburb of Prague where Kafka went frequently). Nevertheless, he will be reprimanded for not meeting the Court's vaguely formulated demands.

K.'s first response is to abide by the summons and to make his first appearance also his last one. To get things over with, he even declines the invitation of his Assistant Manager to join a party. Without being aware of making a mistake, K. sets his own time for his first appearance — 9 A.M., since that is the time which courts usually open — and without a fault of his own, he arrives at the place over an hour late. Nobody among the authorities has bothered to tell him details, and yet the Examining Magistrate reproaches him for being late. This is a pattern clearly noticeable throughout the novel: previous little about his pending trial is ever explained, or even mentioned, to K. In fact, the reader is led to believe it is up to K. to take the initiative. This is not altogether wrong. The trouble is that, barely has K. taken it, it turns out he has maneuvered himself into a less favorable position. What the Court wants, or pretends to want, is uttered in such an ambiguous way that, by reacting at all, he sinks into an ever deeper quagmire. Whatever steps K. takes, the Court latches on to and uses against him. In connection with this first interrogation it is interesing to note that the German original for "interrogation" is "Verhör," a word with clear connotations of "hearing incorrectly." This is one of Kafka's great themes: if, indeed, there is a Law, a message, issued from the highest echelons, it is bound to become inaudible, unintelligible, or at least distorted, by the time it reaches the common people. Applied to K.'s situation this means that there is no rational, legal way of establishing contact, let alone rapport, with the Court.

As K. errs through the delapidated Juliusstrasse to locate the Court offices, he recalls the words of the warder Willem that an "attraction existed between the Law and guilt, from which it followed that the Court must abut on the particular flight of stairs which K. happened to choose." Frustrated by this lack of orientation, K. takes Willem's words to heart. He decides to use the name of Captain Lanz, his neighbor at Frau Grubach's, to find the whereabouts of the Court. There is of course no man by that name anywhere, nor could the young woman whom he asks for Lanz's place possibly know the Captain. Nevertheless, she directs K. to the office he is looking for and insists on closing the door behind him because "nobody else must come in." The logic of the dream world prevails: though K. gets there through a series of absurd questions and answers, the Court seems to have assembled where he is looking for it and, what is more, apparently only to receive him. Yet nobody pays any attention to K. and when they finally do, it is only to chide him for having violated a rule they never bothered to let him know: "You should have been here an hour and five minutes ago," the judge says twice.

The impossible location, the sordid atmosphere, and the small, dog-eared law book are all signs of the complete indifference the authorities are displaying toward K. The Examining Magistrate even has K.'s profession down as that of a house painter. K. has made up his mind to keep the initiative and lets the judge know he has not really expected anything but inefficiency anyway. He is still certain, even overbearing; "It is only a trial if I recognize it as such," he says, thereby making a major mistake: he accepts the trial, even if only temporarily and out of a readiness to compromise, perhaps of sheer curiosity, basically because he does not take it seriously. He simply cannot conceive of being guilty. His claim to fight the Court not merely for himself but also for all the others who are indicted shows that he is by no means the only one accused. To be sure, not everybody is guilty to the same degree and not everybody will be punished alike, but perhaps Kafka's point is that to live means to become involved in evil-doing. Also, not everybody is aware of his guilt, as K. certainly proves. In all this we must not forget that the novel's major theme is not K.'s guilt but the way in which he seeks to handle the procedure he is involved in.

K.'s determination to reproach the Court for the manner in which it conducted his arrest turns into sheer anger when he notices secret signs being exchanged between the Examining Magistrate and members of the packed courtroom. His point-blank attack on the lethargy and corruption of all levels of the Court is met by more indifference. The badges K. notices on everybody present confirm his suspicion that he is facing some closed organization whose mind is already made up on the very subject they are supposed to deal with. When he seeks to escape the stifling atmosphere, he is held back by the Magistrate who warns him that, "Today you have flung away with your own hand all the advantages which an interrogation invariably confers on an accused man."

Because he does not understand his situation, K. at first decides that "attack is the best defense." Both the women showing him the way to the office and the applause of the audience present encourage K. in his aggressiveness. He is led to believe that he can progress without having to worry about serious obstacles. His downfall is that in a superficial way he seems to make headway. It always turns out soon, however, that his thrusts lose themselves in empty space. Like a spider caught in a web, K. keeps himself from further entanglement only when he is near exhaustion.

Chapter 3

K. does not show the slightest understanding of his situation. He is surprised and even irritated that the Court has evidently taken seriously his initial refusal to be tried and has, as a result, not issued a specific date for the next session with the authorities on a Sunday morning, "assuming tacitly" that this is what they want him to do. The now familiar pattern prevails: K.'s initiative leads him nowhere, and the authorities recede before him whenever he addresses them. As a person under arrest, and one who has been previously reprimanded for showing up late, K. has every reason to make sure he acts in compliance with the Court. The sad fact is, however, that, even though he shows up at the most plausible time, there simply is no session scheduled for that time.

K. runs into the same promiscuous woman who interrupted the first interrogation by giving in to the advances of a student, a potentially powerful assistant of the Court. She knows her way around and her husband, the usher, meets K.'s need for inside information about the Court. It turns out that all she wants is to seduce K. The dirtiness of the setting—the Chief Magistrate's "law book" is a sex magazine—reflects the decadence of the Court. The names "Hans" and "Grete" on the book cover, taken from a very popular German fairy tale, suggest its unreal quality. Most importantly, the intricate pattern of hierarchial rungs gives K. a first glance of the impenetrable wall of indolence and conspiracy he is up against: the woman, the student-assistant, and the Magistrate—they all represent three levels of bureaucratic decadence tied together by sexual appetite. Like everywhere else in Kafka's writings, erotic contacts happen suddenly and because they do, they also lead to immediate disappointment through roused expectations. Deprivation is a feature of these sudden encounters: K. does not even get near the woman here, who does not put up much resistance when she is dragged away from K. and taken upstairs to her boss. The deprivation is a symptomatic feature of the world of *The Trial*: Fräulein Bürstner, too, is not available to K. after their first embrace; and her return at the end of the novel repeats this pattern.

With the help of the cuckolded usher, K. gains access to the Court offices which are located, strangely but appropriately enough, in the garret. As opposed to the usher, K. still thinks his case is by no means "a foregone conclusion," and he follows him with great curiosity. Like all members of the middle strata of the Court, the usher has long since resigned himself to his fate and is bewildered by anyone still optimistically engaged in fighting his case. K. meets a whole roomful of defendants who all rise courteously because they mistake him for the judge. In Chapter 8, Block will tell K. that they stood up, not for him, whom they recognized as a defendant, but for the usher as a potentially helpful person whose good will is to be cherished. A tall man, whose natural superiority is still noticeable despite the dumbfounded reaction he displays when K. addresses him, stands as a grim illustration of the debilitating effect of the Court: he has handed in several affidavits concerning his case but has never received a reply. The resulting uncertainty has rendered him helpless. At this point K. is still convinced of his superior businesslike approach in tackling his own case and he pushes the "weakling" aside.

K. arrives before the gentleman from the Court's Clerk of Inquiries, who is introduced to him with the following words: "He supplies all the information the clients need; since our procedure is not too well known among the people, many of them ask for information. He has an answer ready for each question; if you feel like trying him out, go ahead." At this crucial point where K. is led to believe, as is the reader, that he is very close to the fulfilment of his desire to get at the innermost circles of the Court, his strength fails him. His only wish now is to escape the stale air and dizzying narrowness of the garret. Again the familiar pattern of the highest Court receding before K.'s advances prevails. The parallel to the scene in *The Castle* is obvious, where K. falls asleep at exactly the moment he is on the verge of obtaining everything he wants from Bürgel.

Chapter 4

The opening paragraphs make it clear that Fräulein Bürstner is not going to grant K. his wish for another date. Her decision to move in with the pale and weakly Fräulein Montag is her precautionary step against possible advances on K.'s part. Speaking for her roommate, Fräulein Montag argues that "interviews are neither deliberately accepted nor refused," but that someone may just "see no point in them." This argument is very much like the one with whose help the authorities keep K. at bay. Note, too, that when Fräulein Bürstner sends her roommate as an intermediary, it is on a Sunday of all things, a day which is bound to remind K. of his first interrogation. As a result, a certain, perhaps only symbolic, relationship exists between the three. The message Fräulein Montag brings to K. is to suggest that he talk to her instead of her friend: in terms of K.'s scheme this means that he has not found any sympathy, let alone recourse, in Fräulein Bürstner—she is seemingly disinterested in his case, possibly because he cannot tell her anything about legal matters in which she claims to be interested.

K. assesses Fräulein Bürstner incorrectly: recalling Frau Grubach's derogatory remarks about her loose behavior, he convinces himself that it is only a question of perseverence until she yields to him. This continued sensual yearning coupled with self-delusion about her are an indication of his confusion, which is the direct result of his unwillingness and inability to come to terms with his case.

It will turn out that her refusal to listen to K. could have worked to his advantage, had he taken her advice that he should rely on himself. We must add, however, that this argument makes sense only if we assume that his proper handling of his own case could eventually lead to his acquittal. We must see clearly, though, that there are at least as many passages in *The Trial* that foreshadow the opposite. It cannot be emphasized often enough that the "guilt" K. incurs by mishandling his case is not the same as the original guilt on whose account he has been arrested in the first place. The former is more like a series of tactical errors, whereas the latter results from his basic moral insensitivity. Of course they are connected with each other in the sense that K. fails to defend himself adequately because his moral deficiency keeps him from assessing the nature of his case and the seriousness of his position correctly.

The overall mood of the chapter is one of K. feeling ridiculed and deceived by the two women, individually and as a team, as well as by the suave Captain Lanz. K. feels, above all, watched. K.'s preoccupation with feeling watched, actually being watched, and watching others himself, deserves special mention. It is an indication of K.'s (and Kafka's) almost neurotic desire to pin down every single aspect of every single ramification of everything going on around or within him. It is the psychological expression of his craving for total transparency against which the priest will warn him: "It is not necessary to accept everything as true, only as necessary."

Chapter 5

The strange timeless and developmentless atmosphere of the world portrayed finds a most adequate expression in the title of this chapter,

"The Whipper." It stands out because it shows the continued repetition of the one event it deals with. Everything is reduced to certain fixed habits, a reflection of the inaneness of the Court.

This chapter affords us a glimpse into the terroristic facets of the Court. K. himself is not exposed to punishment, but the two warders whom he has accused of illegal practices during his arrest are to be whipped. K. is understandably shocked at this, not only because he had not planned to have them beaten, but because by punishing them the Court takes away from K.'s attack on it: by responding to K.'s complaint in this way the Court demonstrates that K.'s charges of indifference and inaccessibility are not universally valid. Of course, K. would prefer no beatings for this reason. However, the overseer calms him down: "The punishment is as just as it is inevitable." By implication this sentence makes clear that K. is guilty and that nobody can escape his just punishment.

What makes the scene so particularly frightening to K. is the stereotyped repetition of the whipping. A reflection of his own hopeless situation, it is this repetition that tortures him most: he is almost tempted to "take off his clothes and to offer himself to the whippers." He is already caught in the vicious, senseless cycle of floundering about. This motion around in a circle is the structural equivalent of his life's justification, which he craves but cannot obtain.

Chapter 6

K. is taken to the lawyer Huld by his obtrusive Uncle Karl (who greets his lawyer-friend by calling himself Albert), whose main worry is the shame his nephew is about to bring on the whole family by his involvement in a trial. A representative of the shallow bourgeois mentality, Uncle Karl cannot help but resort to the dubious, though publicly esteemed, Dr. Huld. This episode is also heavily autobiographical: Kafka always had to defend himself, as a person and an artist, against such well-intended but boorish and at any rate inefficient intrusions. Yet even his uncle knows enough to comment that "things like this don't occur suddenly, they pile up gradually, there must have been indications." This is an unequivocal view of K.'s life as the cause of his present involvement.

Leni is nothing but a tool of the Court. This is why she urges K. not to act stubbornly against the authorities. As opposed to the usher's wife, who is not depraved enough to want to be enslaved to the Court's lewd officials, Leni does not even desire her freedom from Huld. The diction used in her description is full of possessives and such little symbols of deformation as "claws" and "webbed hand." It is with these that Leni pulls down K. to the floor in an attempt to make herself his mistress. In a perversion of the old fairy tale motif of "loving girl breaks the spell cast on poor boy," Leni cannot and does not help him. Her erotic playfulness, rehearsed in long years with her employer, Huld, only serves to enslave K. physically. Later on, Block meets the same fate at her greedy lips.

Proportionately to the degree that K. is gradually becoming aware of the seriousness of his case, he thinks Leni might be able to help him. The truth is that he is even more distracted from relying on himself. He does not realize what she is doing until after the humiliation she inflicts upon Block on behalf of and with the help of Huld. The point of the chapter is that, whatever K.'s reason or rationalization for accepting outside help from anybody, the effect is bound to be negative.

Chapter 7

More than even the previous chapter, this one reveals the hierarchy of mediators and contact people with whose aid K. aspires to free himself. What Huld and Titorelli have in common is that they point to the invisible, inaccessible, highest Court without being able to help K. In their capacity as K.'s mediators, they are accessible to him only through other contacts, such as Uncle Karl and the Manufacturer. This principle of mediation is deeply entrenched in the world of *The Trial*: an entire staff will be instrumental in bringing about the meeting between K. and the priest (they are the Bank Director, an Italian visitor, Leni, and the Verger).

Who are the three figures after whom the chapter is named? The lawyer Huld has inside knowledge of the Court in the sense that he sees the confusion and jealousies prevailing among its members. He makes no efforts to hide these difficulties from K.; in fact, he stresses the insurmountable obstacles to a meaningful defense in this thicket of assumptions, opinions, and half-truths. He makes it clear to K. that his only chance at all lies in K.'s allegiance with him. But there is more: Huld wants nothing short of complete subservience from K. (he demands and gets it also from Leni, and Leni, in turn, wants it from K.) as a *sine qua non* for any effort. In this connection it is important to realize that "Huld" means "meekness" or "grace" in German. Huld dissuades K. from drawing up petitions to the higher levels himself because "defense was not actually countenanced by the Law, but only tolerated." Besides, even if one could accomplish some minor point, "any benefit arising from that would profit clients in the future only, while one's own interests would be immeasurably injured by attracting the attention of the ever vengeful officials."

Some interpretations see Huld as a divine mediator who sacrifices himself to the highest Court on behalf of his clients. If we accept this interpretation, his sickness assumes a new dimension beyond that of sloth and decadence. If he takes it upon himself to suffer for his clients, then his sickness radiates a sacrificial quality. The trouble with this argument is that, even if we accept it, the lawyer's "Huld" ("grace") turns out to be a perverted one: it is not that of religion, but that of secularized messianism.

Huld reveals his true nature when he describes himself as being concerned, not with "ordinary cases," but as a lawyer who "lifts his client on his shoulders from the start and carries him bodily without once letting him down until the verdict is reached, and even beyond it." His perversion lies in the assumption that he can solve each client's case. In spite of his limits – he keeps bragging about connections, but they fail to produce results – he thinks he can "carry" others. In his scintillating back-and-forth between his presumptuousness and weakness lies his guilt. He distorts the essentially positive quality of uncompromising faith into humiliation. Huld acts like Jesus, but in a world that lacks the religious foundation for such an approach.

It is perhaps more plausible to see Huld as a representative of all those forces in our confused world that want to make life "easier" for people, thereby depriving it of its meaning. Leni is of the same kind. They both humiliate their clients – Leni by degrading them sexually and by making them believe she can help them, and Huld by insisting that he has all the answers as long as his clients are willing to give up their personalities. If we substitute "consumerism," "sexual permissiveness," or some form of political totalitarianism for their plan, we have no trouble seeing them as typical representatives of our time. Their common desire is to "help" us escape from freedom and responsibility.

The scene between the Assistant Manager and the Manufacturer reflects K.'s waning self-assurance. He even has the feeling that he is made the "object" of a business deal: "It seemed to L. as though two giants of enormous size were negotiating above his head about himself." The Assistant Manager's remark, "Thanks, I know that already," means that the Court is not the least bit interested in K.'s petition. It also shows that the world of the Bank and that of the trial cannot be separated. The reason the Court would not accept K.'s petition is simply that, even if it were perfect and arrived at the proper place (unlikely in the anonymity of the Court), it would contain only the justification of his life in retrospect. It would not, however, prove his innocence or exempt him from punishment.

Titorelli, too, is part of the Court. He is in charge of doing the portraits of the various judges. His studio is filled with the same stifling air which prevails in all other attics, and it borders on some of these judges' hideaways. Like Huld, he claims he has connections with the higher levels of the Court, but, unlike Huld, he does not soothe K. by promising him his acquittal. When he advises K., he does it as a private individual and not as his counsel of defense. As a result, K. follows his advice willingly. Titorelli's position is unique because he is neither completely outside the Court, like K., nor entrusted with a function by it, at least not as far as K.'s case goes. This sets him apart from the many officials who cannot help K. because "they are caught up in legal matters by day and night."

Titorelli is a beautiful-sounding Italian name that evokes associations with such historical painters as Tintoretto. It is also an assumed name—that is, a sort of a lie. We know this from the Manufacturer who learns about K.'s case from the painter, another indication of Titorelli's familiarity with the Court. What we also know from the Manufacturer is that "Titorelli probably also lies." This he no doubt does when he pretends not to know the reason for K.'s visit with him. He also lies because he does not reveal to K. the extent to which he is in the Court's "confidence." It is only by accident that K. discovers the only way to reach the Court, located in the attic, is to go through Titorelli's room—in fact, step over his bed. To K., who has taken it as a good omen that Titorelli's studio is located far away from all the Court offices, this comes as a shock.

None of Titorelli's portraits shows the judges the way they really look. They are all extremely vain, do not really sit on "thrones," but nevertheless insist on being portrayed like their counterparts of days long gone by. Is this a hint that, in ancient days, the visible instances of the Law were not so corrupt? Or does it mean that the discrepancy between the absolute integrity of the Law as such and its miserable human executors has always been equally wide? Again, the two views are not mutually exclusive.

Here, it is important to note that Titorelli is not allowed to paint the judges the way he wants to. Nor are the judges themselves "free": they are subject to the whims and desires of their superiors. This means that the nature of the manifestations of the Law is determined in advance and by necessity tarnished. Since flattery prevails, the portraits look alike with only the distinctions of rank varying. Titorelli has inherited his position from his ancestors; like they, he knows how to paint the judges along "secret" guidelines.

One picture, an allegory of justice, K. cannot even recognize as such. Titorelli explains that it represents "Justice and even the goddess of Victory," which makes K. reply that it really looks like "the goddess of the Hunt." The portrait also shows a judge ready "to jump up the next moment to say something decisive or pronounce a verdict." This is a lie, for no judge of this Court will ever feel such motivation nor pass a verdict.

There are several paintings of one and the same heathscape, each showing two little trees in front of a sunset. Titorelli thinks they are all different, but they are not. As he admits, "before the Law one loses artistic verve." He who has seen through the inexorable sameness of things, he who knows there can be no acquittal, can also see no individual nuances in the paintings any more.

This brings us to Titorelli's "inside knowledge." Though he does not want to know the ultimate secrets of the highest Court, unattainable for him who has not read "their books" either, he nevertheless has knowledge which he has inherited from his ancestors and acquired through experience. He knows that there has never been an acquittal ("only in legends"), and he also knows the Court is convinced of each defendant's guilt. As opposed to Huld, he speaks his mind freely. In the fragment entitled "The House," added to the Vintage Books' edition of the novel, the Titorelli episode is continued with a most remarkable sentence: "K. was not disconcerted by Titorelli's shameless smile, directed with lifted head into empty space." He who has seen the truth, stared into the abyss of nothingness, has resigned himself to painting the same pictures over and over again.

When K. complains to Titorelli about his contradictory argumentation, the latter reminds him: "In the code of the Law . . . it is of course laid down on the one hand that the innocent shall be acquitted, but it is not stated on the other hand that the Judges are open to influence." This is a variation on Kafka's famous aphorism that "the correct understanding of a matter and the misunderstanding of the same matter do not entirely exclude each other."

Titorelli advises him to keep postponing his case because "by keeping it from getting beyond the first stages he escapes the danger of new sudden arrests." He convinces K. of the wisdom of opting for this approach rather than "ostensible" acquittal and is quite willing to attest to his innocence (knowing, however, this would not help a bit). What Titorelli wants is that K. resign himself to what is feasible. Every other solution is impossible because, as Titorelli elaborates, "even while they are pronouncing the first acquittal, the Judges foresee the possibility of the new arrest."

The mediators Huld and Titorelli are involved with the Court, though in very different ways. The outward signs are the atmosphere of sloth and illness around Huld (disregarding the "religious" interpretation now) and one of promiscuity around Titorelli. He transcends Huld in the sense that he confronts K. with the realities of the Court and his case. What they and the Manufacturer do to K. to a mounting and plausible degree is function as a series of brakes on his self-defeating search for outside help. Expressing it differently, K.'s awareness of his situation has grown to a point where one more piece of circumstantial evidence will make him draw the consequences: Block is about to furnish it.

Chapter 8

Huld continues to emerge as a paradoxical character: he pretends to have influence with the higher-ups and yet pleads with K. not to dismiss him. He claims he loves to help him and would truly regret it if a "misunderstanding" forced him to withdraw his help (he cannot grasp the fact that K. might want to cease relying on him for rational reasons), and yet he keeps K. enslaved. He demands submissiveness from K. and Block, and yet he tells them the Court dislikes them *because* of their submissiveness. He forces Block to read the same legal documents over and over again, justifying his treatment of him by saying Block does not understand them. At the same time, it is obvious that he himself does not believe in the writings: "After a certain stage in my practice nothing really new happens." Huld simply uses the documents to keep Block dependent and to demonstrate that by reading legal documents nobody can learn even a basic fact, such as whether or not his case has been opened yet.

Block's self-deprecation is a masterpiece of psychological insight into the mechanism of mutual influence between the awareness of guilt (imaginary or real) in the accused and its effect on the accuser. It is Huld who summons Block, and yet it is Block's automatic slavish compliance that causes Huld to react as if his client were intruding. He even accuses Block, who literally lives in his lawyer's house to be near him at all times, of appearing at the wrong moment. When the tradesman, overly anxious to read the lawyer's whims, meekly asks whether he should leave again, he almost forces Huld to humiliate him. Through self-doubt and a disgustingly fawning attitude, Block maneuvers himself into a position of apparent guilt. That he is really guilty (everybody is guilty to some degree in the sense that K. is guilty long before he is arrested), is another subject. The point here is that people, by acting in a self-effacing manner, drive others to treat them "like dogs." The same thing happened to K. at his arrest and then before the Examining Magistrate: by showing bewilderment and indecision at the wrong moment, he let the authorities take the initiative and believe his guilt. (The fact that he really is guilty before the highest Law is a different issue again: the arresting officials know and care nothing about that). Leni and Huld find K. attractive because he is, or, as far as they know, *appears* guilty. The same psychological phenomenon operated in Fräulein Bürstner, who also found K. attractive for the same reason. The mere charge results in an awareness of guilt (real or imagined) which, in turn, tends to drive the accused into the arms of the Court. The syndrome Kafka deals with here is that which makes Raskolnikov give himself up in Dostoevski's *Crime and Punishment*. As everywhere in Kafka's writings, the boundary lines between imagined guilt, projected guilt, and actual guilt are not clear-cut.

Because his case is much older (five years as opposed to K.'s six months), Block has stooped much lower in his eagerness to gain some form of help. At first, he even treats K. as if he owned him something, only to turn against him the minute this appears opportune. Because his case is so much older, he realizes that his case is "beyond reason" and that, if help comes at all, it will come through Huld, unlikely though this is. As opposed to K., he has neither the desire nor the strength to dismiss the lawyer.

K. is utterly repulsed by Block's fawning behavior and by Huld's attempt to impress him through treating the tradesman "like a dog." "Had he not chased him away sooner, he [Huld] would have achieved just that through this scene," the narrator says. Huld's pseudo-legal, or at least inefficient legal actions, Block's self-effacing duplicity, and Leni's role as a mistress to everybody in the name of the Law strike K. like a continuously repeated ritual: " . . . as if K. was listening to a well rehearsed conversation that had been and would be repeated many times and which would keep its novelty only for Block."

K. is entirely justified in feeling and thinking the way he does. What he does not know yet is that nobody can really escape this subservience and entanglement completely. He, too, has prostrated himself before several women by now, is eager to sound out the contemptible Block in search of clues that might help him, and, in the end, will also be compared to a dog (as Block is here). In the parable "Before the Law," Kafka reduces K.'s and Block's behavior before the inaccessibility of the Law to its most succinct form when he shows us how the man from the country even seeks to win the sympathy of the fleas in the doorkeeper's fur coat.

The recapitulation of K.'s visit to the Court offices in Chapter 3 affords us a glimpse into the Court's arbitrariness and superstitiousness. It turns out, through Block, that the confusion which K. noticed in a defendant then (and which K. interpreted to be the result of his own aggressive behavior toward that defendant) was really the consequence of the latter's shock over K.'s doom. He claimed he could tell K.'s doom by looking at his lips — an absurd statement, but symptomatic of the arbitrary nature of top decisions.

K., too, has fallen victim to self-delusion, following even the most unlikely leads rather than focusing on his own conscience. Block makes the point that, absurd though the idea of reading a defendant's guilt from his lips may be, "if you live among these people it's difficult to escape the prevailing opinions."

The world in which K. seeks to find his bearings confounds him more with each step toward acting "reasonably." Tempting though it is, we should not jump to the conclusion from this that K. could have extricated himself from his entanglement had he actually dismissed Huld. In this chapter, K. is on the road toward doing just that, but did not finish it, quite in keeping with the notion of the "broken off radiuses." To believe that his dismissal of Huld would have altered his fate pre-supposes that K.'s case is essentially a rational and legal one that can be fought along rational and legal lines.

Chapter 9

The Bank picks K. as a guide for an Italian visitor because he speaks the language and is knowledgeable about art. As far as the structure of the novel goes, Kafka uses this connection to demonstrate one more time how utterly inseparable K.'s world of the Bank is from that of his case.

While waiting for his visitor in the cathedral, K. notices a picture and scans it with his flashlight. The cathedral, by the way, is Prague's fourteenth-century St. Vitus Cathedral, under whose Gothic spires Kafka grew up. This is important because Kafka's proverbial love of Prague has been used to argue *for* the arrangement of Chapter 9 as the culmination point immediately before the final chapter. Note, too, that one of the pictures shows a knight who "seemed to watch an event carefully which went on before his eyes. It was surprising that he did not go nearer." An underlying pattern of Kafka's world, a combination of strong intentionality and absence of motion, becomes visible here. We have dealt with it before in the form of desire and immediate deprivation; here, it is hesitancy that keeps him from following up his intention of looking at it more clearly. The picture brings to mind the doorkeeper of the parable "Before the Law," when K. remarks that the "knight could have been meant to stand guard."

Upon reading the parable, we sense that it mixes concrete and abstract images, that it is an artistic attempt at expressing the basically inexpressible. We will revert to this point after dealing with it in detail. The man from the country, who has not expected "to run into any great troubles," suddenly learns at the door to the Law that he cannot gain admission *now*. It is astounding that the question he immediately asks is not why he is being denied admission *now* but, rather, whether perhaps he might be allowed to enter *later*. Kafka's all-pervading pattern begins to assume contours already: the man from the country has a fatal way of giving away the advantage of initiative. Rather than insisting on clarifying this first essential item, he yields to pressure that at first does not manifest itself as such. The answer he receives to his second, less relevant, question—whether he will be permitted to enter later—is vague, so vague that it reinforces his already strong hesitancy to act. The doorkeeper's statements that he is "powerful" and "only the lowest doorkeeper" intimidate the man from the country enough to prevent his asking any further questions, much less his trying to enter. His aim having been thwarted (this, anyway, is what he thinks has happened), he gradually loses interest in it and permits himself to be distracted. More and more he becomes attracted by the doorkeeper's face, his beard, and even the fleas in his fur coat. His fixation on these irrelevant details mounts, rendering him ever more incapable of acting on his own. The doorkeeper is not described as inhuman. Quite the contrary: he offers the man from the country a chair by the entrance. There he spends the better part of his life and it becomes obvious that Kafka is here, among other things, also portraying a complex mental process. As the years pass, the man from the country develops the *idée fixe* that the man supposedly keeping him away from the Law is the only obstacle. The man from the country retrogresses, his vision becoming ever more myopic, which is beautifully expressed in his dwindling eyesight. That he sees the "radiance" of the Law only as he dies is a theme which we find in many of Kafka's pieces, most prominently perhaps in "The Penal Colony": it is only in the face of death that we recognize the beauty or even the mere existence of the Law (the Absolute?). Though his single-mindedness of purpose has slackened considerably, the man from the country still has moods in which he pursues his original aim. This is exactly the point that Kafka tries to make: he is inconsistent, dependent on moods, and casting about for outside help, as is K. He humiliates himself further by trying to bribe the doorkeeper. But this is in vain: the doorkeeper accepts, but only to keep the man from thinking that he has left one approach untried. The man from the country thus proves the inaccessibility of the Law, but also his unceasing quest. The one decisive question he never asks is this: why is he not being admitted? As he is about to pass away, he asks something he must have noticed for some time—why nobody else besides him has tried to enter through this door. The doorkeeper's reply is most frightening because it shows that our seeker's recognition of the "radiance," his awareness of insight into the Absolute, has come too late—if, indeed, it could have altered his fate at all. The reply is, "No one but you could gain admittance through this door, since this door was intended for you. I am now going to shut it."

This means that the man has not been mistaken in his belief that there is potential meaning to his life. It is just that this meaning turns out to be inaccessible to him, at least as he might benefit from it. The fundamental question is whether he could have attained cognizance of the "radiance" if he acted differently. The man from the country is a man doomed to remain in the antechamber of paradise, who nonetheless hopes to gain admission through perseverence. The tragedy is that he perseveres by waiting pointlessly rather than by determining the right road for himself. But as one of Kafka's famous aphorisms says, "There is a goal, but no road. What we term 'road' is nothing but hesitating." The man from the country, then, or K., realizes as he dies (is led away to his execution) that his battle has taken place in front of the door set aside for him alone and that, for a cursed reason beyond his understanding, he has lost it. Let us remember again that, though the man from the country may very well be guilty of a lack of initiative or determination, thereby possibly forfeiting his chance of entry, this does in no way explain why he is condemned to such a harrowing situation in the first place. Translated into the language of the novel this means that K.'s possible, even probable, mishandling of his case has nothing to do with his fundamental guilt, with which he is burdened from the outset. The mishandling of his case may be the result of his fundamental guilt, but it does not explain it.

There have been countless interpretations of the parable, but they all can be classified under two categories. Each has to come to terms with the crucial question: would the doorkeeper have held back the man from the country if he had simply walked through the door? Let us first discuss the line of interpretation which answers with a clear "no." In order to be consistent, it will also have to pronounce K. guilty in the sense that he mishandles his case, thus forfeiting his chance of acquittal.

That the doorkeeper goes to shut the door at precisely the moment the man dies illustrates that the two men are but two aspects of the same phenomenon and are dependent upon each other. They both represent aspects of our innermost struggle between activity and passivity, initiative and hesitancy, or conviction and doubt. In other words, the doorkeeper's vagueness and ambivalence is a direct function of the supplicant's failure to try to enter. His determination would have forced the doorkeeper either to yield to demands or to turn the man away by force. If we ask the doorkeeper within us for permission instead of acting on our own, we will certainly not be permitted in, for it is the doorkeeper's function to say "no." The lesson of the parable is that the man from the country should have tested the alleged power of the guard. He might very well have discovered that the guard's power is a figment of his imagination, the result of his own hesitation. He would also have discovered that, once the first "doorkeeper" is behind us, the others look far less invincible: a psychological mechanism sets in, reinforcing our self-assurance with each successive step. Within itself this argument makes sense. The trouble is, however, that it grants a degree of freedom to the man from the country which he simply does not have. His severe mishandling of his case is the inevitable consequence of guilt accumulated throughout his life. Both lie buried in his insensitivity and amorality.

The other line of interpretation argues that it is the fate of the man from the country to have to fight a battle he cannot possibly win. As far as K.'s case is concerned, certainly, there are many more lines in *The Trial,* as well as in Kafka's stories and letters, in favor of this more pessimistic outlook. At any rate, this outlook takes issue with the key sentence of the first interpretation: the doorkeeper would not have held back the man if he had merely tried to walk through. The argument is now, from the doorkeeper's reply, "the door was intended for you; I am now going to shut it." The parable draws its enormous tension—the tension between the *certainty* of a goal and the *impossibility* of reaching it. It argues that "Before the Law," as, indeed, the whole novel, would not be a parable but only a thrilling exercise in brinkmanship if the doorkeeper's reaction were made subject to the supplicant's determination. The very point of the novel, runs the argument, is that the human condition is vis-a-vis logically insolvable paradoxes—that is, a human obligation to come to terms with them by accepting them as necssssary. This interpretation argues that there can be no clear-cut answer to the question of how the man from the country should have acted because this is a false or irrelevant question in the first place. Why pose this question once we know he cannot escape his punishment, the just and inevitable consequence of the guilt he loaded upon himself long before his thirtieth birthday?

Ambivalence also characterizes the conversation K. has with the priest about the interpretation of the parable. As a member of the Court, the priest reproaches K. for deluding himself about the nature of the Law which he has to "serve." Yet none of the interpretations they discuss emerges as absolutely correct. The priest warns K. not to pay too much attention to mere "opinions." The main insights of this round of intellectual one-upmanship are, as the priest puts it, that "it is not necessary to accept everything as true, but only as necessary," and that, as K. counters, "both conclusions are to some extent compatible." This is a variation of the priest's statement at the beginning of their discussion, a most revealing comment on the nature of both the Law and Kafka's writing: "The right perception of any matter and the misunderstanding of the same matter do not wholly exclude each other."

Perhaps the most mature way of looking at the parable, and thus the novel, is contained in a famous section from the short story "The Great Wall of China" (1918):

Many complain that the words of the wise are always merely symbols and of no use in daily life, which is the only life we have. When the wise man says "Go over," he does not mean that we should cross over to some actual place, which we could do anyhow if it were worth the effort; he means some miraculous beyond, something unknown to us, something he too cannot define more precisely, and therefore cannot help us here in the least. All these symbols merely express that the incomprehensible is incomprehensible, and we have known that before. But the cares we have to struggle with every day: that is a different matter.

Concerning this a man once said: Why such reluctance? If you only followed the symbols you would become symbols yourselves, and thus rid of all your daily cares.

Another said: I bet this is also a symbol. The first said: You have won.

The second said: But unfortunately only symbolically. The first said: No, in reality; symbolically you have lost.

The upshot is that the parable seems to have been invented with the explicit intention of defying interpretation.

The pictorial quality of K.'s language assumes a rare density in the parable. It is amazing how distinctly we can see both the doorkeeper and the man from the country before us. Nothing really seems abstract and we almost forget that the man has waited all his lifetime. The doorkeeper's language enhances our vivid impressions of an everyday event as do the sentences beginning with "he," through which we are drawn close to the entrance seeker. His voice we hear only once at the end in the form of a question, a marvelous way of showing his metaphysical loneliness.

Chapter 10

The significance of this chapter, like that of Chapter 1, lies in its chronological explicity. Not only do the two black-frocked men pick up K., also dressed in black, at 9 A.M.—the warders arrested K. (also both in black) before 9 A.M.—but this chapter also deals with the evening preceding K.'s thirty-first birthday. Exactly a year has elapsed between the two chapters. It is at the end of this chapter that the only occurrence of the whole story eluding all speculation takes place: K.'s death.

Death has been a possibility throughout, though always covered up by K.'s counter-measure and pleas of innocence. In fact, at one point in the opening chapter, when K. is left alone by the warders for a moment, he muses over the possibility of suicide only to dismiss it right away as a "senseless act."

It is now more obvious than ever that the Court does not intend to do anything against K.'s will. As the priest put it in the previous chapter, suggesting that the Court is apt to recede before K.'s thrusts: "The Court wants nothing from you. It receives you when you come and it dismisses you when you go." The reason for the Court's compliance is of course that K. is at its complete mercy anyway. The executioners who appear as he has expected them to are even more polite than the warders were. They can afford to be because their grip on K. is total, symbolized by the way they lock him between themselves "in a unity which would have brought all three down together had one of them been knocked over." This description brings back one of the warders' reminder in the opening chapter that he and his colleague "stand closer to you (K.) than any other people in the world." These two sentences have been made the basis for an interpretation of the warders and executioners as parts of K.'s personality, even his superego.

At any rate, the three make their way across the bridge and K. turns toward the rails—a motion toward suicide reminiscent of "The Judgment" (1913), where Georg Bendemann's end also brings his relief. K. does not have the strength to carry out his plan, however. He has another chance to kill himself at the very end when preparations for his execution at the quarry are made: "K. now knew exactly that it would have been his duty to grab the knife passing back and forth over his head and plunge it into his own breast." Again he cannot summon enough willpower. He also cannot accept the responsibility which "rested with whoever had not granted him not enough strength to commit the deed."

Fräulein Bürstner's appearance (perhaps only in his mind?) also supplies a link to the opening chapter. It occurs exactly at the moment when K. considers a last attempt at resisting. This is consistent with the portrait we have of her because she was the only one who admonished him to rely on himself and, consequently, refused to listen to him after their first meeting. Her appearance triggers the realization in K. that he has failed to follow her advice and that resistance to his impending end is senseless now: "I always wanted to attack the world with twenty hands and, also, for a purpose not to be approved. That was wrong. Shall I now demonstrate that not even this one-year-old trial could teach me? Shall I leave this world without common sense? Shall people say after I am gone that at the outset of my case I wanted to carry it to an end and that at the end of it I wanted to start over again? I don't want them to say that." This proves that K. is not interested in showing his innocence any longer. On the other hand, it is hardly possible to construct his guilt out of this admission that he "wanted to attack the world with twenty hands." The sole issue now is the most proper form of his death. If he has not been able to prove his innocence, at least he wants to go down with "common sense" and not as a coward. He has resigned himself to the necessity of his pronouncement as "guilty." We should not forget that the connection between guilt and punishment is not the explicit subject of the novel, although it is K. himself who is eager at the outset to attain a juridically clear interpretation of this connection. This, he believes then, would eventually have to lead to his acquittal.

The last sentence, " 'Like a dog!' It was as if the shame of it must outlive him," reads as if Kafka had wished K.'s unsatisfactory and sad death. In light of a diary entry, according to which Kafka regarded K.'s execution as a direct reference to the humiliations at the hands of his father, this becomes even more plausible. Yet we should at least consider the possibility of K.'s death as a liberation. After all, in the parable mentioned previously, the man from the country experiences the Law's "radiance" precisely at the moment he dies: the moment of death coincides with his awareness of his actual situation. In the context of the novel this means that the more K. "sees through" the world of the Court and his situation, the closer he gets to his death. From this realization it is but a short step to his desire to die.

Without for a moment trying to overrate the autobiographical element, we should still mention that several entries in Kafka's diary suggest that K.'s eventual and positive assessment of his death may well be a reflection of Kafka's repeated desire to commit suicide as a way out of his problems. (The most prominent diary entry is that of November 2, 1911).

Another indication of Kafka's relativization of K.'s death and his remarkable distance toward it is the hero's almost comical question to his executioners," What theater are you playing at?" The answer comes in the form of consternation and silence, suggesting that every possible objection to K.'s execution has already been raised.

The intensity of the last scene is enhanced by the image of a human being flashing across the horizon over the quarry. The questions K. may feel emerging now freeze into one prolonged scream. They have become meaningless and show the complete breakdown of his whole argumentation along the lines of logic. All his life he has chosen this legal-logical approach rather than recognize the actual forces of life, which are not those of legality and logic. "Logic is doubtless unshakeable, but it cannot withstand a man who wants to go on living." The will to life mentioned here is already undermined in Chapter 1, and his inability to commit suicide now is only its final, perverted manifestation. His helpless floundering reflects the utter hopelessness of his fate. The correspondence of this hopelessness with his floundering frenzy is one of the elementary appeals of all of Kafka's writings. The almost complete absence of verbal expression, much less metaphysical speculation, increases this appeal. As Kafka once put it, "I have to write like one who can only help himself by wildly throwing around his arms."

ON K.'S GUILT, THE COURT, AND THE LAW

Certainly *The Trial* has many layers of meaning which not even the most "scientific" analysis can decode, be it psychoanalytically or, more recently, linguistically oriented. The probably inevitable result of the novel's multi-level makeup is that certain components are stressed while others are not. Yet it seems that, in spite of this danger, our view of K. will pretty much determine our interpretation.

Both the philosophical-theological and the autobiographical interpretations shed light on two important layers. If we view the Court only as a description of a corrupt bureaucratic system, or as a projection of Kafka's personal problems, K. winds up as the miserable victim whose story grants mankind absolutely no hope in a totally alienated world. The same is true if we take the parable, the novel's artistic focal point, and view it as the tribunal where K., elevated to an absolute level, is forced to vindicate himself as a representative of mankind without really knowing why or how.

If we look at K. as guilty, as a man who is part and parcel of this faulty world and whose aberrations result in severe, though logically consistent occurrences, then we must acknowledge a higher Law toward whose absolute standards K. is stumbling. Looking at *The Trial* this way makes it appear, not only as a portrayal of human desperation, but also as one of Kafka's faith: not faith in the sense of salvation, or even orientation, to be sure, but faith in his eventual acceptance of his sinful life and its consequences.

In this interpretation, K. does not die as a result of his involved and absurd situation, but because he was already dead *inwardly* at his arrest. From the very outset of the story he does not love anybody or anything, does not aim for anything beyond his immediate physical needs, is insensitive and egotistical. His assets are limited to purely economic concerns to a point which keeps him from comprehending the nature of his own new situation. But his self-assurance and defiance against the bizarre authorities, which seem to amount to justified protest in the eyes of the reader—at this point still sympathetic to him—gradually disappear. The longer the trial lasts, the more K. becomes aware that the strange Court with all its bizarre and corrupt officials may have the right to investigate against him after all. As the priest warns K. during their discussion about the meaning of the parable, "It may be that you don't know the nature of the Court you are *serving*." It makes sense, therefore, to see the many scenes of K.'s trial as sequences of his evolving consciousness (and conscience; the two words are cognates). In this case the final scene with all its horror represents the last consequence of guilt in the form of a nightmare. If we accept this view, then the confusing and contradictory aspects of the Court are also a reflection of K.'s inner condition.

It is important to understand that there are many levels of the Court, most of them tangible, corrupt, and dealing with K. in a most haphazard way. The highest level is, above all, elusive. The levels at which K. fights mirror the shortcomings of this life (his included, as said above) and are therefore in no position to pass judgment. The representatives of these levels become bogged down in unresolved and unresolvable issues and utter "diverse viewpoints" at best. Their ranks "mount endlessly so that not even the initiated can survey the hierarchy as a whole" and each level "actually knows less than the defense." Even the "high judges" are "common" and, contrary to popular belief, sit only on "kitchen chairs." These officials represent the sensual unhampered forces of life itself. Their power is such that nobody can escape them. At the same time, and this makes for their paradoxical nature, they are forever caught up in reflecting and registering in a rather abstract realm removed from life. "They were often utterly at a loss; they did not have any right understanding of human relations."

Beyond these bungling levels of the Court, there is the highest seat of Law itself, absolute and inaccessible, yet weighing more and more heavily on K., who becomes increasingly aware of its existence and its relevance to his case. It marks that point of the endless legal pyramid where the notions of justice and inevitability come together, where the countless contradictions and errors of its organs are reconciled. It is the instance which K. becomes drawn to, of which he has an increasingly definite feeling that he has been summoned before it to justify his life. This is the Law he has to serve and which he has violated by being unaware of its existence.

The indifferent and corrupt authorities "are merely sent out by the highest Court." They do not know their superiors. They stand clearly below this "highest Law." This is why the doorkeeper of the parable stands *before* the Law rather than *in* it.

THE NEUROTIC ELEMENT IN KAFKA'S ART

In 1917 Kafka learned about his tubercular condition, which appeared in one night with heavy bleeding. When it happened it did not only scare him, but also relieved him of chronic insomnia. Surprising though this aspect of relief may be on first glance, it becomes understandable when we consider that he was well aware of the profound effect it had on his future: it forced him to dissolve his engagement with Felice Bauer and to give up all marriage plans, tentative though they may have been. The idea of marriage, however, meant more than the decision about his future with another human being in Kafka's life—it was, literally speaking, the one mode of life he extolled. To be married, to have a family, to be able to face life by escaping loneliness and by belonging—these were the ambitions which he never had the strength to realize.

The humiliation he suffered at the hands of his father is a subject all by itself but has to be mentioned because one cannot see his disease or his understanding of it apart from it. Suffice it to say here that he felt humiliated, not only by his father's insensitivity and brutality (*Letter to His Father*), but also by his mere existence. To Kafka, he belonged to those wholesome, big, life-affirming characters whose very practicality instilled both envy and fear in him. This father could never be wrong. As far as his disease goes, this meant that Kafka agreed with his father's view that, as the only male descendant of the family, he had the duty to have a son. It is ironical that Kafka did have a son with Grete Bloch, Felice's friend, but that was out of wedlock and, besides, he never knew about him.

Yet Max Brod said in 1917 that Kafka presented his disease as psychological, as a sort of "life-saver from marriage." Kafka himself is quoted as saying to Brod, "My head is in cahoots with my lungs behind my back." To put it differently, to write all the fantastic things he wrote, Kafka could not allow himself to sink his roots into the practical sphere of his father, if, indeed, he had been able to do so at all. Yet he had identified himself with the aspirations of his father. Out of this conflict a crisis was bound to arise: what he could not solve in his mind was solved, in a sense, by his body. In a letter written in 1922 he refers to himself as a "poor little man obsessed by all sorts of evil spirits" and adds that it is "undoubtedly the merit of medicine to have introduced the more consoling concept of neurasthenia in place of obsession." Aware that a cure could only come through the exposure of the actual cause of a disease, he added that "this makes a cure more difficult."

Parallel to his awareness that he could not possibly gain spiritual relief, and certainly not salvation, in this world, Kafka's tuberculosis progressed. He spent more and more time taking rest cures, then the only therapy. "I am mentally ill, my lung condition is merely a flooding over the banks of a mental disease," he wrote to his second fiancée Milena Jesenská. This disease consisted of an undissolvable dissonance, a deeply ingrained opposition within him. He had two main opponents, one in the sum total of the characteristics he admired in his father but which he loathed at the same time; the other in his craving to write about that which he was experiencing himself with such intensity—his lack of protection, his nagging skepticism, his withdrawal and alienation. His uncompromising attempt to depict the world almost solely in terms of this dilemma has been called his neurosis. Yet we should at least be aware of the fact that he himself also called it a first step toward insight, in the sense that a mental disease, too, can be an essential window through which to view truth. It is in this light that we should interpret his professions that he has not found a way to live out of his own strength "unless tuberculosis is one of my strengths."

The actual horror of his disease, as he saw it, was not his physical suffering. His father thought it was an infection, and Brod believed it resulted from his fragile constitution and his unsatisfactory work as a lawyer. Kafka saw beyond these at best superficial explanations and saw it as an expression of his metaphysical vulnerability. Viewed in this manner, it becomes a sort of sanctuary that prevented him from falling victim to nihilism. As he put it himself, "All these alleged diseases, be they ever so sad, are facts of faith, man's desperate attempts at anchoring in some protective soil. Thus psychoanalysis (with which he was familiar) does not find any other basis of religion but that which lies at the bottom of the individual's disease."

We have made the point elsewhere that in *The Trial* the Court and its paradoxes may be seen as the reflection of K.'s unresolvable problems. In connection with what we have said here it is interesting to note that several attempts have been made to read K.'s story as that of a medical patient. The very title in German, *Der Prozess*, definitely also means a medical process. Also, it is possible to read entire passages without changing anything if we substitute physician for lawyer, disease for guilt, medical examination for interrogation, nurse for usher, patient for the accused, and cure for acquittal. We would not jeopardize the meaning of the story at all; whatever would remain as parabolic is also present in the original version. Certainly the argument that Kafka was not aware of his failing health when he was writing the novel is not a good counter-argument because, first, his deep spiritual dilemma existed of course long before its physical manifestation (that is, tuberculosis according to his own view) occurred; second, because his hypersensitivity would certainly have enabled him to write from within the view of a consumptive. The point made here is not to prove that Kafka really had this in mind when he worked on K.'s case: on the contrary, the mere possibility of such meaningful interchangeability rather proves that K.'s fundamental situation is open to several readings which need not be at odds with each other.

All this is not supposed to demonstrate that Kafka simply equated faith and health or the absence of faith and disease. Certainly, however, there is a relationship between his uncompromising search for total truth and his vulnerability, his limitless self-exposure to the difficulties of life. It must take super-human strength to continuously snatch every bit of firm ground away from under one's feet in an almost maniacal effort to doubt one's own position. Kafka was notoriously incapable of living by the many little white lies the average person adopts as a means of surviving, and he both marveled at and envied those who could, as Milena Jesenska wrote, "He is without the slightest asylum . . . That which has been written about Kafka's abnormality is his great merit. I rather believe the whole world is sick and he the only healthy one, the only one to understand, feel correctly, the only pure human being. I know he does not fight life as such, only against this kind of life." The confessions of a woman in love?

The ultimate question is whether it is not precisely this fixation on purity and perfection that are his spiritual disease, his neurosis, his sin. Every fiber of Kafka would have yearned to exclaim with Browning's *Andrea del Sarto:* "Ah, but a man's reach should exceed his grasp, Or what's a heaven for?"

It was his fate that reach and grasp, in his world, were doomed to remain synonyms simply because there was no possibility of heaven.

STRUCTURE AND ORDER OF CHAPTERS

As we follow K.'s stumbling through the story we get the distinct feeling that there is not much of a development he goes through. Not even Huld, for instance, with all his insight and connections, knows whether K.'s case has ever gotten off the ground. There is no "way," or, more appropriately, whatever appears to be K.'s "way" assumes an altogether different meaning in the thicket of the Court's endless mazes. Kafka once wrote, "The true way leads over a rope which is not strung up in the air but a little above ground; it seems designed to cause us to stumble rather than be walked on." What we have in *The Trial* is a detailed depiction of K.'s directionless stumbling.

The abrupt beginning is a good case in point. We know nothing about K.'s background, and his attempt to vindicate himself through a written petition referring to his past fails miserably before he has a chance of carrying it through. To argue that a major structural reason for this absence of a "way" lies in the closely defined time span of the novel is not very convincing. Many twentieth-century novels also deal with strictly defined time spans and yet do not confront the reader with such a complete *tabula rasa* of their heroes' backgrounds.

Each chapter has the pronounced tendency to start all over again because thematic interconnections are unclear if not absent altogether. The entire section with Titorelli, for instance, is but a variation of the section with Huld. Both scenes rely on a mediator to even get K. in touch with

Huld and Titorelli, respectively. This repetitiveness is important, especially if we see the authorities as a reflection of K.'s ruminating consciousness (conscience). Kafka freely admitted that the multiplicity of possible directions was a subject that was close to him personally: "I always had to tackle the radius and then to break it off . . . The center of the imaginary circle is full of beginnings." The broken off "radiuses" of this novel are the many chapter fragments. Frequently, they do not seem to lead anywhere except to ever-new beginnings—to K.'s former girl friend Elsa, to his mother, to the lawyer's regular get-togethers at the pub (fragments included at the end of the 1969 Vintage Book edition used here).

Kafka himself was aware of the fragmentary character of his work (about four-fifths, fragments) and also recognized his inability to complete things. This inability lay buried in his overly keen perception of the infinite possibilities following from each kaleidoscopic situation and his uncompromising desire for writing the "true" rather than the "necessary," to use the priest's final comment to K. He was, as he said himself, obsessed with writing and yet doomed as a writer because he could never hope to trace the manifold ramifications of each aspect or nuance. It is important to see that his repeated breaking off of "beginning radiuses" is not a flaw of this particular novel, but the consistent result of his temperament that corresponded to his frustratingly imperfect, and hence fragmentary, world view. Kafka was by temperament and outlook committed to remain uncommitted.

It does not follow from this, however, that there is no unity in the novel. The Court is, as Titorelli says, "everywhere" and it does indeed hold together the diverse radiuses of action. The Court holds them together in the sense that all scenes are pervaded by incomprehensibility which unites all of K.'s flounderings. It is of course true that this statement of cohesion is a negative one: to the extent it exists, it is the result of the absence of direction, commitment, a "way"—one radius traveled to the end.

The Trial has a particular problem because there has been considerable disagreement as to the order of several chapters. It has been argued that, well-rounded though the scenes and the central pieces within this novel are ("Before the Law," for instance), some of the chapters are almost interchangeable as far as their placement goes. This is said to be the direct result of the lack of coherence of the novel—that is, the virtual absence of a plot. Though there is something to this argument, "interchangeability" is probably too harsh a word. It would presuppose that Kafka, the exceedingly conscientious writer, deliberately refrained from an overall pattern for the novel.

Brod's arrangement of the chapters was valid, or at least accepted as such, until a new arrangement was attempted by Herman Uyttersprot in his detailed study, On the Structure of Kafka's "Trial" (Brussels, 1953). His argument is that Brod's arrangement is wrong in several instances, especially as far as the novel's time factor goes. Uyttersprot discovered that the events of the novel cannot be fitted into the time interval between K.'s thirtieth and thirty-first birthdays. How can, he argues, winter (Chapter 7) precede autumn (Chapter 9) in the course of the *one* year of K.'s trial? He rearranged a few chapters, even included a few fragments that had been added as loose ends by Brod. He places Chapter 4 right after Chapter 1, arguing that the sentences in Chapter 4 referring to Frau Grubach's insults against Fräulein Bürstner in Chapter 1 find a more logical continuation this way. His main argument, however, concerns the crucial Chapter 9.

Whether one adheres to Brod's original arrangement of this chapter in next-to-last position or prefers the new order of Chapter 9 preceding Chapter 7, the parable chapter is the artistic culmination point of the novel. If one accepts the new arrangement, the scene between K. and the priest loses its paramount position as the major pointer to K.'s immediate end. It rather assumes the role of a portentous warning to K. One can certainly argue that it makes more sense to have the priest reprimand K. in Chapter 7 while there is still time (this presupposes that K. *does* have alternatives while fighting his case), rather than only before his end. In fact, the frantic involvement with his case begins only after the priest's parable and subsequent discussion.

Plausible though the new arrangement is, all we know for a fact is that Kafka did not finish *The Trial*. Moreover, several possible arrangements are certainly compatible with each other. It may well be that Brod and Uyttersprot give us the original and later arrangement, respectively. What we do know is that these problems result from Brod's inexact notes and rather free way of editing, which, in turn, are partly the consequence of his lifelong and intense friendship with Kafka.

COMPOSITION AND RECEPTION

Almost simultaneously with "In the Penal Colony," Kafka began to write *The Trial* in the summer of 1914, a date which has unfortunately convinced many people that the novel is primarily a work foreshadowing political terror. Of course he was painfully aware of the interconnections between World War I and his own problems, but never in the sense that the novel was supposed to be a deliberate effort to write about the political scene.

From all we know, it is much closer to the facts to view *The Trial* in connection with the enormous tension under which he lived during his two years with Felice Bauer. It can be shown that especially his first engagement to her in June 1914 and his subsequent separation from her six weeks later found their expression in the novel: the engagement is reflected in K.'s arrest and his separation in K.'s execution. Even certain details fit easily: the initials F.B. are both Felice's and those Kafka used to abbreviate "Fräulein Bürstner"; K.'s arrest takes place in Fräulein Bürstner's room, which he knows well, and Kafka's engagement took place in Felice's apartment, which he knew well; K. is asked to dress up for the occasion, strangers are watching, and the bank employees he knows are present; at Kafka's engagement, both friends and strangers were present – an aspect which the reserved Kafka abhorred particularly. Most significantly perhaps for a demonstration of the parallel, K. is permitted to remain at large after his arrest. In Kafka's diary we read that he "was tied like a criminal. If I had been put in chains and shoved in the corner with police guarding me . . . it would not have been worse. And that was my engagement." We can translate K.'s escort to his execution into Kafka's painful separation in Berlin: there Felice presided, their mutual friend Grete Bloch and Kafka's writer-friend Ernst Weiss defended him, but Kafka himself said nothing, only accepted the verdict.

At any rate, Kafka took great pains to record his emotional upheaval during these years, which largely coincides with his composition of *The Trial*. A selection of a few diary entries will do:

August 21, 1914: "Began with such high hopes, but was thrown back . . . today even more so."

August 29, 1914: "I must not rely on anything. I am alone."

October 10, 1914: "I've written little and poorly . . . that it would get this bad I had no way of knowing."

November 30, 1914: "I cannot go on. I have reached the final limit, in front of which I may well sit for years again – to start all over on a new story which would again remain unfinished. Their destiny haunts me."

January 18, 1915: "Started a new story because I am afraid to ruin the old ones. Now there are 4 or 5 stories standing up around me like horses before a circus director."

The main reasons Brod decided not to abide by his friend's request to burn certain fragments, preferably without reading them, are set forth in his *Postscript to the First Edition* of 1925, which includes Kafka's original request. Brod took the manuscript in 1920, separated the incomplete from the complete chapters after Kafka's death in 1924, arranged the order of chapters, gave the piece the title it has, though Kafka himself used only the title to refer to the story without ever calling it *The Trial*. Brod admitted he had to use his own judgment arranging the chapters because they carried titles rather than numbers. Since Kafka had read most of the story to him, Brod was reasonably certain he proceeded correctly, something which had been doubted for a long time and was finally revised. Brod also recorded that Kafka himself regarded the story as unfinished, that a few scenes were supposed to have been placed before the final chapter to describe the workings of the secretive trial. Since Kafka repeatedly argued, according to Brod, that K.'s trial should never go to the highest level, the novel was really unfinishable or, which is the same, extendable *ad infinitum*.

When Brod edited *The Trial* posthumously in 1925, it did not have any repercussions and, as late as 1928, there was no publisher to be found. It was Schocken, then located in Berlin, that ventured a publication of the complete works in 1935 — but Germany was already under Hitler's authority, and Kafka was Jewish. The whole Schocken Company was shut down by Goebbels's Ministry of Propaganda, and so it is not surprising that Kafka became known outside the German-speaking world first. Schocken Books, Inc., now located in New York, published *The Trial* in 1946.

There have been many well-known writers to recognize and extol Kafka's genius and his impact. Thomas Mann was among the first:

He was a dreamer and his writings are often conceived and formed in the manner of dreams. Down to comical details they imitate the alogical and breath-taking absurdities of dreams, these wondrous shadow games of life.

Albert Camus gets a little closer to the core of things:

We are here placed at the very limits of human thought. Indeed, in this work everything is essential, literally speaking. It certainly represents the problem of the absurd in its totality. . . . It is the fate and possibly also the greatness of this piece that it offers countless possibilities without affirming a single one.

And Hermann Hesse's exhortation reminds us that we should above all steer clear of modish talk about "Kafkaesque" horror:

Whoever is able to really read a poet, that is, without questions, without expecting intellectual or moral results, to absorb in simple readiness what he offers, will receive any answers he is looking for in Kafka's language. He gives us the dreams and visions of his lonely, difficult life, parables of his experiences, anxieties, and enthrallments.

Since the late forties, interpretations have swamped the "Kafka market." Generalizing a bit, one can say that they have all followed either the view of Kafka, the artist, or Kafka, the philosopher.

In 1947, André Gide and Jean-Louis Barrault came out with a well-received dramatization. The German version had its debut three years later. Gottfried von Einem composed an opera (libretto by Boris Blacher), which was first performed in Salzburg, Austria, in 1953. The most recent version is the film by Orson Welles (1962), with Anthony Perkins in the lead role. Though critics have held widely differing opinions on the film — many charging it is more Welles than Kafka — its success seems justified because of all absence of symbolic or allegorical representation and its high-quality cinematic language.

UNDERSTANDING KAFKA

A major problem confronting readers of Kafka's short stories is to find a way through the increasingly dense thicket of interpretations. Among the many approaches one encounters is that of the autobiographical approach. This interpretation claims that Kafka's works are little more than reflections of his lifelong tension between bachelorhood and marriage or, on another level, between his skepticism and his religious nature. While it is probably true that few writers have ever been moved to exclaim, "My writing was about you [his father]. In it, I merely poured out the sorrow I could not sigh out at your breast" [*Letter to His Father*], it is nevertheless dangerous to regard the anxieties permeating his work solely in these terms. Kafka's disenchantment with an eventual hatred of his father were a stimulus to write, but they neither explain the fascination of his writing nor tell us why he wrote at all.

The psychological or psychoanalytical approach to Kafka largely ignores the content of his works and uses the "findings" of the diagnosis as the master key to puzzling out Kafka's world. We know Kafka was familiar with the teachings of Sigmund Freud (he says so explicitly in his diary, after he finished writing "The Judgment" in 1912) and that he tried to express his problems through symbols in the Freudian sense. One may therefore read Kafka with Freud's teachings in mind. As soon as this becomes more than one among many aids to understanding, however, one is likely to read not Kafka, but a text on applied psychoanalysis or Freudian symbology. Freud himself often pointed out that the analysis of artistic values is not within the scope of the analytical methods he taught.

There is the sociological interpretation, according to which Kafka's work is but a mirror of the historical-sociological situation in which he lived. For the critic arguing this way, the question is not what Kafka really says but the reasons why he supposedly said it. What the sociological and the psychological interpretations have in common is the false assumption that the discovery of the social or psychological sources of the artist's experience invalidate the meaning expressed by his art.

Within the sociological type of interpretation, one of the most popular methods of criticism judges Kafka's art by whether or not it has contributed anything toward the progress of society. Following the Marxist-Leninist dictum that art must function as a tool toward the realization of the classless society, this kind of interpretation is prevalent not merely in Communist countries, but also among the New Left critics this side of the Iron and Bamboo Curtains. Marxist criticism of Kafka has shifted back and forth between outright condemnation of Kafka's failing to draw the consequences of his own victimization by the bourgeoisie and between acclamations stressing the pro-proletarian fighting quality of his heroes. That Kafka was the propagator of the working class as *the* revolutionary class has been maintained not only by official Communist criticism, but also by Western "progressives." And it is true that Kafka did compose a pamphlet lamenting the plight of workers. Yet in a conversation with his friend Janouch, he spoke highly of the Russian Revolution, and he expressed his fear that its religious overtones might lead to a type of modern crusade with a terrifying toll of lives. Surely a writer of Kafka's caliber can describe the terror of a slowly emerging totalitarian regime (Nazi Germany) without being a precursor of communism, as Communist criticism as often claimed. One can also read *The Trial* as the story of Joseph K.'s victimization by the Nazis (three of Kafka's sisters died in a concentration camp); it is indeed one of the greatest tributes one can pay to Kafka today that he succeeded in painting the then still latent horror of Nazism so convincingly. But one must not neglect or ignore the fact that Kafka was, above all, a poet; and to be a poet means to give artistic expression to the many levels and nuances of our kaleidoscopic human condition. To see Kafka as a social or political revolutionary because his country doctor, for instance, or the land surveyor of *The Castle* seeks to change his fate through voluntary involvement rather than outside pressure is tantamount to distorting Kafka's universal quality in order to fit him into an ideological framework.

Closely connected with the quasi-religious quality of Marxist interpretations of Kafka's stories are the countless philosophical and religious attempts at deciphering the make-up of his world. They range from sophisticated theological argumentation all the way to pure speculation. Although Kafka's religious nature is a subject complex and controversial enough to warrant separate mention, the critics arguing along these lines are also incapable, as are their sociological and psychological colleagues, of considering Kafka simply as an artist. What they all have in common is the belief that Kafka's "real meaning" lies beyond his parables and symbols, and can therefore be better expressed in ways he himself avoided for one reason or another. The presumptuousness of this particular approach lies in the belief that the artist depends on the philosopher for a translation of his ambiguous modes of expression into logical, abstract terms. All this is not to dispute Kafka's philosophical-religious cast of mind and his preoccupation with the ultimate questions of human existence. It is just that he lived, thought, and wrote in images and not in "coded" conceptual structures. Kafka himself thought of his stories merely as *points of crystallization* of his problems: Bendemann, Samsa, Gracchus, the hunger artist, the country doctor, Josef K., and K. of *The Castle* — all these men are close intellectual and artistic relatives of Kafka, yet it will not do to reduce his deliberately open-ended images to a collection of data.

Interpretations are always a touchy matter and, in Kafka's case, perhaps more so than in others. The reason for this is that his works are 1) essentially outcries against the inexplicable laws that govern our lives; 2) portrayals of the human drama running its course on several loosely interwoven levels, thus imparting a universal quality to his work; and 3) very much imbued with his high degree of sensitivity which responded differently to similar situations at different times. Particularly this last aspect suggests incohesion and paradox to the mind which insists on prodding Kafka's stories to their oftentimes irrational core. Kafka's pictures stand, as Max Brod never tired of pointing out, not merely for themselves but also for something beyond themselves.

These difficulties have prompted many a scholar to claim that Kafka rarely thought of anything specific in his stories. From this view, it is but a short step to the relativistic attitude that every interpretation of Kafka is as good as every other one. To this, one may reply that "to think of nothing specific" is by no means the same thing as "to think of many things at the same time." Kafka's art is, most of all, capable of doing the latter to perfection. Paradoxical though it may seem at first, viewing Kafka's work from a number of vantage points is not an invitation to total relativism, but a certain guarantee that one will be aware of the many levels of his work.

Despite the many differences in approaching Kafka's writings, all of them must finally deal with a rather hermetically sealed-off world. Whatever Kafka expresses is a reflection of his own complex self amidst a concrete social and political constellation, but it is a reflection broken and distorted by the sharp edges of his analytical mind. Thus the people whom his heroes meet and whom we see through their eyes are not "real" in a psychological sense, not "true" in an empirical sense, and are not "natural" in a biological sense. Their one distinctive mark is that of being something *created*. Kafka once remarked to his friend Janouch, "I did not draw men. I told a story. These are pictures, only pictures." That he succeeded in endowing them with enough plausibility to raise them to the level of living symbols and parables is the secret of his art.

Kafka's stories should not tempt us to analyze them along the lines of fantasy versus reality. An unchangeable and alienated world unfolds before us, a world governed by its own laws and developing its own logic. This world is our world and yet it is not. "Its pictures and symbols are taken from our world of phenomena, but they also appear to belong somewhere else. We sense that we encounter people we know and situations we have lived through in our own everyday lives, and yet these people and situations appear somehow estranged. They are real and physical, and yet they are also grotesque and abstract. They use a sober language devoid of luster in order to assure meaningful communication among each other, and yet they fail, passing one another like boats in an impenetrable fog. Yet even this fog, the realm of the surreal (super-real), has something convincing about it. We therefore have the exciting feeling that Kafka's people say things of preeminent significance but that it is, at the same time, impossible for us to comprehend.

Finally, the reader seems to be left with two choices of how to "read" Kafka. One is to see Kafka's world as full of parables and symbols, magnified and fantastically distorted (and therefore infinitely more real), a world confronting us with a dream vision of our own condition. The other choice is to forego any claim of even trying to understand his world and to expose oneself to its atmosphere of haunting anxiety, visionary bizarreness, and — occasionally — faint promises of hope.

KAFKA'S JEWISH INFLUENCE

Prague was steeped in the atmosphere of Jewish learning and writing until the social and political turmoil of the collapsing Austrian Empire put an end to its traditional character. The first Jews had come to Prague in the tenth century, and the earliest written document about what the city looked like was by a Jewish traveler. According to him, Prague was a cultural crossroads even then. Pulsating with life, the city produced many a lingering myth during the subsequent centuries, and they, in turn, added to its cultural fertility. The myth of the *golem* is probably its most well known: *golem* ("clay" in Hebrew) was the first chunk of inanimate matter that the famed Rabbi Loew, known for his learnedness as well as his alchemistic pursuits, supposedly awakened to actual life in the late sixteenth century. This myth fathered a whole genre of literature written in the haunting, semimystical atmosphere of Prague's Jewish ghetto. It is this background, medieval originally, but with several layers of subsequent cultural impulses superimposed on it, that pervades the world of Franz Kafka, supplying it with a very "real" setting of what is generally and misleadingly known as "Kafkaesque unrealness."

One of the unresolved tensions that is characteristic of Kafka's work occurs between his early (and growing) awareness of his Jewish heritage and the realization that modern Central European Jewry had become almost wholly assimilated. This tension remained alive in him quite apart from his situation as a prominent member of the Jewish-German intelligentsia of Prague. The problem concerned him all the more directly because his family clung to Jewish traditions only in a superficial way. Although perhaps of a more orthodox background than her husband — and therefore not quite so eager to attain total assimilation into gentile society — even Kafka's mother made no great effort to cherish Jewish ways. On one level, then, Kafka's animosity toward his father and his entire family may be explained by his mounting interest in his Jewish heritage which they did not share.

Kafka felt drawn to Jews who had maintained their cultural identity, among them the leader of a Yiddish acting group from Poland. He attended their performances in 1911, organized evenings of reading Yiddish literature, and was drawn into fierce arguments about this subject with his father, who despised traveling actors, as did the Jewish establishment of Prague. It was at that time that Kafka began to study Hebrew. As late as 1921, however, he still complained about having no firm knowledge of Jewish history and religion.

What fascinated Kafka about the various members of this group was their firmness of faith and their resistance to being absorbed into the culture of their gentile environment. There are numerous letters and diary entries which point to Kafka's awareness of the essential difference between Western and Eastern Jews concerning this matter. Kafka felt a great affinity with the chassidic tradition (*chassidic* means "pious" in Hebrew; it was an old conservative movement within Judaism which came to flower again in the eighteenth century in eastern Europe). Kafka admired very much their ardent, this-worldly faith, their veneration of ancestry, and their cherishing of native customs. He developed a powerful contempt for Jewish artists who, in his estimation, too willingly succumbed to assimilation and secularization.

Kafka was particularly interested in Zionism, the movement founded by Theodor Herzl (*The Jewish State*, 1890) to terminate the dissemination of Jews all over the world by promoting their settlement in Palestine. Zionism preached the ancient Jewish belief that the Messiah would arrive with the re-establishment of the Jewish state, and Kafka's desire for such a Jewish state and his willingness to emigrate should be noted. Kafka published in a Zionist magazine, planned several trips to Palestine (which never materialized because of his deteriorating health), and was most enthusiastic about the solidarity, the sense of community, and the simplicity of the new *kibbuzim*.

While it is true that Kafka's friend Max Brod influenced him in supporting the ideals of Zionism, it is incorrect to say that without Brod's influence Kafka would never have developed an interest in the movement. His Hebrew teacher Thieberger, a friend and student of Martin Buber, was also a major influence on Kafka. Thieberger emphasized Jewish responsibility for the whole world and believed that everybody is witness to everybody else. Oddly enough, Kafka's father's steady exhortations to "lead an active life" may have added to his growing esteem for the Jewish pioneer ideal. Another source of Kafka's growing interest in Jewish tradition was, of course, his sickness, the very sickness that kept him from carrying out his plans to emigrate to Palestine and live there as a simple artisan. The more Kafka became aware of his approaching end, the more he delved into the study of his identity. A year before his death, he started attending the Berlin Academy of Jewish Studies, and it was during that same year, 1923, that he met Dora Dymant, who was of chassidic background and further accented his search and love for his Jewish roots.

It is clear that Kafka's interest and love for the various aspects of Jewry are not merely an attempt on his part to make up for past omissions in this matter. They are, above all, the result of his religious concerns — "religious" in the wider sense of the word — that is, religious by temperament, religious in the sense of ceaselessly searching and longing for grace.

KAFKA — A "RELIGIOUS" WRITER?

To know Kafka is to grapple with this problem: was Kafka primarily a "religious" writer? The answer seems to depend on the views one brings to the reading of his stories rather than on even the best analyses. Because so much of Kafka's world remains ultimately inaccessible to us, any such labeling will reveal more about the reader than about Kafka or his works. He himself would most likely have refused to be forced into any such either/or proposition.

Perhaps one of the keys to this question is Kafka's confession that, to him, "writing is a form of prayer." Everything we know about him suggests that he probably could not have chosen any other form of expressing himself but writing. Considering the tremendous sacrifices he had made to his writing, it is only fair to say that he would have abandoned his art had he felt the need to get his ideas across in some philosophical or theological system. At the same time, one feels that what Kafka wanted to convey actually transcended literature and that, inside, art alone must have seemed shallow to him — or at least inadequate when measured against the gigantic task he set for himself — that is, inching his way toward at least approximations of the nature of truth. Each of Kafka's lines is charged with multiple meanings of allusions, daydreams, illusions and reflections — all indicating a realm whose "realness" we are convinced of, but whose nature Kafka could not quite grasp with his art. He remained tragically aware of this discrepancy throughout his life.

This does not contradict the opinion that Kafka was a "philosopher groping for a form rather than a novelist groping for a theme." "Philosopher" refers here to a temperament, a cast of mind, rather than to a man's systematic, abstract school of thought. Whatever one may think of Kafka's success or failure in explaining his world, there is no doubt that he always deals with the profoundest themes of man's fate. The irrational and the horrible are never introduced for the sake of literary effect; on the contrary, they are introduced to express a depth of reality. And if there is one hallmark of Kafka's prose, it is the complete lack of any contrived language or artificial structure.

Essentially, Kafka desired to "extinguish his self" by writing, as he himself put it. In terms of craftsmanship, this means that much of his writing is too unorganized, open-ended, and obscure. Even allowing for the fact that he was concerned with a realm into which only symbols and parables can shed some light (rather than, say, metaphors and similes which would have tied his stories to the more concrete and definitive), it is doubtful whether Kafka can be called an "accomplished writer" in the sense that Thomas Mann, for instance, can.

Kafka was, then, a major writer, but not a good "craftsman." And he was a major thinker and seer in the sense that he registered, reflected, and even warned against the sickness of a whole age when contemporaries with a less acute consciousness still felt secure.

The question of Kafka's being a religious writer has been going on for decades, but has often been meaningless because of the failure of critics or readers to explain what they mean by "religious." It is essential to differentiate between those who call Kafka and Kafka's works religious in the wider sense of the term—that is, religious by temperament or mentality—and those who assert that his stories reflect Kafka as a believer in the traditional Judaic-Christian sense of the word. Of this latter group, his lifelong friend and editor Max Brod was the first and probably most influential. A considerable number of critics and readers have followed Brod's "religious" interpretations—particularly, Edwin Muir, Kafka's principal English translator. However, for some time now, Kafka criticism has not investigated the "religious" aspect. This is so partly because the psychoanalytical approach and the sociological approach have been more popular and fashionable (especially in the United States), and also because critics and biographers have proven beyond doubt that Brod committed certain errors while editing and commenting on Kafka. While the original attitude toward Brod was one of absolute reverence (after all, he saw Kafka daily for over twenty years, listened to his friend's stories, and advised him on changes), the consensus of opinion has more recently been that, although we owe him a great deal as far as Kafka and his work are concerned, he was a poor researcher. He was simply too self-conscious about his close friendship with Kafka and therefore too subjective: he would never admit the obviously neurotic streak in Kafka's personality. While we may trust Brod when he claims that Kafkas's aphorisms are much more optimistic and life-asserting than his fiction, it is difficult to consider Kafka primarily as a believer in the "indestructible core of the universe" or more pronouncedly Jewish-Christian tenets. His famous remark, striking the characteristic tone of self-pity, "Sometimes I feel I understand the Fall of Man better than anyone," is more to the point. We have no reason to doubt Brod's judgment about Kafka's personally charming, calm, and even humorous ways. It is that in Kafka's fiction, calmness is too often overshadowed by fear and anxiety, and the rare touches of humor are little more than convulsions of what in German is known as *Galgenhumor* ("gallows humor")—that is, the frantic giggle before one's execution.

In summary one can argue in circles about Kafka's work being "religious," but one thing is clear: Kafka's stories inevitably concern the desperate attempts of people to do right. And as noted elsewhere, Kafka and his protagonists are identical to an amazing extent. This means that the main characters who try to do right but are continuously baffled, thwarted, and confused as to what it really means to do right are also Kafka himself. Viewed in this way, Kafka becomes a religious writer *par excellence:* he and his protagonists are classical examples of the man in whose value system the sense of duty and of responsibility and the inevitability of moral commandments have survived the particular and traditional code of a religious system — hence Kafka's yearning for a frame of reference which would impart meaning to his distinct sense of "shalt" and "shalt not." If one takes this all-permeating desire for salvation as the main criterion for Kafka's "religiousness" rather than the grace of faith which he never found, how could anyone *not* see Kafka as a major religious writer? "He was God-drunk," a critic wrote, "but in his intoxication his subtle and powerful intellect did not stop working."

KAFKA AND EXISTENTIALISM

Kafka's stories suggest meanings which are accessible only after several readings. If their endings, or lack of endings, seem to make sense at all, they will do so immediately and not in unequivocal language. The reason for this is that the stories offer a wide variety of possible meanings without confirming any particular one of them. This, in turn, is the result of Kafka's view — which he shares with many twentieth-century writers — that his own self is a parcel of perennially interacting forces lacking a stable core; if he should attain an approximation of objectivity, this can come about only by describing the world in symbolic language and from a number of different vantage points. Thus a total view must inevitably remain inaccessible to him. Such a universe about which nothing can be said that cannot at the same time — and just as plausibly — be contradicted has a certain ironic quality about it — ironic in the sense that each possible viewpoint becomes relativized. Yet the overriding response one has is one of tragedy rather than irony as one watches Kafka's heroes trying to piece together the debris of their universe.

Kafka's world is essentially chaotic, and this is why it is impossible to derive a specific philosophical or religious code from it — even one acknowledging chaos and paradox as does much existential thought. Only the events themselves can reveal the basic absurdity of things. To reduce Kafka's symbols to their "real" meanings and to pigeonhole his world-view as some "ism" or other is to obscure his writing with just the kind of meaningless experience from which he liberated himself through his art.

Expressionism is one of the literary movements frequently mentioned in connection with Kafka, possibly because its vogue in literature coincided with Kafka's mature writing, between 1912 and his death in 1924. Of course, Kafka does have certain characteristics in common with expressionists, such as his criticism of the blindly scientific-technological world-view, for instance. However, if we consider what he thought of some of the leading expressionists of his day, he certainly cannot be associated with the movement: he repeatedly confessed that the works of the expressionists made him sad; of a series of illustrations by Kokoschka, one of the most distinguished representatives of the movement, Kafka said: "I don't understand. To me, it merely proves the painter's inner chaos." What he rejected in expressionism is the overstatement of feeling and the seeming lack of craftsmanship. While Kafka was perhaps not the great craftsman in the sense that Flaubert was, he admired this faculty in others. In terms of content, Kafka was highly skeptical and even inimical toward the expressionist demand for the "new man." This moralistic-didactic sledgehammer method repulsed him.

Kafka's relationship with existentialism is much more complex, mainly because the label "existentialist" by itself is rather meaningless. Dostoevsky, Nietzsche, and Kierkegaard all have a certain existentialist dimension in their writings, as do Camus, Sartre, Jaspers and Heidegger, with whose works the term existentialism has been more or less equated since World War II. These various people have rather little in common concerning their religious, philosophical, or political views, but they nevertheless share certain characteristic tenets present in Kafka.

Kafka certainly remained fascinated and overwhelmed by the major theme of all varieties of existentialist thinking, namely the difficulty of responsible commitment in the face of an absurd universe. Deprived of all metaphysical guidelines, a man is nevertheless obligated to act morally in a world where death renders everything meaningless. He alone must determine what constitutes a moral action although he can never foresee the consequences of his actions. As a result, he comes to regard his total freedom of choice as a curse. The guilt of existentialist heroes, as of Kafka's, lies in their failure to choose and to commit themselves in the face of too many possibilities — none of which appears more legitimate or worthwhile than any other one. Like Camus' Sisyphus, who is doomed to hauling a rock uphill only to watch it roll down the other side, they find themselves faced with the fate of trying to wring a measure of dignity for themselves in an absurd world. Unlike Sisyphus, however, Kafka's heroes remain drifters in the unlikely landscape they have helped create. Ulrich in Musil's *The Man Without Quality* and Mersault in Camus' *The Stranger*—these men are really contemporaries of Kafka's "heroes," drifters in a world devoid of metaphysical anchoring and suffering from the demons of absurdity and alienation. And in this sense, they are all modern-day relatives of that great hesitator Hamlet, the victim of his exaggerated consciousness and overly rigorous conscience.

The absurdity which Kafka portrays in his nightmarish stories was, to him, the quintessence of the whole human condition. The utter incompatibility of the "divine law" and the human law, and Kafka's inability to solve the discrepancy are the roots of the sense of estrangement from which his protagonists suffer. No matter how hard Kafka's heroes strive to come to terms with the universe, they are hopelessly caught, not only in a mechanism of their own contriving, but also in a network of accidents and incidents, the least of which may lead to the gravest consequences. Absurdity results in estrangement, and to the extent that Kafka deals with this basic calamity, he deals with an eminently existentialist theme.

Kafka's protagonists are lonely because they are caught midway between a notion of good and evil, whose scope they cannot determine and whose contradiction they cannot resolve. Deprived of any common reference and impaled upon their own limited vision of "the law," they cease to be heard, much less understood, by the world around them. They are isolated to the point where meaningful communication fails them. When the typical Kafka hero, confronted with a question as to his identity, cannot give a clear-cut answer, Kafka does more than indicate difficulties of verbal expression: he says that his hero stands between two worlds — between a vanished one to which he once belonged and between a present world to which he does not belong. This is consistent with Kafka's world, which consists not of clearly delineated opposites, but of an endless series of possibilities. These are never more than temporary expressions, never quite conveying what they really ought to convey — hence the temporary, fragmentary quality of Kafka's stories. In the sense that Kafka is aware of the limitations which language imposes upon him and tests the limits of literature, he is a "modern" writer. In the sense that he does not destroy the grammatical, syntactical, and semantic components of his texts, he remains traditional. Kafka has refrained from such destructive aspirations because he is interested in tracing the human reasoning process in great detail up to the point where it fails. He remains indebted to the empirical approach and is at his best when he depicts his protagonists desperately trying to comprehend the world by following the "normal" way.

Because they cannot make themselves heard, much less understood, Kafka's protagonists are involved in adventures which no one else knows about. The reader tends to have the feeling that he is privy to the protagonist's fate and, therefore, finds it rather easy to identify with him. Since there is usually nobody else within the story to whom the protagonist can communicate his fate, he tends to reflect on his own problems over and over again. This solipsistic quality Kafka shares with many an existential writer, although existentialist terminology has come to refer to it as "self-realization."

Kafka was thoroughly familiar with the writings of Kierkegaard and Dostoevsky, and it pays to ponder the similarities and differences between their respective views. The most obvious similarity between Kafka and Kierkegaard, their complex relationships with their respective fiancées and their failures to marry, also points up an essential difference between them. When Kafka talks of bachelorhood and a hermit's existence, he sees these as negative. Kierkegaard, on the other hand, was an enthusiastic bachelor who saw a divine commandment in his renunciation of women. For Kafka, bachelorhood was a symbol of alienation from communal happiness, and he thought of all individualism in this manner. This makes him a poor existentialist.

Unlike Kierkegaard, who mastered his anguish through a deliberate "leap into faith," leaving behind all intellectual speculation, Kafka and his heroes never succeed in conquering this basic anguish: Kafka remained bound by his powerful, probing intellect, trying to solve things rationally and empirically. Kafka does not conceive of the transcendental universe he seeks to describe in its paradoxical and noncommunicable terms; instead, he sets to describing it rationally and, therefore, inadequately. It is as if he were forced to explain something which he himself does not understand—nor is really supposed to understand. Kafka was not the type who could *will* the act of belief. Nor was he a man of flesh and bones who could venture the decisive step toward action and the "totality of experience," as did Camus, for instance, who fought in the French Underground against the Nazi terror. Kafka never really went beyond accepting this world in a way that remains outside of any specific religion. He tended to oppose Kierkegaard's transcendental mysticism, although it might be too harsh to argue that he gave up all faith in the "indestructible nature" of the universe, as he called it. Perhaps this is what Kafka means when he says, "One cannot say that we are lacking faith. The simple fact in itself that we live is inexhaustible in its value of faith."

In the case of Dostoevsky, the parallels with Kafka include merciless consciousness and the rigorous conscience issuing from it. Just as characters in Dostoevsky's works live in rooms anonymous and unadorned, for example, so the walls of the hunger artist's cage, the animal's maze, and Gregor Samsa's bedroom are nothing but the narrow, inexorable and perpetual prison walls of their respective consciences. The most tragic awakening in Kafka's stories is always that of consciousness and conscience. Kafka surpasses Dostoevsky in this respect because that which is represented as dramatic relation—between, say, Raskolnikov and

Porfiry in *Crime and Punishment* — becomes the desperate monologue of a soul in Kafka's pieces.

Kafka's philosophical basis, then, is an open system: it is one of human experiences about the world and not so much the particular *Weltanschauung* of a thinker. Kafka's protagonists confront a secularized diety whose only visible aspects are mysterious and anonymous. Yet despite being continually faced with the essential absurdity of all their experiences, these men nevertheless do not cease trying to puzzle them out. To this end, Kafka uses his writing as a code of the transcendental, a language of the unknown. It is important to understand that this code is not an escape from reality, but the exact opposite — the instrument through which he seeks to comprehend the world in its totality — without ever being able to say to what extent he may have succeeded.

SELECTED BIBLIOGRAPHY

Brod, Max. *Über Franz Kafka*. Frankfurt, Heidelberg: Fischer, 1966. This volume was the first to contain Brod's three important pieces on Kafka. For over twenty years Brod saw his friend daily and discussed his work with him. Because of Brod, four-fifths of Kafka's work was not burned, as Kafka had requested it to be.

Emrich, Wilhelm. *Franz Kafka*. Frankfurt: Athenaeum Verlag, 1958. Dealing with a cross section of Kafka's work, the author argues that an autonomous logic prevails in Kafka's world of images. The book, which even Politzer lists as having most influenced his own *Parable and Paradox,* is permeated by an atmosphere of intimate contact with Western philosophical-religious tradition. The excellent bibliography warrants mention.

Flores, Angel, ed. *The Kafka Problem*. New York: New Directions, 1946. A collection of essays on various philosophical, literary, and biographical aspects. Themes of special interest for a further study of Kafka are given preference over interpretations of individual pieces, although the two main novels figure prominently.

Flores, Angel, and Swander, Homer, eds. *Franz Kafka Today*. Madison: University of Wisconsin Press, 1958. The three parts deal with specific stories, the novels, and diaries and letters, respectively. Of special value is a complete bibliography of all of Kafka's works that have appeared in English and a complete bibliography of secondary material.

Gray, Ronald, ed. *Kafka: A Collection of Critical Essays*. Englewood Cliffs, New Jersey: Prentice-Hall, 1962. The volume contains fourteen critical and interpretive essays from a wide variety of writers and critics. It attempts to do justice to the reading of Kafka by presenting his work from many different viewpoints, some of them strongly disagreeing with most Kafka criticism.

Heller, Erich. *The Disinherited Mind.* Cambridge, England: Bowes and Bowes, 1952. The tenor of the essay "The World of Franz Kafka" (the other two deal with other aspects of modern literature) is that Kafka, although fully aware of his own sickness and the sickness of the age, could at no point even begin to extricate himself from his personal tragedies. He would not and could not venture the "leap into faith" and can under no circumstances be called a believer.

Janouch, Gustav. *Gesprache mit Kafka* (Conversations with Kafka). Frankfurt: Fischer, 1951. Janouch, who met Kafka in 1920, participated in several translations of Kafka's work into Czech. The volume is a collection of letters, notes, diary entries, and personal memories. The material is therefore rather personal in character, expressing Kafka's views in the form of parables, aphorisms, and anecdotes.

Kafka, Franz. *Letter to His Father.* New York: Schocken, 1966.

_____. *Selected Short Stories.* New York: Modern Library, 1952.

Politzer, Heinz. *Franz Kafka: Parable and Paradox.* Cornell University Press, 1962. Politzer's Austrian-Jewish background and his friendship with Kafka were largely responsible for his undertaking the task, together with Brod, of editing Kafka's *Collected Works.* Foremost in this volume, which was started in the early thirties as his thesis, is the concern with Kafka's work as a literary document. The emphasis is on the three novel fragments.

Reimann, Paul, ed. *Franz Kafka aus Prager Sicht.* (Franz Kafka Viewed from Prague) Prague: Voltaire, 1966. This collection of lectures delivered at the now famous Kafka Symposium of 1963 marked a turning point in the Communist appraisal of Kafka. For the first time, the relevance of his work was admitted for Socialist countries as well. In the meantime, this cautious new approach has been completely reversed, especially since the Warsaw Pact Invasion of August, 1968. Once more, Kafka's work is regarded as decadent and irrelevant for Socialist societies. Since all contributions are by noted Communist critics and politicians—many of whom emigrated to the West after Dubcek's fall—the emphasis is on such concepts as realism, alienation, and the function of art in a Socialist society.

Wagenbach, Klaus. *Franz Kafka in Selbstzeugnissen und Bilddokumenten.*
(Franz Kafka: Testimonials and Picture Documents of Himself) Reinbek bei Hamburg: Rowohlt, 1964. Largely biographical, this study
shows the diverse personal, political, and literary influences shaping
and changing Kafka's views.

This is the TITLE INDEX, indexing the over 200 titles available by Series, by Library and by Volume Number for both the BASIC LIBRARY SERIES and the AUTHORS LIBRARY SERIES.

TITLE	SERIES	LIBRARY	Vol
Absalom, Absalom!	Basic	American Lit	4
	Authors	Faulkner	3
Adonais (in Keats & Shelley)	Basic	English Lit	1
Aeneid, The	Basic	Classics	1
Aeschylus' Oresteia (in Agamemnon)	Basic	Classics	1
Agamemnon	Basic	Classics	1
Alice in Wonderland	Basic	English Lit	3
All That Fall (in Waiting for Godot)	Basic	European Lit	1
All the King's Men	Basic	American Lit	6
All Quiet on the Western Front	Basic	European Lit	2
All's Well That Ends Well	Basic	Shakespeare	1
	Authors	Shakespeare	8
American, The	Basic	American Lit	2
	Authors	James	6
American Tragedy, An	Basic	American Lit	3
Animal Farm	Basic	English Lit	5
Anna Karenina	Basic	European Lit	3
Antigone (in Oedipus Trilogy)	Basic	Classics	1
Antony and Cleopatra	Basic	Shakespeare	2
	Authors	Shakespeare	9
Apology (in Plato's Euthyphro....)	Basic	Classics	1
Aristotle's Ethics	Basic	Classics	1
Arms and the Man (in Shaw's Pygmalion....)	Basic	English Lit	6
	Authors	Shaw	11
"Artificial Nigger, The" (in O'Connor's Short Stories)	Basic	American Lit	7
As I Lay Dying	Basic	American Lit	4
	Authors	Faulkner	3
Assistant, The	Basic	American Lit	6
As You Like It	Basic	Shakespeare	1
	Authors	Shakespeare	8
Autobiography of Benjamin Franklin	Basic	American Lit	1
Autobiography of Malcolm X, The	Basic	American Lit	6
Awakening, The	Basic	American Lit	2
Babbitt	Basic	American Lit	3
	Authors	Lewis	7
"Bear, The" (in Go Down, Moses)	Basic	American Lit	4
	Authors	Faulkner	3
Bear, The	Basic	American Lit	4
	Authors	Faulkner	3
Bell Jar, The	Basic	American Lit	6
Beowulf	Basic	Classics	3
Billy Budd	Basic	American Lit	1
Birds, The (in Lysistrata....)	Basic	Classics	1
Black Boy	Basic	American Lit	4

TITLE	SERIES	LIBRARY	Vol
Black Like Me	Basic	American Lit	6
Bleak House	Basic	English Lit	3
	Authors	Dickens	1
Bourgeois Gentleman, The (in Tartuffe....)	Basic	European Lit	1
Brave New World	Basic	English Lit	5
Brave New World Revisited (in Brave New World)	Basic	English Lit	5
Brothers Karamozov, The	Basic	European Lit	3
	Authors	Dostoevsky	2
Caesar and Cleopatra (in Shaw's Man and Superman....)	Basic	English Lit	6
	Authors	Shaw	11
Call of the Wild, The	Basic	American Lit	3
Candide	Basic	European Lit	1
Canterbury Tales, The	Basic	Classics	3
"Cask of Amontillado, The" (in Poe's Short Stories)	Basic	American Lit	1
Catch-22	Basic	American Lit	6
Catcher in the Rye, The	Basic	American Lit	6
Choephori (in Agamemnon)	Basic	Classics	1
Clouds, The (in Lysistrata....)	Basic	Classics	1
Color Purple, The	Basic	American Lit	6
Comedy of Errors, The	Basic	Shakespeare	1
	Authors	Shakespeare	8
Connecticut Yankee in King Arthur's Court, A	Basic	American Lit	2
	Authors	Twain	13
Count of Monte Cristo, The	Basic	European Lit	1
Crime and Punishment	Basic	European Lit	3
	Authors	Dostoevsky	2
Crito (in Plato's Euthyphro....)	Basic	Classics	1
Crucible, The	Basic	American Lit	6
Cry, the Beloved Country	Basic	English Lit	5
Cyrano de Bergerac	Basic	European Lit	1
Daisy Miller	Basic	American Lit	2
	Authors	James	6
David Copperfield	Basic	English Lit	3
	Authors	Dickens	1
Day of the Locust, The (in Miss Lonelyhearts....)	Basic	American Lit	5
Death of a Salesman	Basic	American Lit	6
Deerslayer, The	Basic	American Lit	1
"Delta Autumn" (in Go Down, Moses)	Basic	American Lit	4
Demian	Basic	European Lit	2
Diary of Anne Frank, The	Basic	European Lit	2
"Displaced Person, The" (in O'Connor's Short Stories	Basic	American Lit	7
Divine Comedy I: Inferno	Basic	Classics	3
Divine Comedy II: Purgatorio	Basic	Classics	3
Divine Comedy III: Paradiso	Basic	Classics	3
Doctor Faustus	Basic	Classics	3
Doll's House, A (in Ibsen's Plays I)	Basic	European Lit	4
Don Quixote	Basic	Classics	3
Dr. Jekyll and Mr. Hyde	Basic	English Lit	3

TITLE	SERIES	LIBRARY	Vol
Dracula	Basic	English Lit	3
Dune	Basic	American Lit	6
Electra (in Euripides' Electra & Medea)	Basic	Classics	1
Emerson's Essays	Basic	American Lit	1
Emily Dickinson: Selected Poems	Basic	American Lit	2
Emma	Basic	English Lit	1
Endgame (in Waiting for Godot)	Basic	European Lit	1
Enemy of the People, An (in Ibsen's Plays II)	Basic	European Lit	4
Ethan Frome	Basic	American Lit	3
Eumenides (in Agamemnon)	Basic	Classics	1
Euripides' Electra	Basic	Classics	1
Euripides' Medea	Basic	Classics	1
Euthyphro (in Plato's Euthyphro....)	Basic	Classics	1
Eve of St. Agnes, The (in Keats & Shelley)	Basic	English Lit	1
"Everything That Rises Must Converge" (in O'Connor's Short Stories)	Basic	American Lit	7
Faerie Queene, The	Basic	Classics	4
"Fall of the House of Usher, The" (in Poe's Short Stories)	Basic	American Lit	1
Far from the Madding Crowd	Basic	English Lit	3
	Authors	Hardy	4
Farewell to Arms, A	Basic	American Lit	4
	Authors	Hemingway	5
Fathers and Sons	Basic	European Lit	3
Faust, Pt. I and Pt. II	Basic	European Lit	2
"Fire and the Hearth, The" (in Go Down, Moses)	Basic	American Lit	4
Flies, The (in No Exit & The Flies)	Basic	European Lit	1
For Whom the Bell Tolls	Basic	American Lit	4
	Authors	Hemingway	5
"Four Quartets, The" (in T.S. Eliot's Major Poems and Plays)	Basic	English Lit	6
Frankenstein	Basic	English Lit	1
French Lieutenant's Woman, The	Basic	English Lit	5
Frogs, The (in Lysistrata....)	Basic	Classics	1
Ghosts (in Ibsen's Plays II)	Basic	European Lit	4
Giants in the Earth	Basic	European Lit	4
Glass Menagerie, The	Basic	American Lit	6
Go Down, Moses	Basic	American Lit	4
	Authors	Faulkner	3
Good Country People (in O'Connor's Short Stories)	Basic	American Lit	7
Good Earth, The	Basic	American Lit	4
Good Man is Hard to Find, A (in O'Connor's Short Stories)	Basic	American Lit	7
Grapes of Wrath, The	Basic	American Lit	4
	Authors	Steinbeck	12
Great Expectations	Basic	English Lit	3
	Authors	Dickens	1
Great Gatsby, The	Basic	American Lit	4
Greek Classics	Basic	Classics	2
Gulliver's Travels	Basic	English Lit	1

TITLE	SERIES	LIBRARY	Vol
Hamlet	Basic	Shakespeare	2
	Authors	Shakespeare	9
Hard Times	Basic	English Lit	3
	Authors	Dickens	1
Heart of Darkness	Basic	English Lit	5
Hedda Gabler (in Ibsen's Plays I)	Basic	European Lit	4
Henry IV, Part 1	Basic	Shakespeare	3
	Authors	Shakespeare	10
Henry IV, Part 2	Basic	Shakespeare	3
	Authors	Shakespeare	10
Henry V	Basic	Shakespeare	3
	Authors	Shakespeare	10
Henry VI, Pts. 1,2, & 3	Basic	Shakespeare	3
	Authors	Shakespeare	10
Hobbit, The (in The Lord of the Rings)	Basic	English Lit	5
House of the Seven Gables, The	Basic	American Lit	1
Huckleberry Finn	Basic	American Lit	2
	Authors	Twain	13
"A Hunger Artist" (in Kafka's Short Stories)	Basic	European Lit	2
Ibsen's Plays I	Basic	European Lit	4
Ibsen's Plays II	Basic	European Lit	4
Iliad, The	Basic	Classics	1
Invisible Man, The	Basic	American Lit	7
Ivanhoe	Basic	English Lit	1
Jane Eyre	Basic	English Lit	3
Joseph Andrews	Basic	English Lit	1
Jude the Obscure	Basic	English Lit	3
	Authors	Hardy	4
Julius Caesar	Basic	Shakespeare	2
	Authors	Shakespeare	9
Jungle, The	Basic	American Lit	3
Kafka's Short Stories	Basic	European Lit	2
Keats & Shelley	Basic	English Lit	1
Kidnapped (in Treasure Island & Kidnapped)	Basic	English Lit	4
King Lear	Basic	Shakespeare	2
	Authors	Shakespeare	9
King Oedipus (in The Oedipus Trilogy)	Basic	Classics	1
Krapp's Last Tape (in Waiting for Godot)	Basic	European Lit	1
Last of the Mohicans, The	Basic	American Lit	1
Le Morte d'Arthur	Basic	Classics	4
Leaves of Grass	Basic	American Lit	1
Les Miserables	Basic	European Lit	1
"The Life You Save May Be Your Own" in O'Connor's Short Stories)	Basic	American Lit	7
Light in August	Basic	American Lit	4
	Authors	Faulkner	3
Lord Jim	Basic	English Lit	5
Lord of the Flies	Basic	English Lit	5
Lord of the Rings, The	Basic	English Lit	5

TITLE	SERIES	LIBRARY	Vol
Lost Horizon	Basic	English Lit	5
"Love Song of J. Alfred Prufrock, The" (in	Basic	English Lit	6
T.S. Eliot's Major Poems and Plays)			
Love's Labour's Lost (in Comedy of Errors....)	Basic	Shakespeare	1
	Authors	Shakespeare	8
Lysistrata & Other Comedies	Basic	Classics	1
Macbeth	Basic	Shakespeare	2
	Authors	Shakespeare	9
Madame Bovary	Basic	European Lit	1
Main Street	Basic	American Lit	3
	Authors	Lewis	7
Man and Superman (in Shaw's Man and Superman)	Basic	English Lit	6
	Authors	Shaw	11
Manchild in the Promised Land	Basic	American Lit	7
Mayor of Casterbridge, The	Basic	English Lit	3
	Authors	Hardy	4
Measure for Measure	Basic	Shakespeare	1
	Authors	Shakespeare	8
Medea (in Euripides' Electra & Medea)	Basic	Classics	1
Merchant of Venice, The	Basic	Shakespeare	1
	Authors	Shakespeare	8
Merry Wives of Windsor, The (in All's Well....)	Basic	Shakespeare	1
	Authors	Shakespeare	8
"Metamorphosis, The" (in Kafka's Short Stories)	Basic	European Lit	2
Middlemarch	Basic	English Lit	4
Midsummer Night's Dream, A	Basic	Shakespeare	1
	Authors	Shakespeare	8
Mill on the Floss, The	Basic	The English Lit	4
Misanthrope (in Tartuffe....)	Basic	European Lit	1
Miss Lonelyhearts	Basic	American Lit	5
Moby Dick	Basic	American Lit	1
Moll Flanders	Basic	English Lit	1
Mother Night (in Vonnegut's Major Works)	Basic	American Lit	7
Mrs. Dalloway	Basic	English Lit	5
Much Ado About Nothing	Basic	Shakespeare	1
	Authors	Shakespeare	8
"Murder in the Cathedral" (in T.S. Eliot's Major	Basic	English Lit	6
Poems and Plays)			
My Antonia	Basic	American Lit	3
Mythology	Basic	Classics	1
Native Son	Basic	American Lit	5
New Testament	Basic	Classics	4
Nichomachean Ethics (in Aristotle's Ethics)	Basic	Classics	1
Nineteen Eighty-Four	Basic	English Lit	6
No Exit	Basic	European Lit	1
Notes from the Underground	Basic	European Lit	3
	Authors	Dostoevsky	2
O'Connor's Short Stories	Basic	American Lit	7
Odyssey, The	Basic	Classics	1

TITLE	SERIES	LIBRARY	Vol
Oedipus at Colonus (in The Oedipus Trilogy)	Basic	Classics	1
Oedipus the King (in The Oedipus Trilogy)	Basic	Classics	1
Oedipus Trilogy, The	Basic	Classics	1
Of Human Bondage	Basic	English Lit	6
Of Mice and Men	Basic	American Lit	5
	Authors	Steinbeck	12
Old Man and the Sea, The	Basic	American Lit	7
	Authors	Hemingway	5
"Old People, The" (in Go Down, Moses)	Basic	American Lit	4
Old Testament	Basic	Classics	4
Oliver Twist	Basic	English Lit	4
	Authors	Dickens	1
One Day in the Life of Ivan Denisovich	Basic	European Lit	3
One Flew Over the Cuckoo's Nest	Basic	American Lit	7
One Hundred Years of Solitude	Basic	American Lit	6
"On First Looking Into Chapman's Homer" (in Keats & Shelley)	Basic	English Lit	1
Othello	Basic	Shakespeare	2
	Authors	Shakespeare	9
Our Town	Basic	American Lit	5
Ox-Bow Incident, The	Basic	American Lit	7
"Ozymandias" (in Keats & Shelley)	Basic	English Lit	1
"Pantaloon in Black" (in Go Down, Moses)	Basic	American Lit	4
Paradise Lost	Basic	English Lit	2
Passage to India, A	Basic	English Lit	6
Patience (in Sir Gawain and the Green Knight)	Basic	Classics	4
Pearl, The	Basic	American Lit	5
	Authors	Steinbeck	12
Pearl (in Sir Gawain and the Green Knight)	Basic	Classics	4
Phaedo (in Plato's Euthyphro....)	Basic	Classics	1
Pilgrim's Progress, The	Basic	English Lit	2
Plague, The	Basic	European Lit	1
Plato's Euthyphro, Apology, Crito & Phaedo	Basic	Classics	1
Plato's The Republic	Basic	Classics	1
Poe's Short Stories	Basic	American Lit	1
Portrait of the Artist as a Young Man, A	Basic	English Lit	6
Portrait of a Lady, The	Basic	American Lit	2
	Authors	James	6
Power and the Glory, The	Basic	English Lit	6
Prelude, The	Basic	English Lit	2
Pride and Prejudice	Basic	English Lit	2
Prince, The	Basic	Classics	4
Prince and the Pauper, The	Basic	American Lit	2
	Authors	Twain	13
Purity (in Sir Gawain and the Green Knight)	Basic	Classics	4
"Purloined Letter, The" (in Poe's Short Stories)	Basic	American Lit	1
Pygmalion (in Shaw's Pygmalion....)	Basic	English Lit	6
	Authors	Shaw	11

TITLE	SERIES	LIBRARY	Vol
Red and the Black, The	Basic	European Lit	1
Red Badge of Courage, The	Basic	American Lit	2
Red Pony, The	Basic	American Lit	5
	Authors	Steinbeck	12
Republic, The (in Plato's The Republic)	Basic	Classics	1
Return of the Native, The	Basic	English Lit	4
	Authors	Hardy	4
Richard II	Basic	Shakespeare	3
	Authors	Shakespeare	10
Richard III	Basic	Shakespeare	3
	Authors	Shakespeare	10
Robinson Crusoe	Basic	English Lit	2
Roman Classics	Basic	Classics	2
Romeo and Juliet	Basic	Shakespeare	2
	Authors	Shakespeare	9
Scarlet Letter, The	Basic	American Lit	1
Secret Sharer, The (in Heart of Darkness)	Basic	English Lit	5
Separate Peace, A	Basic	American Lit	7
Shakespeare's Sonnets	Basic	Shakespeare	3
	Authors	Shakespeare	10
Shane	Basic	American Lit	7
Shaw's Man and Superman & Caesar and Cleopatra	Basic	English Lit	6
Shaw's Pygmalion & Arms and the Man	Basic	English Lit	6
Shelley (in Keats and Shelley)	Basic	English Lit	1
Siddhartha (in Steppenwolf & Siddhartha)	Basic	European Lit	2
Silas Marner	Basic	English Lit	4
Sir Gawain and the Green Knight	Basic	Classics	4
Sister Carrie	Basic	American Lit	3
Slaughterhouse Five (in Vonnegut's Major Works)	Basic	American Lit	7
Sons and Lovers	Basic	English Lit	6
Sound and the Fury, The	Basic	American Lit	5
	Authors	Faulkner	3
Steppenwolf	Basic	European Lit	2
Stranger, The	Basic	European Lit	1
Streetcar Named Desire, A (in The Glass Menagerie....)	Basic	American Lit	6
Sun Also Rises, The	Basic	American Lit	5
	Authors	Hemingway	5
T.S. Eliot's Major Poems and Plays	Basic	English Lit	6
Tale of Two Cities, A	Basic	English Lit	4
	Authors	Dickens	1
Taming of the Shrew, The	Basic	Shakespeare	1
	Authors	Shakespeare	8
Tartuffe	Basic	European Lit	1
Tempest, The	Basic	Shakespeare	1
	Authors	Shakespeare	8
Tender is the Night	Basic	American Lit	5
Tess of the D'Urbervilles	Basic	English Lit	4
	Authors	Hardy	4

TITLE	SERIES	LIBRARY	Vol
Three Musketeers, The	Basic	European Lit	1
To Kill a Mockingbird	Basic	American Lit	7
Tom Jones	Basic	English Lit	2
Tom Sawyer	Basic	American Lit	2
	Authors	Twain	13
Treasure Island	Basic	English Lit	4
Trial, The	Basic	European Lit	2
Tristram Shandy	Basic	English Lit	2
Troilus and Cressida	Basic	Shakespeare	1
	Authors	Shakespeare	8
Turn of the Screw, The (in Daisy Miller....)	Basic	American Lit	2
	Authors	James	6
Twelfth Night	Basic	Shakespeare	1
	Authors	Shakespeare	8
Two Gentlemen of Verona, The (in Comedy of Errors...)	Basic	Shakespeare	1
	Authors	Shakespeare	8
Typee (in Billy Budd & Typee)	Basic	American Lit	1
Ulysses	Basic	English Lit	6
Uncle Tom's Cabin	Basic	American Lit	2
Unvanquished, The	Basic	American Lit	5
	Authors	Faulkner	3
Utopia	Basic	Classics	4
Vanity Fair	Basic	English Lit	4
Vonnegut's Major Works	Basic	American Lit	7
Waiting for Godot	Basic	European Lit	1
Walden	Basic	American Lit	1
Walden Two	Basic	American Lit	7
War and Peace	Basic	European Lit	3
"Was" (in Go Down, Moses)	Basic	American Lit	4
"Waste Land, The" (in T.S. Eliot's Major Poems and Plays)	Basic	English Lit	6
White Fang (in Call of the Wild & White Fang)	Basic	American Lit	3
Who's Afraid of Virginia Woolf?	Basic	American Lit	7
Wild Duck, The (in Ibsen's Plays II)	Basic	European Lit	4
Winesburg, Ohio	Basic	American Lit	3
Winter's Tale, The	Basic	Shakespeare	1
	Authors	Shakespeare	8
Wuthering Heights	Basic	English Lit	4

This is the AUTHOR INDEX, listing the over 200 titles available by author and indexing them by Series, by Library and by Volume Number for both the BASIC LIBRARY SERIES and the AUTHORS LIBRARY SERIES.

AUTHOR	TITLE(S)	SERIES	LIBRARY	Vol
Aeschylus	Agamemnon, The Choephori, & The Eumenides	Basic	Classics	1
Albee, Edward	Who's Afraid of Virginia Woolf?	Basic	American Lit	7
Anderson, Sherwood	Winesburg, Ohio	Basic	American Lit	3
Aristophanes	Lysistrata * The Birds * Clouds * The Frogs	Basic	Classics	1
Aristotle	Aristotle's Ethics	Basic	Classics	1
Austen, Jane	Emma	Basic	English Lit	1
	Pride and Prejudice	Basic	English Lit	2
Beckett, Samuel	Waiting for Godot	Basic	European Lit	1
Beowulf	Beowulf	Basic	Classics	3
Beyle, Henri	see Stendhal			
Bronte, Charlotte	Jane Eyre	Basic	English Lit	3
Bronte, Emily	Wuthering Heights	Basic	English Lit	4
Brown, Claude	Manchild in the Promised Land	Basic	American Lit	7
Buck, Pearl	The Good Earth	Basic	American Lit	4
Bunyan, John	The Pilgrim's Progress	Basic	English Lit	2
Camus, Albert	The Plague * The Stranger	Basic	European Lit	1
Carroll, Lewis	Alice in Wonderland	Basic	English Lit	3
Cather, Willa	My Antonia	Basic	American Lit	3
Cervantes, Miguel de	Don Quixote	Basic	Classics	3
Chaucer, Geoffrey	The Canterbury Tales	Basic	Classics	3
Chopin, Kate	The Awakening	Basic	American Lit	2
Clark, Walter	The Ox-Bow Incident	Basic	American Lit	7
Conrad, Joseph	Heart of Darkness & The Secret Sharer * Lord Jim	Basic	English Lit	5
Cooper, James F.	The Deerslayer * The Last of the Mohicans	Basic	American Lit	1
Crane, Stephen	The Red Badge of Courage	Basic	American Lit	2
Dante	Divine Comedy I: Inferno * Divine Comedy II: Purgatorio * Divine Comedy III: Paradiso	Basic	Classsics	3
Defoe, Daniel	Moll Flanders	Basic	English Lit	1
	Robinson Crusoe	Basic	English Lit	2
Dickens, Charles	Bleak House * David Copperfield * Great Expectations * Hard Times	Basic	English Lit	3
	Oliver Twist * A Tale of Two Cities	Basic	English Lit	4
	Bleak House * David Copperfield * Great Expectations * Hard Times * Oliver Twist * A Tale of Two Cities	Authors	Dickens	1

AUTHOR	TITLE(S)	SERIES	LIBRARY	Vol
Dickinson, Emily	Emily Dickinson: Selected Poems	Basic	American Lit	2
Dostoevsky, Feodor	The Brothers Karamazov * Crime and Punishment * Notes from the Underground	Basic	European Lit	3
	The Brothers Karamazov * Crime and Punishment * Notes from the Underground	Authors	Dostoevsky	2
Dreiser, Theodore	An American Tragedy * Sister Carrie	Basic	American Lit	3
Dumas, Alexandre	The Count of Monte Cristo * The Three Musketeers	Basic	European Lit	1
Eliot, George	Middlemarch * The Mill on the Floss * Silas Marner	Basic	English Lit	4
Eliot, T.S.	T.S. Eliot's Major Poets and Plays: "The Wasteland," "The Love Song of J. Alfred Prufrock," & Other Works	Basic	English Lit	6
Ellison, Ralph	The Invisible Man	Basic	American Lit	7
Emerson, Ralph Waldo	Emerson's Essays	Basic	American Lit	1
Euripides	Electra * Medea	Basic	Classics	1
Faulkner, William	Absalom, Absalom! * As I Lay Dying * The Bear * Go Down, Moses * Light in August	Basic	American Lit	4
	The Sound and the Fury * The Unvanquished	Basic	American Lit	5
	Absalom, Absalom! * As I Lay Dying * The Bear * Go Down, Moses * Light in August The Sound and the Fury * The Unvanquished	Authors	Faulkner	3
Fielding, Henry	Joseph Andrews	Basic	English Lit	1
	Tom Jones	Basic	English Lit	2
Fitzgerald, F. Scott	The Great Gatsby	Basic	American Lit	4
	Tender is the Night	Basic	American Lit	5
Flaubert, Gustave	Madame Bovary	Basic	European Lit	1
Forster, E.M.	A Passage to India	Basic	English Lit	6
Fowles, John	The French Lieutenant's Woman	Basic	English Lit	5
Frank, Anne	The Diary of Anne Frank	Basic	European Lit	2
Franklin, Benjamin	The Autobiography of Benjamin Franklin	Basic	American Lit	1
Gawain Poet	Sir Gawain and the Green Night	Basic	Classics	4
Goethe, Johann Wolfgang von	Faust - Parts I & II	Basic	European Lit	2
Golding, William	Lord of the Flies	Basic	English Lit	5
Greene, Graham	The Power and the Glory	Basic	English Lit	6
Griffin, John H.	Black Like Me	Basic	American Lit	6

AUTHOR	TITLE(S)	SERIES	LIBRARY	Vol
Haley, Alex see also Little, Malcolm	The Autobiography of Malcolm X	Basic	American Lit	6
Hardy, Thomas	Far from the Madding Crowd * Jude the Obscure * The Mayor of Casterbridge	Basic	English Lit	3
	The Return of the Native * Tess of the D'Urbervilles	Basic	English Lit	4
	Far from the Madding Crowd * Jude the Obscure * The Mayor of Casterbridge The Return of the Native * Tess of the D'Urbervilles	Authors	Hardy	4
Hawthorne, Nathaniel	The House of the Seven Gables* The Scarlet Letter	Basic	American Lit	1
Heller, Joseph	Catch-22	Basic	American Lit	6
Hemingway, Ernest	A Farewell to Arms * For Whom the Bell Tolls	Basic	American Lit	4
	The Old Man and the Sea	Basic	American Lit	7
	The Sun Also Rises	Basic	American Lit	5
	A Farewell to Arms * For Whom the Bell Tolls The Old Man and the Sea The Sun Also Rises	Authors	Hemingway	5
Herbert, Frank	Dune & Other Works	Basic	American Lit	6
Hesse, Herman	Demian * Steppenwolf & Siddhartha	Basic	European Lit	2
Hilton, James	Lost Horizon	Basic	English Lit	5
Homer	The Iliad * The Odyssey	Basic	Classics	1
Hugo, Victor	Les Miserables	Basic	European Lit	1
Huxley, Aldous	Brave New World & Brave New World Revisited	Basic	English Lit	5
Ibsen, Henrik	Ibsen's Plays I: A Doll's House & Hedda Gabler * Ibsen's Plays II: Ghosts, An Enemy of the People, & The Wild Duck	Basic	European Lit	4
James, Henry	The American * Daisy Miller & The Turn of the Screw * The Portrait of a Lady	Basic	American Lit	2
	The American * Daisy Miller & The Turn of the Screw * The Portrait of a Lady	Authors	James	6
Joyce, James	A Portrait of the Artist as a Young Man * Ulysses	Basic	English Lit	6
Kafka, Franz	Kafka's Short Stories * The Trial	Basic	European Lit	2
Keats & Shelley	Keats & Shelley	Basic	English Lit	1
Kesey, Ken	One Flew Over the Cuckoo's Nest	Basic	American Lit	7
Knowles, John	A Separate Peace	Basic	American Lit	7

AUTHOR	TITLE(S)	SERIES	LIBRARY	Vol
Lawrence, D.H.	Sons and Lovers	Basic	English Lit	6
Lee, Harper	To Kill a Mockingbird	Basic	American Lit	7
Lewis, Sinclair	Babbit * Main Street	Basic	American Lit	3
	Babbit * Main Street	Authors	Lewis	7
Little, Malcolm see also Haley, Alex	The Autobiography of Malcolm X	Basic	American Lit	6
London, Jack	Call of the Wild & White Fang	Basic	American Lit	3
Machiavelli, Niccolo	The Prince	Basic	Classics	4
Malamud, Bernard	The Assistant	Basic	American Lit	6
Malcolm X	see Little, Malcolm			
Malory, Thomas	Le Morte d'Arthur	Basic	Classics	4
Marlowe, Christopher	Doctor Faustus	Basic	Classics	3
Marquez, Gabriel Garcia	One Hundred Years of Solitude	Basic	American Lit	6
Maugham, Somerset	Of Human Bondage	Basic	English Lit	6
Melville, Herman	Billy Budd & Typee * Moby Dick	Basic	American Lit	1
Miller, Arthur	The Crucible * Death of a Salesman	Basic	American Lit	6
Milton, John	Paradise Lost	Basic	English Lit	2

Moliere, Jean
  Baptiste
	Tartuffe, Misanthrope &
	  Bourgeois Gentleman
		Basic	European Lit	1

More, Thomas	Utopia	Basic	Classics	4
O'Connor, Flannery	O'Connor's Short Stories	Basic	American Lit	7
Orwell, George	Animal Farm	Basic	English Lit	5
	Nineteen Eighty-Four	Basic	English Lit	6
Paton, Alan	Cry, The Beloved Country	Basic	English Lit	5
Plath, Sylvia	The Bell Jar	Basic	American Lit	6

Plato	Plato's Euthyphro, Apology,
	  Crito & Phaedo * Plato's
	  The Republic
		Basic	Classics	1

Poe, Edgar Allen	Poe's Short Stories	Basic	American Lit	1
Remarque, Erich	All Quiet on the Western Front	Basic	European Lit	2
Rolvaag, Ole	Giants in the Earth	Basic	European Lit	4
Rostand, Edmond	Cyrano de Bergerac	Basic	European Lit	1
Salinger, J.D.	The Catcher in the Rye	Basic	American Lit	6
Sartre, Jean Paul	No Exit & The Flies	Basic	European Lit	1
Scott, Walter	Ivanhoe	Basic	English Lit	1
Shaefer, Jack	Shane	Basic	American Lit	7

Shakespeare,
  William
	All's Well that Ends Well & The
	  Merry Wives of Windsor * As
	  You Like It * The Comedy of
	  Errors, Love's Labour's Lost, &
	  The Two Gentlemen of Verona *
	  Measure for Measure * The
	  Merchant of Venice * Midsum-
	  mer Night's Dream * Much Ado
	  About Nothing * The Taming
	  of the Shrew * The Tempest *
		Basic	Shakespeare	1

AUTHOR	TITLE(S)	SERIES	LIBRARY	Vol
Shakespeare, William	Troilus and Cressida * Twelfth Night * The Winter's Tale	Basic	Shakespeare	1
	All's Well that Ends Well & The Merry Wives of Windsor * As You Like It * The Comedy of Errors, Love's Labour's Lost, & The Two Gentlemen of Verona * Measure for Measure * The Merchant of Venice * Midsummer Night's Dream * Much Ado About Nothing * The Taming of the Shrew * The Tempest * Troilus and Cressida * Twelfth Night * The Winter's Tale	Authors	Shakespeare	8
	Antony and Cleopatra * Hamlet * Julius Caesar * King Lear * Macbeth * Othello * Romeo and Juliet	Basic	Shakeapeare	2
	Antony and Cleopatra * Hamlet * Julius Caesar * King Lear * Macbeth * Othello * Romeo and Juliet	Authors	Shakespeare	9
	Henry IV Part 1 * Henry IV Part 2 * Henry V * Henry VI Parts 1,2,3 * Richard II * Richard III * Shakespeare's Sonnets	Basic	Shakespeare	3
	Henry IV Part 1 * Henry IV Part 2 * Henry V * Henry VI Parts 1,2,3 * Richard II * Richard III * Shakespeare's Sonnets	Authors	Shakespeare	10
Shaw, George Bernard	Man and Superman & Caesar and Cleopatra * Pygmalion & Arms and the Man	Basic	English Lit	6
	Man and Superman & Caesar and Cleopatra * Pygmalion & Arms and the Man	Authors	Shaw	11
Shelley, Mary	Frankenstein	Basic	English Lit	1
Sinclair, Upton	The Jungle	Basic	American Lit	3
Skinner, B.F.	Walden Two	Basic	American Lit	7
Solzhenitsyn, Aleksandr	One Day in the Life of Ivan Denisovich	Basic	European Lit	3
Sophocles	The Oedipus Trilogy	Basic	Classics	1
Spenser, Edmund	The Faerie Queen	Basic	Classics	4
Steinbeck, John	The Grapes of Wrath *	Basic	American Lit	4
	Of Mice and Men * The Pearl * The Red Pony	Basic	American Lit	5

AUTHOR	TITLE(S)	SERIES	LIBRARY	Vol
Steinbeck, John	The Grapes of Wrath * Of Mice and Men * The Pearl * The Red Pony	Authors	Steinbeck	12
Stendhal	The Red and the Black	Basic	European Lit	1
Sterne, Lawrence	Tristram Shandy	Basic	English Lit	2
Stevenson, Robert Louis	Dr. Jekyll and Mr. Hyde *	Basic	English Lit	3
	Treasure Island & Kidnapped	Basic	English Lit	4
Stoker, Bram	Dracula	Basic	English Lit	3
Stowe, Harriet Beecher	Uncle Tom's Cabin	Basic	American Lit	2
Swift, Jonathan	Gulliver's Travels	Basic	English Lit	1
Thackeray, William Makepeace	Vanity Fair	Basic	English Lit	4
Thoreau, Henry David	Walden	Basic	American Lit	1
Tolkien, J.R.R.	The Lord of the Rings & The Hobbit	Basic	English Lit	5
Tolstoy, Leo	Anna Karenina * War and Peace	Basic	European Lit	3
Turgenev, Ivan Sergeyevich	Fathers and Sons	Basic	European Lit	3
Twain, Mark	A Connecticut Yankee * Huckleberry Finn * The Prince and the Pauper * Tom Sawyer	Basic	American Lit	2
	A Connecticut Yankee * Huckleberry Finn * The Prince and the Pauper * Tom Sawyer	Authors	Twain	13
Virgil	The Aeneid	Basic	Classics	1
Voltaire, Francois	Candide	Basic	European Lit	2
Vonnegut, Kurt	Vonnegut's Major Works	Basic	American Lit	7
Walker, Alice	The Color Purple	Basic	American Lit	7
Warren, Robert Penn	All the King's Men	Basic	American Lit	6
West, Nathanael	Miss Lonelyhearts & The Day of the Locust	Basic	American Lit	5
Wharton, Edith	Ethan Frome	Basic	American Lit	3
Whitman, Walt	Leaves of Grass	Basic	American Lit	1
Wilder, Thornton	Our Town	Basic	American Lit	5
Williams, Tennessee	The Glass Menagerie & A Streetcar Named Desire	Basic	American Lit	6
Woolf, Virginia	Mrs. Dalloway	Basic	English Lit	5
Wordsworth, William	The Prelude	Basic	English Lit	2
Wright, Richard	Black Boy	Basic	American Lit	4
	Native Son	Basic	American Lit	5

INDEX OF SERIES

BASIC LIBRARY (24-0)

THE SHAKESPEARE LIBRARY: 3 Volumes, 26 Titles (25-9)
- V. 1 - The Comedies 12 titles (00-3)
- V. 2 - The Tragedies, 7 titles (01-1)
- V. 3 - The Histories; The Sonnets, 7 titles (02-X)

THE CLASSICS LIBRARY: 4 Volumes, 27 Titles (26-7)
- V. 1 - Greek & Roman Classics, 11 titles (03-8)
- V. 2 - Greek & Roman Classics, 2 titles (04-6)
- V. 3 - Early Christian/European Classics, 7 titles (05-4)
- V. 4 - Early Christian/European Classics, 7 titles (06-2)

ENGLISH LITERATURE LIBRARY: 6 Volumes, 55 Titles (29-1)
- V. 1 - 17th Century & Romantic Period Classics, 7 titles (07-0)
- V. 2 - 17th Century & Romantic Period Classics, 7 titles (08-9)
- V. 3 - Victorian Age, 11 titles (09-7)
- V. 4 - Victorian Age, 10 titles (10-0)
- V. 5 - 20th Century, 10 titles (11-9)
- V. 6 - 20th Century, 10 titles (12-7)

AMERICAN LITERATURE LIBRARY: 7 Volumes, 77 Titles (33-X)
- V. 1 - Early U.S. & Romantic Period, 11 titles (13-5)
- V. 2 - Civil War to 1900, 11 titles (14-3)
- V. 3 - Early 20th Century, 9 titles (15-1)
- V. 4 - The Jazz Age to W.W.II, 11 titles (16-X)
- V. 5 - The Jazz Age to W.W.II, 10 titles (17-8)
- V. 6 - Post-War American Literature, 13 titles (18-6)
- V. 7 - Post-War American Literature, 12 titles (19-4)

EUROPEAN LITERATURE LIBRARY: 4 Volumes, 29 Titles (36-4)
- V. 1 - French Literature, 12 titles (20-8)
- V. 2 - German Literature, 7 titles (21-6)
- V. 3 - Russian Literature, 7 titles (22-4)
- V. 4 - Scandinavian Literature, 3 titles (23-2)

AUTHORS LIBRARY (65-8)

- V. 1 - **Charles Dickens** Library, 6 titles (66-6)
- V. 2 - **Feodor Dostoevsky** Library, 3 titles (67-4)
- V. 3 - **William Faulkner** Library, 7 titles (68-2)
- V. 4 - **Thomas Hardy** Library, 5 titles (69-0)
- V. 5 - **Ernest Hemingway** Library, 4 titles (70-4)
- V. 6 - **Henry James** Library, 3 titles (71-2)
- V. 7 - **Sinclair Lewis** Library, 2 titles (72-0)
- V. 8 - **Shakespeare** Library, Part 1 - The Comedies, 12 titles (73-9)
- V. 9 - **Shakespeare** Library, Part 2 - The Tragedies, 7 titles (74-7)
- V. 10 - **Shakespeare** Library, Part 3 - The Histories; Sonnets, 7 titles (75-5)
- V. 11 - **George Bernard Shaw** Library, 2 titles (76-3)
- V. 12 - **John Steinbeck** Library, 4 titles (77-1)
- V. 13 - **Mark Twain** Library, 4 titles (78-X)

Moonbeam Publications ISBN Prefix: 0-931013-

CLIFFS NOTES

HARDBOUND LITERARY LIBRARIES

INDEX OF LIBRARIES

This is the INDEX OF LIBRARIES, listing the volumes and the individual titles within the volumes for both the BASIC LIBRARY SERIES (24 Volumes, starting below) and the AUTHORS LIBRARY SERIES (13 Volumes, see Page 6).

BASIC LIBRARY SERIES (24 Volumes)

THE SHAKESPEARE LIBRARY: 3 Volumes, 26 Titles

Vol 1 - The Comedies (12 titles)
*All's Well that Ends Well & The Merry Wives of Windsor * As You Like It * The Comedy of Errors, Love's Labour's Lost, & The Two Gentlemen of Verona * Measure for Measure * The Merchant of Venice * A Midsummer Night's Dream * Much Ado About Nothing * The Taming of the Shrew * The Tempest * Troilus and Cressida * Twelfth Night * The Winter's Tale*

Vol 2 - The Tragedies (7 titles)
*Antony and Cleopatra * Hamlet * Julius Caesar * King Lear * Macbeth * Othello * Romeo and Juliet*

Vol 3 - The Histories; The Sonnets (7 titles)
*Henry IV Part 1 * Henry IV Part 2 * Henry V * Henry VI Parts 1,2,3 * Richard II * Richard III * Shakespeare's Sonnets*

THE CLASSICS LIBRARY: 4 Volumes, 27 Titles

Vol 1 - Greek & Roman Classics Part 1 (11 titles)
*The Aeneid * Agamemnon * Aristotle's Ethics * Euripides' Electra & Medea * The Iliad * Lysistrata & Other Comedies * Mythology * The Odyssey * Oedipus Trilogy * Plato's Euthyphro, Apology, Crito & Phaedo * Plato's The Republic*

THE CLASSICS LIBRARY (cont'd)

Vol 2 - Greek & Roman Classics Part 2 (2 titles)
*Greek Classics * Roman Classics*

**Vol 3 - Early Christian/European Classics Part 1
(7 titles)**
*Beowulf * Canterbury Tales * Divine Comedy - I. Inferno
* Divine Comedy - II. Purgatorio * Divine Comedy - III.
Paradiso * Doctor Faustus * Don Quixote*

**Vol 4 - Early Christian/European Classics Part 2
(7 titles)**
*The Faerie Queene * Le Morte D'Arthur * New Testament * Old Testament * The Prince * Sir Gawain and the
Green Knight * Utopia*

ENGLISH LITERATURE LIBRARY: 6 Volumes, 55 Titles

**Vol 1 - 17th Century & Romantic Period Classics
Part 1 (7 titles)**
*Emma * Frankenstein * Gulliver's Travels * Ivanhoe *
Joseph Andrews * Keats & Shelley * Moll Flanders*

**Vol 2 - 17th Century & Romantic Period Classics
Part 2 (7 titles)**
*Paradise Lost * Pilgrim's Progress * The Prelude * Pride
and Prejudice * Robinson Crusoe * Tom Jones * Tristram
Shandy*

Vol 3 - Victorian Age Part 1 (11 titles)
*Alice in Wonderland * Bleak House * David Copperfield
* Dr. Jekyll and Mr. Hyde * Dracula * Far from the Madding Crowd * Great Expectations * Hard Times * Jane
Eyre * Jude the Obscure * The Mayor of Casterbridge*

ENGLISH LITERATURE LIBRARY (cont'd)

Vol 4 - Victorian Age Part 2 (10 titles)
*Middlemarch * The Mill on the Floss * Oliver Twist * The Return of the Native * Silas Marner * A Tale of Two Cities * Tess of the D'Urbervilles * Treasure Island & Kidnapped * Vanity Fair * Wuthering Heights*

Vol 5 - 20th Century Part 1 (10 titles)
*Animal Farm * Brave New World * Cry, The Beloved Country * The French Lieutenant's Woman * Heart of Darkness & The Secret Sharer * Lord Jim * Lord of the Flies * The Lord of the Rings * Lost Horizon * Mrs. Dalloway*

Vol 6 - 20th Century Part 2 (10 titles)
*Nineteen Eighty-Four * Of Human Bondage * A Passage to India * A Portrait of the Artist as a Young Man * The Power and the Glory * Shaw's Man and Superman & Caesar and Cleopatra * Shaw's Pygmalion & Arms and the Man * Sons and Lovers * T.S. Eliot's Major Poems and Plays * Ulysses*

AMERICAN LITERATURE LIBRARY: 7 Volumes, 77 Titles

Vol 1 - Early U.S. & Romantic Period (11 titles)
*Autobiography of Ben Franklin * Billy Budd & Typee * The Deerslayer * Emerson's Essays * The House of Seven Gables * The Last of the Mohicans * Leaves of Grass * Moby Dick * Poe's Short Stories * The Scarlet Letter * Walden*

AMERICAN LITERATURE LIBRARY (cont'd)

Vol 2 - Civil War to 1900 (11 titles)
The American * The Awakening * A Connecticut Yankee in King Arthur's Court * Daisy Miller & The Turn of the Screw * Emily Dickinson: Selected Poems * Huckleberry Finn * The Portrait of a Lady * The Prince and the Pauper * Red Badge of Courage * Tom Sawyer * Uncle Tom's Cabin

Vol 3 - Early 20th Century (9 titles)
An American Tragedy * Babbitt * Call of the Wild & White Fang * Ethan Frome * The Jungle * Main Street * My Antonia * Sister Carrie * Winesburg, Ohio

Vol 4 - The Jazz Age to W.W.II Part 1 (11 titles)
Absalom, Absalom! * As I Lay Dying * The Bear * Black Boy * A Farewell to Arms * For Whom the Bell Tolls * Go Down, Moses * The Good Earth * The Grapes of Wrath * The Great Gatsby * Light in August

Vol 5 - The Jazz Age to W.W.II Part 2 (10 titles)
Miss Lonelyhearts & The Day of the Locust * Native Son * Of Mice and Men * Our Town * The Pearl * The Red Pony * The Sound and the Fury * The Sun Also Rises * Tender is the Night * Unvanquished

Vol 6 - Post-War American Literature Part 1 (13 titles)
100 Years of Solitude * All the King's Men * The Assistant * The Autobiography of Malcolm X * The Bell Jar * Black Like Me * Catch-22 * The Catcher in the Rye * The Color Purple * The Crucible * Death of a Salesman * Dune and Other Works * The Glass Menagerie & A Streetcar Named Desire

AMERICAN LITERATURE LIBRARY (cont'd)

Vol 7 - Post-War American Literature Part 2 (12 titles)

The Invisible Man * *Manchild in the Promised Land* *
O'Connor's Short Stories * *The Old Man and the Sea* *
One Flew Over the Cuckoo's Nest * *The Ox-Bow Incident*
* *A Separate Peace* * *Shane* * *To Kill a Mockingbird* *
Vonnegut's Major Works * *Walden Two* * *Who's Afraid
of Virginia Woolf?*

EUROPEAN LITERATURE LIBRARY: 4 Volumes, 29 Titles

Vol 1 - French Literature (12 titles)

Candide * *The Count of Monte Cristo* * *Cyrano de
Bergerac* * *Les Miserables* * *Madame Bovary* * *No Exit &
The Flies* * *The Plague* * *The Red and the Black* * *The
Stranger* * *Tartuffe, Misanthrope & Bourgeois Gentlemen*
* *The Three Musketeers* * *Waiting for Godot*

Vol 2 - German Literature (7 titles)

All Quiet on the Western Front * *Demian* * *The Diary of
Anne Frank* * *Faust Pt. I & Pt. II* * *Kafka's Short Stories*
* *Steppenwolf & Siddhartha* * *The Trial*

Vol 3 - Russian Literature (7 titles)

Anna Karenina * *The Brothers Karamozov* * *Crime and
Punishment* * *Fathers and Sons* * *Notes from the Underground* * *One Day in the Life of Ivan Denisovich* * *War
and Peace*

Vol 4 - Scandinavian Literature (3 titles)

Giants in the Earth * *Ibsen's Plays I: A Doll's House &
Hedda Gabler* * *Ibsen's Plays II: Ghosts, An Enemy of the
People & The Wild Duck*

AUTHORS LIBRARY

Vol 1 -Charles Dickens Library (6 titles)
Bleak House * David Copperfield * Great Expectations * Hard Times * Oliver Twist * A Tale of Two Cities

Vol 2 - Feodor Dostoevsky Library (3 titles)
The Brothers Karamazov * Crime and Punishment * Notes from the Underground

Vol 3 - William Faulkner Library (7 titles)
Absalom, Absalom! * As I Lay Dying * The Bear * Go Down, Moses * Light in August * The Sound and the Fury * The Unvanquished

Vol 4 - Thomas Hardy Library (5 titles)
Far from the Madding Crowd * Jude the Obscure * The Major of Casterbridge * The Return of the Native * Tess of the D'Urbervilles

Vol 5 - Ernest Hemingway Library (4 titles)
A Farewell to Arms * For Whom the Bell Tolls * The Old Man and the Sea * The Sun Also Rises

Vol 6 - Henry James Library (3 titles)
The American * Daisy Miller & The Turn of the Screw * The Portrait of a Lady

Vol 7 - Sinclair Lewis Library (2 titles)
Babbitt * Main Street

Vol 8 - Shakespeare Library, Part 1 - The Comedies (12 titles)
*All's Well that Ends Well & The Merry Wives of Windsor
* As You Like It * The Comedy of Errors, Love's Labour's
Lost & The Two Gentlemen of Verona * Measure for
Measure * The Merchant of Venice * A Midsummer
Night's Dream * Much Ado About Nothing * The Taming
of the Shrew * The Tempest * Troilus and Cressida *
Twelfth Night * The Winter's Tale*

Vol 9 - Shakespeare Library, Part 2 - The Tragedies (7 Titles)
*Antony and Cleopatra * Hamlet * Julius Caesar * King
Lear * Macbeth * Othello * Romeo and Juliet*

Vol 10 - Shakespeare Library, Part 3 - The Histories; Sonnets 7 titles)
*Henry IV Part 1 * Henry IV Part 2 * Henry V * Henry VI
Parts 1,2,3 * Richard II * Richard III * Shakespeare's The
Sonnets*

Vol 11 - George Bernard Shaw Library (2 titles)
*Pygmalion & Arms and the Man * Man and Superman &
Caesar and Cleopatra*

Vol 12 - John Steinbeck Library (4 titles)
*The Grapes of Wrath * Of Mice and Men * The Pearl *
The Red Pony*

Vol 13 - Mark Twain Library (4 titles)
*A Connecticut Yankee in King Arthur's Court * Huckle-
berry Finn * The Prince and the Pauper * Tom Sawyer*